Lecture Notes in Computer Science

AF166359

Lecture Notes in Artificial Intelligence   15446

Founding Editor

Jörg Siekmann

Series Editors

Randy Goebel, *University of Alberta, Edmonton, Canada*
Wolfgang Wahlster, *DFKI, Berlin, Germany*
Zhi-Hua Zhou, *Nanjing University, Nanjing, China*

The series Lecture Notes in Artificial Intelligence (LNAI) was established in 1988 as a topical subseries of LNCS devoted to artificial intelligence.

The series publishes state-of-the-art research results at a high level. As with the LNCS mother series, the mission of the series is to serve the international R & D community by providing an invaluable service, mainly focused on the publication of conference and workshop proceedings and postproceedings.

Max Bramer · Frederic Stahl
Editors

Artificial Intelligence XLI

44th SGAI International Conference
on Artificial Intelligence, AI 2024
Cambridge, UK, December 17–19, 2024
Proceedings, Part I

 Springer

Editors
Max Bramer
University of Portsmouth
Portsmouth, UK

Frederic Stahl
DFKI Niedersachsen
Oldenburg, Germany

ISSN 0302-9743   ISSN 1611-3349 (electronic)
Lecture Notes in Artificial Intelligence
ISBN 978-3-031-77914-5   ISBN 978-3-031-77915-2 (eBook)
https://doi.org/10.1007/978-3-031-77915-2

LNCS Sublibrary: SL7 – Artificial Intelligence

This Springer imprint is published by the registered company Springer Nature Switzerland AG
The registered company address is: Gewerbestrasse 11, 6330 Cham, Switzerland

If disposing of this product, please recycle the paper.

Preface

Artificial Intelligence XLI comprises the refereed papers presented at the 44 SGAI International Conference on Innovative Techniques and Applications of Artificial Intelligence, held in December 2024. It is published as two volumes containing papers for the technical stream and the application stream, respectively. The conference was organised by SGAI, the British Computer Society Specialist Group on Artificial Intelligence. This year 80 papers were submitted and all were single-blind peer reviewed by either 2 or 3 reviewers plus the expert members of the Executive Program Committee for each stream of the conference.

This year's Donald Michie Memorial Award for the best refereed technical paper was won by a paper entitled 'NER Explainability Framework: Utilizing LIME to Enhance Clarity and Robustness in Named Entity Recognition' by Morten Grundetjern, Per-Arne Andersen, Morten Goodwin and Karl Audun Borgersen (University of Agder, Norway).

This year's Rob Milne Memorial Award for the best refereed application paper was won by a paper entitled 'Adaptive CNN Method For Prostate MR Image Segmentation Using Ensemble Learning' by Lars Jacobson, Mohamed Bader-El-Den, Adrian Hopgood, Shamsul Masum, Vincenzo Tamma (University of Portsmouth, UK), David Prendergast (Innovative Physics Ltd., UK) and Peter Osborn (Portsmouth Hospitals, University NHS Trust, UK).

The other technical stream full papers included are divided into sections on Neural Nets, Deep Learning, Large Language Models, Machine Learning, Evolutionary and Genetic Algorithms, and Knowledge Management. The other application stream full papers are divided into sections on Machine Vision, Evaluation of AI Systems, Applications of Machine Learning and Other AI Applications. Both volumes also include the text of short papers presented as posters at the conference.

On behalf of the conference Organising Committee, we would like to thank all those who contributed to the organisation of this year's programme, in particular the Program Committee members, the Executive Program Committees and our administrators Mandy Bauer and Bryony Bramer.

September 2024

Max Bramer
Frederic Stahl

Organisation

Conference Committee

Conference Chair

Max Bramer — University of Portsmouth, UK

Technical Program Chair

Max Bramer — University of Portsmouth, UK

Application Program Chair

Frederic Stahl — DFKI: German Research Center for Artificial Intelligence, Germany

Workshop Organiser

Adrian Hopgood — University of Portsmouth, UK

Treasurer

Rosemary Gilligan — SGAI, UK

Poster Session Organiser

Juan Augusto — Middlesex University London, UK

Panel Session Organiser

Andrew Lea — PersuasionXP, UK

FAIRS Organiser

Giovanna Martinez — University of Nottingham, UK

Conference Administrator

Mandy Bauer   BCS, UK

Paper Administrator

Bryony Bramer   SGAI, UK

Technical Executive Program Committee

Max Bramer (Chair)   University of Portsmouth, UK
Frans Coenen   University of Liverpool, UK
Adrian Hopgood   University of Portsmouth, UK
John Kingston   Nottingham Trent University, UK
Jixin Ma   University of Greenwich, UK

Application Executive Program Committee

Frederic Stahl (Chair)   DFKI: German Research Center for Artificial
                               Intelligence, Germany
Richard Ellis   RKE Consulting, UK
Rosemary Gilligan   SGAI, UK
Lars Nolle   Jade University of Applied Sciences, Germany
Richard Wheeler   University of Edinburgh, UK

Technical Program Committee

Per-Arne Andersen   University of Agder, Norway
Mercedes Arguello Casteleiro   University of Southampton, UK
Matt Armstrong-Barnes   HPE, UK
Juan Augusto   Middlesex University London, UK
Raed Sabri Hameed Batbooti   Southern Technical University/ Basra Engineering
                               Technical College, Iraq
Karl Audun Borgersen   University of Agder, Norway
Soufiane Boulehouache   University of 20 Août 1955-Skikda, Algeria
Max Bramer   University of Portsmouth, UK
Ken Brown   University College Cork, Ireland
Marcos Bueno   Radboud University, The Netherlands
Darren Chitty   Aston University, UK

Frans Coenen	University of Liverpool, UK
Bertrand Cuissart	Université de Caen Normandie, France
Nicolas Durand	Aix-Marseille University, France
Frank Eichinger	DATEV eG, Germany
Michael Free	BT, UK
Martin Fyvie	Robert Gordon University, UK
Hossein Ghodrati Noushahr	University of Leicester, UK
Adrian Hopgood	University of Portsmouth, UK
Chris Huyck	Middlesex University London, UK
Mohamed Ihmeida	Buckinghamshire New University, UK
Stelios Kapetanakis	Distributed Analytics, UK
Mathias Kern	BT, UK
Ivan Koychev	University of Sofia, Bulgaria
Andrew Langworthy	BT, UK
Nicole Lee	University of Hong Kong, China
Haiming Liu	University of Southampton, UK
Jixin Ma	University of Greenwich, UK
Giovanna Martinez-Arellano	University of Nottingham, UK
Ken McGarry	University of Sunderland, UK
Silja Meyer-Nieberg	Universität der Bundeswehr München, Germany
Daniel Neagu	University of Bradford, UK
Lars Nolle	Jade University of Applied Sciences, Germany
Joanna Isabelle Olszewska	University of the West of Scotland, UK
Daniel O'Leary	University of Southern California, USA
Sanjib Raj Pandey	Royal Marsden NHS Foundation Trust, UK
Fernando Saenz-Perez	Universidad Complutense de Madrid, Spain
Pradeep Kumar Saraswathi	Salesforce, USA
Simon Thompson	GFT Technology, UK
M. R. C. van Dongen	University College Cork, Ireland

Application Program Committee

Manal Almutairi	University of Reading, UK
Saif Alzubi	University of Exeter, UK
Ines Arana	Robert Gordon University, UK
Vasileios Argyriou	Kingston University, UK
Juan Carlos Augusto	Middlesex University London, UK
Lakshmi Babu Saheer	Anglia Ruskin University, UK
Ken Brown	University College Cork, Ireland
Nikolay Burlutskiy	ContextVision AB, Sweden
Xiaochun Cheng	Swansea University, UK

Sarah Jane Delany	Technological University Dublin, Ireland
Tarek El-Mihoub	German Research Center for Artificial Intelligence GmbH (DFKI), Germany
Richard Ellis	RKE Consulting, UK
Ahmed Elsayed	German Research Center for Artificial Intelligence GmbH (DFKI), Germany
Xiaohong Gao	Middlesex University London, UK
Rosemary Gilligan	University of Hertfordshire, UK
John Gordon	AKRI Ltd, UK
Holmer Hemsen	German Research Center for Artificial Intelligence GmbH (DFKI), Germany
Chris Hinde	Loughborough University, UK
Chris Huyck	Middlesex University London, UK
Carl James-Reynolds	Middlesex University London, UK
Colin Johnson	University of Nottingham, UK
Stelios Kapetanakis	Distributed Analytics, UK
Mathias Kern	BT, UK
Daniel Lukats	German Research Center for Artificial Intelligence GmbH (DFKI), Germany
Christoph Manß	German Research Center for Artificial Intelligence GmbH (DFKI), Germany
Andre Miedtank	German Research Center for Artificial Intelligence GmbH (DFKI), Germany
Lars Nolle	Jade University of Applied Sciences, Germany
Sanjib Raj Pandey	Royal Marsden NHS Foundation Trust, UK
Jing Qi	University of Essex, UK
Robert Rettig	German Research Center for Artificial Intelligence GmbH (DFKI)
Sam Richardson	AstraZeneca, UK
Miguel A. Salido	Universitat Politècnica de València, Spain
Georgios Samakovitis	University of Greenwich, UK
Janina Schneider	German Research Center for Artificial Intelligence GmbH (DFKI), Germany
Frederic Stahl	German Research Center for Artificial Intelligence GmbH (DFKI), Germany
Daphpne Theodorakopoulos	German Research Center for Artificial Intelligence GmbH (DFKI), Germany
Christoph Tholen	German Research Center for Artificial Intelligence GmbH (DFKI), Germany
Richard Wheeler	European Sustainable Energy Innovation Alliance, TU Graz, Austria

Contents – Part I

Large Language Models

Machine Learning

Evolutionary and Genetic Algorithms

Knowledge Management

Short Technical Papers

Contents – Part II

Applications of Machine Learning

Other AI Applications

Short Application Papers

Technical Papers

NER Explainability Framework: Utilizing LIME to Enhance Clarity and Robustness in Named Entity Recognition

Morten Grundetjern$^{(\boxtimes)}$ (ID), Per-Arne Andersen (ID), Morten Goodwin (ID), and Karl Audun Borgersen (ID)

University of Agder, Jon Lilletuns vei 9, Grimstad, Norway
post@uia.no
https://www.uia.no/

Abstract. Named Entity Recognition (NER) is crucial for many Natural Language Processing (NLP) applications, yet current models often lack explainability and robustness, particularly against lexical variations. While methods like Local Interpretable Model-agnostic Explanations (LIME) have enhanced explainability in text classification, their application to sequence-based tasks like NER remains an open challenge. This paper introduces the NER Explainability Framework (NEF), a novel approach that transforms the sequence-based NER task into a multi-classification problem. This transformation enables the application of LIME to any NER architecture. NEF provides precise, interpretable insights into model decisions by highlighting which parts of the input text most influence tagging decisions, significantly advancing explainability in NER. To address the critical gap in assessing model resilience, we also present the Misspelling Robustness Score (MRS), a new metric designed to quantify NER model resilience against lexical variations, particularly misspellings. MRS offers a comprehensive evaluation of model performance in the face of spelling variations and errors. We apply NEF to four widely used NER models (SpaCy, Flair, Stanza, and RoBERTa) using the CoNLL-2003 dataset, revealing critical patterns and weaknesses in model behavior. Our method enables targeted improvements, demonstrated by fine-tuning the SpaCy model to achieve a significant 17.5% increase in robustness against misspellings. These findings lay the groundwork for developing more robust, accurate, and interpretable NER systems, providing practical strategies to address existing challenges in NLP. The universal applicability of NEF across NER architectures and the insights provided by MRS offers valuable tools for researchers and practitioners in advancing the field of NER.

Keywords: NER · LIME · Explainability · NLP · Robustness

1 Introduction

NER stands at the forefront of natural language processing, critical in applications ranging from question-answering systems to machine translation [8]. By

M. Bramer and F. Stahl (Eds.): SGAI 2024, LNAI 15446, pp. 3–15, 2025.
https://doi.org/10.1007/978-3-031-77915-2_1

identifying and classifying key information elements in text, NER forms the backbone of many AI-driven language understanding tasks.

Recent years have witnessed significant advancements in NER methodologies, particularly with the advent of deep learning models. However, this progress has come at a cost: increased model complexity has rendered these systems opaque, making it virtually impossible to understand the reasoning behind their predictions [18]. This "black-box" nature presents a significant challenge, especially when models encounter the noisy, variable data typical of real-world scenarios. Linguistic variations and misspellings, for instance, can substantially degrade model performance [4].

While the importance of model explainability has gained recognition across various AI domains [3,16], NER has received comparatively little attention in terms of developing interpretable solutions. This oversight is particularly concerning given NER's fundamental role in NLP applications and its vulnerability to real-world data variations.

To address these interconnected challenges, we introduce NEF. Our approach transforms NER's traditional sequence-labeling task into a classification problem, enabling the generation of accurate and interpretable explanations using LIME. NEF operates independently of models' underlying confidence scores, ensuring its universal applicability across all NER architectures.

A key innovation of NEF is its integration of overall model performance metrics, including our newly developed MRS. Combining MRS's global explanations with LIME's local explanations gives NEF a comprehensive view of model behavior. It evaluates robustness against lexical variations, particularly misspellings, and provides detailed insights into individual prediction decisions.

Our experiments with NEF have yielded promising results. For instance, we discovered that misspellings have a surprisingly negative effect on model performance. However, we also found that targeted fine-tuning guided by NEF insights can mitigate this performance drop by as much as 17%. These findings demonstrate the practical value of our framework and open new avenues for improving the robustness and reliability of NER systems in real-world applications.

2   Related Work

Research on explainability in NER has primarily focused on model performance at the dataset level, addressing biases such as the impact of sentence length or capitalization [7,11]. While these studies provide valuable insights into overall model behavior, they often lack granularity in explaining individual predictions. A notable exception is the EXSEQREG framework by Güngör et al. [9], which explores prediction-specific explanations for NER models in morphologically rich languages. EXSEQREG combines NER and POS tagging models, dividing text into regions for analysis. To the best of our knowledge, EXSEQREG and our work are among the few approaches focusing on local explanations for NER predictions. However, our work differs in its aim to develop a more generalizable method applicable to any NER model, regardless of the underlying architecture or language. The connection between NER model explainability and robustness is well-established in the literature. Traditional evaluation metrics such as precision, recall, and F1-score have been extended to assess robustness by evaluating model performance under perturbed conditions [20]. These metrics provide a foundation for understanding model behavior, but they often lack specificity in isolating particular types of perturbations. More specialized approaches have emerged to address specific aspects of robustness. Adversarial robustness metrics evaluate a model's ability to withstand malicious inputs [22], while metrics measuring generalization across different domains assess the model's adaptability to domain shifts [21]. Interpretability metrics help identify weaknesses or biases affecting robustness [6], and composite indices offer a holistic view of model resilience [21]. However, existing measures often conflate various types of input perturbations, making it challenging to isolate and address issues related specifically to orthographic errors. This limitation is particularly crucial in NER tasks, where entity names are prone to typographical errors. Our proposed MRS addresses this gap by offering a focused evaluation of a model's ability to handle misspellings. The MRS complements existing robustness metrics by providing a targeted measure for assessing the impact of orthographic variations on NER performance. Our work thus contributes to the field by introducing a generalizable explanation method for NER predictions and a specialized metric for assessing robustness against misspellings, addressing key limitations in current NER model evaluation and interpretation approaches.

3 Methodology

NEF is a novel approach that transforms the sequence-based NER task into a multi-classification problem. This transformation enables the application of powerful explainability techniques, such as LIME, to NER models—a capability previously limited by the sequential nature of NER tasks. Our study demonstrates NEF's effectiveness on four prominent NER models: Stanza, SpaCy, Flair, and RoBERTa, using the CoNLL-03 dataset. NEF's design ensures its applicability to any NER model, regardless of its underlying architecture. Figure 1 provides an overview of our framework.

The NEF process begins with an input text processed by an NER model. NEF then transforms this NER task into a classification problem by generating input perturbations, focusing on specific words. For example, "John Smith ate pizza" might be perturbed to "0000 Smith ate pizza" or "John 0000 ate pizza", with each version classified by the model.

LIME is then applied to provide interpretative insights, analyzing how perturbations affect the model's predictions. This analysis visualized using Sankey diagrams, illustrates the flow from input words to their contributions and final classifications, highlighting which parts of the input text most influence the tagging decisions.

While our study uses MRS to evaluate model performance against lexical variations and misspellings, NEF's flexible design allows for integrating various evaluation metrics tailored to specific research objectives. The MRS, in our case, assesses the model's accuracy when confronted with misspellings, calculated as the ratio of correct identifications on misspelled inputs to those on original inputs.

The combined output of LIME explanations and the chosen evaluation metric (MRS in our study) provides a comprehensive view of local predictions and overall model behavior. These insights guide actionable steps for model improvement, creating a feedback loop for continuous enhancement when the process is rerun.

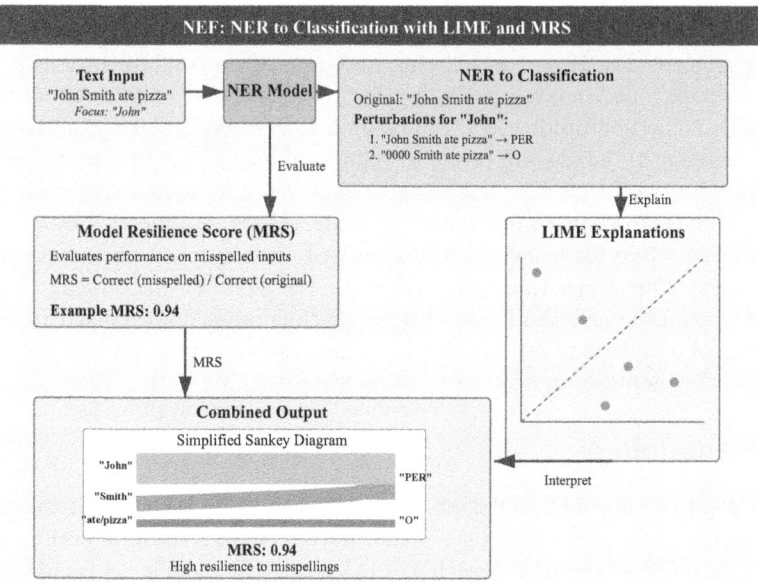

Fig. 1. Overview of NEF. The diagram illustrates the transformation of NER tasks into classification problems, the application of LIME for interpretability, and the use of the MRS for performance evaluation. The framework creates a feedback loop to improve NER model interpretability and robustness continuously.

3.1   Models

This study analyzes four NER models: Stanza, SpaCy, Flair, and RoBERTa. These models were selected based on their distinct approaches to NER and their extensive adoption within the NLP community [2,13,15], offering a comprehensive overview of the state-of-the-art in NER technology. Stanza employs a neural network-based pipeline featuring a BiLSTM-CNNs-CRF architecture, which combines bidirectional Long Short-Term Memory networks, Convolutional Neural Networks, and Conditional Random Fields to achieve high accuracy in NER tasks [15]. SpaCy utilizes a transition-based parsing method with a Convolutional

Neural Networks model for efficient and production-ready text processing. It is renowned for its speed and integration with deep learning frameworks, making it suitable for real-time applications [10]. Flair uses contextual string embeddings derived from a character-level language model to capture nuanced contextual information. Its framework integrates various embeddings, such as Flair embeddings, BERT, and ELMo, to enhance NER performance [2]. RoBERTa, an optimized version of BERT, employs a transformer-based architecture to capture intricate contextual dependencies. It improves on BERT by training with larger mini-batches, longer sequences, and dynamic masking [13].

3.2 Data Acquisition and Preparation

The CoNLL-03 dataset [19] is a standard benchmark in NER, containing annotated text for English, German, Spanish, and Dutch. Introduced in 2003 as a shared task for NER, it has since become the most widely used dataset for testing NER models. This study focuses on the English portion, with sentences annotated for Person (PER), Organization (ORG), Location (LOC), and Miscellaneous (MISC) entities in the IOB format. The dataset comprises:

- **Training Set**: 14,987 sentences with 203,621 tokens and 23,499 named entities.
- **Validation Set**: 3,466 sentences with 51,362 tokens and 5,942 named entities.
- **Test Set**: 3,684 sentences with 46,435 tokens and 5,648 named entities.

The samples used for data pattern analysis were taken from the test set of the CoNLL-03 dataset, specifically where the NER models failed in their predictions. The base dataset for MRS consists of all sentences in the test set of CoNLL-03 containing a PER entity, totaling 865 sentences. We focused on the PER label due to its high precision and recall across datasets such as CoNLL-03, Wikipedia, and MUC-6 [1,5,8].

3.3 Applying LIME to NER Tasks

Adapting LIME to explain NER models presents unique challenges due to the sequential nature of NER tasks. Figure 2 illustrates our novel approach to transform this sequence labeling problem into a classification task suitable for LIME analysis. This transformation enables us to leverage LIME's interpretability power for NER models, providing insights that were previously difficult to obtain.

The key innovation in our approach lies in how we decompose the NER task into localized classification problems. By focusing on individual tokens and their contexts, we can apply LIME's perturbation-based explanations to understand the model's decision-making process for each entity label.

Our method begins with sampling, creating perturbed versions of the input text. This step is crucial as it allows us to explore the model's behavior under various input conditions, simulating different contexts for each word. The subsequent feature representation stage translates these textual perturbations into a numerical format, preserving the essence of word presence and absence.

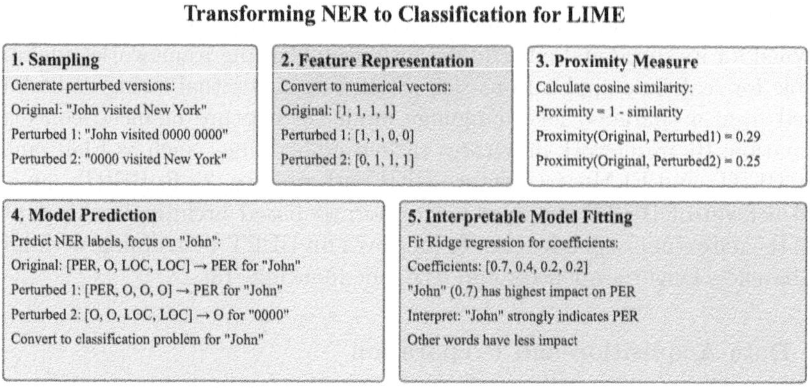

Transforming NER to Classification for LIME

1. Sampling	2. Feature Representation	3. Proximity Measure
Generate perturbed versions:	Convert to numerical vectors:	Calculate cosine similarity:
Original: "John visited New York"	Original: [1, 1, 1, 1]	Proximity = 1 - similarity
Perturbed 1: "John visited 0000 0000"	Perturbed 1: [1, 1, 0, 0]	Proximity(Original, Perturbed1) = 0.29
Perturbed 2: "0000 visited New York"	Perturbed 2: [0, 1, 1, 1]	Proximity(Original, Perturbed2) = 0.25

4. Model Prediction	5. Interpretable Model Fitting
Predict NER labels, focus on "John":	Fit Ridge regression for coefficients:
Original: [PER, O, LOC, LOC] → PER for "John"	Coefficients: [0.7, 0.4, 0.2, 0.2]
Perturbed 1: [PER, O, O, O] → PER for "John"	"John" (0.7) has highest impact on PER
Perturbed 2: [O, O, LOC, LOC] → O for "0000"	Interpret: "John" strongly indicates PER
Convert to classification problem for "John"	Other words have less impact

Fig. 2. Process of transforming NER to a classification problem for LIME explanation.

A critical component of our approach is the proximity measure, which quantifies the similarity between perturbed samples and the original text. This measure plays a vital role in weighing the importance of each perturbation, ensuring that the final explanation is anchored close to the original input's neighborhood in the feature space.

The model prediction step bridges the gap between NER and classification. By focusing on individual tokens and vectorizing their predicted labels, we effectively transform the NER output into a format that LIME can interpret. This localized view allows us to explain the model's decisions for each word independently while considering its context.

Finally, the interpretable model fitting stage generates local and faithful explanations to the original NER model. Using Ridge regression, we balance model fidelity and explanation simplicity, producing coefficients that quantify each word's impact on the prediction.

This approach allows us to explain individual NER decisions and provides a framework for understanding the model's overall behavior. It opens up new possibilities for debugging NER models, identifying potential biases, and gaining insights into the linguistic patterns the model has learned.

3.4 MRS Evaluation Methodology

The MRS evaluates NER models' resilience to misspellings in entity names. The process involves:

1. **Data Preparation**: Create two datasets:
   - Set A: Entities with original spellings.
   - Set B: Same entities with introduced misspellings.
2. **Misspelling Generation**: Apply the following techniques to Set B:
   - **Skip**: Removes a character at a random position if the word length exceeds one.

- **Swap**: Swaps a character with its subsequent character, ensuring there is a character to swap with.
- **Duplicate**: Duplicates a character at a random position.
- **Substitute**: Replaces a character with a random letter.
- **Insert**: Inserts a random letter at a random position.
- **Phonetic**: Replaces parts of the word based on common phonetic substitutions.

The MRS is calculated as:

$$MRS = \frac{\text{Correct identifications in Set B}}{\text{Correct identifications in Set A}} \qquad (1)$$

MRS values range from 0 to 1, 1 indicating perfect resilience to misspellings. MRS offers a targeted approach to identifying and addressing misspelling-related vulnerabilities in NER systems by isolating misspelling effects, assessing contextual understanding, and simulating real-world typographical errors. This complements existing general input resilience metrics [12,14], enabling a more precise evaluation of NER model robustness.

3.5 Analysis

We analyzed the models using the NEF framework, focusing on a series of samples where all models failed their predictions. This analysis revealed that the CoNLL-03 dataset contained many documented errors [17]. A common finding in our NEF analysis was that misspellings consistently negatively affected model performance. Notably, the SpaCy model was selected for further investigation because it was the most negatively affected by misspellings. In response, we fine-tuned the SpaCy model on a subset of 5,000 sentences from the CoNLL training dataset, in which all PER tags were intentionally misspelled. We then used the NEF to compare the performance of the fine-tuned model against the original model, specifically evaluating its resilience to misspellings.

4 Experiments and Results

This section presents our experimental findings on evaluating and improving NER models' robustness against misspellings. Our NEF framework, as shown in Fig. 1, comprises three key components:

1. Metrics Evaluation: Assessing MRS effectiveness in evaluating NER model robustness.
2. LIME Explanations: Generating visualizations to understand word influence on predictions.
3. Actionable Insights: Implementing NEF insights to enhance model performance, demonstrated through SpaCy model fine-tuning.

4.1   MRS Evaluation

The following results highlight the effectiveness of the MRS in evaluating the robustness of various NER models against misspellings, particularly in their ability to identify PER tags correctly. As shown in Table 1, the performance of different models varies significantly when faced with misspelled inputs. Accuracy loss indicates the percentage decrease in model accuracy when processing misspelled inputs compared to correctly spelled inputs.

Table 1. MRS and Accuracy Loss for NLP Models

Model	MRS	Accuracy Loss
Stanza on PER tag	0.8968	10% loss
Spacy on PER tag	0.7634	24% loss
Spacy fine-tuned for misspellings	0.9358	6.5% loss
Flair on PER tag	0.9613	3.9% loss
Roberta on PER tag	0.9175	8.8% loss

The Stanza model demonstrates strong resilience with an MRS of 0.8968, indicating it successfully maintains 89.68% of its accuracy in the presence of misspelled inputs. The slight accuracy reduction by about 10.32% points to potential areas for improvement in handling more complex misspelling scenarios. Stanza's architecture, which includes bidirectional LSTM networks, allows it to use contextual information, contributing to its robustness effectively [15].

Conversely, the SpaCy model shows a more noticeable struggle with an MRS of 0.7634, retaining only 76.34% of its accuracy when processing misspelled inputs. This significant decrease by approximately 23.66% highlights a critical vulnerability to misspellings and underscores the need for enhanced training or algorithmic adjustments to improve its robustness. SpaCy's transition-based parsing method may not leverage context as effectively as other models, contributing to its lower resilience. However, the fine-tuned version of SpaCy shows a marked improvement, achieving an MRS of 0.9358 and reducing the accuracy loss to 6.5% [10].

The Flair model exhibits the highest resilience among the evaluated models, with an MRS of 0.9613 and a minimal accuracy loss of 3.9%. Flair's use of contextual string embeddings and integration of various embeddings, such as BERT and ELMo, allow it to capture nuanced contextual information, making it highly effective at handling misspelled inputs and maintaining performance despite orthographic errors [2].

Roberta also shows strong resilience, with an MRS of 0.9175 and an accuracy loss of 8.8%. As a transformer-based model optimized from BERT, Roberta effectively captures intricate contextual dependencies, contributing to its robustness against misspellings [13]. However, it still has some room for improvement.

4.2   Case Study: Effective Classification of Target Word

In a demonstration of effective entity recognition, we analyzed the influence of contextual words on the classification of the target word "John" from the sentence "John Smith ate Pizza." This analysis was visualized using a Sankey diagram, which illustrates the influence flow from the surrounding words toward the classification decision for "John." The text was tested on all the models in this study and most showed a close variation to Sankey diagram shown in Fig. 3. The diagram shows that the words "John" and "Smith" have a significant impact on pulling the classification toward "Person" indicating that these words collectively contribute to recognizing "Joh" as part of a person's name. Conversely, "at" and "Pizza" exert influence towards a classification of "None," suggesting that these words, when considered in isolation, do not support the classification of "John" as a person entity.

This selective impact demonstrates the model's nuanced ability to weigh the relevance of contextual words in classifying a target word. While "John" and "Smith" reinforce each other to strengthen the 'Person' category, the non-relevant words "ate" and "Pizza" are correctly deemed inconsequential to the entity recognition of "John," highlighting NEF capacity to focus on contextual cues for accurate classification.

John Smith ate pizza

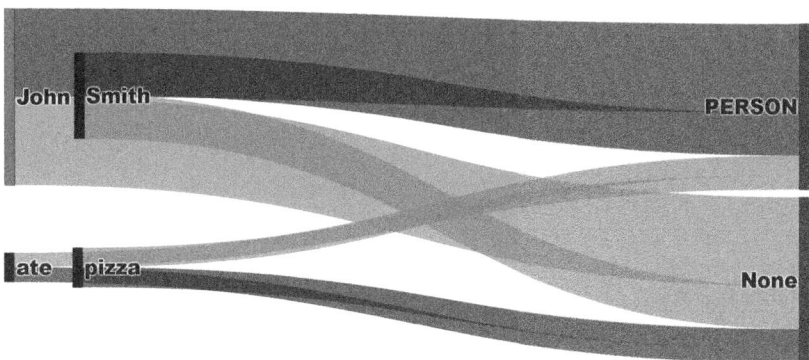

Fig. 3. Sankey diagram illustrating the influence of contextual words on the classification of the target word "John" in the sentence "John Smith ate pizza." Dark gray flows indicate positive influence, while light gray flows represent negative influence on the model's classification decision.

4.3   Case Study: 'Lloyd' vs. 'Loyd'

In our experiments, we analyzed many samples where the models had failed on the CoNLL-03 dataset. We chose the following example to illustrate the complexity of handling lexical variations that do not constitute typical misspellings. The text we analyzed is: "Lloyd did not say what form the discipline would take." The name "Lloyd" is a variation of "Loyd" found in Welsh, further illustrating the challenges NER systems face with such variations.

Using LIME to generate explanations and Sankey diagrams to visualize these challenges, we observed that multiple models struggled to identify the target words Lloyd and its variant Loyd. The models often classified Lloyd as an organization entity instead of a person. This is likely because there are organizations named Lloyd. Still, the models should understand the difference from context, as many organizations are named after persons.

Analyzing the models' responses using LIME revealed interesting patterns. A diagram (see Fig. 4) created using the Stanza model shows that the name "Lloyd" predominantly impacts the classification towards the organization category. However, the rest of the contextual words, represented on the right side of the diagram by a black bar, positively influence the identification of "Lloyd" as a person entity, except for the word "not". Removing the word "not" or substituting "Lloyd" with "Loyd" leads the model to classify it as a person correctly.

Lloyd did not say what form the discipline would take

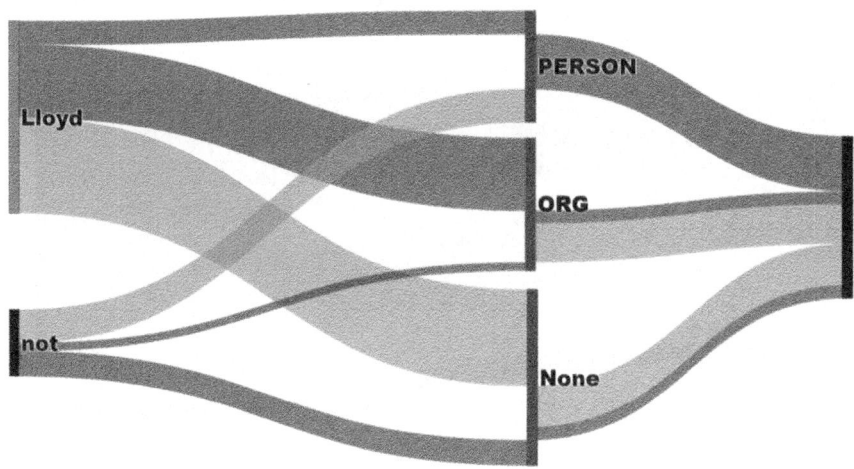

Fig. 4. Sankey diagram illustrating the model's predictions when 'Lloyd' is recognized.

4.4   Fine-Tuning Experiment on SpaCy for Improving MRS Scores

Following fine-tuning, the SpaCy model's MRS improved markedly from 0.7634 to 0.9358. This enhanced MRS indicates that misspellings now reduce the model's accuracy in entity recognition by only approximately 6.5%, a significant improvement from the 24% accuracy loss observed in the pre-tuning performance, resulting in a 17.5% improvement. This development highlights the effectiveness of targeted improvements using the NEF to gain insights and enhance model performance. The analysis utilizing LIME provided further insights into this improvement. It indicated that the increase in MRS might not necessarily be attributed to better utilization of contextual information. Instead, LIME analysis suggests that the model's improvement is primarily due to its enhanced ability to recognize variations and misspellings of names directly. This points to the model becoming more robust in identifying misspelled tokens as belonging to the person category without necessarily relying more heavily on the surrounding context.

5 Discussion

The analysis of NER models using our proposed NEF framework provides significant insights into their behavior when faced with lexical variations. Our case studies highlight the challenges and differences in how various models process and weigh contextual information surrounding entity names.

1. **Model Performance**: NEF reveals notable differences in how each model processes context:
   - **Stanza and SpaCy**: These models show limitations in handling lexical variations effectively, with SpaCy relying heavily on exact word matches. Showing high vulnerability to lexical variations.
   - **Flair and RoBERTa**: These models demonstrate higher resilience to misspellings, likely due to their use of contextual embeddings and transformer-based architectures.

Future research could expand the application of NEF to different languages and pair it with different metrics that could provide more insights into model behavior and robustness across diverse linguistic contexts. We should seek to enhance models' tolerance to input variations while carefully managing the trade-off with increased model complexity. Our results indicate different paths for increased robustness with specialized fine-tuning or expanding the model's ability to utilize context.

6 Conclusion

This study presents advancements in the domain of NER by introducing the method NEF, developing the metric MRS, and insightful findings on model performance. NEF is a pioneering approach designed to enhance the explainability and robustness of NER models. Uniquely, NEF transforms the sequence-based NER task into a multi-class classification problem and integrates a version of LIME using the ridge regression model, providing precise and interpretable insights into model decisions. One of the standout features of NEF is its ability to operate independently of underlying confidence scores, making it one of the few methods available for explaining NER in this manner and the only one to our knowledge that offers this level of simplicity and broad applicability. Our study tested NEF on various NER models, including Stanza, SpaCy, Flair, and RoBERTa, demonstrating its universal applicability.

We introduce the MRS, a novel metric designed to evaluate NER models' resilience to lexical variations, specifically misspellings in target words. MRS measures a model's ability to accurately identify entities despite orthographic deviations, reflecting real-world challenges of typographical errors and enhancing our understanding of model robustness.

Our experiments reveal that models like Flair and RoBERTa, which leverage extensive contextual information, are more resilient to misspellings than SpaCy and Stanza. This conclusion is based on a broad range of case studies and experimental results, highlighting each model's strengths and weaknesses.

Implementing NEF has enabled the identification of critical patterns in model performance, particularly regarding how different NER models process and respond to contextual cues and orthographic deviations. For example, fine-tuning the SpaCy model on misspelled data significantly improved its robustness, reducing accuracy loss from 24% to 6.5%. This finding underscores the practical value of targeted model adjustments informed by NEF.

To build upon this study's findings, future research could expand the application of NEF to different languages and more complex entity recognition tasks. Additionally, refining metrics like the MRS and extending fine-tuning strategies to address other model weaknesses will be essential for capturing comprehensive performance dynamics revealed through explainability studies.

References

1. Agarwal, O., Yang, Y., Wallace, B.C., Nenkova, A.: Interpretability analysis for named entity recognition to understand system predictions and how they can improve. Comput. Linguist. **47**(1), 117–140 (2021)
2. Akbik, A., Bergmann, T., Blythe, D., Rasul, K., Schweter, S., Vollgraf, R.: FLAIR: an easy-to-use framework for state-of-the-art NLP. In: Proceedings of the 2019 Conference of the North American Chapter of the Association for Computational Linguistics (Demonstrations), pp. 54–59 (2019)
3. Alam, M.N., Kaur, M., Kabir, M.S.: Explainable AI in healthcare: enhancing transparency and trust upon legal and ethical consideration. Int. Res. J. Eng. Technol. **10**(6), 1–9 (2023)
4. Augenstein, I., Derczynski, L., Bontcheva, K.: Generalisation in named entity recognition: a quantitative analysis. Comput. Speech Lang. **44**, 61–83 (2017)
5. Balasuriya, D., Ringland, N., Nothman, J., Murphy, T., Curran, J.R.: Named entity recognition in wikipedia. In: Proceedings of the 2009 Workshop on the People's Web Meets NLP: Collaboratively Constructed Semantic Resources (People's Web), pp. 10–18 (2009)
6. Doshi-Velez, F., Kim, B.: Towards a rigorous science of interpretable machine learning. Stat **1050**, 2 (2017)

7. Fu, J., Liu, P., Neubig, G.: Interpretable multi-dataset evaluation for named entity recognition. In: Proceedings of the 2020 Conference on Empirical Methods in Natural Language Processing (EMNLP), pp. 6058–6069 (2020)

8. Grishman, R., Sundheim, B.M.: Message understanding conference-6: a brief history. In: COLING 1996 volume 1: The 16th International Conference on Computational Linguistics (1996)

9. Güngör, O., Güngör, T., Uskudarli, S.: EXSEQREG: explaining sequence-based nlp tasks with regions with a case study using morphological features for named entity recognition. PLoS ONE **15**(12), e0244179 (2020)

10. Honnibal, M., Montani, I.: spaCy 2: natural language understanding with bloom embeddings, convolutional neural networks and incremental parsing. To appear **7**(1), 411–420 (2017)

11. Lassen, I.M.S., Almasi, M., Enevoldsen, K., Kristensen-McLachlan, R.D.: Detecting intersectionality in NER models: a data-driven approach. In: Proceedings of the 7th Joint SIGHUM Workshop on Computational Linguistics for Cultural Heritage, Social Sciences, Humanities and Literature, pp. 116–127 (2023)

12. Lin, B.Y., Gao, W., Yan, J., Moreno, R., Ren, X.: RockNER: a simple method to create adversarial examples for evaluating the robustness of named entity recognition models. In: Proceedings of the 2021 Conference on Empirical Methods in Natural Language Processing, pp. 3728–3737 (2021)

13. Liu, Y., et al.: Roberta: a robustly optimized bert pretraining approach. arXiv preprint arXiv:1907.11692 (2019)

14. Moradi, M., Samwald, M.: Evaluating the robustness of neural language models to input perturbations. In: Proceedings of the 2021 Conference on Empirical Methods in Natural Language Processing, pp. 1558–1570 (2021)

15. Qi, P., Zhang, Y., Zhang, Y., Bolton, J., Manning, C.D.: Stanza: a python natural language processing toolkit for many human languages. In: Proceedings of the 58th Annual Meeting of the Association for Computational Linguistics: System Demonstrations, pp. 101–108 (2020)

16. Ribeiro, M.T., Singh, S., Guestrin, C.: "Why should i trust you?" Explaining the predictions of any classifier. In: Proceedings of the 22nd ACM SIGKDD International Conference on Knowledge Discovery and Data Mining, pp. 1135–1144 (2016)

17. Rueda, A., Mellado, E.A., Lignos, C.: CoNLL#: Fine-grained Error Analysis and a Corrected Test Set for CoNLL-03 English (2024). http://arxiv.org/abs/2405.11865. arXiv:2405.11865

18. Räz, T., Beisbart, C.: The importance of understanding deep learning. Erkenntnis **89**(5), 1823–1840 (2024)

19. Sang, E.F.T.K., De Meulder, F.: Introduction to the CoNLL-2003 Shared Task: Language-Independent Named Entity Recognition (2003). http://arxiv.org/abs/cs/0306050. arXiv:cs/0306050

20. Sekine, S.: Extended named entity ontology with attribute information. In: LREC (2008)

21. Wang, W., Wang, R., Wang, L., Wang, Z., Ye, A.: Towards a robust deep neural network against adversarial texts: a survey. IEEE Trans. Knowl. Data Eng. **35**(3), 3159–3179 (2021)

22. Zügner, D., Akbarnejad, A., Günnemann, S.: Adversarial attacks on neural networks for graph data. In: Proceedings of the 24th ACM SIGKDD International Conference on Knowledge Discovery & Data Mining, pp. 2847–2856 (2018)

Neural Nets

Revealing Limitations of ResNet Models for Deep Evaluation in Chess

Jakub Zeman$^{(\boxtimes)}$ and Ladislava Smítková Janků

Czech Technical University Prague, Thákurova 9, 16000 Prague, Czech Republic
{zemanj37,smitkul}@fit.cvut.cz
https://www.fit.cvut.cz

Abstract. Convolutional neural networks have become core parts of many modern chess engines. CNNs with their ability to predict the next move from the current board configuration can be utilized as a replacement for heuristic functions intended to prune the game tree. This prediction can however serve as a standalone chess engine. This paper studies the ability to predict the best move by searching the game tree with a comparison to CNN prediction. Particularly, this paper reveals some limitations of CNNs, specifically ResNet models, to predict the best move in certain scenarios. This paper also proposes a method for measuring chessboard complexity, which can be very helpful for the identification of board configurations, where CNNs struggle with prediction.

Keywords: Convolutional Neural Networks · ResNet · Searchless Chess · Move Prediction

1 Introduction

The primary objectives of CNNs in chess engines are the evaluation of board positions and the prediction of the next move. Using visible elements such as piece count and their distribution across the board, CNNs can extract and utilize features such as king safety, pawn structures, pawns near promotion, movable rooks, or blocked bishops. While these features are highly correlated with the probability of winning, when aiming for the most accurate evaluation or move selection, it is important to take into account possible future gameplay from the current configuration. Some kind of deeper chess understanding, which includes future possibilities is very important for achieving a high Elo playing style. Elo is a metric used to measure a player's skill level in chess and is adjusted based on the outcomes of the games. This described deeper understanding can have many forms. Humans, for instance, switch perspectives and simulate gameplay mentally. Computers typically construct a game tree, evaluate it, and backpropagate using the MiniMax or Monte Carlo tree search algorithm. There are, however, chess engines that do not require to search a game tree. Its decision-making process relies solely on a single forward pass of a CNN. Examples of these are Li-Chess bots from the Maia chess project [1].

M. Bramer and F. Stahl (Eds.): SGAI 2024, LNAI 15446, pp. 19–32, 2025.
https://doi.org/10.1007/978-3-031-77915-2_2

2   Related Work

The game of chess has been extensively studied in the artificial intelligence domain since the beginnings of computers. The first expert systems relied heavily on a broad search of the game tree, expertly designed heuristic functions, and a database of prior knowledge. However, this approach was not feasible for some board games due to the enormous branching factor of the game tree and the impossibility of algorithmically describing heuristic functions. A prime example is the game Go.

With the use of neural networks, it is possible to overcome obstacles of the game Go by reducing the demands on the search and generalizing heuristic functions to learn complex patterns from data. This advancement made it possible to create a framework that is easily transferable to different board games and can be trained completely without human supervision by self-play even without knowledge of the rules [2–5].

This progress also enhanced state-of-the-art engines like Stockfish, which increased its performance through the use of neural networks [6]. Neural networks have not only improved performance but also enabled training systems for entirely different tasks, such as predicting the moves a human player would make and personalizing these moves [1,7].

Chess has long been a benchmark for AI, and very recently, there have been numerous successful applications of language modeling by transformer architectures at the scale of chess to test their capabilities [8–11].

An evident trend is the minimization of the search part of the algorithm. Or even a complete replacement of the search with a single forward pass of the NN [1,12]. This approach offers framework/model maximum flexibility but on the other hand, has its limits. Estimating an architecture's ability to model decisions that require an understanding of the game tree structure is crucial for designing such systems and thus is the core subject of study of this paper.

3   Hypothesis Formulation

The capabilities of CNNs to predict the best moves of human players or computer engines with a high degree of accuracy and the fact, that a CNN with its single forward pass can substitute the whole move selection process at the high Elo rating lays a foundation for the main hypothesis of this paper:

Theorem 1. *CNNs can serve as a viable alternative to the MiniMax or MCTS algorithm for best move selection or board evaluation. Specifically, CNNs can achieve this objective in consideration of possible future gameplay in a single forward pass, without requiring a game tree.*

This hypothesis is too inexplicit in order to reject it formally. Due to this reason, another 2 supplementary hypotheses will be proposed for 2 experiments. Rejecting these supplementary hypotheses rejects indirectly the main hypothesis.

3.1   More Detailed Explanation Using Example

To further illustrate the hypothesis, this section provides a practical example explaining the issue with a complex board configuration.

Certain board configurations may appear visually similar but have significant differences in evaluation due to information hidden in the game tree. An example of such configuration can be seen in Fig. 1.

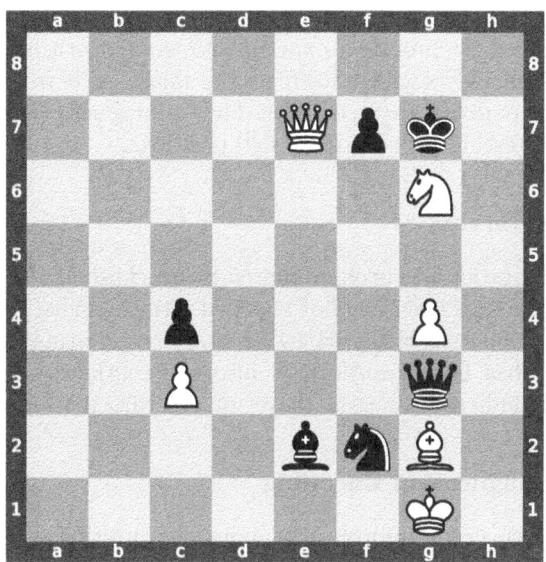

Fig. 1. Example (black on the move)

There are two possible outcomes of the game:

- Black can make Kxg6, has material advantage and ends with draw after Qg5+
- Alternatively, black can play Nxg4 and has a high chance of winning

Although these two positions can look very similar from the pixel-image perspective and possible extracted features[1], there is a significant difference in the probability of winning. The key difference is hidden in the game tree.

This paper aims to study such examples and determine whether CNNs can accurately select the best move and evaluate such configurations. The inability of CNNs to predict moves like Nxg4, where impactful information is hidden in the game tree, would contradict the mentioned hypothesis.

---

[1] Similar pieces count, similar positions, similar space controlled, no pieces are under attack.

4   Technical Background for Experiments

In this paper, two experiments utilizing training a neural network for move prediction and board evaluation on an algorithmically generated dataset are evaluated. This section provides technical details covering dataset generation, encoding, neural network architecture, and training process.

4.1   Board Configurations Generation

Board configurations for proposed experiments were algorithmically generated by letting Stockfish play against itself at the depth of 6 with 20% of moves randomly selected to diversify the dataset. The training set consists of 10 million positions and the testing set consists of 640 positions.

4.2   Assigning Targets

Each board configuration has been evaluated by Stockfish at the required depth. The suggested move has been one hot encoded into the move vector. The move vector consists of 4096 positions. 64*64 for start and destination squares. The board evaluation has been transformed into the continuous range of $[-1, 1]$, where the value 1 indicates that the player on the turn is winning.

4.3   Board Configuration Encoding

Firstly, the network needs information about the position of pieces. For that purpose, the input to the CNN consists of several layers. There exist 6 types of pieces for each player in the game of chess and the positions of each kind of piece are represented in its own layer. Positions of pieces within a chess board are represented by a 2D array of $8 * 8$ dimensions with the value 1 for a present piece and 0 if this type of piece is not present. To represent all these pieces' positions, a total of 12 2D layers is required. Additionally, the input includes one additional layer for each player with values 1 on squares where the current player can place any of its pieces had it been on the turn and 0 otherwise.

The perspective is switched on the opponent's turn, eliminating the need for an additional feature to indicate the current player.

4.4   Neural Network Architecture

Experiments employ training multiple ResNet neural networks [13]. Dual-head ResNet architecture was utilized similarly as in the AlphaZero [2] project. Specifically ResNet 18, 50, and 152 modified to take 14 color profiles as an input. The feature extraction part is the same for both heads. The output is then split using fully connected linear layers into both heads. The policy head predicts the probabilities of the next moves, while the value head evaluates the board position. No further modifications to standard ResNet architecture have been made.

4.5   Training Process

The training process consisted of 10 thousand training steps. In each step, 40,960 board configurations were fed forward to the neural network in 10 batches of 4,096 board positions and backpropagated by utilizing the Adam optimizer. The policy head was trained using cross-entropy loss. The value head was trained using MSE. During each step, the training was conducted over three epochs, with the learning rate being updated using a geometric sequence with a hyper-parameter *gamma* = 0.9. After each epoch, all of the 40,960 positions were randomly shuffled. After each step, half of these 40,960 positions were randomly swapped with random positions in the training set. Finally, a small amount of L2 regularization was applied to prevent overfitting.

5   Experiment 1

The first experiment aims to measure the ability of CNN to utilize information extracted from deep tree searches. To measure this ability two training datasets can be created with different depths. The dataset with greater depth contains more information from deep search of the game tree. The initial intuition is that a CNN trained on a deeper dataset may have the ability to comprehend and utilize this information and might perform better. In case any performance gain is not observed we may conclude that CNN is not able to utilize such information. Thus, the hypothesis for this experiment can be formulated like this:

Theorem 2. *Models trained on a dataset of depth 12 will have better performance than models trained on a dataset of depth 6 when both evaluated on the testing set of depth 12.*

The proposed algorithm for rejecting or proving the hypothesis is stated as follows:

1. Generate training and testing sets at the depth of 6 as well as at the depth of 12.
2. Train ResNet 18, 50, and 152 on both training sets.
3. After each training step, evaluate the models' ability to classify the correct move and evaluate the board on the testing set of depth corresponding to the training depth. Additionally, evaluate the models trained on depth 6 on the testing set of depth 12.

Finally, the move classification results of the proposed experiment can be seen in Fig. 2 and board evaluation results can be seen in Fig. 3. To smooth fluctuations, the results were averaged over 1000 training steps.

5.1   Discussion

To begin with, the ResNet types show no significant differences from one another. On the same dataset, ResNet18 can fit the data similarly to ResNet152. The only

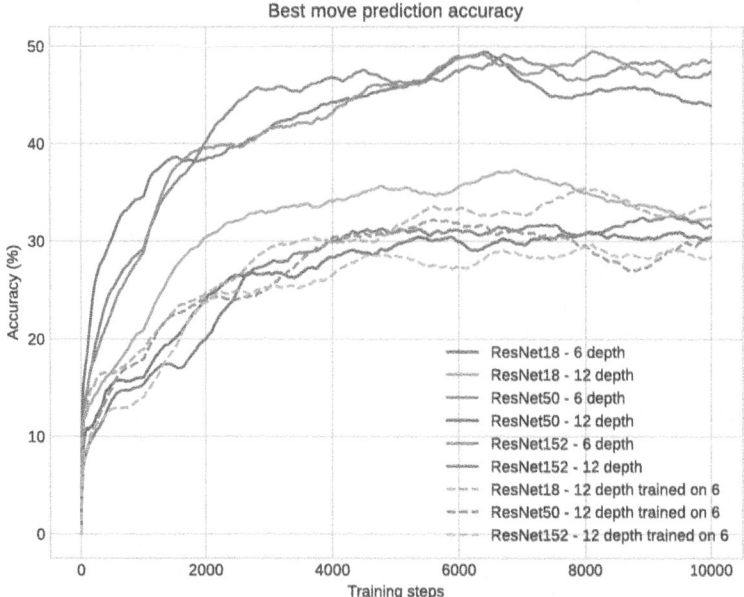

Fig. 2. Results for move classification

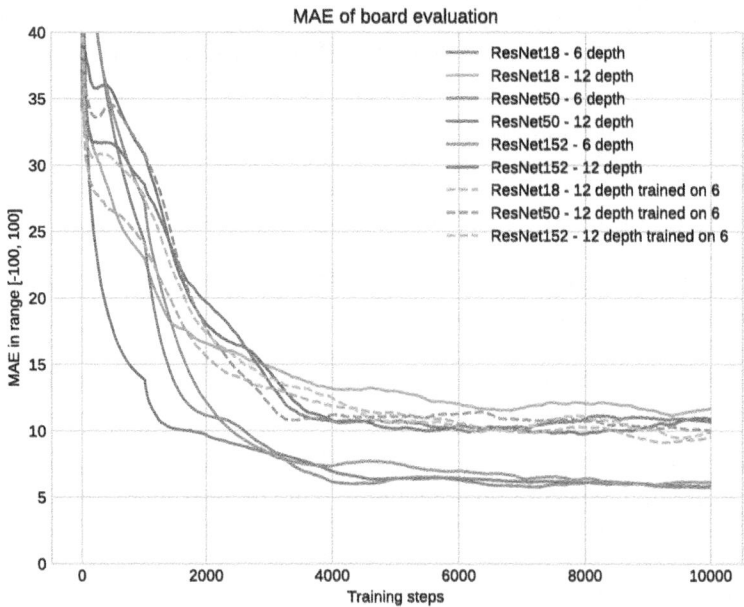

Fig. 3. Results for board evaluation

difference is that ResNet18 learns faster from the beginning, which is expected since ResNet18 is a much less complex model.

In case CNNs were able to approximate the result of the MiniMax algorithm, then fitting evaluations yield by MiniMax run to higher depths would correspond to approximating more complex functions. As a result, there would be a connection between the depth of the generated dataset and the complexity of the model used. The absence of this connection indicates that the selected models' complexity is sufficient for the proposed task or that fitting MiniMax run to higher depths is a fundamentally impossible task.

Overall, there are negligible differences between all models within the same testing set, however, there is a significant gap between testing sets at different depths, regardless of the complexity of the model applied to them. Depth 6 exhibits an average classification accuracy of around 50% over 1000 steps. In contrast, depth 12 is correctly classified only around 30% on average over 1000 steps. A similar pattern can be seen in the board evaluation. Predicting lower depths with higher accuracy is expected due to the reduced complexity of the task. While it is possible to achieve accuracy over 99% in classic image recognition problems [14], such a task is not comparable to the complex classification task of predicting chess moves, where saturation of around 50% in a single forward pass is expected. This expectation is supported by empirical evidence from the Maia chess project, which achieved similar accuracy [1], and is conceptually grounded in the observation that, in many configurations, multiple moves are either similarly powerful or present personal strategic choices.

The most important revelation is that incorporating additional depth in the training data did not improve the performance on the testing data. Interestingly, the final best move prediction performance on the depth 12 test set was achieved by the ResNet18 model that was trained on the depth of 6, additionally all less deeply trained models achieved slightly better final evaluation performance than more deeply trained models on the deeper test set. This observation dismisses the hypothesis proposed for this experiment as well as the main hypothesis of this paper. This suggests that CNNs cannot select the best move or evaluate board configuration in consideration of possible future gameplay, and thus cannot serve as a viable alternative to algorithms with such capabilities.

6 Board Complexity

The results obtained from the previous experiments revealed that the ability of CNNs to learn from higher-depth searches of the MiniMax algorithm was severely limited, as the error rates remained similar to the models trained on lower-depth searches.

6.1 Necessity of Measuring a Board Complexity

Nevertheless, CNNs were able to predict about 30% of moves correctly to the Stockfish brute-force MiniMax algorithm implementation run to depth 12.

Achieving such accuracy may seem impressive at first glance. However, the final performance in the game of chess is determined by the sequence of moves leading to a win or a loss. Therefore, assessing the ability of a subject to predict the next move on a single position is inadequate without the consideration of the complexity of the position and the difficulty of understanding and evaluating it in order to select the next move. While some positions in a professional game may be predicted by a beginner, such as the second move of a trade, others may be much more complex.

To gain a deeper understanding of the relationship between the MiniMax algorithm and the neural network's forward pass, it is important to algorithmically measure the difficulty of the best move prediction for a given board configuration. By doing so, it can be determined whether there are any special cases in which the neural network can accurately predict the MiniMax algorithm or whether this is fundamentally an impossible task.

6.2   Explaining the Board Complexity

Let us consider board positions in Fig. 4 and Fig. 5 to examine the impact of board complexity on the ability to understand and evaluate the next move.

In the position 4, where black is on the turn, the optimal move is easily recognizable by any player, regardless of their skill level or by any chess engine used, regardless of the depth of search. It is evident that black should capture the white queen with the king.

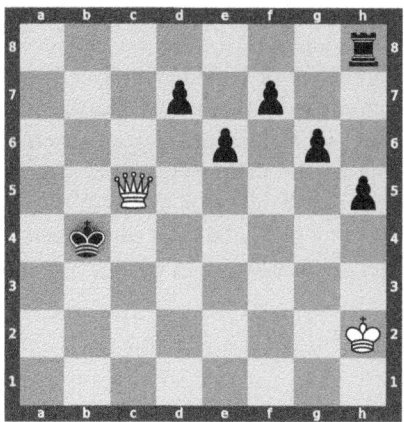

Fig. 4. Clear move (black on turn)

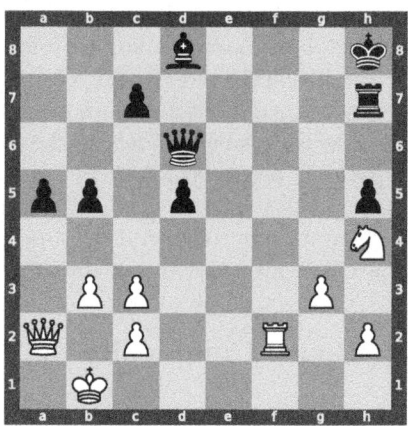

Fig. 5. Surprising move (white on turn)

In contrast, the position 5 is more challenging. While a beginner may choose to capture the hanging pawn on a5 with his queen, a more sophisticated move, which requires deeper analysis, is to move the rook to protected square f8.

To further examine this position, we can analyze the probabilities of the next moves at various depths for both positions.

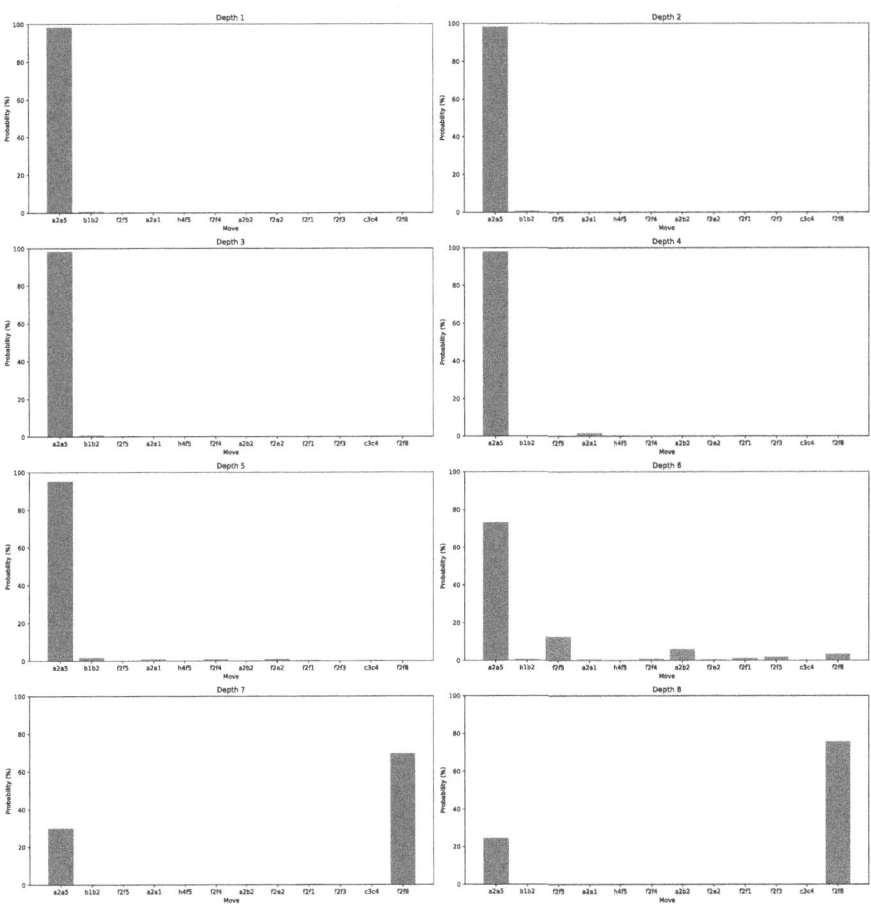

Fig. 6. Move probabilities according to particular depths

In comparison to position 4, position 5 has a more complex game tree, with various best moves as the search depth increases. Taking the hanging pawn is the best move until the depth of 7, where f2f8+ suddenly arises as the best move from an almost negligible initial evaluation. This implies that some important information is hidden in the game tree, and to uncover it, a search up to depth 7 is required. Move probabilities according to particular depths for position 5 are visualized in Fig. 6.

The main difference between the two positions is that in the first position, the benefit of the optimal move is immediately apparent, while in the second position, the advantage is hidden in the game tree.

These examples illustrate how board complexity affects the ability to understand and evaluate a chess position and highlight the importance of considering the complexity level of each position in assessing the ability to predict the next move.

6.3   Meassuring the Board Complexity Algorithmically

The proposed board complexity metric allows to measure these expertly observed results algorithmically. The algorithm progressively searches deeper and deeper until it finds a move satisfying the following conditions. The move was initially evaluated with a probability below 5% but newly has the highest probability of being played with a probability over 40%. The algorithm for obtaining probability distribution is described in Subsect. 6.4 In case no such example was found in the game tree of depth of 12, the complexity evaluation for that board position is assigned as 0. If such a move was found, the value of the proposed metric is the depth where the move was found.

Practical usage of this metric indeed assigns complexity 0 to the board in the Fig. 4 and complexity 7 to the board in the Fig. 5.

6.4   Move Probability Prediction

This subsection provides a function estimating move probabilities from Stockfish's centipawn evaluation, which was used to calculate board complexity.

The first step is to calculate the gain of every move in centipawns.

$$gain = \text{evaluation before move} - \text{evaluation after move} \qquad (1)$$

In the second step, 25% of weak outliers are removed as significantly suboptimal. This percentage is based on the practical observation that keeping these moves skews the distribution over all the remaining moves.

The reduced data is then further transformed using MinMax scaler resulting in a nearly uniform distribution.

However, the goal was achieving of more exponential-like distribution. To accomplish this goal, each value was raised to the power of four, thus creating a greater difference between high and low values.

Finally, the probabilities were then calculated by dividing each value by the sum of all values of all moves. This process generated a target that closely approximates an exponential probability distribution, with a sum equal to 1. The algorithm's pseudocode is as follows:

```
1: function MOVE_PROB(board)
2:     base ← eval_board(board)
3:     moves ← [(m, eval_move(board, m) − base) for m in board.legal_moves]
4:     if len(moves) ≥ 4 then
5:         moves ← Top75Percent(moves)
6:     end if
7:     probs ← MinMaxScaler(moves)
```

8:      probs ← [pow(x, 8) for x in probs]
9:      **return** $[x/\text{sum(probs)}$ for x in probs]
10: **end function**

7   Experiment 2

With the use of the board complexity metric, a straightforward experiment has been proposed. The experiment involves comparing the best-move matching accuracy on two sets of board positions, one with a complexity level of 0 and the other with a complexity level of 6.

This experiment introduces a supplementary hypothesis. Rejecting this supplementary hypothesis indirectly rejects the main hypothesis. Finally, the hypothesis for the second experiment is stated as follows:

Theorem 3. *The best move matching accuracy of CNN trained on the dataset of depth 6 will be significantly higher when compared to random predictions. This gain will be observable on both testing sets of complexity 0 and 6.*

7.1   Experiment Execution

Testing sets of sizes of 100 board configurations for 0 and 6 were generated. Due to some problems with board complexity mentioned in Sect. 8, the testing set for complexity 6 has to be manually checked and cleaned. The ResNet152 model, which exhibited the highest accuracy at the depth of 6 on the testing set during the training process of experiment 1, was selected for testing purposes. This model achieved an average accuracy of approximately 50% accuracy over 1000 training steps. To establish a solid baseline for comparison, random predictions were averaged over 100 testing iterations. Finally, the results are shown in the Fig. 7.

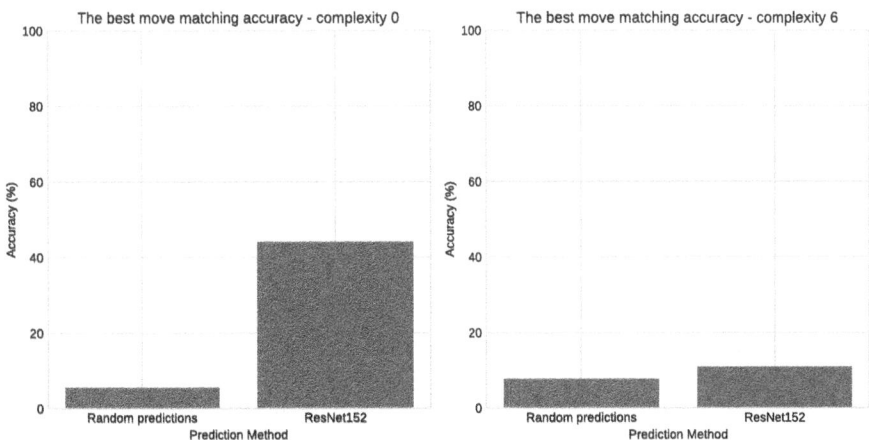

Fig. 7. Graphical representation of results

7.2 Discussion

As expected, the results obtained on board positions with a complexity level of 0 were similar to those achieved on the whole testing set regardless of the complexity split. The best move matching accuracy on the testing set of complexity 6 is, however, significantly lower and is comparable to random predictions. This fact contradicts the supplementary hypothesis, and thus indirectly rejects the main hypothesis.

8 Open Issues with Complexity Metric

Although the board complexity metric looks solid, it has certain weaknesses.

Firstly there are some special cases, where according to this metric, the board has high complexity and the key information is hidden deep in the game tree, however, in practice, the information is clearly visible. An example of such a board configuration involves pushing the last pawn multiple squares to the promotion. Technically, the information is hidden deep in the game tree, but it is still obvious for any beginner.

Secondly, there is a huge problem with this specific complexity metric implementation using Stockfish that the metric relies on initial evaluation at the depth of 1. The Stockfish chess engine is not intended and fine-tuned to run at the depth of 1, so the results are sometimes very odd, even in quite simple cases.

This wasn't a problem for this testing purpose, because expertly checking one hundred boards wasn't that difficult. Also, minor deviations from the actual complexity shouldn't hinder the experiment as this experiment was only a supplementary experiment to the first one, which is algorithmically reproducible. However, for autonomous deployment, this metric should be fine-tuned and probably use some more simple engine fine-tuned to run in shallow depths.

9 Possible Applications

Understanding the limitations of CNNs to predict moves selected based on deep evaluation has possible applications in human move prediction in projects similar to the Maia chess [1]. The newly discovered limitations indicate that there is a limit to the performance that CNNs can achieve in one forward pass. Thus when aiming to predict human moves at the high Elo rating, who are typically capable of deep analysis, board complexity metrics, when properly implemented, may help with the identification of board configurations that are easy enough for players at the given Elo rating to predict, but too complex for CNN. In such cases, a deep search is still necessary, either by completely replacing CNN or by providing this information to CNN as an input. In the end, such steps may help to improve human prediction models to surpass a performance limit and align them to the higher-rated players not only by their game style but also by their performance and ability to search the game tree.

10   Conclusion

In conclusion, the experiments in this paper aimed to investigate the capabilities of CNNs to predict moves based on deep evaluation of the game tree.

The first experiment utilized training multiple models at the depths of 6 and 12 of a game tree and testing them at the depth of 12. The results revealed that providing additional depth in the training data did not improve performance. This finding contradicts the hypothesis that CNNs can serve as a viable alternative to the algorithms searching the game tree.

In the second experiment, the board complexity metric was introduced and then used to generate deep and shallow testing sets. The resNet152 prediction accuracy was compared to the random predictions on both testing sets. The results of this experiment further demonstrate the inability of CNNs to deal with higher-complexity board configurations and highlight the importance of tree search.

Despite the promising accuracy of CNNs in the prediction of algorithmically selected moves, the findings of this paper suggest that there are certain limitations to their ability to predict moves where the key information is hidden in the game tree. The importance of considering board complexity was proposed as a viable factor when selecting an optimal prediction method. Future work could explore more advanced models or hybrid approaches.

After we completed our research, a new paper in the field of chess without search came out and had a huge impact on the searchless chess domain. The authors of that paper trained multiple models of transformer architecture to predict Stockfish moves with great success. In conclusion, the authors stated: *"that is possible to distill an approximation of Stockfish 16 into a feed-forward transformer via standard supervised training. The resulting predictor generalizes well to unseen board states, and, when used in a policy, leads to strong chess play"* [15]. This work showcases the capabilities of attention-based architectures to serve not only as statistical pattern recognizers but also as general algorithm approximations. Our work thus adds to this conclusion by highlighting the gap in the capabilities of CNNs and transformers. In the end, as artificial intelligence is constantly evolving, the limitations of current state-of-the-art models and approaches are opportunities for future architectures.

Acknowledgments. This work was supported by the Student Summer Research Program 2023 of FIT CTU in Prague.

References

1. McIlroy-Young, R., Sen, S., Kleinberg, J., Anderson, A.: Aligning superhuman AI with human behavior: chess as a model system. In: Proceedings of the 26th ACM SIGKDD International Conference on Knowledge Discovery & Data Mining, pp. 1677–1687. Association for Computing Machinery, New York (2020). https://doi.org/10.1145/3394486.3403219

2. Silver, D., et al.: A general reinforcement learning algorithm that masters chess, shogi, and go through self-play. Science **362**(6419), 1140–1144 (2018). https://doi.org/10.1126/science.aar6404

3. Silver, D., et al.: Mastering the game of go without human knowledge. Nature **550**(7676), 354–359 (2017). https://doi.org/10.1038/nature24270

4. Silver, D., et al.: Mastering the game of go with deep neural networks and tree search. Nature **529**(7587), 484–489 (2016). https://doi.org/10.1038/nature16961

5. Schrittwieser, J., et al.: Mastering Atari, Go, Chess and Shogi by Planning with a Learned Model. arXiv preprint arXiv:1911.08265 (2019). http://arxiv.org/abs/1911.08265

6. The Stockfish developers (see AUTHORS file): SF NNUE · Issue #2728 · official-stockfish/Stockfish · GitHub. https://github.com/official-stockfish/Stockfish/issues/2728#issuecomment-650523408. Accessed 20 Apr 2023

7. McIlroy-Young, R., Wang, R., Sen, S., Kleinberg, J.M., Anderson, A.: Learning Personalized Models of Human Behavior in Chess. arXiv preprint arXiv:2008.10086 (2020). https://arxiv.org/abs/2008.10086

8. Feng, X., et al.: ChessGPT: bridging policy learning and language modeling. In: Advances in Neural Information Processing Systems, vol. 36 (2024)

9. Karvonen, A.: Emergent world models and latent variable estimation in chess-playing language models. arXiv preprint arXiv:2403.15498 (2024)

10. Czech, J., Blüml, J., Kersting, K.: Representation Matters: The Game of Chess Poses a Challenge to Vision Transformers. arXiv preprint arXiv:2304.14918 (2023)

11. Toshniwal, S., Wiseman, S., Livescu, K., Gimpel, K.: Chess as a testbed for language model state tracking. In: Proceedings of the AAAI Conference on Artificial Intelligence, vol. 36, no. 10, pp. 11385–11393 (2022)

12. Maesumi, A.: Playing Chess with Limited Look Ahead. arXiv preprint arXiv:2007.02130 (2020). https://arxiv.org/abs/2007.02130

13. He, K., Zhang, X., Ren, S., Sun, J.: Deep residual learning for image recognition. In: Proceedings of the IEEE Conference on Computer Vision and Pattern Recognition, pp. 770–778 (2016)

14. Wölflein, G., Arandjelović, O.: Determining chess game state from an image. J. Imaging **7**(6), 94 (2021). https://doi.org/10.3390/jimaging7060094

15. Ruoss, A., et al.: Grandmaster-Level Chess Without Search. arXiv preprint arXiv:2402.04494 (2024). https://arxiv.org/abs/2402.04494

Quasi Biologically Plausible Category Learning

Christian Huyck[✉]

Middlesex University, London NW4 4BT, UK
c.huyck@mdx.ac.uk
https://cwa.mdx.ac.uk/chris/chrisroot.html

Abstract. This paper explores machine learning using adaptive spiking neurons and spike timing dependent plasticity (STDP). This is shown to work on two categorisation tasks. It is neuro-biologically flawed but works with a small number of point neurons, and is much closer to biology than multi layer perceptrons. The work is derived from mathematical exploration and the portion of the parameter space where categorisation works is small. This is just a proof of concept that categorisation can be done by these spiking competitive nets with STDP. The parameter space could be further explored to find better results, or how to apply this to new categorisation tasks. This work provides support for further exploration of neurobiologically plausible category learning.

Keywords: Spiking Neurons · Spike Timing Dependent Plasticity · Categorisation · MNIST

1 Introduction

The human brain is the basis of intelligent behaviour, including categorisation. Many machine learning algorithms are used to categorise, but none accurately duplicates the behaviour of the brain. Despite using neuron-like units, most neural network learning algorithms do not attempt to duplicate the brain's behaviour. Part of the problem is that the academic community does not completely understand how the brain works in general, or how it learns to categorise in particular.

None the less, things are known about the brain that are widely ignored in machine learning. Neurons spike, as opposed to have continuous valued outputs; the structure of the network of neurons is not layered, but instead is recurrently connected; and learning is done by a Hebbian learning rule instead of gradient descent to reduce an error gradient.

This paper presents a categorisation system using spiking neurons, with recurrent connections, and learning using spike timing dependent plasticity [1], a Hebbian learning rule. There are inconsistencies with biology (discussed in Sect. 4), but the overall system is much closer to a biological system than typical machine learning algorithms.

M. Bramer and F. Stahl (Eds.): SGAI 2024, LNAI 15446, pp. 33–46, 2025.
https://doi.org/10.1007/978-3-031-77915-2_3

In the brain, most if not all learning is Hebbian [2]. If the pre-synaptic neuron tends to cause the post-synaptic neuron to spike, the weight of the excitatory synapses will tend to increase. There are many variations of this rule, but a great deal of biological evidence supports STDP [1]. Bi and Poo [1] have perhaps the first published example that shows the performance of the changing efficiency of biological synapses, and Song et al. [3] have developed an idealised curve that fits the biological data.

The simulations described below are a modification of the work of Diehl and Cook [4], described more fully in Sect. 2.2. The simulations use spiking neurons with dynamic thresholds for some of the neurons. A three population topology is used with plastic synapses (using STDP) between the Input and Categorisation populations, and recurrent connections between the Categorisation and Inhibition populations.

The algorithm is unsupervised. A training, category setting and testing regime is used to generate results that are reasonable on the Iris task and a version of the MNIST digit recognition task (see Sect. 3).

Parameter and hyper parameter settings and exploration mechanisms are described in the hopes that new categorisation tasks can be implemented relatively easily using these mechanisms. Biological plausibility and future work are discussed in Sect. 4.

2   Literature Review

The work reported in this paper is the fourth in a series of papers using biologically motivated simulated neurons and learning rules. The first two papers in the series [5,6] were based on simulations that used a feed forward topology with input neurons connected to category neurons. The third was based on competitive topology with three populations [7]. This topology and mechanism are derived from work by Diehl and Cook [4]. This is the basic topology, shown in Fig. 1, used by the simulations described below.

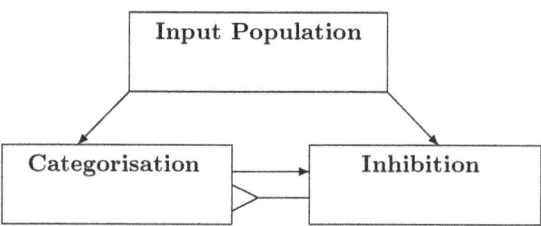

Fig. 1. The boxes represent populations of simulated neurons. The arrows represent excitatory synapses from neurons in the pre-synaptic population to neurons in the post-synaptic population. The fork represents inhibitory synapses from neurons in the pre-synaptic population to neurons in the post-synaptic population. The recurrent connections between the Categorisation population and the Inhibition population lead the Categorisation neurons to compete for firing.

2.1 The Story so Far

My colleagues and I have worked on spiking nets for decades, frequently working with learning, and almost always Hebbian learning. A paper [8] used leaky integrate and fire neurons, and compensatory Hebbian learning, implemented in a neural simulator I made, to categorise items. On the widely used Iris task, the system got 93.67% (see Sect. 3.2). Work on the Human Brain Project and the need for easier duplicability of results led the group to move to PyNN [9] and Nest [10] instead of the groups' own simulator (see Sect. 2.3).

I am on the faculty of a British University, and as such supervise many BSc and MSc theses. Many of these students are interested in machine learning so work was begun on learning systems with PyNN and Nest and standard synaptic and neural models. This led to the first paper [5], which merely had a neuron for each feature value and one neuron for each category. The results for the Iris task here were 90.6% (again see Sect. 3.2).

The subsequent paper, including work from an MSc thesis, [6] extended the prior work to a new task, and looked at feature combination. A third paper, including work from an MSc thesis, [7] used competitive nets. Having read Diehl and Cook [4] (see Sect. 2.2), it seemed that results were relatively straight forward to generate. However, Diehl and Cook used a non-standard neural model with a dynamic threshold. While new neural models can be added to Nest, and used from PyNN, existing models were explored. The use of adaptive neurons was not particularly successful, and a compensatory weight adjustment between training runs was also not successful. A version of the MNIST digit categorisation task was used (see Sect. 3.3). It had 64 inputs with each value between 0 and 16. One of the benefits compared to Huyck [5] was the feature presentation mechanism, which used 64 input neurons instead of 1088. It turned out that the competitive nets did relatively well without learning, getting around 32% while chance is 10%. Merely randomly placing the categorisation neurons in the 64 dimensional input space, then associating each with a category, led to results better than chance.

This was not particularly satisfying. Another group using competitive spiking nets, a version of the neurons with dynamic threshold [4], and STDP made the code for their paper [11] available. This code was used to generate a result for the Iris task (Sect. 3.2), getting 84% on the training set. It was clear that this was a system that worked. However, this was written in PyNest, and translation to PyNN and Nest led to a system that got 70%. Ostensibly, the same system (considering randomness) was performing significantly worse. Moreover, on an initial attempt at the digit task, it was not clear what parameter settings to use.

2.2 Unsupervised Learning Using STDP

Perhaps the best known example of spiking nets learning using Hebbian rules is by Diehl and Cook [4]. Each input feature has one neuron, and the higher the value of the feature, the more spikes are fired and the sooner they are fired. These neurons are connected to two populations, excitatory neurons that are the categorisation neurons, and inhibitory neurons. These are in turn connected to each other, an instance of the topology in Fig. 1.

The system is trained by presenting instances of the data items to the input population, each for an epoch including a rest interval with no input between epochs. The only plastic synapses are those from the *Input* population to the *Categorisation* population. This is unsupervised behaviour, and to this point the category labels have not been presented.

Once the training is complete, the plastic synapses are replaced by static synapses with the synaptic weights that were learned from training. The test items can be presented, and the spiking behaviour of the category neurons determines the category that is selected.

This behaviour resembles that of a self organising map (SOM) [12]. The nodes of the SOM are like category neurons. The SOM nodes move to a place that responds to particular inputs, and moves away from other nodes. When the category neurons are learning properly, they also respond to particular inputs and not others. If one wants to categorise with a SOM network, each of the nodes can be assigned a particular category. (Unlike SOM nodes, the neurons can also each give support to different categories and then spiking during a test can be used to determine the category of the input features.) Novel input can then be categorised by the category of the node (or nodes) that responds.

This work is derived from work on spiking networks for expectation maximization [13]. Here the networks have even fewer biological constraints with only a two layer system, inputs to category neurons. The category neurons inhibit each other to make a winner takes all network. There is instantaneous spiking, time is continuous, and synaptic transfer is immediate. The homeostatic dynamics from the title of that paper refers to the dynamic threshold. The mathematics describe how neurons are forced to their own place in the input space so that they can represent inputs, and thus successfully categorise.

There is a fair amount of work in extending the work of Habenschuss et al. [13] towards more biological plausibility. Indeed Diehl and Cook [4] (and others e.g. [11]) have extended this work to include neurons that are either excitatory or inhibitory and a reasonable amount of time for synaptic transfer.

2.3   PyNN, Nest and PyNest

There are hundreds of published neural models, and the use of standard simulators has increased reproducibility and reusability. Consequently, the simulations below have been performed in Nest [10], a widely used simulator. Nest typically comes with many neural and synaptic models, but there is a mechanism to include unsupported models. Moreover, it is often useful for topologies to run in different simulators, or indeed in neuromorphic hardware. A middleware package, PyNN [9], can be used to define a topology and runtime side effects, and then use those on different backends (simulators or hardware). Somewhat confusingly, Nest also comes with its own Python front end, PyNest [14].

The code that started the work in this paper (see Sect. 2.1) was in PyNest, though it did use the Nest simulator. The modified code is in PyNN, also using the Nest simulator. Code can be found on https://cwa.mdx.ac.uk/spikeLearn/spikeLearn.html.

2.4 Neurons and Synapses

The neural model used for the excitatory Categorisation neurons and the inhibitory Inhibition neurons is a leaky integrate and fire (LIF) model with a dynamic threshold, which is a form of adaptation. It extends a standard LIF model [15], by making the threshold dynamic. When it spikes, the threshold is increased, so it becomes more difficult to emit another spike.

Equations 1 to 3 are standard input mechanisms and Eq. 4 is the leak. Together, these describe the leaky integrator component of the neuron. Equations 5 and 6 explain the synaptic transfer over time. Equations 7 and 8 explain the firing and the dynamic threshold components of the neuron. Equations 9 and 10 explain the STDP rule.

The activation is the current voltage V_M. Equation 1 describes the change in voltage, V_M is the membrane potential and C_M is the membrane capacity. The four currents are the leak current, the currents from excitatory and inhibitory synapses, and the input current (from some external source). The variable currents are governed by Eqs. 2, 3 and 4. In Eqs. 2 and 3 E_{Ex}^{rev} and E_{In}^{rev} are the reversal potentials; excitation and inhibition change respectively slow as the voltage approaches these reversal potentials. In Eq. 4, V_{rest} is the resting potential of the neuron, and τ_M is the leak constant.

$$\frac{dV_M}{dt} = \frac{(-I_{Leak} - I_{Ex}^{syn} - I_{In}^{syn} + I_{Ext})}{C_M} \qquad (1)$$

$$I_{Exc}^{syn} = G_{Ex} \times (V_M - E_{Ex}^{rev}) \qquad (2)$$

$$I_{Inh}^{syn} = G_{In} \times (V_M - E_{In}^{rev}) \qquad (3)$$

$$I_{Leak} = \frac{C_M(V_M - V_{rest})}{\tau_M} \qquad (4)$$

$$G_{Ex}(t) = k_{Ex} \times t \times e^{-\frac{t}{\tau_{Ex}^{syn}}} \qquad (5)$$

$$G_{In}(t) = k_{In} \times t \times e^{-\frac{t}{\tau_{In}^{syn}}} \qquad (6)$$

In Eqs. 5 and 6, G_{Ex} and G_{In} are the conductance in mS/cm^2 to scale the post-synaptic potential amplitudes used in Eq. 2, and 3. t is the time step. The constant k_{Ex} and k_{In} are chosen so that $G_{Ex}(\tau_{Ex}^{syn}) = 1$ and $G_{In}(\tau_{In}^{syn}) = 1$. The τ_{Ex}^{syn} and the τ_{In}^{syn} are the decay rate of excitatory and inhibitory synaptic current.

The dynamic threshold is implemented by increasing the threshold V_{th} by a constant θ^+, Eq. 7, when the neuron spikes. When it does not spike, the threshold drifts back toward a constant θ^{rest} at a rate determined by another constant t_θ, as shown in Eq. 8.

$$V_{th} = V_{th} + \theta^+ \tag{7}$$

$$V_{th} = -1 * (V_{th} - \theta^{rest})/t_\theta \tag{8}$$

When the voltage reaches the threshold, there is a spike and the voltage is reset. No current is transferred during the refractory period τ_{ref}.

The synaptic plasticity model is spike timing dependent plasticity with a symmetric nearest neighbour spike pairing scheme. As usual, the weight only changes if both pre and post-synaptic neuron spike. When a presynaptic spike occurs, the temporally nearest spike determines whether it causes depression (Eq. 10) or potentiation (Eq. 9).

Equation 9 shows the weight increase when there is a potentiation event with the initial weight w, the learning rate λ, the difference in time between the pre and post-synaptic spikes $\Delta(t)$, the maximum synaptic weight W_{max}, μ_+ the weight potentiation exponent, and the increase time constant τ_+.

$$\Delta w^+ = \lambda * (1 - (w/W_{max}))^{(\mu_+ * |\Delta(t)|/\tau_+)} \tag{9}$$

Equation 10 shows the weight decrease when there is a depression event, with α a constant that skews potentiation vs. depression, μ_- the weight depression exponent, and the decrease time constant τ_-.

$$\Delta w^- = \alpha * \lambda * ((w/W_{max})^{(\mu_- * |\Delta(t)|/\tau_-)} \tag{10}$$

The only plastic synapses used in these simulations are those between the input and Categorisation neurons. They are only plastic during the training phase.

So, using simulated neurons, data is presented to the network one item at a time. The synaptic weights change in response to neuron spikes using an STDP rule to implement unsupervised learning. After training, the spiking net can be used to categorise novel input.

3   Methods

Simulations are run in Ubuntu, with a Nest [10] simulator in this case Nest 3.5 [16], using PyNN [9] to develop the topology and interface with the simulator. Calculations on spikes from the Categorisation neurons are used to determine the categories in Python.

The topology works from input neurons (four in the case of the Iris task, and 64 in the case of the digit task), stimulated by poisson sources. The input neurons are parrot neurons, which merely forward the same spikes from the poisson sources. Following Fig. 1, there are an equal number of Categorisation neurons and Inhibition neurons. Both Categorisation and Inhibition neurons are LIF neurons with dynamic thresholds.

Both Categorisation and Inhibition neurons are stimulated directly from the input via the parrot neurons, and these synapses are relatively sophisticated. First, they are sparse, so that each input only connects to a (randomly selected) portion of the Inhibition and Categorisation neurons. Secondly, the synaptic delay varies randomly between synapses. Thirdly, the initial synaptic weights are randomly selected. Finally, the synaptic weights from input to Categorisation neurons are plastic during training.

Connectivity from Categorisation neurons to Inhibition neurons is one to one. Those weights are all the same and the default delay and parameters are used. The weights from Inhibition to Categorisation neurons are all to all except to the neuron's pair (the one it gets activated by). Again the weights are all the same and the synaptic defaults for delay and synaptic parameters are used. These two populations stand in for the categorisation neurons in the winner take all network from Habenshcuss et al. [13], though they do not duplicate it.

Biological neuron simulations run for a period of simulated time with the neuron behaving throughout the period. When a neuron spikes, activation spreads from it to other neurons that have synapses from it. The initial topology has a great deal of randomness, and the system is run for a considerable amount of time. As the system runs, the LIF neurons with dynamic thresholds can come to be quite different (due to stored variables V_m and V_{th}) than the original neurons. During training, the input to Categorisation synapses can also change quite a bit.

The systems learn via a Hebbian learning rule, and the simulations in this paper use the STDP with nearest neighbour spike pairing describe in Sect. 2.4. Synaptic weights change via STDP, increasing when pre-synaptic neurons spikes before post-synaptic neurons, and decreasing when pre-synaptic neurons spikes after the post-synaptic neurons.

Initial values for voltage used in both tasks are non-standard. The initial voltage variable for the Categorisation and Inhibition neurons are −50.0 and −40.0 respectively in all simulations. Parameter values for the neurons are described below (mostly in Sect. 3.2).

3.1   Running the Categorisation System

The standard running mechanism presents the data via poisson sources, with higher values having larger poisson median values. The parrot neurons then convert these to spikes, and these send current to the Categorisation and Inhibition neurons. The data is presented in three types of phases, learning (training), category setting, and testing.

In the first phase, learning, the system is presented with the data in a series of epochs, one epoch for each input item. In this paper, all learning phases present each training item exactly once. All of the epochs last 400 ms with the poisson spike source being active for 350 ms followed by a rest period of 50 ms. (All times are simulated times.) Spikes can occur in this rest period, due to residual activity from spiking within the period. So, the duration of an Iris training phase (or the other phases) is $(400 * 75) = 30000$ ms as there are 75 training items. The synaptic weights between the parrot and the Categorisation neurons change, and are saved.

In the category setting phase, the system loads the saved synaptic weights from the parrot neurons to the Categorisation neurons onto the now static synapses and reuses the rest of the topology. The data is again presented, but this time the spikes from the Categorisation neurons are stored. These spikes are then used to determine how often each neuron spikes for each category. Training is entirely unsupervised, but here the category values for each Categorisation neuron is determined. Note that a neuron may not spike at all, or spike for any number of categories.

The final phase is the testing phase. Again, the topology is exactly the same as the final topology of the training phase (after learning), and the category setting phase. The system is now presented with the test data, and the spikes from the Categorisation neurons are stored. These spikes along with the amount of spikes from the categorisation neurons during the category setting phase are used to determine the category of each test item. This is the sum of the neurons that spiked in the test epoch weighted by those neurons' category weight ratios and overall spiking in the categorisation phase.

3.2   Iris Categorisation

In the Iris simulations, the three phases are run in sequence. There is two fold cross validation. Each phase takes 30000 ms., or 30 s, so each simulation is run for 90 simulated seconds.

Initially, I explored the digit classifying system in PyNest but it quickly became apparent that the laptop I was using was not powerful enough nor did it have enough memory. So, I moved to the much smaller Iris task. I got this running in PyNest, but was not getting a categorisation value. So, I switched to PyNN, using the non-standard neuron with dynamic threshold, and the non-standard STDP synapse. I spent a great deal of time exploring parameters and hyperparameters before deciding to just figure out the PyNest system and follow it.

It was clear from Habenshcuss et al. [13] and the spiking behaviour of the PyNest system, that it was important that only one or a very few Categorisation neurons spiked in each epoch. This, in collaboration with learning, prevents one or a small number of neurons dominating, which would lead to poor categorisation. This was the problem in Huyck and Erekpaine [7].

I figured out the hyperparameters; in particular I found that sparse connectivity between input and the Categorisation neurons, and input and the Inhibition neurons was important. I also started using the 1 to 1 Categorisation to Inhibition connections, along with 1 to all but one Inhibition to Categorisation connections.

There are several hyperparameters. Input to inhibition synapses are allocated randomly 10% of the time. The delay for each synapse is randomly allocated between 0 and 5 ms., but greater than 0. The weight of the synapse is randomly set between 0 and 0.0002.

Input to categorisation synapses are allocated randomly 60% of the time. The delay for each synapse is randomly allocated between 0 and 10, greater than 0. The initial weight of the synapse is randomly set between 0 and 0.01.

There are 100 Inhibition neurons, and 100 Categorisation neurons. There are four inputs. Note that the input values are not normalized.

An important hyperparameter is the time step. The original PyNest experiments were run in .1 ms time steps. Unsurprisingly, this takes roughly 10 times as long to run as with 1 ms time steps. Perhaps more surprisingly, the categorisation results are quite similar.

There are also system parameters. In particular, I could not find a straight forward translation from the PyNest to Nest systems for weighting the input. So, I introduced the really quite important parameter, Rate Multiplier. I set this to 20.0 so that the parrot neurons spiked on all input values, though, obviously, more for higher values. I also explored normalizing inputs, but found that it was unnecessary.

Parameters for the Categorisation neurons and the Inhibition neurons differed. They are shown in Table 1. The parameters for the synapses, and the system wide parameters are also shown in that table.

Table 1. System Parameters

Name	Symbol	Categorisation Neuron	Inhibition Neuron
Neuron			
Capacitance	C_M	100.0.0	10.0
Rest Threshold	θ^{rest}	−72.0	−40.0
Exc. Rev. Potential	E_{Ex}^{rev}	0.0	0.0
Inh. Rev. Porential	E_{In}^{rev}	−100.0	−100.0
Rest Potential	V_{rest}	−65.0	−60.0
Leak Time	τ_M	100.0	10.0
Exc. Current Rate	τ_{Ex}^{syn}	1.0	1.0
Inh. Current Rate	τ_{In}^{syn}	2.0	2.0
Threshold Increase	θ_{plus}	0.2	0.0
Refractory Period	τ_{ref}	5.0	2.0
Plastic Synapse			
Potentiation Time	τ_+	20.0	
Potentiation Exponent	μ_+	0.0	
Depression Exponent	μ_-	0.0	
Learning Rate	λ	0.01	
Potentiation Depression Skew	α	0.55	
System			
Rate Multiplier		20.0	
Input to Inhib		0.0002	
Cat to Inhib		0.0104	

Once a reasonably successful parameter set was found, hill climbing was used on one paramater at a time to find improvements. This was directed by the firing behaviour as individual category neurons should not fire in most training epochs.

When the system was run in PyNest, it got 84% on the training set. It was awkward to manage, but a direct translation to PyNN led to a system with 70.67% on the training set a 67.3% on the test set, both in a two fold test. A minor change in the system parameters, Input to Inhib to 0.0005 and Cat to Inhib to 0.03 led to a system with 75.33% on the training set a 76% on the test set. See Table 2 for a comparison. A different spiking net achieves 93.67% on the test set, again with two fold cross validation. It is not that the system developed here is superior, but that it performs reasonably well. These results are from one value of the random seed. Other seeds give other, but similar, results.

Table 2. Selected Iris Results

System	Train	Test
PyNest	84%	
Orig Params	70.67%	67.33%
Orig Params .1 ms	68%	71.33%
Novel Params	75.33%	76%
[5]	92%	90.6%
[8]		93.67%

3.3   Digit Categorisation

The digit categorisation task is a smaller version of the common task [17]. It has 5620 instances each with 64 input integer valued features between 0 and 16. This has been used over the last several years as a task for an undergraduate AI class, and a standard result on a two fold test using nearest neighbour gets 98.25% correct (see Table 3).

With no advice on how to set parameters for a new categorisation task, the parameters from the Iris task were initially used. It was clear that what was needed was to have one or a few categorisation neurons spiking once in each training epoch. So an initial modification to the Rate Multiplier was set to 10.0, and the Input to Inhibition median was left at 0.0002. In the initial simulations 100 Categorisation and 100 Inhibition neurons were used.

The initial simulation ran the training phase, categorisation setting phase, and testing phase all in one simulation. Unfortunately, the computer was not able to cope with the 2810 inputs for a two fold test, so initially a 20 fold test, with 1 training and 19 tests, was used. The average test result over the 20 training runs was 50.11% (see Table 3).

The training data set was used as a test both during training, and then during testing. Table 3 reports the train results during the testing phase, 59.84%.

The result during the training run in testing phase was 57.69%. As this lower result was with the neurons retaining the voltage and threshold values from the training and category setting phases, it was expected that it would do better. So, this result is somewhat surprising.

This led to simulations on a 10 fold test with each phase running separately, yielding the 10 fold result in Table 3. Both of these results had 100 Categorisation and Inhibition neurons. This was changed to 200 of each, and run for the final system result. Unsurprisingly, the 10 fold test was better than the 20 fold test, influenced by more training. Similarly, unsurprisingly, the 200 neuron test did better than the 100 neuron test.

Though better than chance, the MNIST results are poor. Part of problem is that it takes a few days to simulate a 10 fold test, which trains on one data set and tests on nine. A better machine or neuromorphic system should help here. It would also allow more neurons to be used, which should improve results.

Table 3. Selected MNIST Results

System	Train	Test
20 Fold	59.84%	50.11%
10 Fold	60.05%	52.98%
10 Fold 200 Neurons	69.62%	59.34%
Nearest Neighbour		98.25%

4 Discussion

The brain is a poorly understood organ, but it is clear that its 65 billion neurons [18] are used to, for instance, classify digits. All of the neurons are not critical to the task, but as it involves the primary visual cortex, billions of neurons are. With 264 neurons, the digit categorisation system described above is clearly not a complete model of the human neural network for solving the task.

The work described here and the work it is derived from [4,13] notes that the biology is important, and to some degree tries to model it. For categorisation, it is important that none of the categorisation neurons win very often. This is a main point of Habenshcuss [13] and is the reason for the use of the dynamic threshold neurons.

Some things are obviously biologically inaccurate; for example, in the brain input is not via poisson sources but from complex sensory organs and a complex neural interpretation mechanism. The neurons are not devoted to a single task. Learning is not turned off, at least easily.

Other biological inaccuracies can be more readily addressed. Output of the category is not by calculating spike ratios of Categorisation neurons on the training set, and then using those ratios on spikes from the same neurons during a test. However, it is reasonably easy to imagine a system that uses those spikes, connects to other neurons, which in turn yield a category decision, which is then conveyed to the environment. Indeed this is largely what has been done by Huyck and Mitchell [8].

The neural models, even though they spike, are poor models of biological neurons. For computational simplicity this seems like a reasonable assumption. However, the parameters for the neural models are not aligned with biological parameters. In Huyck and Erekpaine [7], neurons with adaptation [15] were used, but an effective parameter set for categorisation was not found. It is not clear that there is one. The model used in this paper, with a dynamic threshold, is a type of adaptive neuron. However, the adaptation lasts for much longer than the adaptation and adaptation recovery values allowed by the Brette neurons used in Huyck and Erekpaine [7]. I am unaware of any mapping between the dynamic threshold neuron models and biological neurons, unlike the Brette neurons.

So, my group's earlier system [8] for categorisation, though also flawed as a biological model, is closer to biology. It uses something like cell assemblies [2]. Learning remains on.

A more biologically plausible circuit could involve at least three different types of cell assembly based topologies. The first, like Huyck and Mitchell [8], would have persistently firing cell assemblies; these could overlap between the three categories with some neurons in both or even all three. The second could involve thalamacoritcal circuits [19] or circuits through other areas. Here the neurons do not need to fire at such a high rate, but are reactivated as waves of firing flow through the neural net. A third system would be in between the other two in localization, involving laminar architecture [20]. Here projections between the different layers of a small section of cortex could, at least initially, be wired in a biologically plausible way. The weights could then be modified by STDP; structural plasticity could also be used. All three of these mechanisms could lead to improved categories over time.

Despite these simulations using few neurons it is surprising that it is so slow to simulate. This might be fixed by caching the input spikes away and removing the poisson source from the simulation. It could also be fixed using a better simulator or neuromorophic hardware.

There are several things that could easily be explored as future work. For instance, can the dynamic threshold neurons be replaced by simple leaky integrate and fire neurons, at least in the Inhibition neurons? What happens when the number of Categorisation neurons and Inhibition neurons do not match? Will different STDP rules work, particularly those that are in the default Nest build? How will it work on different tasks? What is the relationship between tasks and parameters? Can this be improved by training on multiple passes of the training input? The portion of the parameter space where it works is small. Is there a mathematical solution to support parameter selection? Can this be integrated with the work of Huyck and Mitechell [8]? This integration might include modifying the learning rule to make it compensatory, running continuously with learning on, and integrating with input and output systems.

5 Conclusion

So, it is clear that these adaptive spiking neuron systems learning with STDP can be used for categorisation. This is not novel, but the basics of this mechanism have been described above and it has been extended to a novel digit recognition task. As a machine learning mechanism, it is initially an unsupervised system. It does not need to normalize inputs. Theoretically [13], this type of system can be used to optimize the internal model of the environment.

The novelty of this paper, particularly as compared to Diehl and Cook [4], is that the parameters are shown. The translation from Habenschuss et al. [13] to neurons makes mathematically determining parameters difficult. This paper, and associated code, show these values for two novel tasks.

The origin of this mechanism has come from mathematical proof, but it has matured to include a more biologically plausible system. Though this system is not fully neurobiologically plausible, it does provide support for further exploration of biologically plausible learning topologies; exploration can be done both in simulation and from neurobiology to see how it is done in brains and in petri dishes. It is quasi-neurobiologically plausible learning.

References

1. Bi, G., Poo, M.: Synaptic modifications in cultured hippocampal neurons: dependence on spike timing, synaptic strength, and postsynaptic cell type. J. Neurosci. **18**(24), 10464–10472 (1998)
2. Hebb, D.: The Organization of Behavior: A Neuropsychological Theory. Wiley, New York (1949)
3. Song, S., Miller, K., Abbott, L.: Competitive hebbian learning through spike-timing-dependent synaptic plasticity. Nat. Neurosci. **3**(9), 919–926 (2000)
4. Diehl, P., Cook, M.: Unsupervised learning of digit recognition using spike-timing-dependent plasticity. Front. Comput. Neurosci. **9**, 99 (2015)
5. Huyck, C.: Learning categories with spiking nets and spike timing dependent plasticity. SGAI **2020**, 139–144 (2020)
6. Huyck, C., Samey, C.: Extended category learning with spiking nets and spike timing dependent plasticity. SGAI **2021**, 33–43 (2021)
7. Huyck, C., Erekpaine, O.: Competitive learning with spiking nets and spike timing dependent plasticity. In: Bramer, M., Stahl, F. (eds.) SGAI 2022. LNCS, vol. 13652, pp. 153–166. Springer, Cham (2022). https://doi.org/10.1007/978-3-031-21441-7_11
8. Huyck, C., Mitchell, I.: Post and pre-compensatory Hebbian learning for categorisation. Comput. Neurodyn. **8**(4), 299–311 (2014)
9. Davison, A., Yger, P., Kremkow, J., Perrinet, L., Muller, E.: PyNN: towards a universal neural simulator API in python. BMC Neurosci. **8**(S2), P2 (2007)
10. Gewaltig, M., Diesmann, M.: NEST (NEural Simulation Tool). Scholarpedia **2**(4), 1430 (2007)
11. Rybka, R., Davydov, Y., Vlasov, D., Serenko, A., Sboev, A., Ilyin, V.: Comparison of bagging and sparcity methods for connectivity reduction in spiking neural networks with memristive plasticity. Big Data Cogn. Comput. **8**(3), 22 (2024)

12. Kohonen, T.: Self-Organizing Maps. Springer, Heidelberg (1997). https://doi.org/10.1007/978-3-642-56927-2
13. Habenschuss, S., Bill, J.J., Nessler, B.: Homeostatic plasticity in Bayesian spiking networks as expectation maximization with posterior constraints plasticity. In: Advances in Neural Information Processing Systems, vol. 25 (2012)
14. Eppler, J., Helias, M., Muller, E., Diesmann, M.M., Gewaltig, M.: Pynest: a convenient interface to the nest simulator. Front. Neuroinform. **2**, 363 (2009)
15. Brette, R., Gerstner, W.: Adaptive exponential integrate-and-fire model as an effective description of neuronal activity. J. Neurophysiol. **94**, 3637–3642 (2005)
16. Haug, N., Well, S., Mørk, H., Plesser, H., et al.: Nest 3.5 (2024)
17. Bache, K., Lichman, M.: UCI machine learning repository (2013)
18. Churchland, P., Sejnowski, T.: The Computational Brain. MIT Press, Cambridge (1999)
19. Granger, R.: Engines of the brain: the computational instruction set of human cognition. AI Mag. **27**(2), 15–32 (2006)
20. Raizada, R., Grossberg, S.: Towards a theory of the laminar architecture of cerebral cortex: computational clues from the visual system. Cereb. Cortex **13**(1), 100–113 (2003)

On the Development of a Pixel-Wise Plastic Waste Identification System for Multispectral Remote Sensing Applications

Christoph Tholen[1(✉)], Eike Rodenbäck[1,2], Lars Nolle[1,2], Robert Rettig[1], and Frederic Stahl[1]

[1] German Research Center for Artificial Intelligence, Oldenburg, Germany
{christoph.tholen,eike.rodenbaeck,lars.nolle,robert.rettig,
frederic_theodor.stahl}@dfki.de
[2] Jade University of Applied Sciences, Wilhelmshaven, Germany
lars.nolle@jade-hs.de

Abstract. This paper presents the development of a pixel-wise plastic waste identification system for multispectral remote sensing data, based on artificial intelligence methods. The system will be used as part of a two stage approach to identify and quantify plastic waste in waterways and onshore utilizing airborne based remote sensing and Artificial Intelligence. This work investigates the performance and generalization capabilities of Artificial Neural Networks (ANN), Random Forests (RF), Support Vector Machines (SVM), Logistic Regression (LR), and Decision Trees (DT) on two different multispectral datasets. All models are trained and tested on a dataset with artificial plastic waste targets, covering three different undergrounds, i.e. sand, grass and water. To investigate the generalization capabilities of the models, further tests on a dataset from a real landfill are conducted without retraining. On dataset #1, ANN and RF demonstrated superior performance, both achieving 98.4% accuracy, followed closely by DT at 97.4%. SVM and LR showed lower but comparable accuracies of 87.7% and 87.4%, respectively. RF exhibited the best generalization with 90.4% accuracy, while SVM showed improved relative performance at 88.1% on dataset #2. Furthermore, it was shown that an ensemble of all five methods achieved 91.3% accuracy on dataset #2 without retraining, demonstrating a clear trade-off between false positives and false negatives.

Keywords: PlasticObs+ · Plastic Pollution · Machine Learning · Plastic Waste Classification · Ensemble Methods

1 Introduction

Marine plastic pollution poses a significant environmental threat, with rivers annually depositing millions of metric tons of plastic waste into oceans globally [1]. To address this issue, it's essential to implement innovative and cost-effective monitoring strategies that enhance waste and plastic management in marine environments. These approaches

© The Author(s), under exclusive license to Springer Nature Switzerland AG 2025
M. Bramer and F. Stahl (Eds.): SGAI 2024, LNAI 15446, pp. 47–60, 2025.
https://doi.org/10.1007/978-3-031-77915-2_4

should enable the identification of litter sources and quantities across various localities, regions, and nations. Furthermore, data on plastic litter types, including polymer classifications, is crucial for developing targeted policies and legislation aimed at collecting and recycling priority plastic items. These efforts align with major political initiatives such as the EU Marine Strategy Framework Directive's descriptor 10 [2], the Single-use Plastics Directive 2019 [3], UN Sustainable Development Goal 14 (target 14.1), and the UN Decade of Ocean Science for Sustainable Development (2021–2030), all of which strive to mitigate marine pollution and enhance ocean health [4]. Detecting pollution on the ocean surface is vital for preserving marine ecosystems and ensuring the safety of human activities. While previous studies have explored plastic detection using remote sensing techniques [5, 6], continuous monitoring of extensive, contiguous marine areas remains unestablished. Consequently, current models and estimates of plastic waste are primarily based on temporally and spatially limited measurements. The highly heterogeneous distribution of plastic makes it challenging to draw comprehensive conclusions about its sources, distribution patterns, accumulation sites, and temporal evolution.

In recent work different Artificial Intelligence (AI) methods, like Linear Discriminant Analysis [7], Support Vector Machines [8, 9], Random Forests [9, 10], Feed-Forward Neural Networks [11, 12] or Convolutional Neural Networks [13], were used for plastic waste assessment in remote sensing applications. In most studies CNNs were used for the identification and quantification of plastic waste in marine environments [14], especially on high resolution images [13, 15]. However, for the analysis of low resolution images pixelwise classification methods, i.e. treating each single individually, might be advisable since spatial information like shape of small objects cannot be retrieved from low resolution images.

In this research, five different models were built, based on Artificial Neural Networks (ANNs), Logistic Regression (LR), Random Forest (RF), Support Vector Machines (SVM) and Decision Trees (DTs). ANNs are computational models inspired by the structure and function of biological neural networks in the brain. They consist of interconnected nodes or artificial neurons that can learn from data and capture complex non-linear relationships between inputs and outputs [16]. LR accomplishes binary classification tasks by predicting the probability of an outcome, event, or observation. It analyzes the relationship between one or more independent variables and classifies data into discrete classes, extensively used in predictive modeling, where a model estimates the mathematical probability of whether an instance belongs to a specific category or not [17]. Support Vector Machines (SVMs) generate a linear model used for classification and regression tasks, effectively addressing both linear and non-linear problems. The fundamental idea behind SVMs is to construct a line or hyperplane that separates the data into distinct classes. The algorithm seeks to identify the Maximum Margin Hyperplane that optimally divides the classes, with the closest data points to this hyperplane being termed support vectors [18]. Top-Down Induction of Decision Trees is a heuristic for constructing DT models. It places the most influential variable at the root and recursively builds subtrees based on the subfunctions. The goal is to create an approximation of a target function [19].

2 System Overview

The long-term goal of the project is to develop an airborne method for monitoring plastic waste on the water surface. The system, developed in the PlasticObs+ project, is based on an overview sensor (VIS-Line scanner), a fast VIS-AI for anomaly detection, an AI based system for candidate selection [20] and a detail sensor, i.e. adjustable camera (EOIR), to further investigate candidates selected. The images taken by the EOIR are further analysed after the flight using AI methods. The concept of the system, together with the block diagram of the different components is shown in Fig. 1. This paper will focus on the development of the VIS-AI system.

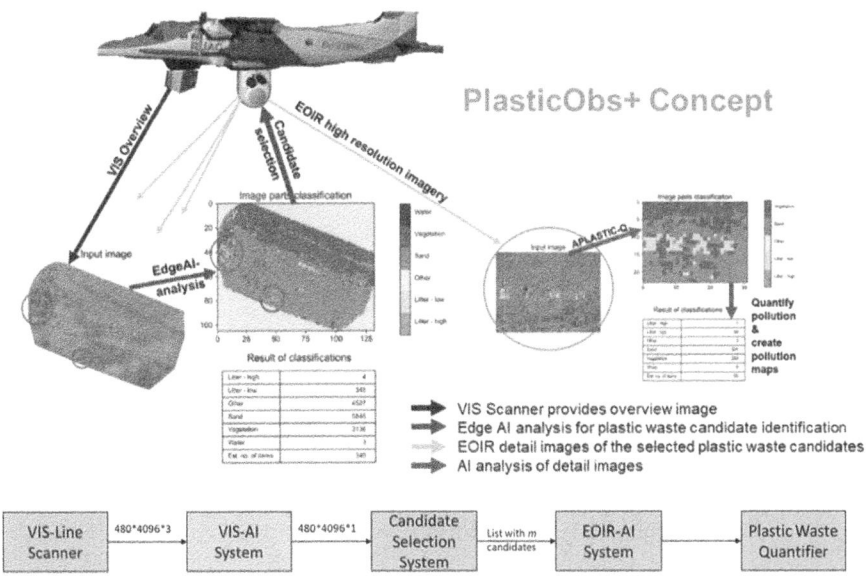

Fig. 1. PlasticObs+ Concept including VIS line scanner and EOIR mounted on the aircraft and indicating different AI systems developed in PlasticObs+, beneath showing the system overview as a block diagram.

3 VIS-AI System

In general, the output of the VIS-Line scanner are single lines of pixels, i.e. $1 \times n$ pixels. During the survey, subsequent lines can be combined to images used for anomaly detection. Convolutional Neural Networks or Auto Encoder models could be used for anomaly detection in those images. However, to align the different lines requires additionally precise real-time information about the movement of the aircraft in all six degrees of freedom, which is a challenge. Therefore, to avoid processing the images, a pixel-wise classification approach will be discussed in this research. However, a pixel-wise classification approach cannot make use of context information, for example contour information, and needs to rely on the information of each pixel only. Here, multispectral information can provide additional information for the identification of plastic waste items. In this research, a multispectral camera system with five bands is used for data acquisition. This data acquisition and processing is described in the next section.

4 Dataset Preparation

This work is based on data collected during three different field tests, covering different kinds of undergrounds and setups. The data was recorded using a DJI Mavic M210 equipped with a Micasense Altum multispectral camera. The camera covers six different spectral bands, i.e. blue, green, red, red edge, near infrared and thermal infrared. In this research, the thermal infrared information is not used, due to the different spatial resolution of this band, compared to the others [21]. Property information of the different bands is summarised in Table 1. The drone was operated in an altitude of 75 m and the single images, ensuring a front and side overlap higher than 80%, were used to create an orthomosaic, employing Pix4Dmapper V.4.6.4 [22], for further processing.

Table 1. Summary of spectral information of Micasense Altum AL04 after [21].

Band#	Name	Center wavelength (nm)	Bandwith (nm)
1	Blue	475 nm	20 nm
2	Green	560 nm	20 nm
3	Red	668 nm	10 nm
4	Red edge	717 nm	10 nm
5	Near Infrared (NIR)	840 nm	40 nm
6	Thermal Infrared	11 μm	6 μm

In the first and second field tests artificial plastic waste targets were used. Five different kinds of plastic i.e. LDPE blue (low density Polyethylene), LDPE transparent, PS white (Polystyrene), PS cream and PP black (Polypropylene), were used to form artificial targets. The use of artificial targets to determine the limits of detectability of remote sensing applications was also applied by Topouzelis et al. [5]. The targets were placed on three different surface types, i.e. grass, sand and water. The experimental setup on the three different undergrounds are shown in Fig. 2.

The third field test was conducted on a German land fill, and therefore contains different, but unknown types of plastic waste (Fig. 3). The data was captured following the same procedure as for the first two experiments using the same equipment.

The data from the first two experiments are combined to one dataset, while the data from the third experiment is used as a second dataset. For both datasets, the ground truth with the corresponding class is also required. For this purpose, the images are labelled using the CVAT tool [23]. This tool can be used to export an image mask, where each pixel is coloured according to its assigned class. The labelling process is summarised in

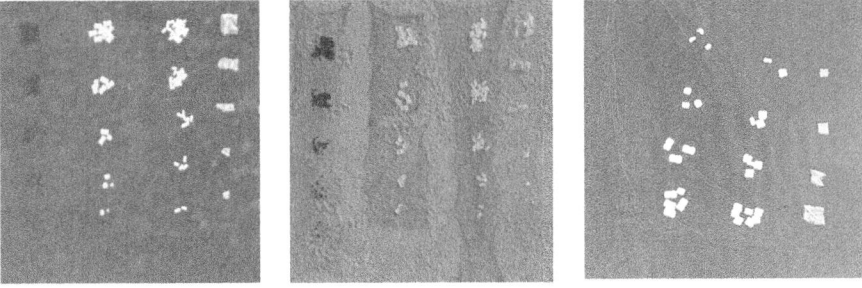

Fig. 2. Experimental set-up of the field tests on grass and sand soil and on the water surface.

Fig. 4. From this mask and the five orthomosaics, vectors for each pixel can be created. As the dataset generated in this way is unbalanced (there are significantly more pixels that do not contain plastic), random undersampling is used [24]. In the labelling process different classes were used, including the different kinds of plastic, meadow, water and beach. For each of these classes, a random selection of up to 1,000 pixels per image are used for dataset #1. Due to the smaller number of pixels containing plastic, for dataset #2 a maximum of 300 pixels per class are used. The dataset is then normalised and converted to the binary *plastic/no plastic* classification dataset. The final dataset #1 contains 58,245 elements, where 41.6% of the instances belong to the category *plastic,* and 58.4% to the category *no plastic*. The second dataset is comprised of 1,026 elements where 41.5% belong to the category *plastic* and 58.5% to the *no plastic* category.

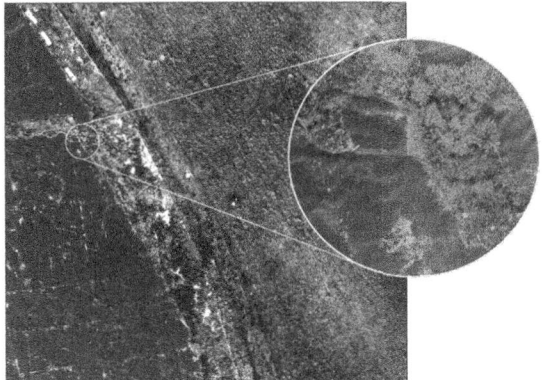

Fig. 3. Experimental setup at German landfill.

5   Experiments

In this research five different AI models, i.e. an artificial neural network (ANN), a logistic regression (LR), a Random Forest (RF), a support vector machine (SVM) and a Decision Tree (DT) are used to address the pixel-wise classification of plastic waste identification.

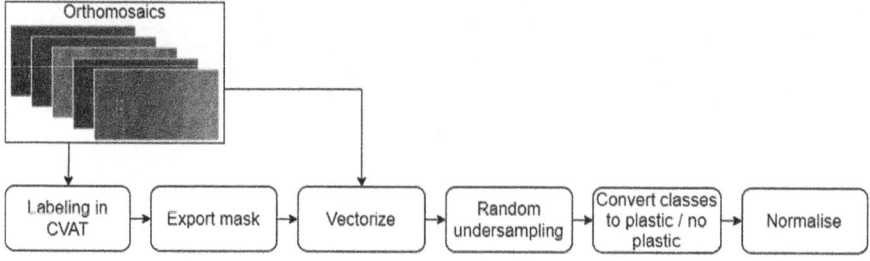

Fig. 4. Labelling process block diagram.

All experiments, except of the training of the ANN was undertaken using the KNIME Analytics platform [25, 26].

Most AI-models require fine-tuning of control parameters to maximise their capability of solving the problem at hand [27]. Therefore, the models used in this research were fine tuned to maximise the classification accuracy of the models. For the ANN network architecture, i.e. number of hidden layers and number of neurons per layer were optimised using the pytorch library [28]. The results of the optimisation are shown in Fig. 5. As it can be observed from the figure, networks with 100 nodes per layer achieve the best results. In the associated table, the p-values were calculated using the t-test, which can be used to show that there is no significant change with more than three hidden layers. A network with three hidden layers containing 100 neurons each is therefore suitable. This network architecture is used in KNIME for the experiments during this research.

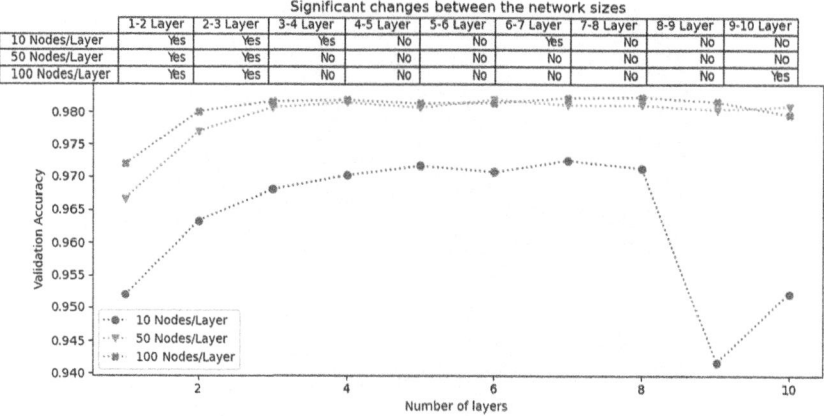

Fig. 5. Accuracy of the trained neural networks with associated table for analysing significant changes between the network sizes.

The optimisation of the RF and the DT were conducted in KNIME. For the RF, two parameters, i.e. tree depth (d_{tree}) and number of trees (n_{trees}), were optimised. The ranges for both parameters are given as follows:

$$\{d_{tree} \in \mathbb{N} | 1 \leq d_{tree} \leq 100\} \tag{1}$$

$$\{n_{trees} \in \mathbb{N} | 1 \leq n_{trees} \leq 500\} \tag{2}$$

For the DT one parameter, i.e. minimum number of samples ($n_{samples}$), was optimised. The parameter was optimised in the range:

$$\{n_{samples} \in \mathbb{N} | 1 \leq n_{samples} \leq 5{,}000\} \tag{3}$$

Tree-structured Parzen Estimator (TPE) [29] was used for both optimisations. The number of iterations was set to 1,000, while the number of warm-up-rounds was chosen to be 100. The best performance was found for a RF with a depth $d_{tree} = 73$ and a number of trees $n_{trees} = 196$. The best performance was found for a DT with a minimum number of samples $n_{samples} = 2$.

No optimisation was undertaken for the SVM and the LR model, i.e. standard parameter settings given by KNIME were used in this research.

In the first set of experiments, dataset 1 is used to train the different models used, i.e. ANN, RF, SVM, LR, and DT. The dataset is split into 70% for training and 30% for testing, using random sampling without replacement. The VIS-AI system will be used in different environments; thus, a good generalisation ability of the system is required. To test the generalisation ability of the different models, a second set of experiments was conducted, applying the trained models on dataset 2 without retraining or modification of the models. The modelling approach is visualised in Fig. 6.

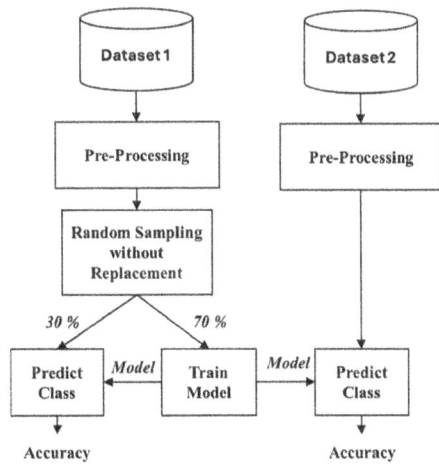

Fig. 6. Block diagram of the modelling approach.

In this work, five different models with different strengths and weaknesses are used. Potentially not a single model can achieve a good result for the generalization, but an ensemble of the models can. Therefore, a third set of experiments is carried out, using a combination of all five models trained on dataset 1. In the first step, a data tuple is evaluated by each model separately. Afterwards, the number of predictions of class *plastic* are summarized and compared to the threshold *a*. The threshold *a* is chosen as follows:

$$\{a \in \mathbb{N} | 1 \leq a \leq 5\} \tag{4}$$

If the sum is higher than the threshold *a*, the current input is classified as *plastic*, otherwise it is classified as *no plastic*. The process is visualized in Fig. 7.

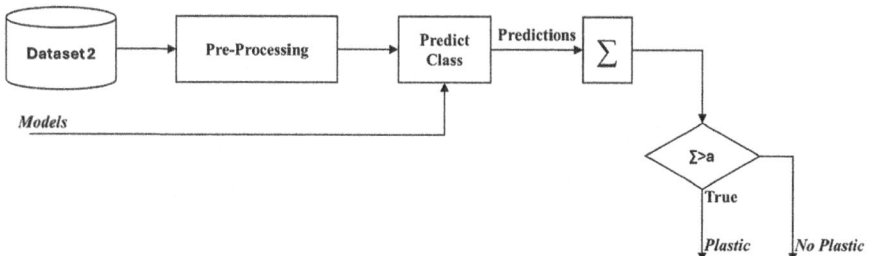

Fig. 7. Block diagram of ensemble evaluation process.

The results of the three sets of experiments are presented in the next section.

6 Results

As shown in Fig. 6, the five models are trained with 70% of the data contained in dataset 1. Afterwards the models are applied to predict the remaining 30% of dataset 1. The results of this prediction are summarized in Table 2. One can see that ANN and RF performed best, both with an accuracy of 0.984, followed by DT with an accuracy of 0.974. SVM accuracy was 0.877, while LR showed a comparable performance, i.e. accuracy of 0.874. In Fig. 8 accuracy, precision, recall and F1-score of the different models trained are given.

Table 2. Summarized Results for the different models on the test data from dataset #1.

Model	True Positives	False Positives	True Negatives	False Negatives	Accuracy
ANN	7151	146	10047	130	0.984
RF	7109	172	10085	108	0.984
SVM	6170	1039	9154	1111	0.877
LR	6194	1118	9075	1087	0.874
DT	7016	195	9998	265	0.974

In the second step of experiments, the models trained on dataset 1 are applied on dataset 2 without retraining or adaptation of the models (Fig. 6). The results of this set

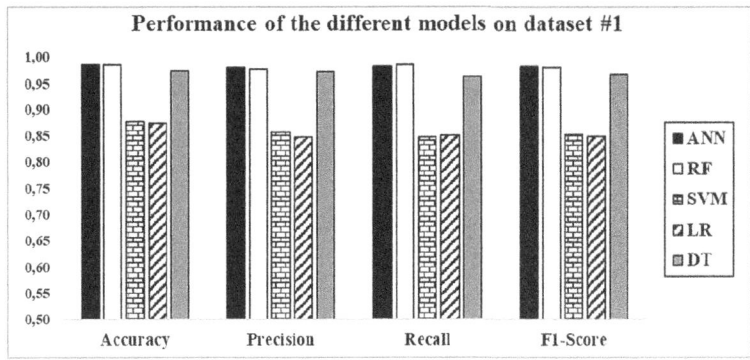

Fig. 8. Accuracy, Precision, Recall and F1-score for the different models on dataset #1.

of experiments are summarized in Table 3. It can be observed that the best performance, i.e. with an accuracy of 0.904, was achieved by the RF, followed by the SVM achieving an accuracy of 0.881. In Fig. 9 performance indicators for the second set of experiments are visualized. It can be observed from the figure that the SVM and the DT showed the highest precision.

Table 3. Summarized results for the different models on dataset #2.

Model	True Positives	False Positives	True Negatives	False Negatives	Accuracy
ANN	311	60	540	115	0.829
RF	351	75	576	24	0.904
SVM	365	61	539	61	0.881
LR	370	122	478	56	0.827
DT	341	61	539	85	0.858

The results of the third set of experiments are given in Table 4. The highest accuracy of 0.913 is achieved for a threshold of $a = 3$. For smaller and higher values of a, the accuracy is lower. However, it can be noted that the number of false positives decreases with higher values of a, while the number of false negatives increases with higher values of a. This behavior can be expected, due to the direct influence of a on the prediction outcome of the ensemble. In Fig. 10 performance indicators of the ensemble experiments are given. It can be observed from the figure that the precision increases with increasing threshold a, while recall decreases with increasing threshold a.

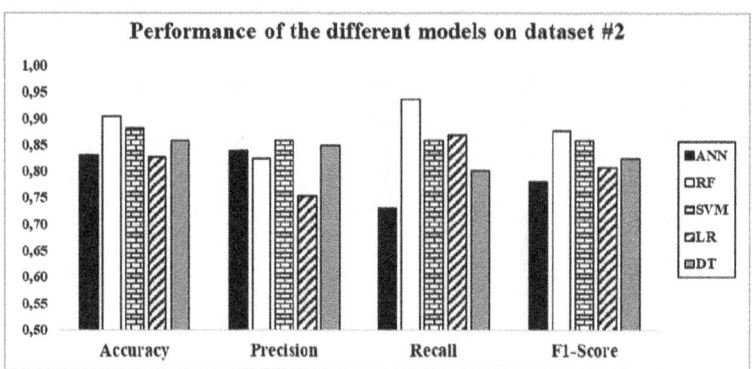

Fig. 9. Accuracy, Precision, Recall and F1-score for the different models on dataset #2.

Table 4. Summarized results for different values of threshold *a* on dataset #2.

Threshold *a*	True Positives	False Positives	True Negatives	False Negatives	Accuracy
1	391	204	396	35	0.767
2	377	87	513	49	0.867
3	359	22	578	67	0.913
4	333	10	590	93	0.900
5	278	5	595	148	0.851

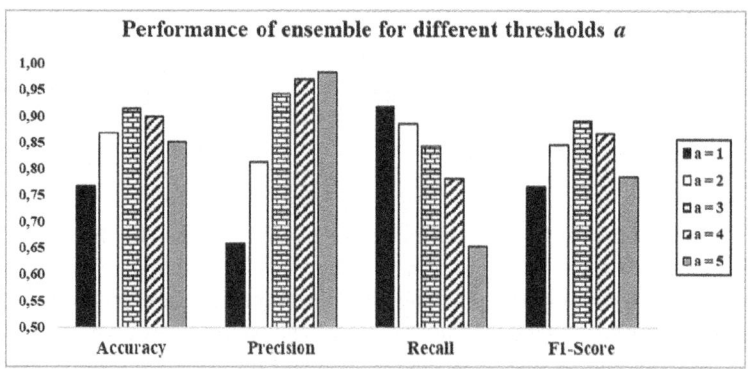

Fig. 10. Accuracy, Precision, Recall and F1-score for the ensemble for different thresholds *a* on dataset #2.

7 Discussion

The first set of experiments, conducted on dataset #1, revealed notable differences in model performance. The ANN and RF demonstrated superior accuracy, both achieving 98.4% on the test set. This high performance suggests that these models were particularly well-suited to capture the underlying patterns in dataset #1. The DT model also performed admirably, with an accuracy of 97.4%, indicating that even a simpler model could effectively learn from this dataset. In contrast, the SVM and LR models showed significantly lower, but similar accuracies, i.e. 87.7% and 87.4%, respectively. This performance gap might indicate that the decision boundary in this dataset is more complex than what these models can efficiently capture, or that the feature space may benefit from additional preprocessing or feature engineering for these algorithms.

For the second set of experiments, the models trained on dataset 1 were applied to the unseen dataset #2, providing crucial insights into the models' generalization capabilities. Interestingly, the RF demonstrated the best generalization, maintaining a high accuracy of 90.4% on the new dataset. This robustness suggests that RF might be capturing more universal features of the problem space, making it a strong candidate for deployment in varied conditions. The SVM model showed improved relative performance on dataset #2, achieving 88.1% accuracy and outperforming the ANN. This result highlights the importance of testing models on diverse datasets, as relative performance can shift in new contexts. The ANN's more significant drop in performance when applied to dataset #2 warrants further investigation. It may indicate a degree of overfitting to dataset #1 or a sensitivity to differences between the two datasets that the other models were more robust against.

The third set of experiments explored the effect of varying the threshold in an ensemble approach. The results demonstrate a clear trade-off between false positives and false negatives as the threshold changes. An optimal threshold of $a = 3$ was identified, yielding the highest accuracy of 91.3%. This finding underscores the importance of threshold tuning in ensemble methods to balance precision and recall according to specific application requirements. As the threshold increased, a decrease in false positives accompanied by an increase in false negatives can be observed. This behavior aligns with theoretical expectations and provides a practical lever for adjusting model performance based on the relative costs of different types of errors in a given application.

The varying performance and generalization capabilities of the models suggest different potential use cases. The Random Forest model, with its high accuracy and strong generalization, appears to be a robust choice for deployment across varied conditions. The SVM improved performance on the new dataset makes it an interesting candidate for applications where adaptability to new data is crucial.

It's important to note that this study is limited to two specific datasets. While this provides valuable insights, further testing on a more diverse range of datasets would be beneficial to fully assess the generalization capabilities of these models. Additionally, exploring the impact of feature selection and engineering on model performance could yield further improvements and insights.

8 Conclusion and Future Work

In this work five different AI-models were trained for pixel-wise plastic waste detection utilizing multispectral information. The models are trained on a dataset containing artificial plastic targets in three different natural environments. The generalization capabilities of the models are examined by applying the trained models on a second dataset recorded on a German landfill. The RF model showed the best generalization capabilities, while the accuracy of the ANN decreases by 15.5%. It is worth noted that the accuracy of the SVM increases by 0.4% when applied on dataset #2 compared to dataset #1.

This work does not review which input channel mostly influences the decision-making process of the five models. Hence explainable AI methods like SHapley Additive exPlanations (SHAP) [30] will be used to enhance the model interpretability. Furthermore, the trained models will be further fine-tuned using data from additional field tests. In addition, it will be examined, if a combination of pixel-wise classification and image-based classification can further improve the classification accuracy. In the final step, the system will be deployed on the surveillance aircraft as part of the PlasticObs+ system.

Acknowledgements. Funded by the German Federal Ministry for the Environment, Nature Conservation, Nuclear Safety and Consumer Protection (BMUV) based on a resolution of the German Bundestag (Grant No. 67KI21014A). The authors would like to thank Tobias Binkele, Gizem Bulut, Michael Butter, Richard Kachel, Martin Kumm, Tobias Schmid, Jens Wellhausen, and Simone Wiegand for their support during field work and Markus Eckhardt for his support during data preparation. The authors would like to thank the "Zweckverband Abfallwirtschaftszentrum Friesland/Wittmund" for their support during fieldwork.

References

1. Lebreton, L.C.M., van der Zwet, J., Damsteeg, J.-W., Slat, B., Andrady, A., Reisser, J.: River plastic emissions to the world's oceans. Nat. Commun. **8**, 15611 (2017). https://doi.org/10.1038/ncomms15611
2. Galgani, F., Hanke, G., Werner, S., De Vrees, L.: Marine litter within the european marine strategy framework directive. ICES J. Mar. Sci. **70**, 1055–1064 (2013). https://doi.org/10.1093/icesjms/fst122
3. Directive (EU) 2019/of the European Parliament and of the Council of 5 June 2019 on the reduction of the impact of certain plastic products on the environment
4. Recuero Virto, L.: A preliminary assessment of the indicators for Sustainable Development Goal (SDG) 14 "Conserve and sustainably use the oceans, seas and marine resources for sustainable development." Mar. Policy **98**, 47–57 (2018). https://doi.org/10.1016/j.marpol.2018.08.036
5. Topouzelis, K., Papageorgiou, D., Karagaitanakis, A., Papakonstantinou, A., Arias, M.: Remote sensing of sea surface artificial floating plastic targets with sentinel-2 and unmanned aerial systems (plastic litter project 2019). Remote Sens. **12**, 2013 (2020). https://doi.org/10.3390/rs12122013
6. Garaba, S.P., et al.: Sensing ocean plastics with an airborne hyperspectral shortwave infrared imager. Environ. Sci. Technol. **52**, 11699–11707 (2018). https://doi.org/10.1021/acs.est.8b02855

7. Balsi, M., Moroni, M., Chiarabini, V., Tanda, G.: High-resolution aerial detection of marine plastic litter by hyperspectral sensing. Remote Sens. **13**, 1557 (2021). https://doi.org/10.3390/rs13081557
8. Zhu, S., Chen, H., Wang, M., Guo, X., Lei, Y., Jin, G.: Plastic solid waste identification system based on near infrared spectroscopy in combination with support vector machine. Adv. Ind. Eng. Polym. Res. **2**, 77–81 (2019). https://doi.org/10.1016/j.aiepr.2019.04.001
9. Cortesi, I., Masiero, A., De Giglio, M., Tucci, G., Dubbini, M.: Random forest-based river plastic detection with a handheld multispectral camera. Int. Arch. Photogram. Remote Sens. Spatial Inf. Sci. XLIII-B1-2021, 9–14 (2021). https://doi.org/10.5194/isprs-archives-XLIII-B1-2021-9-2021
10. Gonçalves, G., Andriolo, U., Pinto, L., Bessa, F.: Mapping marine litter using UAS on a beach-dune system: a multidisciplinary approach. Sci. Total. Environ. **706**, 135742 (2020). https://doi.org/10.1016/j.scitotenv.2019.135742
11. Kako, S., Morita, S., Taneda, T.: Estimation of plastic marine debris volumes on beaches using unmanned aerial vehicles and image processing based on deep learning. Mar. Pollut. Bull. **155**, 111127 (2020). https://doi.org/10.1016/j.marpolbul.2020.111127
12. Pinto, L., Andriolo, U., Gonçalves, G.: Detecting stranded macro-litter categories on drone orthophoto by a multi-class neural network. Mar. Pollut. Bull. **169**, 112594 (2021). https://doi.org/10.1016/j.marpolbul.2021.112594
13. Wolf, M., et al.: Machine learning for aquatic plastic litter detection, classification and quantification (APLASTIC-Q). Environ. Res. Lett. **15**, 114042 (2020). https://doi.org/10.1088/1748-9326/abbd01
14. Jia, T., et al.: Deep learning for detecting macroplastic litter in water bodies: a review. Water Res. **231**, 119632 (2023). https://doi.org/10.1016/j.watres.2023.119632
15. Jia, T., Vallendar, A.J., De Vries, R., Kapelan, Z., Taormina, R.: Advancing deep learning-based detection of floating litter using a novel open dataset. Front. Water. **5**, 1298465 (2023). https://doi.org/10.3389/frwa.2023.1298465
16. Bishop, C.M.: Pattern Recognition and Machine Learning. Springer, New York (2006)
17. Sperandei, S.: Understanding logistic regression analysis. Biochem. Med. **24**, 12–18 (2014). https://doi.org/10.11613/BM.2014.003
18. Cortes, C., Vapnik, V.: Support-vector networks. Mach. Learn. **20**, 273–297 (1995). https://doi.org/10.1007/BF00994018
19. Quinlan, J.R.: C4.5: Programs for Machine Learning. Elsevier (2014)
20. Tholen, C., Wolf, M.: On the development of a candidate selection system for automated plastic waste detection using airborne based remote sensing. In: Bramer, M. and Stahl, F. (eds.) Artificial Intelligence XL, pp. 506–512. Springer, Cham (2023). https://doi.org/10.1007/978-3-031-47994-6_45
21. MicaSense Inc.: Altum Integration Guide. https://support.micasense.com/hc/en-us/articles/360010025413-Altum-Integration-Guide. Accessed 31 May 2024
22. Pix4D: PIX4Dmapper: Professional photogrammetry software for drone mapping. https://www.pix4d.com/product/pix4dmapper-photogrammetry-software. Accessed 04 July 2024
23. CVAT. https://www.cvat.ai/. Accessed 04 July 2024
24. Van Den Broek, W.H.A.M., Wienke, D., Melssen, W.J., Buydens, L.M.C.: Plastic material identification with spectroscopic near infrared imaging and artificial neural networks. Anal. Chim. Acta **361**, 161–176 (1998). https://doi.org/10.1016/S0003-2670(98)00012-9
25. Berthold, M.R., et al.: KNIME - the Konstanz information miner: version 2.0 and beyond. SIGKDD Explor. Newsl. **11**, 26–31 (2009). https://doi.org/10.1145/1656274.1656280
26. Fillbrunn, A., Dietz, C., Pfeuffer, J., Rahn, R., Landrum, G.A., Berthold, M.R.: KNIME for reproducible cross-domain analysis of life science data. J. Biotechnol. **261**, 149–156 (2017). https://doi.org/10.1016/j.jbiotec.2017.07.028

27. Feurer, M., Hutter, F.: Hyperparameter optimization. In: Hutter, F., Kotthoff, L., Vanschoren, J. (eds.) Automated Machine Learning: Methods, Systems, Challenges, pp. 3–33. Springer, Cham (2019). https://doi.org/10.1007/978-3-030-05318-5_1
28. PyTorch. https://pytorch.org/. Accessed 04 July 2024
29. Bergstra, J., Bardenet, R., Bengio, Y., Kégl, B.: Algorithms for hyper-parameter optimization. In: Shawe-Taylor, J., Zemel, R., Bartlett, P., Pereira, F., and Weinberger, K.Q. (eds.) Advances in Neural Information Processing Systems. Curran Associates, Inc. (2011)
30. Lundberg, S.M., Lee, S.-I.: A unified approach to interpreting model predictions. In: Proceedings of the 31st International Conference on Neural Information Processing Systems, pp. 4768–4777. Curran Associates Inc., Red Hook (2017)

Streamlining Attention for Text Classification: Sequence Length Reduction with Pooling Attention

Daniel Biermann[1]([✉]), Fabrizio Palumbo[1,2], Morten Goodwin[1],
and Ole-Christoffer Granmo[1]

[1] Centre for Artificial Intelligence Research (CAIR), Department of ICT, University
of Agder, Grimstad, Norway
`daniel.biermann@uia.no`
[2] Artificial Intelligence Lab (AI Lab), Department of Journalism and Media Studies,
Oslo Metropolitan University, Oslo, Norway

Abstract. Text classification tasks require a reduction from a sequence
of tokens down to a single token. State-of-the-art Transformer models
usually employ a class (`CLS`)-token to represent the entire sequence or
pool all output token representations into a single token. In both schemes,
the sequences are reduced in a single step. Although these approaches
yield commendably high performance, we propose an integration of pooling operations into the scaled dot product mechanism that would facilitate a more nuanced reduction of sequence length. This article introduces
a competitive and innovative pooling attention mechanism that is comparatively efficient and utilizes 2-dimensional pooling operations on the
attention map generated in the scaled dot-product calculation. We further devise a sequence classification model that uses pooling attention
to gradually reduce the input sequence to a single token within 8 or
4 attention steps. Our model performs comparably to well-established
non-attention classification models while offering a promising new approach to nuanced sequence reduction in smaller pure attention models.
A more nuanced approach to sequence reduction can aid explainability in attention models by examining sequences at different granularities
across attention layers and extending the reduction process to multiple
steps. Additionally, the computational cost is saved by processing shorter
sequences in subsequent attention layers, improving overall efficiency.
Our results show a significant speed-up in training time when comparing pooling attention with standard attention approaches. This work
establishes a foundation for future exploration into sequence-reducing
attention models.

Keywords: Deep Learning · Sequence classification · Attention models

1 Introduction

Transformer models have been part of state-of-the-art natural language processing since their inception in 2017 [19]. Transformer-based large language models

M. Bramer and F. Stahl (Eds.): SGAI 2024, LNAI 15446, pp. 61–73, 2025.
https://doi.org/10.1007/978-3-031-77915-2_5

such as BERT models [5,12,17] or XLNet [22] all made significant improvements on the respective state-of-the-art and all current cutting edge chatbot systems such as OpenAI's GPT4 [1], Google's Gemini [18] or the recent Claude 3.5 by Anthropic [2] are based on Transformer systems.

Their power is rooted in the attention mechanism at the heart of the Transformer. The scaled dot-product attention and multi-head attention allow for easy parallel processing while retaining the ability to capture contextual information in sequential data. Typically, state-of-the-art Transformer models are large models trained on vast unlabelled text corpora via a masking pretext task. [5,14]. Using relatively small labeled datasets, the pretrained model can then be fine-tuned for specific tasks. This semi-supervised pretraining-finetuning method surmises the core success of Transformer models.

One unique and necessary core challenge in text—or-sequence classification is reducing a sequence of tokens to a single token. As Transformer-like attention models process all tokens of a sequence in parallel and yield an output for every token, this sequence length reduction is not an inherent part of attention models. Usually, Transformer models rely on two different approaches to reduce a sequence to a single token: A class-token approach and a token pooling approach. In the class-token approach, a specific token, usually denoted as CLS, is added or designated to represent the entire sequence. The sequence containing the CLS-token is then processed, and the CLS-token is used for subsequent classification tasks. On the other hand, the pooling approach usually averages all output tokens of the attention process to yield a single token. For further details see Sect. 2.

Both approaches perform well, and models utilizing them were able to push performance beyond the state-of-the-art of their time. However, while performing satisfactorily, these two approaches do not allow for a more nuanced and stepwise reduction process, which is essential for refining the granularity of information retention during reduction and enhancing the interpretability of results.

Widening the reduction process from a single to multiple steps naturally allows for more fine-grained processing of information and allows the model to evaluate the importance and contribution of single tokens at different stages of the reduction process.

Aligning this multi-step reduction process directly with the attention step has the added benefit of offering a potential increase in explainability. For example, earlier attention layers might better capture the relations between single words on a token-level while later layers, due to handling of fewer tokens, are encouraged to capture the relations between different larger parts of a sentence.

Additionally, the explainability of the reduction process itself is aided by simply being able to look at which reduction step the importance of a feature might have dropped off. Assuming that less important features are discarded earlier in the reduction process, the importance of features could intuitively be measured by how much overall attention is paid to them in later layers.

Recent work started to explore utilizing the ability of the scaled dot-product to manipulate the length of a sequence directly. In Biermann et al. [4], a trainable scaling matrix is added to the scaled dot-product attention mechanism to manipulate the number of output tokens by rescaling the query matrix.

In this work, we extend our exploration of the reduction capabilities inherent to the scaled dot-product attention mechanism. Specifically, we propose an innovative pooling attention mechanism that achieves output token reduction by employing pooling functions on the two-dimensional attention weight matrix. This novel approach is then applied to a text classification task, where sequences are efficiently reduced to a single token through multiple iterations of pooling attention.

We posit that a more refined, gradient-based approach to sequence reduction in attention models will offer a compelling and fruitful research trajectory. Such models hold the promise of providing enhanced explainability over the prevailing standard of single-step sequence reduction. In particular, classification attention models stand to gain from reduced computational cost, given that Transformer-like architectures scale quadratically with sequence length. By incrementally reducing sequences through successive attention steps, subsequent attention layers naturally become more compact, resulting in a streamlined and efficient overall model. This approach not only optimizes computational efficiency but also paves the way for a more interpretable understanding of the attention mechanism's internal dynamics.

2   Related Work

Attention models have been used in text classification tasks with great success. Usually, two different approaches are used to achieve the necessary reduction in sequence length.

The first approach is the common CLS-token method that adds or establishes a designated token that is trained to capture the context of the entire sequence for the purposes of classification tasks. BERT [5], a used Transformer model, adds a CLS-token in the preprocessing step and subsequently uses the output token at the position of the CLS-token as a contextual representation for the entire sequence. The T5 model [15] uses the 'target'-token in classification setups as an equivalent to BERTs CLS-token. Further, Gao et al. [8], Hou et al. [9] and Wang et al. [20] use the CLS-token in a contrastive learning scheme to create sentence embeddings while Feng et al. [7] create sentence embeddings by ℓ_2 normalizing the CLS-token of the last encoder attention block.

The second approach pools all output tokens of the attention model. Reimers and Gurevych [16] create sentence embeddings in a siamese model setup by averaging over the tokens of the last Transformer block. Similarly, Li et al. [11] averaged over the last two Transformer blocks and observed an improved performance compared to a CLS-token approach. The Sentence T5 model [13] uses both approaches and generates sentence embeddings by either using the first token of the encoder output or the average of the encoder outputs.

Deviating from the two more common approaches, Fang et al. [6] reduce a sequence to a single token by introducing a single learnable query vector. In the scaled dot-product attention calculation, the number of query vectors dictates the number of output vectors and, thus, output tokens. Usually, the query vectors are generated from the input sequence, which makes changing the number of query vectors practically challenging. By using a single learnable query vector, Fang et al. are able to reduce the sequence within an attention step. Similarly, recent work by Biermann et al. [4] manipulates the query matrix by introducing a scaling matrix into the scaled dot-product calculation. Specifically, the query matrix is generated from the input sequence and then rescaled via the scaling matrix to subsequently yield fewer output tokens.

This work builds on using the attention mechanism directly to reduce the number of output tokens of the processed sequence. In contrast to Biermann et al. [4], we do not reduce the sequence by manipulating the effective number of query vectors but by employing 2-dimensional pooling functions directly on the attention weight map. To our knowledge, no previous work has investigated manipulating the attention weight map dimension for sequence reduction.

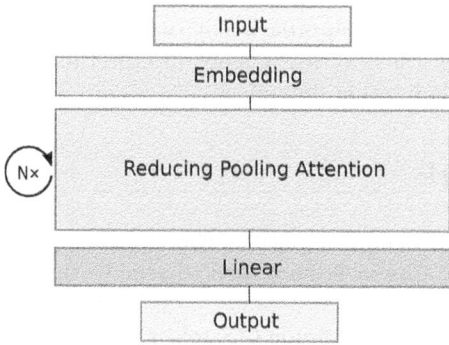

Fig. 1. The general architecture of the reducing classifier. The sequence is reduced by the application of the reducing pooling attention layer. Depending on the desired number of steps, denoted as N, in which the sequence is to be reduced, the reducing pooling attention layer is applied repeatedly.

3   Model

The proposed architecture builds on the fundamental principles of Transformer models, exchanging the scaled dot-product with the novel, reducing pooling attention. The sequences are embedded using a pre-trained BERT tokenizer from Huggingface [21], and a positional encoding is added onto the embedding. Subsequently, the sequences are given to a reducing pooling attention layer. Similar to other Transformer models, repeated application of the attention layers is employed. Figure 1 depicts the overall architecture of the reducing classifier. In this work, the number of attention layers is chosen to be $N = 4$ or $N = 8$.

This corresponds to reducing the input sequence length to one token in 4 or 8 attention steps (see Sect. 3.2).

In a departure from standard Transformer models, residual connections have been omitted due to technical constraints arising from the disparity in sequence lengths before and after each attention step. Finally, after the input sequence is distilled into a single output token, it is passed through a linear layer to a softmax classifier for final prediction.

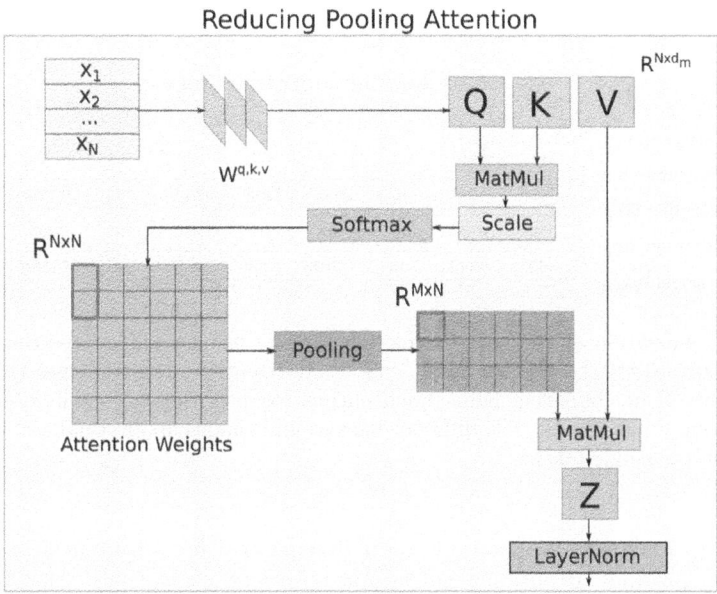

Fig. 2. Structure of the pooling attention layer. The Sequence is reduced from N to M tokens by pooling over the $N \times N$-dimensional attention weight matrix to yield a $M \times N$-dimensional matrix. The two boxes drawn over the attention weight matrices depict an example kernel of `kernel=[2,1]` and the affected value in the pooled matrix.

3.1 Reducing Pooling Attention Layer

The reducing pooling attention builds on the scaled dot-product [19]. Figure 2 depicts the reducing pooling attention architecture. First, query, key, and value vectors are generated from the input. The query and key vectors are used to calculate the attention weight map. If the original sequence has N tokens, the attention weight map has dimension $N \times N$. Because the attention weight map is a 2-dimensional structure, 2D pooling operations can be applied as is standard in convolution models. We use the common max- and average pooling functions to pool the attention weight map and change its shape.

The subsequent matrix multiplication of the value vector and the pooled attention weight map yields the new sequence representation consisting of fewer tokens. This last step also enforces restrictions on the allowed kernel and stride shapes of the pooling process. The width of the pooled attention weight map needs to match the value vector dimension, and thus, the kernel and stride are of the form: `kernel=[k,1]` and `stride=[s,1]`. k and s can be arbitrarily chosen, depending on the desired reduction dynamics and used data.

In addition, layer normalization [3] and dropout are applied after the attention step.

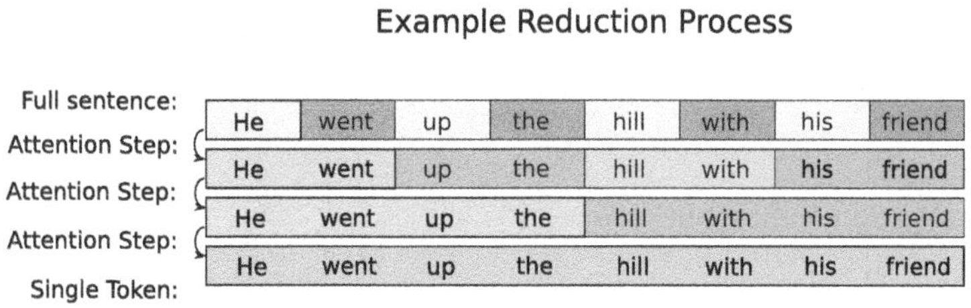

Example Reduction Process

Fig. 3. Visualization of the token reduction process using pooling attention. When choosing `kernel=[2,1]` and `stride=[2,1]`, each attention step combines the attention weights of neighbouring pairs. Each output token is thus a combination of two neighbouring input tokens. The different background shades are a visual aid to better distinguish the single tokens.

Figure 3 illustrates an example reduction process for a sentence. In regular scaled dot-product attention, the output representation of the "He" token is in essence a weighted sum of how much attention the "He" token pays to all other tokens in the sequence. However, using a kernel and stride of [2,1], the attention weights of neighbouring words are combined, effectively combining the weighted sums of neighbouring tokens. In our example, the first output token would be the combination of how much attention the tokens "He" and "went" spent on all other single tokens (including themselves). The reduced token is thus a representation of both input tokens. When reducing sequences in multiple pooling attention steps, we successively go from capturing information by paying attention to tokens representing single words to capturing information by paying attention to tokens representing groups of words.

3.2   4-Step and 8-Step Setup

The input is fixed to the common upper limit in Transformer models of 512 tokens. Sequences exceeding this limit are cut off after 512 tokens, while smaller sequences are padded respectively. The chosen fixed input arises from the chosen reduction dynamics of the classifier. The classifier is designed to reduce the sequence to a single token in a specific number of steps. Biermann et al. were able to reduce sequences down to 50% in a single attention step without significant loss of information. With a fixed input length of 512 tokens, halving the sequence in every attention step will require 8 attention steps to reduce it down to 1 token, while quartering the sequence length necessitates only 4 attention steps. Thus, the reducing classifier is designed to operate in two reduction setups:

8-Step Reduction: To effectively halve a sequence in a single attention step, we must halve the number of rows of the attention weight map. Choosing `kernel=[2,1]` and `stride=[2,1]` yields the desired reduction by pooling two subsequent rows into a single row. As $512 = 2^9$, 512 tokens cannot be halved to a single token in 8 steps. Thus, the last attention step uses `kernel=[4,1]` and `stride=[4,1]` instead of an additional ninth step, as the additional step would only reduce two tokens down to one.

4-Step Reduction: Reducing the sequence to a quarter of its length in each attention step corresponds to pooling 4 subsequent rows of the attention weight map into a single row. This corresponds to `kernel=[4,1]` and `stride=[4,1]` in the first 3 layers, and `kernel=[8,1]` and `stride=[8,1]` in the last layer.

This direct relation between the input dimension and the number of reduction steps imposes a limitation in flexibility regarding the dimensions of the input. In its current form, the model requires a fixed input that is compatible with the chosen number of steps. Meaning that changing one will require changing the other as well. Adding more flexibility to the input dimension that the model can process will prove to be an exciting future direction in this area of research. We argue that this drawback will not significantly hinder applicability in more specific classification tasks, especially cases with more uniformly shaped sequential data.

3.3 Dataset and Hyperparameters

In this work, we use the open-source Web of Science (WOS) dataset [10] for text classification. While the WOS dataset was created and intended for hierarchical document classification, we use it for standard text classification as it complements the fixed input length requirement of the reducing classifier model. The WOS dataset contains abstracts of scientific articles, favoring longer text sample sizes. In fact, the average text length is around 300 tokens with the majority of samples containing more than 200 tokens.

Specifically, we use the WOS-5736 subset containing 5736 text samples categorized into 11 classes. The samples are split into a 80%–20% train-test split. The chosen hyperparameters are depicted in Table 1. We observed that the model required very low learning rates (order of e^{-5}) to effectively learn. The chosen hyperparameters yield from a hyperparameter search, maximizing accuracy.

Table 1. Hyperparameters

Learning rate	$1e^{-5}$
Attention dimension	512
Embedding dimension	512
Max length	512
Dropout	0.1
Loss function	CrossEntropyLoss

4   Results and Discussion

Table 2 summarizes the text classification performance on the WOS-5736 dataset. We trained the classifier for both 4-step and 8-step reduction setups with average or max pooling, respectively. Each simulation ran with a patience of 10 epochs regarding the test loss. The classification accuracy reports the average achieved highest test accuracy across five different model initializations. In addition, we adapt the scaling matrix approach from Biermann et al. [4] and apply it to likewise reduce the sequence in 4 or 8 steps. Further, the table lists the accuracies of other standard models for comparison. We include DNN, RNN, and CNN baseline models, as well as the best-performing HDLTex model from Kowsari et al. [10]. We further show the performances of a BERT and XLNet model. For this, we finetuned Huggingface's pretrained BERT and XLNet models [21] for 3 epochs on the WOS-5736 dataset, each. When compared with these models, our model achieves comparable performances to the non-Transformer models while retaining the potential of the full parallelizability of Transformer models.

Our approach shows similar performances across reduction steps and pooling setups. Overall, for both max and average pooling, reducing the sequence in eight steps yields slightly higher accuracies: 88.75% for max pooling and 88.33% for average pooling compared to their 4-step counterparts of 87.80% and 87.63%. Additionally, max pooling achieved slightly higher performances in both reduction setups with the highest performance achieved in the 8-step max pooling setup.

As reducing the sequence in 4 steps corresponds to quartering the sequence in every attention step, we observe that, on average, it leads to a minor increase in information loss compared to halving the sequence. This agrees with the findings in Biermann et al., where sequences could be reduced down to 50% of the initial length without significant loss in information.

The difference in performance between the different step sizes is especially visible in the scaling matrix approach, with a performance difference of almost 2%. This shows that the scaling matrix approach favors smaller but more steps, while the pooling attention shows a similar but less pronounced inclination.

Interestingly, max pooling demonstrates a slightly higher performance difference between the two reduction step sizes while reaching overall higher accuracy than average pooling. Average pooling, on the other hand, shows a slightly smaller discrepancy in performance regarding the different reduction steps. These findings suggest that the choice of pooling function could be further optimized depending on the specific requirements and characteristics of the application, thus offering valuable insights into the design of more effective attention models.

The higher robustness of average pooling with regard to the reduction steps is likely rooted in the averaging process. When pooling via averaging, we effectively average over 2 or 4 rows for each column in the attention weight map matrix. Here, the averaging process considers information from all reduced rows. In contrast, max pooling only considers the row with the highest value, and the other values are discarded. Thus, increasing the number of reduced rows also increases the number of discarded rows and, thus, the potential amount of lost information.

Table 2. Classification Accuracies

Model	Accuracy	
DNN [10]		86.15
CNN [10]		88.68
RNN [10]		89.46
HDLTex-CNN [10]		90.93
XLNet		93.21
BERT		93.12
Our Model	4-steps	8-steps
max pooling	87.80	88.75
average pooling	87.63	88.33
scaling matrix	85.57	87.49

Our reducing pooling classifier performs comparatively to other well-established text classification models. Comparing with standard DNNs, pooling attention reaches higher accuracy in all reduction setups. Furthermore, the 8-step setup demonstrates equivalent effectiveness with regards to CNN models. However, when pitted against RNN models, the reducing pooling attention exhibits a minor lag in performance. This gap becomes more pronounced when juxtaposed with more complex models like XLNet and BERT. Given the substantial difference in size and extensive pretraining of BERT and XLNet models, it is unsurprising that our more streamlined reducing pooling attention classifier is unable to match their performance levels. BERT and XLNet typically consist of more than 100 million trainable parameters while our pooling attention models reach 18 to 22 million trainable parameters. We are confident that further work into finding suitable pretraining tasks and adding pretraining to pooling attention will significantly lower this mismatch.

Despite these differences, the fact that our approach attains performance levels comparable to established non-transformer models is a testament to the potential of the pooling attention mechanism. Especially, when taking into consideration that while the RNN models show a higher performance, it is to be leveraged against the fully parallelizable nature of the pooling attention approach, a core feature that makes large Transformer models so powerful.

Table 3. Comparison of training times with and without pooling attention

| Model | Training time [s] | | | | |
	Parameters [10^6]	per epoch	per batch [10^{-3}]	norm. per batch [10^{-9}]	Speed-up factor
4-step					
pooling	18.8	2.014	6.536	0.348	0.60
no reduction	18.8	3.785	10.887	0.579	
8-step					
pooling	21.9	2.764	9.932	0.454	0.559
no reduction	21.9	6.353	17.779	0.812	

$$\text{speed-up factor} = \frac{\text{pooling train time}}{\text{standard train time}} \tag{1}$$

We further evaluate the effect of pooling attention on computational efficiency by measuring and comparing the training times observed in our 4- and 8-step pooling attention models. As a direct comparison with BERT and XLNet would not provide any meaningful insight due to the large discrepancy in complexity and trainable parameters, we compare the pooling attention models with test attention models that have an identical architecture to the pooling attention models apart from removing the pooling operation on the attention weights. By removing the pooling attention from the model, it no longer reduces the sequence along its layers and behaves like a standard attention model. Constructing the test attention models in this way ensures models of equal size and complexity. Thus, any change in training time observed can be attributed to the presence or absence of token reduction in-between layers.

Table 3 summarizes the training times observed with and without reduction in-between layers. We are able to observe a significant difference in training time between the pooling attention and the standard attention models. Normalizing the training time with respect to the number of trainable parameters, we see that the 4-step pooling attention model has the lowest normalized per batch training time when compared to its 8-step counterpart. This is due to the fact that a reduction in four steps introduces a more aggressive reduction with a kernel of [4,1] instead of [2,1].

On the other hand, calculating the speed-up factor as the ratio between pooling and reduced training time (Eq. 1) shows that the 8-step pooling model yields the highest overall speed-up, where each training batch only takes about half as long to process compared to the non-reducing counterpart.

This is likely due to the increased number of layers in the 8-step approach resulting in a higher cumulative effect overall. Both pooling models show significant improvements regarding training time with speed-up factors of 0.559 and 0.600, respectively. This speed-up is not caused by a change in model size but by the fact that computational cost scales quadratically with sequence length in attention models. By reducing the sequence with each pooling attention layer, subsequent layers are presented with shorter sequences, thus saving computational cost. This ultimately results in the observed shorter training times.

This underscores the value of our approach as a promising new direction in the field of attention models, offering a more nuanced way of reducing sequence length while maintaining effective and efficient classification capabilities.

5 Conclusion

In this paper, we introduced a novel pooling attention mechanism. We leverage a two-dimensional pooling function on the scaled dot-product attention weight map to facilitate a direct, stepwise reduction of sequence lengths. This innovative approach enhances the reduction capabilities of attention models, offering an efficient and structured means of condensing sequences.

We further demonstrate the utility of this pooling attention mechanism with the introduction of a novel reducing pooling classifier. This classifier compresses sequences down to a single token over the course of four or eight steps, corresponding to halving or quartering the sequence length in every attention step. We reach comparable performance with non-transformer standard classification models while retaining the inherent parallelizable nature of pure attention models.

In additional we are able to observe a significant speed-up in training time when comparing the pooling attention classifier with standard attention models of similar size and complexity.

Future research will aim to bridge the performance gap between this approach and larger Transformer models like BERT or XLNet. It is likely that the performance gap may be attributed to the large difference in model sizes and extensive amount of pretraining. At the same time, the natural reduction in model size when using pooling attention could make attention models more attainable for smaller, more specialized tasks that might not benefit from the large overhead of full LLMs.

A first next step could be to try and pretrain the reducing classifier model with established pretext tasks to gain access to the vast amount of unlabelled data and make use of the powerful pretraining-finetuning approach. Further investigations might go more in-depth and aim to devise suitable pretext tasks for sequence reduction and pooling attention models. Another direction might be the investigation into better pooling functions that capture the underlying contextual data in attention weight maps better than the chosen max- or average pooling functions as well as alleviating the input flexibility limitations observed.

Overall, this work successfully establishes a purely attention-based classification model using pooling attention to reduce sequences in multiple steps, laying a solid foundation for future explorations into sequence-reducing attention models. Our innovative framework not only provides a compelling alternative to traditional attention mechanisms but also opens new doors for research into compact, efficient, and highly parallelizable attention-based architectures and more nuanced approaches to reducing sequences.

References

1. Achiam, J., et al.: GPT-4 technical report. arXiv preprint arXiv:2303.08774 (2023)
2. Anthropic: Claude 3.5 sonnet (2024). https://www.anthropic.com/news/claude-3-5-sonnet
3. Ba, J.L., Kiros, J.R., Hinton, G.E.: Layer normalization. arXiv preprint arXiv:1607.06450 (2016)
4. Biermann, D., Palumbo, F., Goodwin, M., Granmo, O.C.: Harnessing attention mechanisms: efficient sequence reduction using attention-based autoencoders. arXiv preprint arXiv:2310.14837 (2023)
5. Devlin, J., Chang, M.W., Lee, K., Toutanova, K.: Bert: pre-training of deep bidirectional transformers for language understanding (2019). https://arxiv.org/abs/1810.04805
6. Fang, L., Zeng, T., Liu, C., Bo, L., Dong, W., Chen, C.: Transformer-based conditional variational autoencoder for controllable story generation. arXiv preprint arXiv:2101.00828 (2021)
7. Feng, F., Yang, Y., Cer, D., Arivazhagan, N., Wang, W.: Language-agnostic bert sentence embedding (2022). https://arxiv.org/abs/2007.01852
8. Gao, T., Yao, X., Chen, D.: Simcse: simple contrastive learning of sentence embeddings. In: EMNLP 2021 - 2021 Conference on Empirical Methods in Natural Language Processing, Proceedings, pp. 6894–6910. EMNLP 2021 - 2021 Conference on Empirical Methods in Natural Language Processing, Proceedings, Association for Computational Linguistics (ACL) (2021). Publisher Copyright: 2021 Association for Computational Linguistics; 2021 Conference on Empirical Methods in Natural Language Processing, EMNLP 2021; Conference date: 07-11-2021 Through 11-11-2021
9. Hou, P., Li, X.: Improving contrastive learning of sentence embeddings with focal-infonce. arXiv preprint arXiv:2310.06918 (2023)
10. Kowsari, K., Brown, D.E., Heidarysafa, M., Meimandi, K.J., Gerber, M.S., Barnes, L.E.: Hdltex: hierarchical deep learning for text classification. In: 2017 16th IEEE International Conference on Machine Learning and Applications (ICMLA), pp. 364–371. IEEE (2017)
11. Li, B., Zhou, H., He, J., Wang, M., Yang, Y., Li, L.: On the sentence embeddings from pre-trained language models. In: Proceedings of the 2020 Conference on Empirical Methods in Natural Language Processing (EMNLP), pp. 9119–9130. Association for Computational Linguistics, Online (2020). https://doi.org/10.18653/v1/2020.emnlp-main.733. https://aclanthology.org/2020.emnlp-main.733
12. Liu, Y., et al.: Roberta: a robustly optimized bert pretraining approach. arXiv preprint arXiv:1907.11692 (2019)

13. Ni, J., et al.: Sentence-T5: scalable sentence encoders from pre-trained text-to-text models. In: Findings of the Association for Computational Linguistics: ACL 2022, Dublin, Ireland, pp. 1864–1874. Association for Computational Linguistics (2022). https://doi.org/10.18653/v1/2022.findings-acl.146. https://aclanthology.org/2022.findings-acl.146

14. Radford, A., Narasimhan, K., Salimans, T., Sutskever, I., et al.: Improving language understanding by generative pre-training (2018). https://cdn.openai.com/research-covers/language-unsupervised/language_understanding_paper.pdf

15. Raffel, C., et al.: Exploring the limits of transfer learning with a unified text-to-text transformer. J. Mach. Learn. Res. **21**(1), 5485–5551 (2020)

16. Reimers, N., Gurevych, I.: Sentence-BERT: sentence embeddings using Siamese BERT-networks. In: Proceedings of the 2019 Conference on Empirical Methods in Natural Language Processing and the 9th International Joint Conference on Natural Language Processing (EMNLP-IJCNLP), Hong Kong, China, pp. 3982–3992. Association for Computational Linguistics (2019). https://doi.org/10.18653/v1/D19-1410. https://aclanthology.org/D19-1410

17. Sanh, V., Debut, L., Chaumond, J., Wolf, T.: Distilbert, a distilled version of bert: smaller, faster, cheaper and lighter. arXiv preprint arXiv:1910.01108 (2019)

18. Team, G., et al.: Gemini: a family of highly capable multimodal models. arXiv preprint arXiv:2312.11805 (2023)

19. Vaswani, A., et al.: Attention is all you need. In: Advances in Neural Information Processing Systems, vol. 30 (2017)

20. Wang, H., Dou, Y.: SNCSE: contrastive learning for unsupervised sentence embedding with soft negative samples. In: Huang, D.S., Premaratne, P., Jin, B., Qu, B., Jo, K.H., Hussain, A. (eds.) ICIC 2023. LNCS, vol. 14089, pp. 419–431. Springer, Cham (2023). https://doi.org/10.1007/978-981-99-4752-2_35

21. Wolf, T., et al.: Transformers: state-of-the-art natural language processing. In: Proceedings of the 2020 Conference on Empirical Methods in Natural Language Processing: System Demonstrations, pp. 38–45. Association for Computational Linguistics, Online (2020). https://www.aclweb.org/anthology/2020.emnlp-demos.6

22. Yang, Z., Dai, Z., Yang, Y., Carbonell, J., Salakhutdinov, R.R., Le, Q.V.: Xlnet: generalized autoregressive pretraining for language understanding. In: Wallach, H., Larochelle, H., Beygelzimer, A., d'Alché-Buc, F., Fox, E., Garnett, R. (eds.) Advances in Neural Information Processing Systems, vol. 32. Curran Associates, Inc. (2019). https://proceedings.neurips.cc/paper/2019/file/dc6a7e655d7e5840e66733e9ee67cc69-Paper.pdf

LSTM for Modelling and Predictive Control of Multivariable Processes

Krzysztof Zarzycki[(✉)] and Maciej Ławryńczuk

Institute of Control and Computation Engineering, Warsaw University of Technology,
ul. Nowowiejska 15/19, 00-665 Warsaw, Poland
{krzysztof.zarzycki,maciej.lawrynczuk}@pw.edu.pl

Abstract. This paper presents the use of Long Short-Term Memory (LSTM) networks as models for prediction in the Model Predictive Control (MPC) algorithm. LSTMs are recurrent neural networks often used to model dynamical processes. MPC is an advanced control technique using a process model to calculate online predictions. MPC sets the control policy for the process by solving an optimisation problem to minimise the prediction error and not violate the constraints. This paper compares two LSTM model architectures for MPC in a process with Multiple Inputs and Multiple Outputs (MIMO): a single LSTM model with multiple inputs and multiple outputs (LSTM MIMO) and several parallel LSTM models, each with Multiple Inputs and Single Output (LSTM MISO). The quality of modelling using these two architectures is analysed. Next, the selected MIMO and MISO LSTM models are implemented in the MPC algorithm. Finally, the control quality and execution time are investigated. It is concluded that both MIMO and MISO approaches offer distinct advantages; however, for the benchmark neutralisation reactor, MIMO models provide a more efficient solution for MPC implementation.

Keywords: LSTM · Model Predictive Control · Process Modelling

1 Introduction

Model Predictive Control (MPC) [17] is an advanced control technique used when classical techniques fail, i.e., linear control methods. In particular, MPC is recommended for multivariable processes with multiple inputs and multiple outputs or for processes with highly nonlinear dynamics. The MPC control technique requires a dynamical model of the controlled process to predict future signals of the controlled variables. Various types of models are used, including polynomial structures [13] and fuzzy systems [12]. Additionally, neural networks, such as multilayer perceptrons [10] and radial basis function networks [2], are commonly employed.

Long Short-Term Memory (LSTM) [6] is a type of recurrent neural network frequently used in tasks requiring the analysis, processing, classification, or

© The Author(s), under exclusive license to Springer Nature Switzerland AG 2025
M. Bramer and F. Stahl (Eds.): SGAI 2024, LNAI 15446, pp. 74–87, 2025.
https://doi.org/10.1007/978-3-031-77915-2_6

prediction of time-series data. Namely, LSTMs are used in applications such as speech recognition [5] and machine translation [19]. They also prove very efficient for modelling various dynamic processes, making them suitable for MPC controllers. Applications are mainly limited to Single Input Single Output (SISO) systems, e.g., chemical reactors [14,20], artificial pancreas systems [1], or Heating, Ventilation and Air Conditioning (HVAC) systems [11]. Implementations of MPC controllers relying on LSTMs for predictions are also possible for dynamical systems with Multiple Inputs and Multiple Outputs (MIMO), e.g., multiple tanks systems [7], continuously stirred reactors [18], underwater vehicles [4], vehicle fuel cells [15], or cardiovascular systems [3]. Unfortunately, to the best of the authors' knowledge, the existing literature does not address the selection of the internal structure of MIMO models in relation to the modeling accuracy and control quality possible in MPC.

This paper compares two approaches to modelling dynamic processes using LSTM models. The first approach utilises a single MIMO network. The second approach involves using several LSTM networks with Multiple Inputs and Single Output (MISO), operating in parallel and independently of each other. Three primary objectives are set for this study:

a) determining which approach helps to achieve the lowest possible modelling errors,
b) implementation of the trained LSTM models in the MPC algorithm,
c) analysis of the control errors and average calculation times in the controller with LSTM MIMO and LSTM MISO models.

2   LSTM Models of Dynamical Processes

The LSTM is a recurrent neural network resistant to the vanishing gradient phenomenon, enabling it to retain information over long periods [6]. Two internal states characterise the LSTM network: the cell state, c, and the hidden state, h. The cell state corresponds to the network's long-term memory, while the hidden state corresponds to short-term memory. Figure 1 depicts the architecture of the neuron itself, also known as the cell. It is complex compared to simple Multi-Layer Perceptron (MLP) networks. Four gates inside of each cell control the flow of information through the network: an input gate i adds new relevant information, a forget gate f removes unnecessary data, a state candidate gate g determines the cell's state and an output gate o determines the hidden state. Let $\mathbf{X}(k)$ be the input vector of the LSTM network. The following equations can be used to calculate the outputs of the LSTM network gates in a discrete-time instant k

$$i(k) = \sigma(\boldsymbol{W}_{i}\mathbf{X}(k) + \boldsymbol{R}_{i}\boldsymbol{h}(k-1) + \boldsymbol{b}_{i}) \tag{1}$$

$$\boldsymbol{f}(k) = \sigma(\mathbf{W}_{f}\mathbf{X}(k) + \boldsymbol{R}_{f}\boldsymbol{h}(k-1) + \boldsymbol{b}_{f}) \tag{2}$$

$$\boldsymbol{g}(k) = \tau(\boldsymbol{W}_{g}\mathbf{X}(k) + \boldsymbol{R}_{g}\boldsymbol{h}(k-1) + \boldsymbol{b}_{g}) \tag{3}$$

$$\boldsymbol{o}(k) = \sigma(\boldsymbol{W}_{o}\mathbf{X}(k) + \boldsymbol{R}_{o}\boldsymbol{h}(k-1) + \boldsymbol{b}_{o}) \tag{4}$$

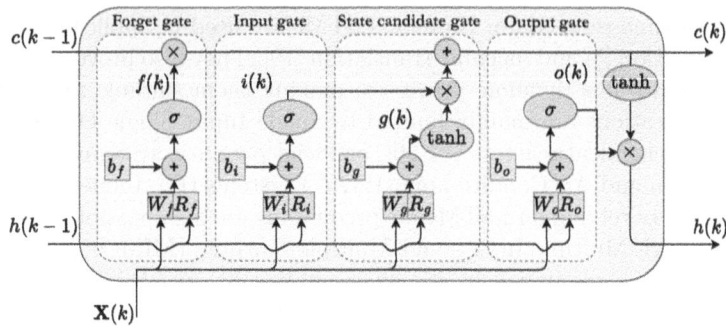

Fig. 1. LSTM cell

where σ and τ represent sigmoid and hyperbolic tangent functions, respectively, $\mathbf{W}$ denotes the weights associated with the input vector $\mathbf{X}$, $\mathbf{R}$ denotes the recursive weights associated with the hidden state $\mathbf{h}(k)$, and $\mathbf{b}$ denotes the bias. The cell state $\mathbf{c}(k)$ is then determined by removing unnecessary information from the state $\mathbf{c}(k-1)$ and adding new information from the candidate state $\mathbf{g}(k)$.

$$\mathbf{c}(k) = \mathbf{f}(k) \circ \mathbf{c}(k-1) + \mathbf{i}(k) \circ \mathbf{g}(k) \tag{5}$$

where the symbol $\circ$ denotes the Hadamard product [16]. Next, the hidden state is calculated based on the current cell state $\mathbf{c}(k)$ by the output gate $\mathbf{o}(k)$

$$\mathbf{h}(k) = \mathbf{o}(k) \circ \tau(\mathbf{c}(k)) \tag{6}$$

Finally, the fully connected layer of the network determines the model's output $y^{\mathrm{LSTM}}(k)$ based on the current hidden LSTM state $\mathbf{h}(k)$

$$y^{\mathrm{LSTM}}(k) = \mathbf{W}_{\mathrm{y}}\mathbf{h}(k) + b_{\mathrm{y}} \tag{7}$$

Let us present two possible approaches to modelling MIMO systems. We use the following notation: n_{u} stands for the number of process inputs, i.e., the manipulated variables, n_{y} defines the number of process outputs, i.e., the controlled variables. The symbols u_i and y_j stand for the input and output signals, where $i = 1, \ldots, n_{\mathrm{u}}$ and $j = 1, \ldots, n_{\mathrm{y}}$, respectively.

2.1   LSTM MIMO Models

The structure of the MIMO model configuration is shown in Fig. 2. In this case, one single LSTM network is used to model the multivariable MIMO dynamic process. Namely, the network calculates values of all n_{y} process output signals. The LSTM input vector, next used in Eqs. (1)–(4), takes into account a set of past measurements of all n_{u} process inputs and n_{y} outputs

$$\mathbf{X}(k) = [u_1(k-1), \ldots, u_1(k-n_{\mathrm{B}}), \ldots, u_{n_{\mathrm{u}}}(k-1), \ldots, u_{n_{\mathrm{u}}}(k-n_{\mathrm{B}}),$$
$$y_1(k-1), \ldots, y_1(k-n_{\mathrm{A}}), \ldots, y_{n_{\mathrm{y}}}(k-1), \ldots, y_{n_{\mathrm{y}}}(k-n_{\mathrm{A}})]^{\mathrm{T}} \tag{8}$$

where the parameters n_{A} and n_{B} describe the dynamic order of the model.

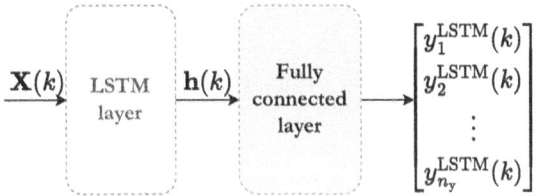

Fig. 2. LSTM MIMO model structure

2.2 LSTM MISO Models

The structure of the MISO model is shown in the Fig. 3. We use n_y independent MISO models with only one scalar output variable in this approach. In contrast to the MIMO structure, each submodel has a different input vector. Namely, each submodel takes as the input vector a set of past signals of all process inputs and only past values of the modelled output

$$\mathbf{X}_m(k) = [u_1(k-1), \dots, u_1(k-n_B^m), \dots, u_{n_u}(k-1) \dots, u_{n_u}(k-n_B^m),$$
$$y_m(k-1), \dots, y_m(k-n_A^m)]^T \tag{9}$$

where $m = 1, \dots, n_y$ is the submodel number. Let us note that the second structure allows the utilisation of different orders of dynamics for the consecutive submodels, which is impossible in the first model structure.

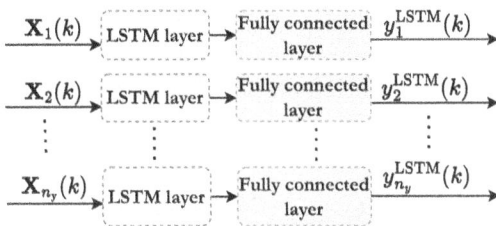

Fig. 3. LSTM MISO model structure

3   Model Predictive Control

In this paper, we utilise a general form of the MPC task. At each discrete time instant k, the controller performs online calculations to determine a vector of optimal control increments.

$$\triangle \boldsymbol{u}(k) = [\triangle u_1(k|k), \ldots, \triangle u_{n_u}(k|k), \ldots,$$
$$\triangle u_1(k + N_u - 1|k), \ldots, \triangle u_{n_u}(k + N_u - 1|k)]^T \tag{10}$$

The notation can be interpreted as follows: $\triangle u_n(k|k)$ is the n–th control increment at time instant k, determined at time instant k; $\triangle u_n(k + 1|k)$ is the n–th increment at time instant $k + 1$, determined at time instant k. The symbol N_u denotes the MPC control horizon. The MPC optimisation task is

$$\min_{\triangle \boldsymbol{u}(k)} J(k) = \sum_{p=1}^{N} \sum_{m=1}^{n_u} \mu_m \left(y_m^{sp}(k + p|k) - \hat{y}_m(k + p|k) \right)^2$$
$$+ \sum_{p=0}^{N_u - 1} \sum_{n=1}^{n_u} \lambda_n \left(\triangle u_n(k + p|k) \right)^2$$

subject to

$$\underline{u}_n \leq u_n(k + i|k) \leq \overline{u}_n, \ i = 0, \ldots, N_u - 1, \ n = 1, \ldots, \ n_u$$
$$\triangle \underline{u}_n \leq \triangle u_n(k + i|k) \leq \triangle \overline{u}_n, \ i = 0, \ldots, N_u - 1, \ n = 1, \ldots, \ n_u$$
$$\underline{y}_m \leq \hat{y}_m(k + i|k) \leq \overline{y}_m, \ i = 1, \ldots, N, m = 1, \ldots, \ n_y \tag{11}$$

where $y_m^{sp}(k + p|k)$ is the set-point for the m–th output at future time $k + p$, known at time k; $\hat{y}(k + p|k)$ is the prediction for time $k + p$, determined at time k; N is the length of the control horizon; and μ_m is the penalty factor. The first component of the minimised function can thus be interpreted as a prediction of future control error. Its second component relates to minimising the n–th control signal increments, with λ_n denoting the penalty coefficient. The input signals, their increments, and the predicted output are constrained. The constraints are defined by the quantities $\underline{u}_n$, $\overline{u}_n$, $\triangle \underline{u}_n$, $\triangle \overline{u}_n$, $\underline{y}_m$, $\overline{y}_m$ respectively. Predictions for the LSTM model are defined as

$$\hat{y}_m(k + p|k) = y_m^{LSTM}(k + p|k) + d_m(k) \tag{12}$$

$y_m^{LSTM}(k)$ denotes the model output for a future time sample k and the prediction error $d_m(k)$ is determined as the difference between the measured value of the output and its estimate from the model.

The MPC task (11) is solved online at each time sample, resulting in a vector of optimal control increments (10). It is important that only the optimal values of the manipulated variables for the current discrete time k are sent to the process. The above-described procedure is repeated at subsequent sampling moments.

4   Simulation Results

Simulation experiments have been conducted in MATLAB using a PC with a Geforce GTX970 graphics card, an Intel i5-3450 processor, and 16 GB of

RAM. MATLAB's Deep Learning Toolbox package has been used to train the LSTM models. Different numbers of LSTM neurons n_N have been considered: $2, 4, 6, 8, 10$. The models have been categorised based on the order of model dynamics. The parameter n_A is 0 in the first category; the values of n_B are $1, 2, 3$. In the second category, $n_A = n_B$; the following dynamics order is considered: $1, 2, 3$. Five models have been trained for each set of parameters (n_N, n_A, n_B), and the model with the best performance on the validation set has been selected. Only the best-performing models for each parameter set are considered in the following analysis. The Adam optimisation algorithm [8], with an initial learning rate of 0.01, has been used to train the LSTM network. The dataset used during training has been divided into training and validation sets in a 70:30 ratio. The training takes a maximum of 2000 epochs, although it is terminated early if no improvement in model quality on the validation set is observed for ten consecutive epochs.

4.1 Benchmark Process: Neutralisation Reactor

MIMO Neutralisation reactor benchmark [9] has been chosen to test the trained neural models and the implemented MPC control algorithm. The base (NaOH) (q_1) and acid (HNO3) (q_3) streams are the inputs of the process. The process outputs are the product's pH value and the liquid column's height in the reactor, denoted as h. The process is characterised by nonlinearity; its static and dynamic properties depend on the operating point. A first-principle model of the reactor in the form of a system of nonlinear differential equations [9] (solved using the Runge-Kutta method) is used to simulate the process and collect training and validation data sets. The sampling time is $10\,\mathrm{s}$.

4.2 Model Structure Comparison: The Number of Parameters

In the context of MPC control, prediction calculation is performed multiple times at each sampling instant online and must be computationally simple. The model should have as few internal parameters as possible. For the LSTM MIMO model structure, consisting of only one neural network, the internal parameters are:

- four $\mathbf{W}$ weights matrices of the LSTM layer, each with dimensions $n_N \times (n_y \times n_A + n_u \times n_B)$,
- four $\mathbf{R}$ recurrent weights matrices of the LSTM layer, each with dimensions $n_N \times n_N$,
- four bias vectors $\mathbf{b}$ of the LSTM layer, each with dimensions $n_N \times 1$,
- $\mathbf{W}_y$ weights matrix and a bias vector of the fully connected layer $\mathbf{b}_y$, with dimensions $n_y \times n_N$ and $n_N \times 1$, respectively.

Hence, the number of parameters of the LSTM MIMO model can thus be expressed as

$$N = 4(n_N(n_y n_A + n_u n_B) + n_N^2 + n_N) + n_N n_y + n_y \qquad (13)$$

In the case of the LSTM MISO model consisting of n_y MISO networks, the internal parameters are:

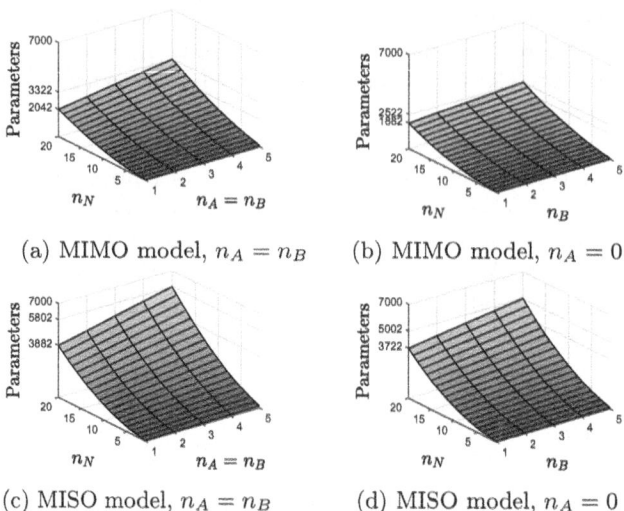

(a) MIMO model, $n_A = n_B$ (b) MIMO model, $n_A = 0$

(c) MISO model, $n_A = n_B$ (d) MISO model, $n_A = 0$

Fig. 4. The number of internal parameters of LSTM MIMO model and two MISO models when $n_u = n_y = 2$. For displaying clarity, we assume that both MISO models have the same values of n_N, n_A, and n_B

- n_y models are used, in each model, the **W** matrices of the LSTM layer have dimensions $n_N \times (n_A + n_u \times n_B)$,
- the **R** matrices and **b** vectors remain unchanged compared to the MIMO model,
- the weight matrix $\mathbf{W}_y$ has dimensions $1 \times n_N$ and the bias b_y is a scalar.

Hence, the number of parameters of the LSTM MISO models is

$$N = 4n_y((n_A + n_u n_B)n_N + n_N^2 + n_N) + n_N n_y + n_y \tag{14}$$

A comparison of the number of internal model parameters for LSTM MIMO and LSTM MISO structures for a process with two inputs and two outputs, i.e., when $n_u = n_y = 2$, is shown in Fig. 4. It is evident that MIMO models have fewer parameters than MISO models. This disproportion is particularly evident as n_N increases.

4.3   Model Structure Comparison: Modelling Accuracy

The modelling results are presented in Tables 1 and 2. The Mean Squared Errors (MSE) for the pH and h variables from the validation dataset are denoted as E_{val}^{pH} and E_{val}^{h}, respectively. P denotes the number of parameters of LSTM MIMO models, while P_1 and P_2 denote the number of parameters of the first and the second MISO submodels comprising the LSTM MISO structure, respectively.

Based on the obtained results, the following conclusions can be drawn:

Table 1. LSTM MIMO model structure: comparison of errors and the number of internal parameters

n_B	n_N	$n_A = 0$			$n_A = n_B$		
		E_{val}^{pH}	E_{val}^{h}	P	E_{val}^{pH}	E_{val}^{h}	P
1	2	0.111	0.075	46	0.182	0.140	62
	4	0.068	0.050	122	0.074	0.460	154
	6	0.047	0.066	230	0.064	0.075	278
	8	0.031	0.027	370	0.063	0.082	434
	10	0.030	0.035	542	0.016	0.061	622
2	2	0.098	0.061	62	0.274	0.400	94
	4	0.079	0.118	154	0.080	0.200	218
	6	0.045	0.078	278	0.080	0.190	374
	8	0.030	0.061	434	0.027	0.060	562
3	2	0.103	0.077	78	0.111	0.067	126
	4	0.046	0.041	186	0.055	0.094	282
	6	0.043	0.096	326	0.053	0.064	470
	8	0.036	0.047	498	0.047	0.068	690
	10	0.027	0.093	702	0.029	0.052	942

Table 2. LSTM MISO model structure: comparison of errors and the number of internal parameters

n_B	n_N	$n_A = 0$				$n_A = n_B$			
		E_{val}^{pH}	P_1	E_{val}^{h}	P_2	E_{val}^{pH}	P_2	E_{val}^{h}	P_2
1	2	0.143	43	0.0099	43	0.177	51	0.1641	51
	4	0.062	117	0.0062	117	0.035	133	0.0034	133
	6	0.034	233	0.0053	233	0.096	247	0.0044	247
	8	0.034	361	0.0039	361	0.011	393	0.0034	393
	10	0.026	531	0.0053	531	0.021	571	0.0015	571
2	2	0.094	59	0.0147	59	0.179	75	0.0091	75
	4	0.117	149	0.0096	149	0.094	181	0.0137	181
	6	0.038	271	0.0081	271	0.057	319	0.0129	319
	8	0.032	426	0.0070	426	0.032	489	0.0032	489
	10	0.026	611	0.0045	611	0.033	691	0.0036	691
3	2	0.101	75	0.0177	75	0.138	99	0.0068	99
	4	0.031	181	0.0095	181	0.096	229	0.0049	229
	6	0.030	319	0.0123	319	0.053	391	0.0081	391
	8	0.039	489	0.0088	489	0.046	585	0.0049	585
	10	0.056	691	0.0054	691	0.045	811	0.0027	811

1. Unsurprisingly, the modelling error for both LSTM MIMO and LSTM MISO model structures decreases significantly as the number of neurons n_N increases.

2. However, the LSTM MISO structure allows for excellent modelling quality even with fewer neurons. It is especially evident for the h output where LSTM MISO models outperformed LSTM MIMO models significantly.
3. Increasing the order of dynamics, defined by n_A and n_B, often helps to reduce modelling errors. However, its influence is much milder compared to the effect of increasing the value of n_N.
4. Models with $n_A = n_B$ in general have smaller errors than models with $n_A = 0$.

The LSTM MIMO models with the smallest weighted error for both output signals are selected. In the case of the LSTM MISO models, modelling of h and pH variables is performed independently. Therefore, selection is based on individual errors of the sub-models. We select the best-performing models:

1. MIMO structure v. 1: $n_N = 8$, $n_A = 0$, $n_B = 1$; the model has $P = 370$ parameters,
2. MISO structure v. 1: $n_N^{pH} = 10$, $n_A^{pH} = 0$, $n_B^{pH} = 1$, $n_N^h = 8$, $n_A^h = 0$, $n_B^h = 1$; the model has $P = P1 + P2 = 892$ parameters,
3. MIMO structure v. 2: $n_N = 10$, $n_A = 1$, $n_B = 1$; the model has $P = 622$ parameters,
4. MISO structure v. 2: $n_N^{pH} = 8$, $n_A^{pH} = 1$, $n_B^{pH} = 1$, $n_N^h = 10$, $n_A^h = 1$, $n_B^h = 1$; the model has $P = P1 + P2 = 1060$ parameters.

Figure 5 shows the relationship between the models' pH output and the validation data set for 3,000 samples. All four models exhibit small but frequent errors, especially in the range of greatest process nonlinearity when the pH value is between 6 and 9. These errors are least frequent for the MIMO $v.$ 2 model.

Figure 6 shows a similar relationship for the h signal. The LSTM MIMO structures display infrequent minor errors, while the LSTM MISO structures model this signal excellently.

Figure 7 compares the outputs of the selected models vs. the first 500 samples of the validation data set. All four models achieve acceptable modelling quality. However, it is noticeable that both models with $n_A = 0$ have larger errors for the pH signal and the MIMO structure v. 1 deviates slightly for the h output.

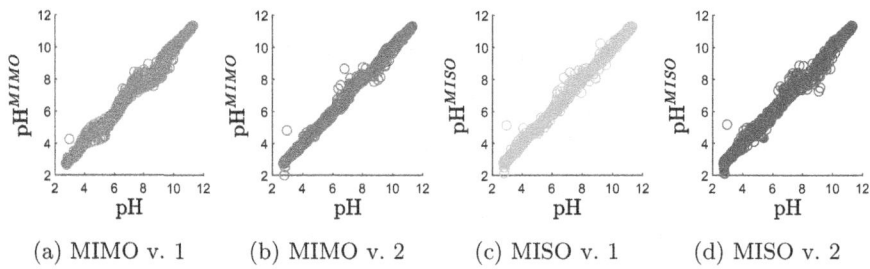

(a) MIMO v. 1   (b) MIMO v. 2   (c) MISO v. 1   (d) MISO v. 2

Fig. 5. The relation between the models' pH output and the validation data set

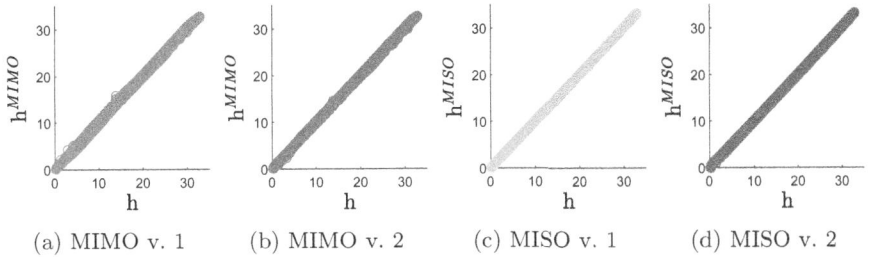

(a) MIMO v. 1   (b) MIMO v. 2   (c) MISO v. 1   (d) MISO v. 2

Fig. 6. The relation between the models' h output and the validation data set

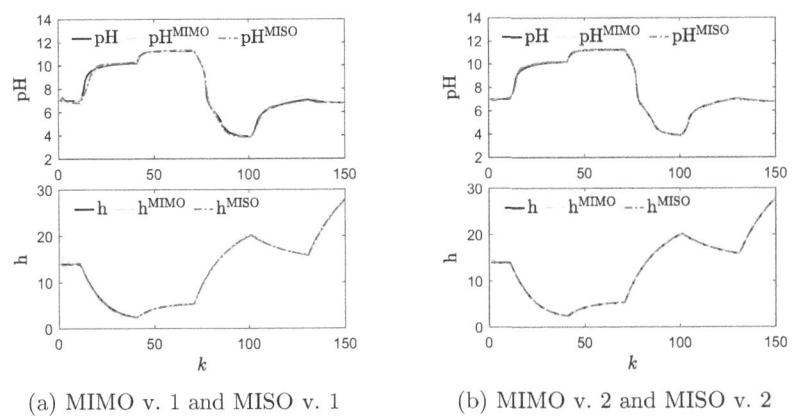

(a) MIMO v. 1 and MISO v. 1   (b) MIMO v. 2 and MISO v. 2

Fig. 7. Best performing model outputs vs. the first 500 samples of validation data.

4.4   Model Structure Comparison: MPC Control Quality

All models presented in Tables 1 and 2 have been implemented into the MPC algorithm. The conditions of the experiments are as follows: the simulation lasts 120 discrete time steps, corresponding to 1200 s. The process is initially at its operating point. At time instant 3, the set-point for the pH value is changed. The set-point is then changed five more times for every 20-time steps. The set-point for h remains constant throughout the simulation. MPC controllers with all models have the same settings, i.e.: $N = 10$, $N_u = 3$, $\mu_1 = \mu_2 = 1$, $\lambda_1 = \lambda_2 = 0.1$. The average cumulative control errors for pH and h controlled variables are determined for each model configuration.

Figure 8 shows the control errors determined for all four categories of models. We can observe the following:

– In Fig. 8a, it can be observed that LSTM MIMO structures with a low number of neurons result in high control error, especially when the order of dynamics is high. As the number of neurons increases, the error decreases rapidly, and for $n_N = 10$, most models reach an error close to 5.

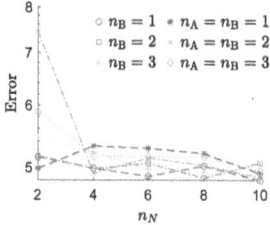

(a) Errors for pH with MIMO model

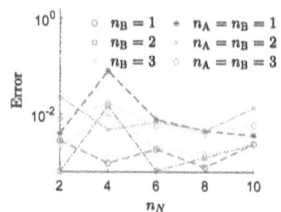

(b) Errors for h with MISO model

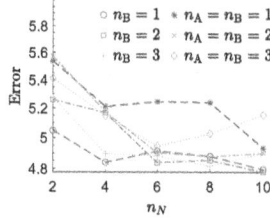

(c) Errors for pH with MISO model

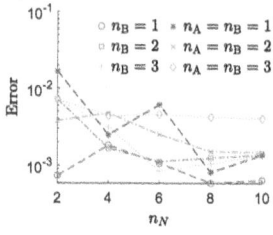

(d) Errors for h with MISO model

Fig. 8. Control errors for different LSTM structures used in the MPC algorithm

- Figure 8c shows the error for LSTM MIMO structures and the h output. Models with $n_A = 0$, small n_B dynamics, and an average (6–8) value of n_B perform better.
- Figure 8b indicates that for the LSTM MISO structures, the error for pH is about 5–6, even for models with fewer internal parameters. As the number of neurons increases, the error decreases, but not rapidly. Models with $n_A = 0$ perform slightly better in MPC.
- Figure 8d shows the error for LSTM MISO structures and the h output. The lowest error is obtained when n_B is low, $n_A = 0$, and the number of neurons is $n_N = 8 - 10$.

Figure 9 shows the average execution time of one iteration of the MPC algorithm with LSTM models. The Sequential Quadratic Programming (SQP) optimisation algorithm is used. The time increases sharply with the increasing order of dynamics. It is also significant that the LSTM MISO structures (Fig. 9b), consisting of two LSTM models with more internal parameters, have a much higher computational cost than the LSTM MIMO structures (Fig. 9a).

In summary, different models perform better in MPC than in the modelling task. It may be counter-intuitive, but in the MPC controller, a merely correct model can yield better regulation quality than a perfect one. This is due to the feedback mechanism in the MPC controller. A model with slightly larger prediction errors causes the controller to generate larger control values, which helps the set-point to be reached faster and reduces control errors. However, the model must be good enough; if the prediction errors are too high, the controller may generate control signals that are too rapid, leading to large oscillations in

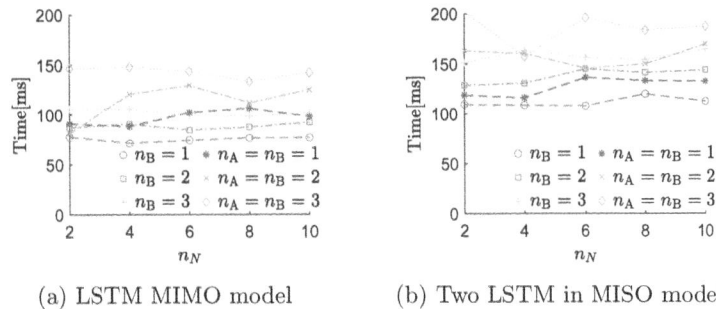

(a) LSTM MIMO model   (b) Two LSTM in MISO model

Fig. 9. The average execution time of one iteration of the MPC algorithm for different LSTM structures

the process output signals. Additionally, the computational cost of the model is important. Predictions from LSTM models with fewer parameters are computed faster. Given that predictions are determined repeatedly by the solver in each iteration of the MPC algorithm, small models should be preferred.

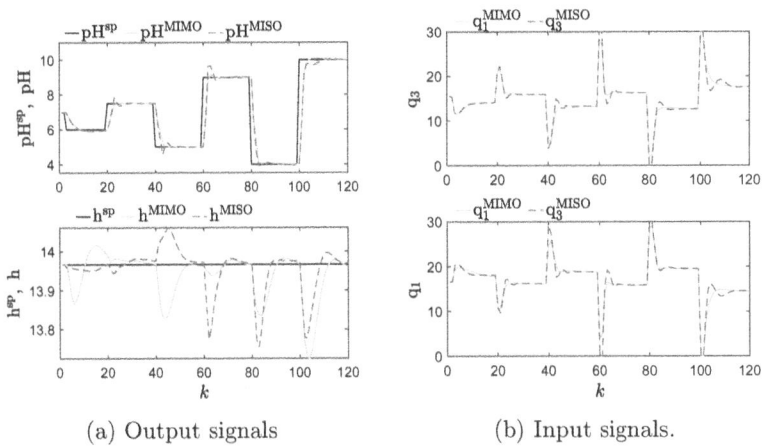

(a) Output signals   (b) Input signals.

Fig. 10. MPC performance using two selected LSTM structures for prediction

Figure 10 shows the controller's performance during simulation with two selected models that exhibit low control errors:

1. MIMO, $n_N = 8$, $n_A = 0$, $n_B = 1$, $P = 434$,
2. MISO, $n_N^{pH} = 8$, $n_A^{pH} = 0$, $n_B^{pH} = 3$, $n_N^h = 10$, $n_A^h = 3$, $n_B^h = 0$, $P = 1018$.

Both MPCs work correctly, with the pH value following the changes in the set-point. The controller with the LSTM MIMO structure demonstrates slightly less overshoot and a shorter control time compared to the one with the structure

MISO structure. For both controllers, the value of h does not deviate from the set-point by more than 0.3. Additionally, the control signals q_1 and q_3 have similar shapes. Given that the LSTM MIMO structure model has almost three times fewer internal parameters, it can be concluded that it is the preferred choice.

5 Conclusion

This work demonstrates two types of LSTM model architectures that can be used for modelling and predictive control of multidimensional processes. Using a representative highly nonlinear multidimensional process example, it is shown that the LSTM MISO structure comprised of a set of sub-models running in parallel can achieve excellent modelling quality. On the other hand, LSTM MIMO structures, which use a single neural network with multiple inputs and outputs, are better suited for implementation in the MPC algorithm due to their lower number of parameters and computational cost. While both approaches have advantages, the LSTM MIMO models provide a more efficient and effective implementation solution in MPC for controlling complex processes.

Acknowledgments. This research was financed by the Warsaw University of Technology in the framework of the research project for the scientific discipline automatic control, electronics and electrical engineering.

Disclosure of Interests. The authors have no competing interests to declare that are relevant to the content of this article.

References

1. Aiello, E.M., Jaloli, M., Cescon, M.: Model predictive control (MPC) of an artificial pancreas with data-driven learning of multi-step-ahead blood glucose predictors. Control. Eng. Pract. **144**, 105810 (2024). https://doi.org/10.1016/j.conengprac.2023.105810
2. Balla, K.M., Nørgaard, J.T., Bendtsen, J.D., Kallesøe, C.S.: Model predictive control using linearized radial basis function neural models for water distribution networks. In: 2019 IEEE Conference on Control Technology and Applications (CCTA), Hong Kong, pp. 368–373 (2019). https://doi.org/10.1109/CCTA.2019.8920627
3. Branen, A., Yao, Y., Kothare, M.V., Mahmoudi, B., Kumar, G.: Data driven control of vagus nerve stimulation for the cardiovascular system: an in silico computational study. Front. Physiol. **13**, 798157 (2022). https://doi.org/10.3389/fphys.2022.798157
4. Cai, M., Wang, Y., Wang, S., Wang, R., Cheng, L., Tan, M.: Prediction-based seabed terrain following control for an underwater vehicle-manipulator system. IEEE Trans. Syst. Man Cybern. Syst. **51**, 4751–4760 (2021). https://doi.org/10.1109/TSMC.2019.2944651
5. Graves, A., Liwicki, M., Fernández, S., Bertolami, R., Bunke, H., Schmidhuber, J.: A novel connectionist system for unconstrained handwriting recognition. IEEE Trans. Pattern Anal. Mach. Intell. **31**, 855–868 (2009). https://doi.org/10.1109/TPAMI.2008.137

6. Hochreiter, S., Schmidhuber, J.: Long short-term memory. Neural Comput. **9**, 1735–1780 (1997). https://doi.org/10.1162/neco.1997.9.8.1735

7. Jung, M., da Costa Mendes, P.R., Önnheim, M., Gustavsson, E.: Model predictive control when utilizing LSTM as dynamic models. Eng. Appl. Artif. Intell. **123**, 106226 (2023). https://doi.org/10.1016/j.engappai.2023.106226

8. Kingma, D.P., Ba, J.: Adam: a method for stochastic optimization (2017). https://arxiv.org/abs/1412.6980

9. Ławryńczuk, M.: On-line set-point optimisation and predictive control using neural Hammerstein models. Chem. Eng. J. **166**, 269–287 (2011). https://doi.org/10.1016/j.cej.2010.07.065

10. Ławryńczuk, M.: Computationally Efficient Model Predictive Control Algorithms: a Neural Network Approach. Studies in Systems, Decision and Control, vol. 3. Springer, Cham (2014). https://doi.org/10.1007/978-3-319-04229-9

11. Ma, L., Huang, Y., Zhang, J., Zhao, T.: A model predictive control for heat supply at building thermal inlet based on data-driven model. Buildings **12** (2022). https://doi.org/10.3390/buildings12111879

12. Marusak, P.M.: A numerically efficient fuzzy MPC algorithm with fast generation of the control signal. Int. J. Appl. Math. Comput. Sci. 31, 59–71 (2021). https://doi.org/10.34768/amcs-2021-0005

13. Ramesh, K., Abd Shukor, S.R., Aziz, N.: Nonlinear model predictive control of a distillation column using NARX model. In: 10th International Symposium on Process Systems Engineering: Part A. Computer Aided Chemical Engineering, vol. 27, pp. 1575–1580 (2009). https://doi.org/10.1016/S1570-7946(09)70653-4

14. Schwedersky, B.B., Flesch, R.C.: Nonlinear model predictive control algorithm with iterative nonlinear prediction and linearization for long short-term memory network models. Eng. Appl. Artif. Intell. **115**, 105247 (2022). https://doi.org/10.1016/j.engappai.2022.105247

15. Song, K., Huang, X., Xu, H., Sun, H., Chen, Y., Huang, D.: Model predictive control energy management strategy integrating long short-term memory and dynamic programming for fuel cell vehicles. Int. J. Hydrogen Energy **56**, 1235–1248 (2024). https://doi.org/10.1016/j.ijhydene.2023.12.245

16. Styan, G.P.: Hadamard products and multivariate statistical analysis. Linear Algebra Appl. **6**, 217–240 (1973). https://doi.org/10.1016/0024-3795(73)90023-2

17. Tatjewski, P.: Advanced Control of Industrial Processes, Structures and Algorithms. Springer, London (2007). https://doi.org/10.1007/978-1-84628-635-3

18. Wang, Z., Tan, W.G.Y., Rangaiah, G.P., Wu, Z.: Machine learning aided model predictive control with multi-objective optimization and multi-criteria decision making. Comput. Chem. Eng. **179**, 108414 (2023). https://doi.org/10.1016/j.compchemeng.2023.108414

19. Yonghui, W., et al.: Google's neural machine translation system: bridging the gap between human and machine translation (2016). https://arxiv.org/abs/1609.08144

20. Zarzycki, K., Ławryńczuk, M.: LSTM and GRU neural networks as models of dynamical processes used in predictive control: a comparison of models developed for two chemical reactors. Sensors **21**, 5625 (2021). https://doi.org/10.3390/s21165625

Structured Radial Basis Function Network: Modelling Diversity for Multiple Hypotheses Prediction

Alejandro Rodriguez Dominguez, Muhammad Shahzad[(✉)], and Xia Hong

Department of Computer Science, University of Reading, Reading, UK
a.j.rodriguezdominguez@pgr.reading.ac.uk,
{m.shahzad2,xia.hong}@reading.ac.uk

Abstract. Multi-modal problems can be effectively addressed using multiple hypothesis frameworks, but integrating these frameworks into learning models poses significant challenges. This paper introduces a Structured Radial Basis Function Network (s-RBFN) as an ensemble of multiple hypothesis predictors for regression. During the training of the predictors, first the centroidal Voronoi tessellations are formed based on their losses and the true labels, representing geometrically the set of multiple hypotheses. Then, the trained predictors are used to compute a structured dataset with their predictions, including centers and scales for the basis functions. A radial basis function network, with each basis function focused on a particular hypothesis, is subsequently trained using this structured dataset for multiple hypotheses prediction. The s-RBFN is designed to train efficiently while controlling diversity in ensemble learning parametrically. The least-squares approach for training the structured ensemble model provides a closed-form solution for multiple hypotheses and structured predictions. During the formation of the structured dataset, a parameter is employed to avoid mode collapse by controlling tessellation shapes. This parameter provides a mechanism to balance diversity and generalization performance for the s-RBFN. The empirical validation on two multivariate prediction datasets—air quality and energy appliance predictions—demonstrates the superior generalization performance and computational efficiency of the structured ensemble model compared to other models and their single-hypothesis counterparts.

Keywords: diversity · ensemble learning · multiple hypotheses prediction · radial basis functions · Voronoi tessellations

1 Introduction

Multi-modality focuses on perception with a set of hypotheses instead of a single output to learn processes. Notable existing approaches include Multiple Choice Learning (MCL) [8,9], Multiple Hypotheses Prediction (MHP) [16], Mixture-Of-Experts [21], Bagging [2], Boosting [7], and Meta-Learning [20]. Among them,

M. Bramer and F. Stahl (Eds.): SGAI 2024, LNAI 15446, pp. 88–101, 2025.
https://doi.org/10.1007/978-3-031-77915-2_7

MCL differs in that it uses the output of different models or hypotheses as inputs to a structured ensemble model (or multiple structured prediction/classification task models), which are heterogeneous ensemble predictors that can vary in size, parameters, and architecture [8]. Diverse Multiple Choice Learning (DivMCL), is an extension proposed for diverse multi-output structured prediction by including a diversity encouraging term in the loss function used for training the models [9]. While DivMCL provides diversity, it trains separate networks which makes information exchange between individual predictors harder. To cope with this, the DivMCL ideas are extended by instead of training separate networks for each choice, the individual hypotheses are combined with Voronoi tessellations formed by the predictors' losses in a shared architecture. This allows sharing of information among predictors during training [16]. But, it is not clear how to optimally combine these predictors into an ensemble. To the best of the authors' knowledge, there is no existing method that optimally combines structured predictions from multiple hypotheses prediction with an ensemble learning model that can be trained with a closed-form solution [8,9,16].

Another important aspect in enhancing generalization of ensembles is the diversity of individual predictors. Diversity in this context has been extensively researched in literature, e.g., using Bias-Variance-Covariance decomposition [18], ambiguity decomposition [10], and their hybrid extensions [3]. However, there is also not a unifying framework for diversity in ensemble learning. Moreover, there is no clear connection in the literature between geometric properties of loss functions for individual predictors and diversity in ensemble learning [19]. This work focuses on the definition of diversity in ensemble learning as the variety of outputs from base learners that can improve the generalization performance of ensemble models [19].

Building on previous aspects [9,16,19], a new approach for multiple hypotheses prediction using a structured ensemble model is presented. In this approach, predictions from a set of base learners or individual predictors are used as inputs for a radial basis function network, with each predictor or hypothesis focusing on a specific basis function. The model is referred to as the Structured Radial Basis Function Network (s-RBFN). During training, the base learners form centroidal Voronoi tessellations (CVT), with each hypothesis or base learner assigned to a particular tessellation. A parametric formula from multiple hypotheses framework [16] is used to weight the updates of the base learner parameters in each iteration of gradient descent, preventing mode collapse and ensuring that all predictions fall within their respective tessellations. In this work, this strategy is applied to control diversity in ensemble learning similar to DivMCL [9] with the mechanism from MHP [16], enhancing generalization performance. The proposed s-RBFN can then be optimized using least squares, providing faster training compared to other existing structured models that rely on gradient descent or non-convex methods [8,9,16].

The paper is organized as follows: Sect. 2 presents a revision of the previous work in structured ensemble learning and diversity; Sect. 3 presents the proposed model; Sect. 4 presents the experimental results and discussions; and finally, Sect. 5 provides the concluding remarks and outlook.

2 Literature Review

Multiple hypotheses prediction (MHP) methods extend semi-supervised ensembles and other single-loss, single-output systems to multiple outputs providing a piece-wise constant approximation of the conditional output space. They differ from mixture density networks by representing the uncertainty through a discrete set of hypotheses [16]. These models initially employed training techniques from multiple choice learning [1,9] and later exploited the geometric properties from Voronoi tessellations formed by losses of the individual predictors as multiple hypothesis [16]. These approaches tend to be based on Winner-Takes-it-All (WTA) loss, meaning that the best base learner among all predictors gets updated during their training. A partial solution is a relaxed version of WTA [16] where in addition to the winner predictor, the other predictors also get updated for each iteration. It alleviates the convergence problem of the WTA, but still leads to hypotheses with incorrect modes. Moreover, when optimizing for a mixture distribution, the issues of numerical instabilities and mode collapsing arise. For this purpose, the evolving WTA loss was proposed [13] which addresses these issues by preserving the distribution, yielding regularly distributed hypotheses. Although this somewhat mitigates the issue but still the problem of how to combine the multiple hypothesis efficiently in a structured ensemble model persists.

Another aspect of MHP is the use of diversity which can serve as effective regularization - leading to possibly worse performance on training data, but better generalization on unseen test data [9]. Traditional diversity measures often assess the correlation or discrepancy between predictions of two models and their collective performance [11]. Recent innovations have introduced the Bias-Variance-Diversity decomposition, a nuanced framework that integrates various functional forms for each loss and directly links diversity to the expectation of ensemble ambiguity [19]. This approach goes beyond the traditional Ambiguity and Bias-Variance-Covariance decompositions, limited to squared-loss and arithmetic-mean combiners [10,18]. In practice, strategies like bagging and boosting facilitate diversity among base learners by manipulating data, thus introducing structural and data diversity. Additional methods quantify diversity through non-maximal predictions and employ metrics such as the logarithm of ensemble diversity (LED) and ensemble entropy [15,20]. More recently, MCL and DivMCL demonstrate superior test accuracy and better generalization compared to traditional multi-output prediction methods [8,9]. These approaches emphasize minimizing oracle loss by focusing on specific hypothesis, contrasting with broader Mixture-of-Expert models [8,9,12,15,20]. Ultimately, the strategic integration of diversity not only serves as an effective regularization mechanism but also critically enhances the predictive accuracy and reliability of ensemble models, especially in managing out-of-distribution data. By optimizing ensemble diversity through sophisticated decomposition models and diverse ensemble strategies, researchers can effectively balance error components to minimize over-all mean-squared error, resulting in significantly improved predictions [4,18].

3   Proposed Methodology

In this section, first the multiple hypotheses prediction with Voronoi Tessella-tions is presented. Later, it is explained how this could be scaled to operate in a structured setting for regression applications. This is done by generating the structured dataset using the MHP base learners' predictions. Finally the opti-mization of the s-RBFN using the structured dataset is efficiently carried out by least squares approach.

In the supervised learning setting, given training instances $\{x_i\}_{i=1}^{N}$ and ground-truth labels $\{y_i\}_{i=1}^{N}$, the multiple hypotheses case involves a set of predic-tion functions $\{f_{\theta_j}(x)\}_{j=1}^{M}$ with corresponding model parameters $\Theta = \{\theta_j\}_{j=1}^{M}$. Assuming the training samples follow the distribution $p(x, y)$, the expected error for a loss function $\mathcal{L}$ is expressed as:

$$\int_X \sum_{j=1}^{M} \int_{\mathcal{Y}_j(f_{\theta_j}(x))} \mathcal{L}(f_{\theta_j}(x), y)\, p(x, y)\, \mathrm{d}y\, \mathrm{d}x \tag{1}$$

During training, the Voronoi tessellation of the label space is induced by the losses computed from M predictors and given as $\mathcal{Y} = \bigcup_{j=1}^{M} \mathcal{Y}_j(f_{\theta_j}(x))$ where $\mathcal{Y}_j(f_{\theta_j}(x_i))$ represents the jth cell with $f_{\theta_j}(x_i)$ being the closest of the M pre-dictions to the label data for each training iteration [16]:

$$\mathcal{Y}_j(f_{\theta_j}(x_i)) = \left\{ y_i \in \mathcal{Y}_j : \mathcal{L}(f_{\theta_j}(x_i), y_i) < \mathcal{L}(f_{\theta_k}(x_i), y_i) \forall k \neq j \right\} \tag{2}$$

While implementing (2), a typical approach adopted to avoid mode collapse is to relax the best-of-M approach by updating all predictors in each iteration [8,9]. Existing works either focus on multi-output prediction or does not provide an efficient way to combine the base learners or multiple hypotheses, often relying on numerical methods [8,9,14]. To this end, the aim of this work is to efficiently combine, in a structured model, the set of hypotheses that form the centroidal Voronoi tessellations. Additionally, the hypothesis that manipulating the shape of the tessellations formed during the training of the predictors, that has direct implications in generalization performance, is validated in the experiments. This is due to the diversity in ensemble learning induced by the predictors.

3.1   Structured Dataset Formation

Two step approach have been taken for structured dataset formation. Firstly, the set of predictors $\{f_{\theta_j}(x)\}_{j=1}^{M}$ are trained with stochastic gradient descent with randomly initialised weights. Secondly, these learned models are used to generate the predictions that form the structured dataset.

In each ith iteration, using the jth prediction $f_{\theta_j}(\boldsymbol{x}_i)$ and the true label y_i, the predictors' parameters are updated using the stochastic gradient descent as follows:

$$\boldsymbol{\theta}_j = \boldsymbol{\theta}_j - \eta_j \left(\frac{\partial \mathcal{L}(f_{\theta_j}(\boldsymbol{x}_i), y_i)}{\partial \boldsymbol{\theta}_j} + \frac{\lambda_p}{N} \boldsymbol{\theta}_j \right) \delta \left(\mathcal{Y}_j \left(f_{\theta_j}(\boldsymbol{x}_i) \right) \right) \tag{3}$$

where η_j denotes the learning rate for the jth predictor and the norm loss is computed as $\mathcal{L}(f_{\theta_j}(\boldsymbol{x}_i), y_i) = \|f_{\theta_j}(\boldsymbol{x}_i) - y_i\|_2^2 + \frac{\lambda_p}{2N} \sum_{j=1}^M \boldsymbol{\theta}_j^2$ with the regularization parameter λ_p. The function $\delta \left(\mathcal{Y}_j \left(f_{\theta_j}(\boldsymbol{x}_i) \right) \right)$ serves as an indicator with a parameter $0 < \varepsilon < 1$ that can alter the shape of the tessellation during training [16]. This parameter enhances diversity in the structured dataset for ensemble generalization by regulating the extent to which non-top predictors' parameters are updated in each training iteration. It is defined as:

$$\delta(y \in \mathcal{Y}_j(f_{\theta_j}(\boldsymbol{x}))) = \begin{cases} 1 - \varepsilon & \text{if is true} \\ \frac{\varepsilon}{M-1} & \text{otherwise} \end{cases} \tag{4}$$

When the training of the predictors is completed, the same set of training instances $\{\boldsymbol{x}_i\}_{i=1}^N$ are used to generate structured dataset. To elaborate, if the prediction obtained after the forward pass for jth predictor on a particular training instance $\boldsymbol{x}_i$ is denoted as $f_{\theta_j}(\boldsymbol{x}_i)$, then the resulting predictions for the entire structured dataset can be written in the matrix form as:

$$\boldsymbol{D}(\varepsilon) = \begin{bmatrix} f_{\theta_1}(\boldsymbol{x}_1) & \cdots & f_{\theta_M}(\boldsymbol{x}_1) \\ \vdots & \ddots & \vdots \\ f_{\theta_1}(\boldsymbol{x}_N) & \cdots & f_{\theta_M}(\boldsymbol{x}_N) \end{bmatrix} \tag{5}$$

with $\boldsymbol{D}(\varepsilon) \in \mathbb{R}^{N \times M}$ being the matrix of predictions for a particular diversity parameter $0 \le \varepsilon \le 1$. Similarly, for any test set with test instances $\{\boldsymbol{x}'_i\}_{i=1}^n$, the structured test set $\boldsymbol{D}(\varepsilon)' \in \mathbb{R}^{n \times M}$ is given by the predictions $\{f_{\theta_j}(\boldsymbol{x}'_i)\}_{i=1}^n$. For any structured test dataset, the predictors use the same set of parameters $\boldsymbol{\Theta}$ obtained after training using stochastic gradient descent.

3.2   s-RBFN Optimisation

The structured dataset is used as input for the radial basis function network, with each jth predictor or hypothesis $f_{\theta_j}(\boldsymbol{x})$ associated to a particular basis function $\phi \left(f_{\theta_j}(\boldsymbol{x}), \mu_j, \sigma_j \right)$, i.e., a map $\boldsymbol{\Phi}(\boldsymbol{D}(\varepsilon)) : \mathbb{R}^{N \times M} \to \mathbb{R}^{N \times M}$ is obtained by applying the basis function $\phi(\cdot)$ to each element of $\boldsymbol{D}(\varepsilon)$, transforming it into:

$$\boldsymbol{\Phi}(\boldsymbol{D}(\varepsilon)) = \begin{bmatrix} \phi(f_{\theta_1}(\boldsymbol{x}_1), \mu_1, \sigma_1) & \cdots & \phi(f_{\theta_M}(\boldsymbol{x}_1), \mu_M, \sigma_M) \\ \vdots & \ddots & \vdots \\ \phi(f_{\theta_1}(\boldsymbol{x}_N), \mu_1, \sigma_1) & \cdots & \phi(f_{\theta_M}(\boldsymbol{x}_N), \mu_M, \sigma_M) \end{bmatrix}$$

In this work, the Gaussian basis function $\phi\left(\cdot\right) = \exp\left(\frac{-1}{2\sigma_j^2}\left|f_{\theta_j}(\boldsymbol{x}_i) - \mu_j\right|^2\right)$ have been used where the centers c_j and scales S_j parameters for the basis functions are computed from each column j of the structured training dataset $\boldsymbol{D}(\varepsilon)$ and are computed by $\mu_j = \frac{1}{N}\sum_{i=1}^{N} f_{\theta_j}(\boldsymbol{x}_i)$, and $\sigma_j = \sqrt{\sum_{i=1}^{N}\frac{\left(f_{\theta_j}(\boldsymbol{x}_i) - \mu_j\right)^2}{(N-1)}}$.

The s-RBFN formulation can now be expressed in matrix form as follows:

$$\hat{\boldsymbol{y}} = \boldsymbol{\Phi}\left(\boldsymbol{D}(\varepsilon)\right)\boldsymbol{w} = \begin{bmatrix} \phi\left(f_{\theta_1}(\boldsymbol{x}_1),\mu_1,\sigma_1\right) & \cdots & \phi\left(f_{\theta_M}(\boldsymbol{x}_1),\mu_M,\sigma_M\right) \\ \vdots & \ddots & \vdots \\ \phi\left(f_{\theta_1}(\boldsymbol{x}_N),\mu_1,\sigma_1\right) & \cdots & \phi\left(f_{\theta_M}(\boldsymbol{x}_N),\mu_M,\sigma_M\right) \end{bmatrix}\begin{bmatrix} w_1 \\ \vdots \\ w_M \end{bmatrix}$$
(6)

The optimal weights $\{w_i\}_{j=1}^{M}$ in (6) can now be simply obtained by least-squares with regularization parameter λ_s for the structured model using:

$$\boldsymbol{w} = \left(\boldsymbol{\Phi}\left(\boldsymbol{D}(\varepsilon)\right)^{\mathrm{T}}\boldsymbol{\Phi}\left(\boldsymbol{D}(\varepsilon)\right) + \lambda_s * \boldsymbol{I}_{(mxm)}\right)^{-1}\boldsymbol{\Phi}\left(\boldsymbol{D}(\varepsilon)\right)^{\mathrm{T}}\boldsymbol{y}$$
(7)

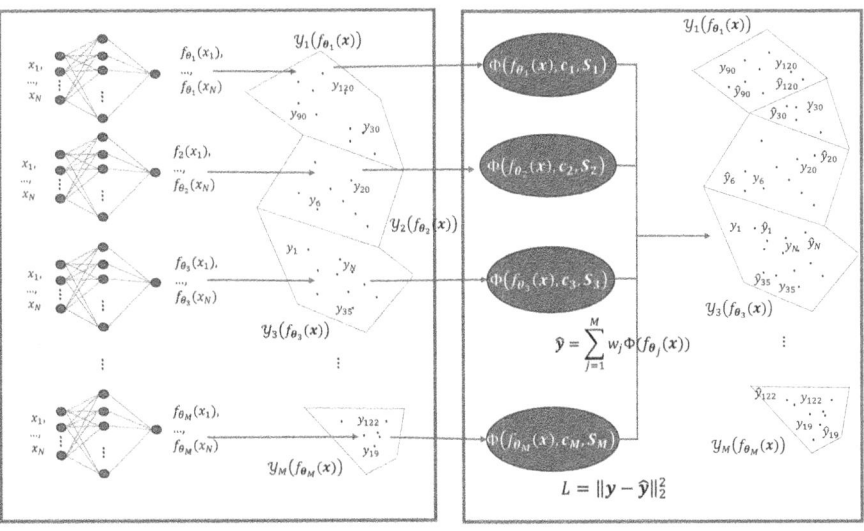

Fig. 1. Model architecture with structured data obtained from neural networks' predictions and the ground-truth labels $\boldsymbol{y}$ forming centroidal Voronoi tessellations based on the neural networks' losses (Left box). The s-RBFN uses these predictions to estimate the ground-truth labels $\hat{\boldsymbol{y}}$, with L representing the s-RBFN norm loss (Right Box).

The whole approach presented above has been summarized in the Fig. 1 where the model is shown with the structured data obtained in the left box, using neural networks as predictors. The label data is assigned to a particular Voronoi tessellations depending on how far it is from the predictions of the base learners.

This tessellation represents the multiple hypotheses prediction target values, y (Left box in Fig. 1). Once training is completed, the predictions from the trained predictors, using all training instances as input, are used as input data for training a radial basis function network (s-RBFN) via least-squares. The estimates $\hat{y}$ in Fig. 1 of the multiple hypotheses prediction ground-truth labels y are given by the output from the s-RBFN (Right box in Fig. 1). L represents the L_2 norm loss between the ground-truth labels and their estimates.

4   Experiments

4.1   Datasets

An Air Quality dataset [6] and the Appliances Energy Prediction dataset [5] are have been employed in this study. The first dataset consists of 9358 instances of hourly averaged responses from five metal oxide chemical sensors embedded in an air quality chemical multisensor device. The data was recorded from March 2004 to February 2005, and represents the longest freely available recordings of on-field responses from deployed air quality chemical sensor devices [6]. The goal is to predict absolute humidity values with the rest of variables in a multivariate regression problem. The second dataset consist of 10 min timestamps for 4.5 months making up over 20 thousand instances from 29 features. The goal is to predict energy appliances in a low energy building [5].

4.2   Models Performance and Comparisons

For the individual predictors, a 2-layer multi-layer perceptron (MLP) have been used with the number of neurons in each layer as κ, learning rates η, multiplicative factor of the initial weights χ, and regularization parameters λ_p. For the s-RBFN model, the number of predictors or hypotheses is given by M, diversity parameter ε, and s-RBFN regularization parameters λ_s. All values used for the hyper-parameters are displayed in Table 1.

For the experiments, the top performing models' versions from the original papers of the two used datasets [5, 6, 17], are replicated for comparison (top competitors). These are the Linear Model (LM), Random Forest (RF), Gradient-Boost (Gboost), and Support Vector Machine Radial Basis Function (SVM-RBF). To elaborate, for the s-RBFN, the experiments are performed with 10 simulations for each combination of hyper-parameters from Table 1. The mean and standard deviations of the RMSE for each of the 10-folds are recorded as performance measures. In total, the experiments have been performed with 80 different model hyper-parameters' configurations (also including the single hypothesis $M = 1$). Additionally, for further comparison, the bench-marking results using the baseline multiple hypothesis prediction (arithmetic combiner) model [16] are also included, in which the ensemble of individual predictors forming Voronoi Tessellations as their arithmetic mean are employed.

Table 1. Sets of values for the s-RBFN hyperparameters

(a) M number of hypotheses, κ number of neurons per layer, η learning rates for the predictors, χ is a multiplicative factor for random initial predictors' weights Θ.

M	κ	η	χ
$[2, 5, 10, 20, 35]$	$[20, 200, 2000]$	$[0.03, 0.3]$	$[0.0001, 0.01, 0.1, 1]$

(b) ε is the diversity parameter, λ_p is the regularization parameter for the predictors, λ_s is the regularization parameter for the s-RBFN.

ε	λ_p	λ_s
$[0, 0.1, 0.35, 0.5]$	$[0, 0.0001, 0.01, 0.07]$	$[0, 3, 5]$

Absolute Humidity Prediction. In Table 2, the 10 cross-folds mean and standard deviation RMSE values for the top performing versions of all models on the test set are presented. The RMSE for the 80 different hyper-parameter configurations are computed and its first and third quartiles are shown in this table. For the rest of the models, 80 different hyper-parameters are applied for comparison.

The best model by generalization performance is the s-RBFN when the hyper-parameters are optimized. The SVM-RBF is the second best performing model. The arithmetic combiner has the lowest standard deviation and consequently has the smallest variation of the mean RMSE for all quartiles. The s-RBFN has a quarter of the 80 different hyper-parameter configurations' mean RMSE values lower than all other models except for the SVM-RBF, due to its higher standard deviation.

Table 2. Absolute humidity prediction: Mean and standard deviation of the 10-fold cross-validation RMSE for the models with the top-performing hyper-parameters configuration in generalization performance. First and third quartiles are shown for all models from 80 different hyper-parameter configurations.

Models	Top Model	std dev	First Quartile	Third Quartile
Linear Model	7692.78	1657.53	8189.84	10488.35
SVM-RBF	**29.83**	**1.99**	34.80	37.65
Random Forest	55.66	15.47	69.00	91.55
Gradient Boosting	55.76	38.73	93.92	151.58
Arithmetic Combiner	39.19	**0.15**	41.75	43.93
s-RBFN	**22.46**	**9.14**	38.98	54.71

Table 3. Energy appliance prediction: Mean and standard deviation of the 10-fold cross-validation RMSE for the models with the top-performing hyper-parameters configuration in generalization performance. First and third quartiles are shown for all models from 80 different hyper-parameter configurations.

Models	Top Model	std dev	First Quartile	Third Quartile
Linear Model	281.76	297.69	321.39	803.31
SVM-RBF	**104.68**	**1.27**	**107.26**	109.01
Random Forest	298.46	29.35	328.48	373.81
Gradient Boosting	292.08	67.26	389.10	476.89
Arithmetic Combiner	115.17	**0.11**	128.54	144.83
s-RBFN	**101.12**	**2.42**	**102.36**	109.96

Energy Appliance Prediction. For the energy appliance dataset the same set of experiments are performed as for the air quality dataset. In line with the results displayed in Table 2, in Table 3 it can be seen how the s-RBFN is the best performing model with less standard deviation than in the previous dataset. This makes the model best performer in the first and third quartiles. The arithmetic combiner is the model with lowest standard deviation and the SVM-RBFN is the second best performing model, in line with the air absolute humidity prediction experiments.

Thus, both the dataset, it has been validated empirically that the s-RBFN is the best performing model in terms of generalization performance and for a range of different hyper-parameters.

4.3 Diversity and Generalization Performance

In this section, the hypothesis of the improvement in generalization performance of the s-RBFN for different values of the diversity parameter ε and the number of hypotheses M is verified. Figures 2 and 3 show, for the air quality and energy appliances test sets respectively, the mean RMSE and 90% confidence interval using 10-fold cross-validation for each hyper-parameter configuration, and for different values of the number of hypotheses M and diversity parameter ε. The horizontal axis represents the pairs of hyper-parameters M and ε.

The results in Fig. 2 indicate, for the absolute humidity prediction experiments with the air quality test set, that the generalization performance increases with the diversity parameter up to a certain number of hypotheses, but decreases if the number of hypotheses is too large. In this set of experiments the optimal pair for $M = 10$ and $\varepsilon = 0.35$ is well defined. For this pair of hyper-parameters the s-RBFN achieves the best performance, equal to the shown in Table 2. It can be shown that increasing ε for two hypotheses worsen the generalization performance, meaning that a minimum number of hypotheses is needed for diversity to improve generalization capabilities.

In Fig. 3, the energy appliances prediction dataset shows the same conclusion with some different results. For relatively large number of hypotheses ($M = 10, 20$) the s-RBFN achieves the best performance in generalization for relatively large $\varepsilon = 0.35$. However, this improvement is not observed for $M = 2$ and $M = 5$, as for five hypotheses the best model has $\varepsilon = 0.1$, with the case of $\varepsilon = 0.35$ being worse than for the case of $\varepsilon = 0$. It is reasonable to believe that for each number of hypotheses there is an optimal level of diversity, or ε, for the s-RBFN model. In the case of two hypotheses ($M = 2$), there is no impact of diversity due to the low number of individual predictors. Moreover, for this case, the performance is very good, suggesting that while diversity can enhance generalization performance for a given number of hypotheses, there may be cases in which the individual predictor alone is good enough for prediction in the test set.

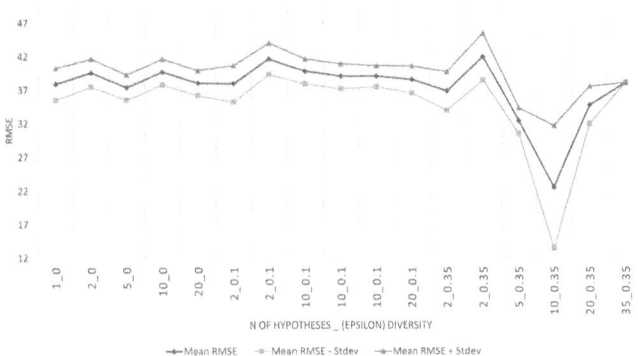

Fig. 2. Air quality test set: Mean RMSE and 90% confidence interval from 10-fold cross-validation for different configurations for hyper-parameters M and ε.

4.4   Impact of Regularization

In this section, the purpose is to understand the contribution of the regularization parameter for the s-RBFN in generalization performance. The regularization parameter λ_s has a clear effect in reducing the uncertainty of the hyper-parameters in the prediction of the structured ensemble model. For the air quality test set, in Fig. 4a, it can be seen that for greater values of the regularization parameter, the mean RMSE for different hyper-parameter configurations remain more constant. Additionally, the standard deviation is lower for greater values of λ_s, as shown in Fig. 4b. The same pattern is observed in the energy appliances test set with Figs. 5a and 5b. It can be concluded that the regularization parameter reduces the uncertainty of the s-RBFN hyper-parameters. It also improves the s-RBFN generalization performance, on average, for any value of the hyper-parameters.

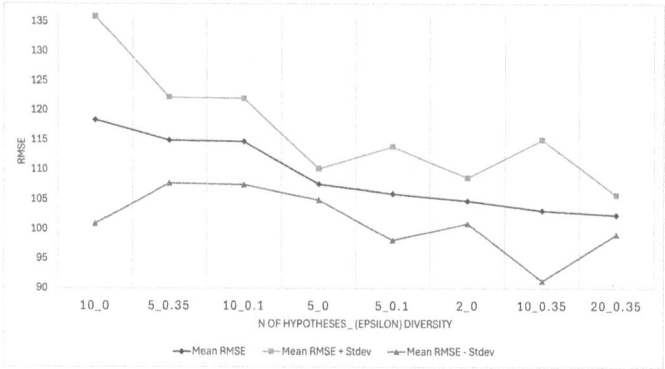

Fig. 3. Energy appliances test set: Mean RMSE and 90% confidence interval from 10-fold cross-validation for different configurations for hyper-parameters M and ε.

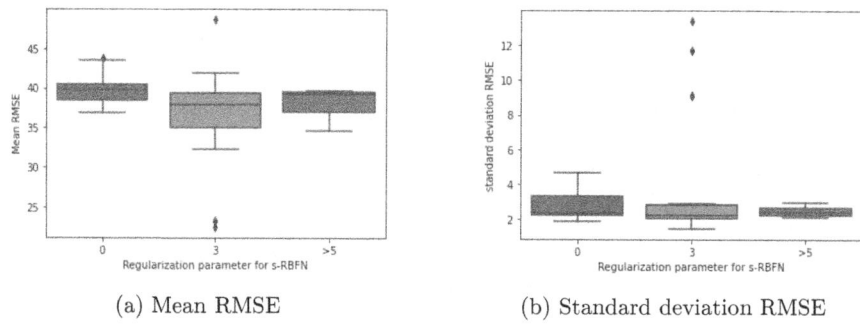

Fig. 4. Air quality test set: (a) Mean and (b) Standard deviation RMSE for 10-Fold cross-validation for different s-RBFN regularization parameters and hyper-parameter configurations.

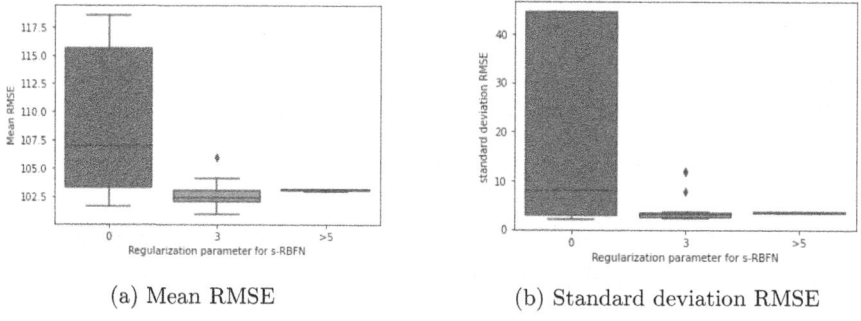

Fig. 5. Energy Appliance test set: (a) Mean and (b) Standard deviation RMSE for 10-Fold cross-validation for different s-RBFN regularization parameters and hyper-parameter configurations.

In summary, the experiments demonstrate that diversity in structured ensemble models, particularly in the s-RBFN, is a distinctive feature of these architectures. There are instances where a single-hypothesis model may perform optimally. This indicates that diversity is not universally beneficial for enhancing generalization performance but rather improves performance contingent on a specific number of hypotheses. The experiments suggest there is indeed an optimal level of diversity, ε, for each number of hypotheses. Conversely, there exists a maximum number of hypotheses beyond which the performance of the ensemble model deteriorates, regardless of the ε level, indicating limits to the benefits of diversification. Similarly, for ε values exceeding 0.35, there is a noticeable decline in overall generalization capabilities.

5   Conclusion

This work introduces a novel structured ensemble model for single-output multiple hypotheses prediction. The presented model incorporates geometric properties of centroidal Voronoi tessellations with the individual predictors' losses during training. By altering the shape of the tessellations through a parametric mechanism, the diversity is introduced to the structured dataset for the s-RBFN model. It has been validated through experiments that the s-RBFN model surpasses other models in generalization performance across a range of hypotheses numbers and diversity parameters. This model is the fastest to train once the structured dataset is prepared using its closed-form expression. Additionally, it facilitates easy control over diversity in structured ensemble learning and multiple hypotheses prediction for single-output regression problems through the diversity parameter. It is crucial to analyze the appropriate number of hypotheses and diversity hyper-parameters for a specific dataset, as these are highly correlated with the generalization performance capabilities of the s-RBFN.

For future work, several areas can be explored to enhance structured ensemble models in multiple hypotheses prediction. For instance, this work uses tabular data for regression with a simple 2-layer network as individual predictors. It would be interesting to employ more datasets from other modalities, e.g., visual or text datasets and use deeper architectures. This would allow to further investigate the relationship between model diversity, complexity and the generalization performance.

Disclosure of Interests. The authors have no competing interests to declare that are relevant to the content of this article.

References

1. Batra, D., Yadollahpour, P., Guzman-Rivera, A., Shakhnarovich, G.: Diverse M-best solutions in Markov random fields. In: Fitzgibbon, A., Lazebnik, S., Perona, P., Sato, Y., Schmid, C. (eds.) ECCV 2012. LNCS, vol. 7576, pp. 1–16. Springer, Heidelberg (2012). https://doi.org/10.1007/978-3-642-33715-4_1

2. Breiman, L.: Bagging predictors. Mach. Learn. **24**(2), 123–140 (1996). https://doi.org/10.1023/A:1018054314350
3. Brown, G.: Diversity in neural network ensembles. Ph.D. thesis, University of Birmingham, United Kingdom (2004). Winner, British Computer Society Distinguished Dissertation Award
4. Brown, G., Wyatt, J., Harris, R., Yao, X.: Diversity creation methods: a survey and categorisation. Inf. Fusion **6**, 5–20 (2005). https://doi.org/10.1016/j.inffus.2004.04.004
5. Candanedo, L.M., Feldheim, V., Deramaix, D.: Data driven prediction models of energy use of appliances in a low-energy house. Energy Build. **140**, 81–97 (2017). https://doi.org/10.1016/j.enbuild.2017.01.083. https://www.sciencedirect.com/science/article/pii/S0378778816308970
6. De Vito, S., Massera, E., Piga, M., Martinotto, L., Di Francia, G.: On field calibration of an electronic nose for benzene estimation in an urban pollution monitoring scenario. Sens. Actuators B Chem. **129**(2), 750–757 (2008). https://doi.org/10.1016/j.snb.2007.09.060. https://www.sciencedirect.com/science/article/pii/S0925400507007691
7. Grandvalet, Y., d'Alché Buc, F., Ambroise, C.: Boosting mixture models for semi-supervised learning, vol. 2130, pp. 41–48 (2001)
8. Guzmán-rivera, A., Batra, D., Kohli, P.: Multiple choice learning: learning to produce multiple structured outputs. In: Pereira, F., Burges, C., Bottou, L., Weinberger, K. (eds.) Advances in Neural Information Processing Systems, vol. 25. Curran Associates, Inc. (2012)
9. Guzman-Rivera, A., Kohli, P., Batra, D., Rutenbar, R.: Efficiently enforcing diversity in multi-output structured prediction. In: Kaski, S., Corander, J. (eds.) Proceedings of the Seventeenth International Conference on Artificial Intelligence and Statistics. Proceedings of Machine Learning Research, Reykjavik, Iceland, vol. 33, pp. 284–292. PMLR (2014). https://proceedings.mlr.press/v33/guzman-rivera14.html
10. Krogh, A., Vedelsby, J.: Neural network ensembles, cross validation, and active learning. In: Tesauro, G., Touretzky, D., Leen, T. (eds.) Advances in Neural Information Processing Systems, vol. 7. MIT Press (1994)
11. Kuncheva, L., Whitaker, C.: Measures of diversity in classifier ensembles and their relationship with the ensemble accuracy. Mach. Learn. **51**, 181–207 (2003). https://doi.org/10.1023/A:1022859003006
12. Lee, S., Purushwalkam, S., Cogswell, M., Ranjan, V., Crandall, D., Batra, D.: Stochastic multiple choice learning for training diverse deep ensembles. In: Proceedings of the 30th International Conference on Neural Information Processing Systems, NIPS 2016, pp. 2127–2135. Curran Associates Inc., Red Hook, NY, USA (2016)
13. Leemann, T., Sackmann, M., Thielecke, J., Hofmann, U.: Distribution preserving multiple hypotheses prediction for uncertainty modeling. CoRR abs/2110.02858 (2021). https://arxiv.org/abs/2110.02858
14. Mienye, I.D., Sun, Y.: A survey of ensemble learning: concepts, algorithms, applications, and prospects. IEEE Access **10**, 99129–99149 (2022). https://doi.org/10.1109/ACCESS.2022.3207287
15. Pang, T., Xu, K., Du, C., Chen, N., Zhu, J.: Improving adversarial robustness via promoting ensemble diversity. In: Chaudhuri, K., Salakhutdinov, R. (eds.) Proceedings of the 36th International Conference on Machine Learning. Proceedings of Machine Learning Research, vol. 97, pp. 4970–4979. PMLR (2019). https://proceedings.mlr.press/v97/pang19a.html

16. Rupprecht, C., et al.: Learning in an uncertain world: representing ambiguity through multiple hypotheses. In: Proceedings of the IEEE International Conference on Computer Vision, pp. 3591–3600 (2017)

17. Saverio Vito: Air quality. The dataset contains 9358 instances of hourly averaged responses from an array of 5 metal oxide chemical sensors embedded in an Air Quality Chemical Multisensor Device., 10.24432/C59K5F (2016)

18. Ueda, N., Nakano, R.: Generalization error of ensemble estimators. In: Proceedings of International Conference on Neural Networks (ICNN 1996), vol. 1, pp. 90–95 (1996)

19. Wood, D., Mu, T., Webb, A.M., Reeve, H.W.J., Luján, M., Brown, G.: A unified theory of diversity in ensemble learning. J. Mach. Learn. Res. **24**(1) (2024)

20. Yang, Y., Lv, H., Chen, N.: A survey on ensemble learning under the era of deep learning. Artif. Intell. Rev. **56**(6), 5545–5589 (2022). https://doi.org/10.1007/s10462-022-10283-5

21. Yuksel, S.E., Wilson, J.N., Gader, P.D.: Twenty years of mixture of experts. IEEE Trans. Neural Netw. Learn. Syst. **23**(8), 1177–1193 (2012). https://doi.org/10.1109/TNNLS.2012.2200299

Deep Learning

Bitcoin Forecasting Using Deep Learning and Time Series Ensemble Techniques

Huma Zafar[1,2](✉) and Stylianos Kapetanakis[1,2]

[1] Middlesex University, London NW4 1DY, UK
[2] Distributed Analytics Solutions, London E14 5RE, UK
{huma,stelios}@dstr.co.uk

Abstract. This research investigates Bitcoin price prediction by reviewing the current state of the art, comparing Time Series and Deep Learning models, evaluating their performance on a range of metrics, and assessing the selected model's real-world applicability. It reviewed existing studies on Deep Learning, Time Series, and Bitcoin, and utilised 44,419 hourly Bitcoin data points for data visualization and mining. The findings showed that ensemble models, particularly stacked ensemble, outperformed other models in predictive accuracy, with the lowest error metrics and highest R^2 value. Deep learning models also performed well, but with slightly higher errors. Time Series models were inadequate for Bitcoin price prediction, as evidenced by their negative R^2 values. These results contribute to our understanding of effective modelling approaches for Bitcoin price prediction. The study also suggests promising avenues for future research, such as fine-tuning ensemble models, incorporating advanced feature engineering techniques, and exploring volatility forecasting. Thus, the study offers a valuable contribution to the field of cryptocurrency research, advancing knowledge on Bitcoin price prediction and fostering a deeper comprehension of the intricacies underlying cryptocurrency markets.

Keywords: Blockchain · Deep Learning · Time Series

1 Introduction

1.1 Background

The inherently volatile nature of the cryptocurrency market necessitates the development of more accurate Bitcoin price prediction models to facilitate informed investment decisions and robust risk management strategies. This study seeks to contribute to the existing body of research by constructing and evaluating a series of enhanced models for Bitcoin price forecasting. This will be achieved through a comparative analysis employing both Time Series and Deep Learning methodologies. Data visualization techniques and performance evaluation metrics will be utilized to assess the efficacy of these models in predicting future Bitcoin prices. Furthermore, the investigation will delve into various model architectures and ensemble methods with the objective of identifying the most effective approach for Bitcoin price prediction.

© The Author(s), under exclusive license to Springer Nature Switzerland AG 2025
M. Bramer and F. Stahl (Eds.): SGAI 2024, LNAI 15446, pp. 105–115, 2025.
https://doi.org/10.1007/978-3-031-77915-2_8

1.2   The Evolution of Bitcoin Price Models

The journey of Bitcoin price prediction models has shifted dramatically, from relying on established time series analysis to embracing the power of deep learning for untangling its complexities. Early studies leaned on ARIMA models, as evidenced by McNally et al. (2018), Shin et al. (2021), and Akyildirim et al. (2021) [2, 14, 18]. The integration of machine learning introduced neural networks and support vector regression (SVR) by Liu et al. (2020) [13]. A significant leap came with deep learning. Pioneering research by Aggarwal et al. (2019) [1] showcased the effectiveness of Convolutional Neural Networks (CNNs), Long Short-Term Memory (LSTM), and Gated Recurrent Units (GRUs) in analysing Bitcoin prices. Lamothe-Fernández et al. (2020) [12] further propelled innovation with Deep Support Vector Regression (DSVR), Deep Neural Decision Trees (DNDTs), and Deep Recurrent Convolutional Neural Networks (DRCNNs).

LSTM models have become dominant due to their ability to capture long-term dependencies. This is supported by research from Aggarwal et al. (2019), Tandon et al. (2019),Liu et al. (2020), and others (Sebastião and Godinho, 2021; Saadah and Whafa, 2020; Derbentsev et al., 2020; Politis et al., 2021) [1, 6, 13, 16, 17, 19].

Despite advancements, challenges such as limited historical data, inherent volatility, and incorporating external factors persist. The current landscape highlights the dominance of deep learning models, particularly LSTMs and CNNs, in deciphering the intricate patterns within Bitcoin price data. However, the need to include explanatory variables beyond historical prices and address overfitting in deep learning models remains crucial.

While deep learning architectures like LSTMs and CNNs have proven superior to traditional time series models in capturing the complexities of Bitcoin price data, achieving accurate predictions requires a comprehensive approach. Incorporating explanatory variables beyond just historical prices is crucial. Macroeconomic indicators and social media sentiment analysis can provide valuable insights into the broader market forces influencing Bitcoin. Finally, addressing overfitting in deep learning models is important. Techniques like dropout layers and regularization help models learn general trends, not just memorize specific patterns, ultimately improving their ability to predict future prices.

Thus, the evolution of Bitcoin price prediction models mirrors the dynamic nature of the cryptocurrency landscape. As artificial intelligence and machine learning technologies progress, further refinements and breakthroughs are expected. Overcoming challenges like data scarcity, model complexity, and rapid market changes is vital for developing robust and accurate models in this ever-evolving financial domain. Researchers and practitioners remain dedicated to enhancing the reliability of Bitcoin price predictions and deepening our understanding of the factors influencing Bitcoin's market behaviour.

2 Time Series Models

The analysis of historical Bitcoin price data is presented, with a focus on modelling and predicting Bitcoin price returns using three statistical methods: ARIMA (Autoregressive Integrated Moving Average), GARCH (Generalized Autoregressive Conditional Heteroskedasticity), and ARCH (Autoregressive Conditional Heteroskedasticity).

In first analysis, we select models like ARCH, GARCH, and ARIMA because they are good at helping us comprehend various aspects of financial data, like how prices change, trends, and seasonal patterns. This assists us gain useful insights. As posited by Engle (1982) [8], ARCH and GARCH models have been instrumental in the spheres of risk management, asset pricing, and an array of financial applications, owing to their proficiency in modelling the dynamics of volatility.

Conversely, ARIMA models, as explained by Wilson (2016) [20], provide a useful way to predict financial data that have trends and patterns that repeat over time. These models use a technique called differencing to make the data easier to work with, and they are effective at making forecasts for the short to medium term. Because of this, ARIMA models are widely used in finance and economics to make better predictions and smarter financial decisions.

To sum up, the choice among ARCH, GARCH, or ARIMA models within financial time series analysis is contingent upon the specific data characteristics and analytical objectives at hand. These models, often employed in tandem, contribute synergistically to the comprehensive understanding and forecasting of financial market behaviour, risk management, and judicious investment decisions.

2.1 Data Preprocessing

In the first stage of data preparation, we focus on selecting the most relevant information for our analysis. Typically, the "close" price column is chosen, as it represents the final trading price of the asset for each hour. This data then undergoes a transformation to capture price fluctuations. We calculate the percentage change between consecutive hours, providing valuable insights into market movements. Finally, to ensure the integrity of our analysis, we address any missing data points or invalid entries, such as "Not-a-Number" values. This meticulous cleaning process results in a high-quality dataset ready for further exploration.

2.2 Model Specifications

ARIMA model (p,d,q) with drift was employed to forecast Bitcoin return series. This model captures the inherent trend in the data by incorporating past values (p), differencing terms (d), a constant term (drift), and past errors (q) into a linear regression framework. In this study, an ARIMA (1,1,1) model was specified for Bitcoin returns. To account for the well-documented phenomenon of volatility clustering in financial time series, a GARCH (1,1) model with a zero-mean assumption was implemented for Bitcoin returns. This model effectively captures the dynamic behaviour of conditional variance, allowing for the generation of volatility forecasts. Similar to GARCH, an ARCH(1) model with a zero-mean assumption was also utilized for Bitcoin returns. While both models address conditional heteroskedasticity, GARCH offers a more comprehensive framework by incorporating past conditional variances into the model.

2.3 Interpretation of Results

Evaluation metrics presented in Table 1, including Mean Squared Error (MSE), Mean Absolute Error (MAE), and Root Mean Squared Error (RMSE), all favoured the ARIMA (1,1,1) model for Bitcoin return forecasting. ARIMA achieved the lowest MSE (6.068), MAE (0.046), and RMSE (0.078) compared to GARCH and ARCH models, suggesting its superior ability to capture overall variability, accuracy of error direction, and closeness of forecasts to actual errors. However, QQ plots and histograms of the residuals (Fig. 1) indicate that ARIMA residuals are closer to a normal distribution, while ARCH and GARCH residuals exhibit non-normality, as expected due to their focus on modelling heteroskedasticity.

While the GARCH model displayed promising characteristics in capturing long-range dependence in volatility through ACF and PACF plots (Fig. 2), these findings also suggest potential limitations in the current model structure for Bitcoin price prediction. The negative R-squared values (Table 1) and the non-normal residuals of ARCH/GARCH models highlight the need for further exploration. Alternative modelling approaches or parameter adjustments might be necessary to achieve a more suitable model for Bitcoin return forecasting.

Table 1. Performance Metrics for ARIMA, ARCH and GARCH.

Model	MSE ($\times 10^{-5}$)	MAE	RMSE ($\times 10^{-5}$)	R^2
ARIMA	6.068	0.046	0.078	−0.0139
GARCH	11.66	0.79	1.08	−0.9482
ARCH	11.73	0.82	1.08	−0.9606

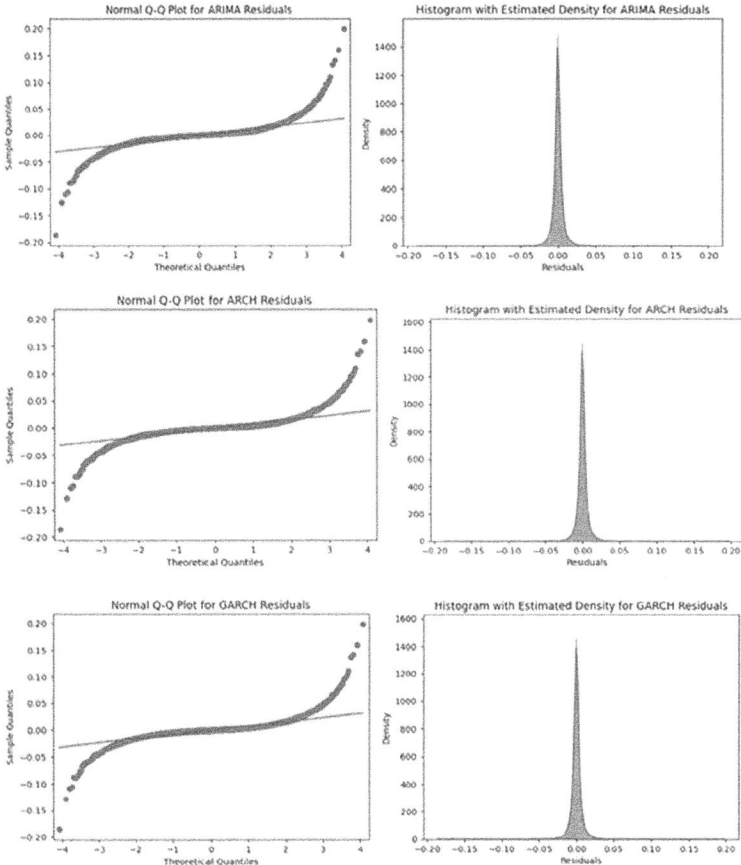

Fig. 1. Graphs showing normal Q-Q plots and histograms for ARIMA, ARCH and GARCH.

3   Deep Learning Models

This section investigated the selection of neural network architectures for predicting Bitcoin's hourly closing price. To achieve a balance between predictive power and computational efficiency, a combination of complex and simple models was chosen. Long Short-Term Memory (LSTM) and Gated Recurrent Unit (GRU) networks were included due to their ability to capture sequential patterns in time series data (Tandon et al., 2019) [19]. These recurrent architectures leverage gating mechanisms specifically designed to remember past data points, making them well-suited for tasks like Bitcoin price prediction (Hochreiter and Schmidhuber, 1997) [10]. The Transformer model was chosen for its effectiveness in modelling long-range dependencies within sequences, employing a self-attention mechanism. In contrast, a Feedforward Neural Network (FNN) was included for its efficient computation, offering a simpler alternative (Chen and Guestrin, 2016) [4].

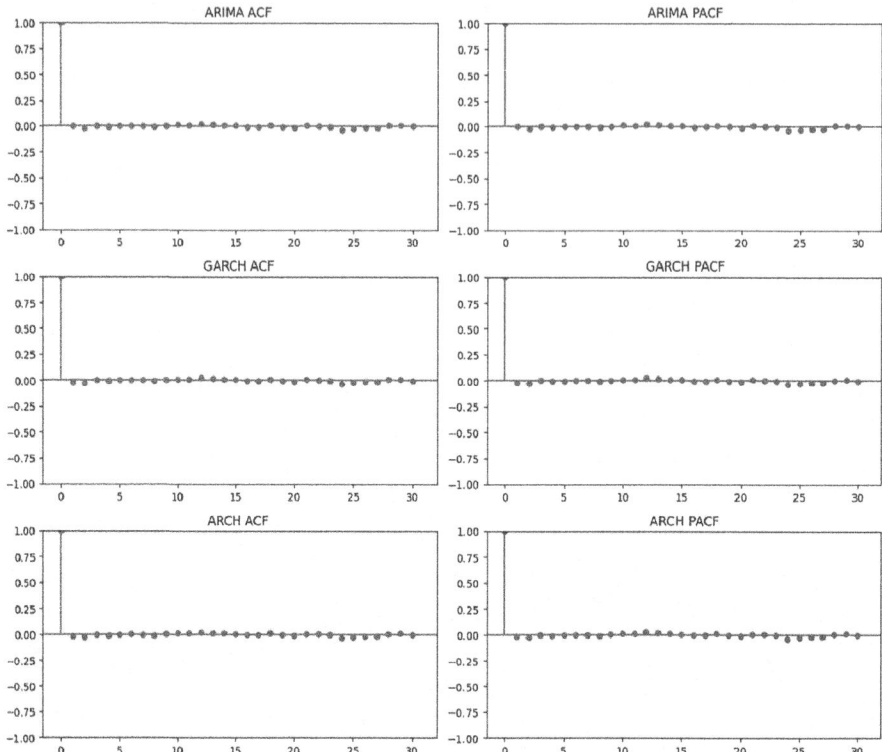

Fig. 2. Graphs illustrating ACF plots and PACF plots for ARIMA, GARCH, and ARCH models.

3.1 Model Specifications

Four models were chosen, offering a balance between complexity and efficiency: LSTM, GRU, Transformer, and FNN. All models utilized a common dropout rate of 0.2 to mitigate overfitting, the Adam optimizer for training, and MSE as the loss function. Training employed a batch size of 32 for 10 epochs.

In short, LSTMs and GRUs, both recurrent architectures known for their ability to capture sequential patterns, employed 3 layers with 50 units per layer. The Transformer model, designed for capturing long-range dependencies, utilized a multi-head attention mechanism with key_dim = 128 within an attention layer followed by a dense layer. The FNN, the simplest model, consisted of two dense layers with 128 and 64 units, respectively.

3.2 Interpretation of Results from Deep Learning Models

Further evaluation examined the effectiveness of various deep learning architectures for Bitcoin price prediction. We compared LSTM, GRU, FNN, and Transformer models. Examining both performance metrics (Table 2) and loss curves (Fig. 3), the LSTM model emerged as the clear winner. LSTM achieved the lowest Mean Squared Error (MSE) and

Root Mean Squared Error (RMSE) in Table 2, indicating the closest predictions to actual prices. Its high R-squared value further strengthens this, signifying a strong correlation between predicted and actual prices.

Figure 3 reinforces this. The LSTM model consistently exhibited the lowest training and validation loss throughout the training process. This demonstrates its superior ability to learn the patterns within Bitcoin price data compared to the other models. While the Transformer model initially reduced loss faster, it ultimately achieved a higher loss than LSTM and GRU. The FNN architecture displayed the slowest learning and highest overall loss.

Therefore, this analysis suggests that the LSTM model is the most effective for time series prediction of Bitcoin prices among the models considered in this study (ARIMA, ARCH, GARCH, LSTM, GRU, FNN, and Transformer).

Table 2. Performance Metrics for the Selected Deep Learning Models.

Model	MSE ($\times 10^{-5}$)	MAE	RMSE ($\times 10^{-5}$)	R^2
LSTM	4.7156	0.0047	0.0069	0.9993
GRU	8.8245	0.0065	0.0094	0.9986
FNN	71.5386	0.0216	0.0267	0.9889
Transformer	516.4715	0.0612	0.0719	0.9201

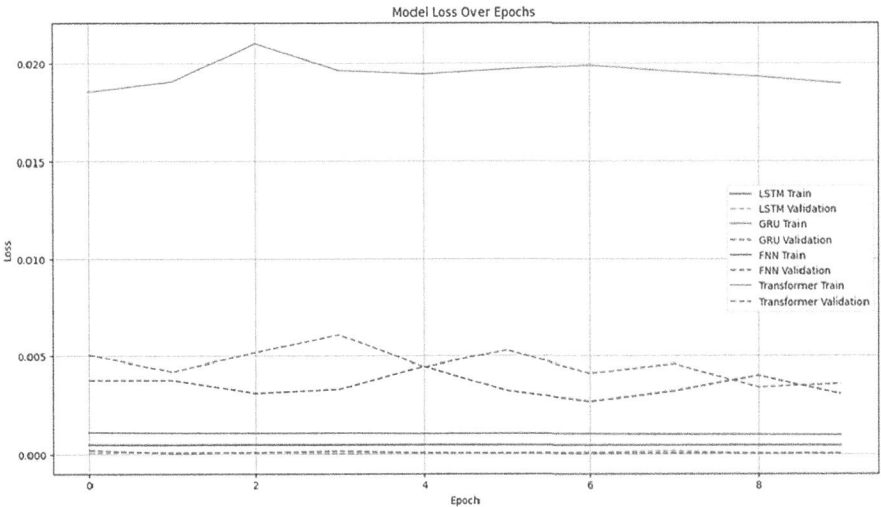

Fig. 3. Reveals the model loss over epoch for different neural network architectures.

3.3 Rationale for Three Ensemble Methodologies

To enhance the robustness and reliability of Bitcoin price predictions, this section explores three ensemble methodologies: Weighted Average Ensemble, Stacked Ensemble, and Simple Average Ensemble.

First approach, Weighted Average Ensemble assigns varying weights to individual model predictions, prioritizing models with demonstrably superior accuracy. In cryptocurrency forecasting, where precision is crucial, this method can significantly improve overall ensemble performance.

Second ones, Stacked Ensemble methodology leverages the strengths of individual models hierarchically. A meta-model is trained on the predictions of the base models [21]. This approach captures complex relationships and interactions between different models' outputs, particularly valuable when dealing with diverse model architectures.

Next, simple Average Ensemble method combines predictions by assigning equal weight to all models [11]. It effectively provides an ensemble prediction that is the average of the individual model outputs. This approach helps mitigate the impact of outliers or extreme predictions, common challenges in cryptocurrency price forecasting [5].

By incorporating these ensemble methodologies, the subsequent section aims to provide a more comprehensive analysis of ensemble modeling's potential in overcoming the inherent challenges of cryptocurrency price forecasting. The Weighted Average Ensemble emphasizes model performance, the Stacked Ensemble captures complex interactions, and the Simple Average Ensemble offers a balanced approach. This combination allows for a deeper understanding of how ensemble techniques can improve Bitcoin price prediction accuracy.

3.4 Interpretation of Results from Ensemble Models

An evaluation of the ensemble models' performance metrics (Table 3) revealed promising results. The Stacked Ensemble achieved the lowest MSE (0.0069) and RMSE (0.0083), demonstrating superior predictive accuracy compared to the other ensemble methods. This finding is further corroborated by the Stacked Ensemble's low MAE (0.0057), suggesting minimal individual prediction errors, and its exceptionally high R-squared value (0.9989), signifying a very strong correlation between predicted and actual Bitcoin prices. The Weighted Average Ensemble exhibited a balance between achieving acceptable accuracy (moderate MSE and RMSE) and mitigating the influence of potentially large individual errors (relatively high MAE). However, the Simple Average Ensemble, while boasting the lowest reported MSE (0.0007), necessitates cautious interpretation due to the possibility of error cancellation. This is further supported by its highest MAE (0.0220), indicating larger individual prediction errors. The Simple Average Ensemble's R-squared value (0.9895) suggests a strong correlation, but not as pronounced as the Stacked Ensemble. In conclusion, these findings underscore the efficacy of ensemble methodologies, particularly the Stacked Ensemble in this study, in significantly enhancing Bitcoin price prediction accuracy compared to individual models.

Table 3. Performance Metrics for Ensemble Models

Model	MSE ($\times 10^{-5}$)	MAE	RMSE ($\times 10^{-5}$)	R^2
Weighted Average	4.179507967	0.5506143208	0.646491142	0.9353310157
Stacked Ensemble	0.0069	0.005652837375	0.008305204384	0.9989327368
Simple Average	0.0006779639791	0.02195876228	0.02603774144	0.9895099513

4   Conclusion

This study investigated the effectiveness of various machine learning models in predicting Bitcoin closing prices. The Stacked Ensemble model emerged as the most optimal choice, achieving demonstrably superior performance metrics. It exhibited the lowest MSR, MAE, and RMSE, signifying exceptional accuracy and resilience to outliers.

The Weighted Average model presented a favourable alternative, offering a well-balanced approach between precise prediction and outlier resistance. The Simple Average model, however, prioritized outlier resistance with a slight trade-off in predictive accuracy, reflected by its marginally lower R^2. Traditional models (LSTM, GRU, FNN) displayed the least favourable performance, highlighting their limitations in this specific context.

It is crucial to acknowledge that ideal benchmarks (zero MSE/MAE and R^2 of 1) are not achievable in practice. However, the Stacked Ensemble model achieved remarkable proximity to these benchmarks. Ultimately, the selection of the most suitable model should be driven by the specific needs and objectives of the prediction task.

This study provides valuable insights for businesses seeking to leverage Bitcoin price prediction. The findings demonstrate the efficacy of ensemble models, particularly during economic uncertainties where such capabilities can provide significant guidance. Notably, ensemble models outperform traditional models in Bitcoin price prediction, offering a clear advantage.

Our exploration has illuminated the strengths and weaknesses of various Bitcoin price prediction models. While challenges like negative R^2 values in Time Series Models exist, they pave the way for innovation in advanced modelling techniques.

As the cryptocurrency market matures, accurate price prediction becomes increasingly important. This study underscores the significance of selecting appropriate models, particularly ensemble approaches, to enhance predictive accuracy. Additionally, ethical considerations and real-time adaptability are paramount for developing robust and dependable models for practical business applications.

Future research has the potential to not only refine Bitcoin price prediction but also to delve deeper into the interplay between external factors, such as socio-political influences, and the evolving financial landscape of cryptocurrencies. By prioritizing innovation, ethical practices, and a comprehensive understanding of these markets, researchers can contribute to the development of highly accurate forecasting models for crypto assets, empowering businesses to make informed decisions.

References

1. Aggarwal, A., Gupta, I., Garg, N., Goel, A.: Deep learning approach to determine the impact of socio-economic factors on bitcoin price prediction. In: 2019 Twelfth International Conference on Contemporary Computing (IC3) (2019). https://doi.org/10.1109/ic3.2019.8844928
2. Akyildirim, E., Cepni, O., Corbet, S., Uddin, G.S.: Forecasting mid-price movement of Bitcoin futures using machine learning. Ann. Oper. Res. (2021). https://doi.org/10.1007/s10479-021-04205-x
3. Borges, T.A., Neves, R.F.: Ensemble of machine learning algorithms for cryptocurrency investment with different data resampling methods. Appl. Soft Comput. **90**, 106187 (2020). https://doi.org/10.1016/j.asoc.2020.106187
4. Chen, T., Guestrin, C.: XGBoost: a scalable tree boosting system. In: Proceedings of the 22nd ACM SIGKDD International Conference on Knowledge Discovery and Data Mining - KDD 2016, pp. 785–794 (2016). https://doi.org/10.1145/2939672.2939785
5. Chen, J.: Analysis of bitcoin price prediction using machine learning. J. Risk Financ. Manag. **16**(1), 51 (2023). https://doi.org/10.3390/jrfm16010051
6. Derbentsev, V., Datsenko, N., Stepanenko, O., Bezkorovainyi, V.: Forecasting cryptocurrency prices time series using machine learning approach. SHS Web Conf. **65**, 02001 (2019). https://doi.org/10.1051/shsconf/20196502001
7. Dutta, A., Kumar, S., Basu, M.: A gated recurrent unit approach to bitcoin price prediction. J. Risk Financ. Manag. **13**(2), 23 (2020). https://doi.org/10.3390/jrfm13020023
8. Engle, R.F.: Autoregressive conditional heteroscedasticity with estimates of the variance of united kingdom inflation. Econometrica **50**(4), 987–1007 (1982)
9. Goodfellow, I., Yoshua Bengio and Courville, A.: Deep Learning. MIT Press, Cambridge (2016)
10. Hochreiter, S., Schmidhuber, J.: Long short-term memory. Neural Comput. **9**(8), 1735–1780 (1997)
11. Hyndman, R.J., Athanasopoulos, G.: Forecasting: Principles and Practice, 3rd edn. Otexts, Heathmont (2021). https://otexts.com/fpp2/
12. Lamothe-Fernández, P., Alaminos, D., Lamothe-López, P., Fernández-Gámez, M.A.: Deep learning methods for modeling bitcoin price. Mathematics **8**(8), 1245 (2020). https://doi.org/10.3390/math8081245
13. Liu, M., Li, G., Li, J., Zhu, X., Yao, Y.: Forecasting the price of bitcoin using deep learning. Finan. Res. Lett. 101755 (2020)
14. McNally, S., Roche, J., Caton, S.: Predicting the price of bitcoin using machine learning. In: 2018 26th Euromicro International Conference on Parallel, Distributed and Network-based Processing (PDP) (2018). https://doi.org/10.1109/pdp2018.2018.00060
15. Politis, A., Doka, K., Koziris, N.: Ether Price Prediction Using Advanced Deep Learning Models. IEEE Xplore (2021). https://doi.org/10.1109/ICBC51069.2021.9461061
16. Saadah, S., Ahmad Whafa, A.A.: Monitoring financial stability based on prediction of cryptocurrencies price using intelligent algorithm. In: International Conference on Data Science and Its Applications (ICoDSA) (2020). https://doi.org/10.1109/icodsa50139.2020.9212968
17. Sebastião, H., Godinho, P.: Forecasting and trading cryptocurrencies with machine learning under changing market conditions. Financ. Innov. **7**(1) (2021). https://doi.org/10.1186/s40854-020-00217-x
18. Shin, M., Mohaisen, D., Kim, J.: Bitcoin price forecasting via ensemble-based LSTM deep learning networks. In: 2021 International Conference on Information Networking (ICOIN) (2021). https://doi.org/10.1109/icoin50884.2021.9333853
19. Tandon, S., Tripathi, S., Saraswat, P., Dabas, C.: Bitcoin price forecasting using LSTM and 10-fold cross validation. IEEE Xplore (2019). https://doi.org/10.1109/ICSC45622.2019.8938251

20. Wilson, G.T.: Time Series Analysis: Forecasting and Control, 5th edn, by George E. P. Box, Gwilym M. Jenkins, Gregory C. Reinsel and Greta M. Ljung. Wiley, Hoboken, p. 712. ISBN 978-1-118-67502-1. J. Time Ser. Anal. **37**(5), 709–711 (2016). https://doi.org/10.1111/jtsa.12194
21. Wolpert, D.H.: Stacked generalization. Neural Netw. **5**, 241–259 (1992)

TRAPL: Transformer-Based Patch Learning for Enhancing Semantic Representations Using Aggregated Features to Estimate Patch-Class Distribution

Sander Riisøen Jyhne[1,2]([✉]) [iD], Per-Arne Andersen[1] [iD], Ivar Oveland[2] [iD], and Morten Goodwin[1] [iD]

[1] Centre for Artificial Intelligence Research, Grimstad, Norway
sandsjyhne@gmail.com
[2] The Norwegian Mapping Authority, Hønefoss, Norway

Abstract. We introduce TRAPL, a Transformer-based Patch Learning technique that enhances semantic representations in segmentation models. TRAPL leverages aggregated features for precise patch-class distribution estimation, gathering features at key layers in the Transformer architecture. The method integrates an auxiliary objective with a convolution-based classifier, enabling robust semantic learning at the patch level. Our experiments demonstrate significant improvements in Intersection-over-Union (IoU) performance across models and datasets. TRAPL is compatible with both flat and hierarchical Transformers, ensuring minimal computational load during training and no extra overhead during inference. Our evaluations across state-of-the-art models and benchmarks demonstrate TRAPL's effectiveness for improving Transformer-based semantic segmentation.

Keywords: Semantic Segmentation · Representation Learning · Transformer

1 Introduction

Semantic segmentation, a cornerstone in computer vision, enables pixel-level class label assignment within images. Its applications span diverse tasks, from building detection [9,10] to autonomous driving [18]. Effective semantic segmentation requires robust and discriminative representations for each class, allowing for better generalization and improved segmentation masks.

Traditional segmentation techniques focus on supervised learning from labeled datasets, while supervised contrastive learning directly targets semantic understanding by comparing similarities between image pairs. However, contrastive learning can be hyperparameter-sensitive and challenging to implement successfully [13].

M. Bramer and F. Stahl (Eds.): SGAI 2024, LNAI 15446, pp. 116–129, 2025.
https://doi.org/10.1007/978-3-031-77915-2_9

In response to these challenges, this paper introduces TRAPL, a novel, end-to-end method designed to learn complex image semantics without relying on elaborate learning objectives. Our approach adopts a supervised objective aiming to estimate patch class distribution, utilizing aggregated patch representations derived at multiple stages within the transformer model. We complement this with a lightweight, convolution-based classification head implemented during the training phase to estimate class distribution at the individual patch level.

The paper's main contributions include an intuitive yet impactful method composed of an auxiliary objective for the aggregated features in the vision transformer architectures. The combination results in enhanced model performance in semantic segmentation tasks, a claim substantiated by our empirical data. The enhancements in IoU scores across various datasets, encoders, and decoders attest to the effectiveness and robustness of TRAPL.

2   Related Work

Vision transformers (ViTs) [3, 8, 15–17] have become popular due to their success in various vision tasks. Unlike convolutional neural networks (CNNs), ViTs flatten images into non-overlapping patches, a technique central to our proposed approach.

Transformers have proven to be highly effective in semantic vision tasks, yet they encounter notable scalability challenges due to their self-attention mechanisms, as discussed in [4]. Thereby, research in recent years has witnessed a surge in efforts to mitigate this computational intensity, all while preserving, if not enhancing, accuracy. A notable contribution in this direction is by the authors of [16], who introduced a hierarchical transformer model that employs shifted windows to reduce the scope of the self-attention mechanism. This strategy substantially reduces the computational demands of self-attention. Other works, such as [17], critique the vision-specific additions in many state-of-the-art ViTs. These scholars argue that while the innovations might boost accuracy and present appealing FLOP counts, they inadvertently introduce complexities that render these models slower than their vanilla ViT counterparts. Furthermore, empirical evaluation demonstrates that when armed with a strong visual pretext task like MAE [5], there is no real imperative for adding extra complexities.

In the quest to enhance semantic representations of images, many research initiatives have tapped into the power of an auxiliary objective known as contrastive learning [6, 11, 12, 14, 21, 25]. A common approach in this field involves two-phase training. Initially, the model is pre-trained with contrastive learning and then finetuned for segmentation. This method, showcased in [24] and [25], uses auxiliary labels in tandem with ground truth for contrastive purposes. However, this method requires substantial memory resources, which can be a limiting factor. Our methodology diverges from the two-phase paradigm using an end-to-end training approach, sidestepping the memory-intensive stages. Notably, other works such as [20] and [1] employ an end-to-end training strategy, but they use a memory bank to store features during training. This storage and retrieval process reduces their efficiency, which our method sidesteps by processing the features in real-time, eliminating the need for temporary storage.

Additional innovative approaches emerge from [14], which integrates end-to-end training with active sampling, guided by a class relationship graph and confidence map-driven key pixel and hard query selection. Meanwhile, [11] harnesses the intrinsic patch structure of ViT, directing contrastive learning towards projected patch features. Our approach differs from the latter in two key ways. First, rather than using a contrastive objective, we introduce an objective focused on evaluating class distribution within patches, directly utilizing the patch features. Second, we consolidate the features and compute the loss once instead of computing the loss at each transformer stage. Moreover, a distinct advantage of our TRAPL approach is its capability to train on the entire batch without the need for selective sampling. This comprehensive batch training ensures consistent exposure to a diverse range of patch features, enhancing the generalizability and robustness of the model.

3 Method

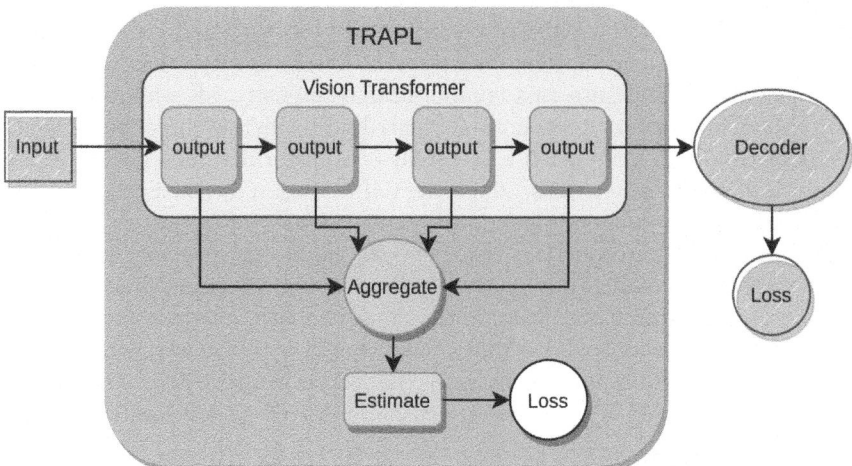

Fig. 1. Schematic representation of the TRAPL technique, which employs Vision Transformers (ViTs) for enhanced patch-based learning. Patches are extracted from different output stages of the ViT, followed by their aggregation to form a comprehensive patch feature. The framework can be adapted to both flat and hierarchical ViT architectures.

ViT has emerged as a dominant architecture for numerous tasks in computer vision. They are primarily characterized by their patch-based design, where an image is divided into non-overlapping patches to process the image. Within this context, the Transformer-based Patch Learning (TRAPL) technique emerges as an innovative learning paradigm. It harnesses the patch-centric design of ViTs to improve the semantic representation of classes for segmentation tasks. A visual summary of TRAPL is provided in Fig. 1. In essence, TRAPL extracts patch features from strategic output indices or stages in a ViT and consolidates them into a single, enriched patch feature. Subsequently, a convolutional layer uses the aggregated features to estimate the class distribution for each patch.

There are mainly two predominant types of ViT architectures. The first is the flat architecture, where both spatial and feature dimensions remain consistent throughout, as exemplified by the original ViT model [3]. The second type is the hierarchical architecture, such as the Swin model [16], characterized by changing spatial and feature dimensions through four distinct stages in the Transformer. This process begins with the highest granularity, and with each subsequent stage, the granularity reduces while the feature dimension is augmented. Given these architectural differences, adapting the feature aggregation process to accommodate both flat and hierarchical ViTs effectively becomes imperative.

For flat architectures, we introduce the Flat TRAPL (F-TRAPL). This approach aggregates representations from four distinct output indices into a single, comprehensive representation. Each feature from the output indices is denoted by (B, C, H, W), where B signifies the batch count, C represents the feature dimension, and H and W indicate the height and width, respectively. After aggregation, the resulting feature has the dimensions $(B, 4C, H, W)$, visualized in Fig. 2.

For hierarchical architectures, we propose the Hierarchical TRAPL (H-TRAPL). This approach systematically interpolates between spatial stages, transitioning from the largest to the smallest patch size. In typical hierarchical transformer models like the Swin Transformer, the feature dimensions for each stage are $S_0(B, C, H, W)$, $S_1(B, 2C, \frac{H}{2}, \frac{W}{2})$, $S_2(B, 4C, \frac{H}{4}, \frac{W}{4})$, and $S_3(B, 8C, \frac{H}{8}, \frac{W}{8})$. Where S_n is the stage number, B signifies the batch count, C represents the feature dimension, and H and W indicate the height and width, respectively. To aggregate these features, we implement a bilinear stepwise interpolation between the stages. Starting with the last stage S_3, the output is interpolated to match the size of the preceding stage S_2 and then concatenated with its features, resulting in a tensor with dimensions $(B, 12C, \frac{H}{4}, \frac{W}{4})$. This tensor is further interpolated to match the shape of S_1, where it is concatenated with the output of that stage. Finally, the result is interpolated to match the shape of S_0, and concatenated once again. Through this step-by-step process, the final tensor attains a shape of $(B, 15C, H, W)$, as visualized in Fig. 3. The aggregation of these features is then used for class-distribution estimation.

TRAPL's design centers on using aggregated features to accurately estimate the patch-class distribution of each unique patch. To achieve this, TRAPL incorporates a single convolution layer with a kernel and step size of 1. This configuration relies on the premise that each patch's internal representation is rich in semantic information, enabling TRAPL to determine the class distribution inde-

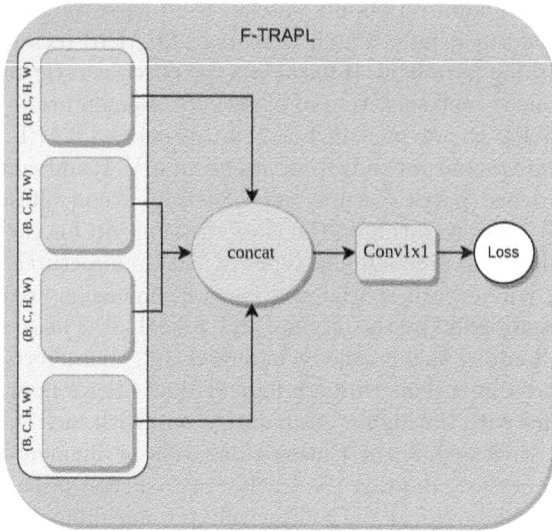

Fig. 2. Illustrative overview of the Flat TRAPL (F-TRAPL) process tailored for flat architectures. Multiple feature representations with identical spatial dimensions are concatenated into a unified representation. Following the concatenation is a convolution layer with a kernel and step size of 1.

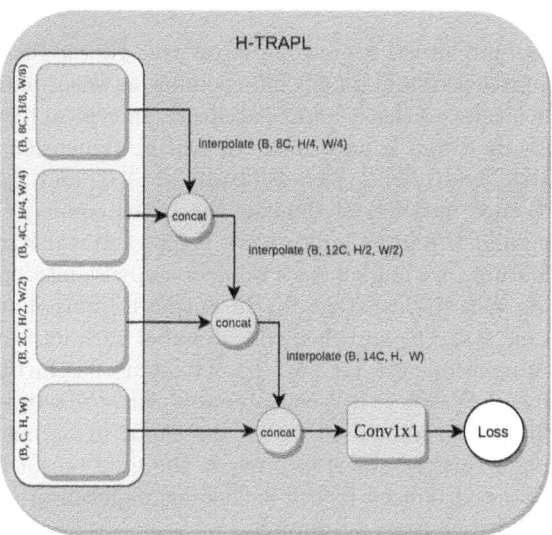

Fig. 3. Diagrammatic representation of the Hierarchical TRAPL (H-TRAPL) method designed for hierarchical architectures. Features from varying spatial stages are interpolated to achieve uniform spatial dimensions, followed by sequential concatenation. The process concludes with the utilization of a convolution layer with a kernel and step size of 1.

pendently without relying on features from adjacent patches. For the auxiliary objective of estimating this distribution for every patch, TRAPL employs the cross-entropy loss function. This function utilizes floating target values, which are directly derived from the actual patch-class distributions in the ground truth data.

Another characteristic of TRAPL is that it is only used during training and thereby does not affect the inference speed of the model. While TRAPL introduces certain modifications during the training phase by leveraging an enriched set of aggregated patch features with the auxiliary objective, it only adds a tiny amount of parameters to the original transformer architecture. This ensures that the computational overhead is kept minimal and does not impact the inference time. As a result, the enhanced semantic understanding achieved with TRAPL does not come at the cost of increased computational complexity for model deployment.

4   Experiments

In this section, we delve into a comprehensive evaluation of our proposed method. Through rigorous experiments conducted across diverse datasets, we aim to underscore the robustness and versatility of our approach. Our results not only validate the efficacy of the method in varied scenarios but also position it in comparison to existing benchmarks and standards.

4.1   Experimental Setup

We assessed the efficacy of the TRAPL technique across three ViTs, namely the Swin Transformer [16], Hiera [17], and vanilla ViT [22]. Each of these transformers was evaluated using the tiny, small, and base versions.

In evaluating the performance of the models, we utilized Intersection over Union (IoU), a widely adopted metric in segmentation tasks. IoU quantifies the overlap between the predicted segmentation and the ground truth by calculating the ratio of their intersection to their union. It provides an intuitive measure of how accurately a model delineates objects in an image, with higher IoU values indicating more precise segmentations. The use of IoU ensures a robust comparison of model efficacy, particularly in scenarios where pixel-level accuracy is paramount, such as the datasets used in our experiments.

To demonstrate the broad applicability of our technique, experiments were conducted on three diverse datasets, namely ADE20K [26], Cityscapes [2], and ISPRS Potsdam [7]. Each model was tested using the UPerNet [23] decoder, with the Hiera and Swin transformers undergoing additional evaluations with the multistage DC [19] decoder.

For consistent and reliable results, every experiment was performed using three distinct seeds, 12, 25, and 42, with the results averaged across these runs. All models commenced their training from pretrained weights. By maintaining a uniform learning rate of $1e^{-4}$ and restricting the training duration to 50 epochs, we ensured that any observed performance disparities arose from intrinsic model variations and not from training inconsistencies.

4.2 ADE20K Dataset

In the initial experiment, the acclaimed ADE20K dataset [26], a benchmark standard for semantic segmentation, was utilized. As illustrated in Table 1, our method showcased significant improvements in IoU and accuracy across all evaluated models. Moreover, Fig. 4 suggests that the TRAPL method imparts a stabilizing effect on model training, contributing to a more consistent and reliable convergence. While these preliminary observations are promising, they underscore the necessity for further systematic investigation to robustly determine the stabilizing dynamics introduced by the TRAPL methodology. Lastly, in Fig. 5 we see a line graph showing the results for all models on the ADE20K dataset, clearly indicating the performance gain for each model by using the TRAPL method compared to the baselines. There are some cases where the validation IoU drops for the base models, which are mainly caused by unstable training runs, as exemplified in Fig. 4 with the HieraDC model.

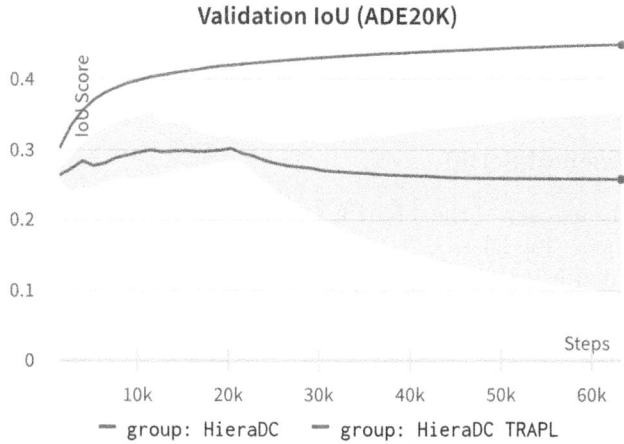

Fig. 4. The plot illustrates the validation IoU scores for HieraDC models on the ADE20K dataset, with TRAPL-enhanced models showing notably higher and steadier IoU trajectories compared to the baseline, indicating enhanced performance and stability.

4.3 Cityscapes Dataset

For our subsequent experiment, we turned to the Cityscapes [2] segmentation benchmark. Similar to ADE20K, Cityscapes is another widely recognized

Table 1. Evaluation scores for all models on the ADE20K dataset, indicating the effectiveness of our learning technique on IoU and accuracy measures.

Backbone	Decoder	Size	Technique	Mean IoU	Δ (%)	Accuracy	Δ (%)
Hiera	UPerNet	Base	-	0.4169	+3.31	0.6740	+3.83
			H-TRAPL	0.4500		0.7123	
		Small	-	0.4044	+3.61	0.7217	+2.99
			H-TRAPL	0.4405		0.7516	
		Tiny	-	0.3935	+3.49	0.6988	+3.23
			H-TRAPL	0.4284		0.7311	
	DC	Base	-	0.3021	+14.77	0.5761	+16.93
			H-TRAPL	0.4498		0.7454	
		Small	-	0.3745	+6.12	0.6733	+6.15
			H-TRAPL	0.4357		0.7348	
		Tiny	-	0.3472	+7.86	0.6420	+8.29
			H-TRAPL	0.4258		0.7249	
ViT	UPerNet	Base	-	0.4599	+2.73	0.7583	+1.77
			F-TRAPL	0.4872		0.776	
		Small	-	0.4329	+2.46	0.7361	+2.05
			F-TRAPL	0.4575		0.7566	
		Tiny	-	0.4061	+1.09	0.7135	+1.10
			F-TRAPL	0.4170		0.7245	
Swin	UPerNet	Base	-	0.4730	+2.82	0.7670	+2.11
			H-TRAPL	0.5012		0.7881	
		Small	-	0.4435	+2.15	0.7476	+1.57
			H-TRAPL	0.4650		0.7633	
		Tiny	-	0.4347	+1.48	0.7371	+1.29
			H-TRAPL	0.4495		0.7500	
	DC	Base	-	0.4468	+5.73	0.7395	+4.67
			H-TRAPL	0.5041		0.7862	
		Small	-	0.4432	+1.84	0.7380	+1.75
			H-TRAPL	0.4616		0.7555	
		Tiny	-	0.4065	+3.43	0.7060	+3.47
			H-TRAPL	0.4408		0.7407	

standard for assessing segmentation models. The evaluation scores detailed in Table 2 underscore the potency of our learning scheme, registering an improvement across all models.

Table 2. Evaluation scores for all models on the Cityscapes dataset, showcasing the effectiveness of our learning technique in IoU and accuracy measures.

Backbone	Decoder	Size	Technique	Mean IoU	Δ (%)	Accuracy	Δ (%)
Hiera	UPerNet	Base	-	0.6613	+1.15	0.9110	+1.51
			H-TRAPL	0.6728		0.9261	
		Small	-	0.3689	+2.30	0.9087	+1.48
			H-TRAPL	0.6830		0.9235	
		Tiny	-	0.6722	+0.59	0.9054	+1.53
			H-TRAPL	0.6781		0.9207	
	DC	Base	-	0.5897	+3.55	0.8775	+4.77
			H-TRAPL	0.6252		0.9252	
		Small	-	0.3689	+3.11	0.8816	+4.04
			H-TRAPL	0.6257		0.9220	
		Tiny	-	0.5769	+4.65	0.8717	+4.72
			H-TRAPL	0.6234		0.9189	
ViT	UPerNet	Base	-	0.6697	+1.68	0.8877	+2.14
			F-TRAPL	0.6865		0.9091	
		Small	-	0.6701	+1.22	0.9035	+1.41
			F-TRAPL	0.6823		0.9176	
		Tiny	-	0.6755	+4.05	0.9003	+1.25
			F-TRAPL	0.7160		0.9128	
Swin	UPerNet	Base	-	0.6419	+1.42	0.9313	+0.89
			H-TRAPL	0.6561		0.9402	
		Small	-	0.3689	+2.11	0.9273	+0.83
			H-TRAPL	0.6583		0.9356	
		Tiny	-	0.6398	+3.21	0.9272	+0.71
			H-TRAPL	0.6719		0.9343	
	DC	Base	-	0.6243	+1.23	0.9071	+3.30
			H-TRAPL	0.6366		0.9401	
		Small	-	0.6210	+0.65	0.9119	+2.14
			H-TRAPL	0.6275		0.9333	
		Tiny	-	0.6089	+2.28	0.9016	+3.04
			H-TRAPL	0.6317		0.9320	

4.4   Potsdam Dataset

In our third evaluation, we tested our model using the ISPRS Potsdam [7] dataset, a benchmark specifically designed to segment aerial images featuring objects like buildings, cars, and roads. The results presented in Table 3 further affirm the efficacy of our approach. We observed a consistent uptick in the IoU across all models.

Table 3. Evaluation scores for all models on the Potsdam dataset, showcasing the effectiveness of our learning technique in IoU and accuracy measures.

Backbone	Decoder	Size	Technique	Mean IoU	Δ (%)	Accuracy	Δ (%)
Hiera	UPerNet	Base	-	0.7370	+1.53	0.8805	+1.51
			H-TRAPL	0.7523		0.8956	
		Small	-	0.7345	+1.60	0.8789	+1.56
			H-TRAPL	0.7505		0.8945	
		Tiny	-	0.7336	+1.50	0.8775	+1.53
			H-TRAPL	0.7486		0.8928	
	DC	Base	-	0.6932	+5.70	0.8023	+9.19
			H-TRAPL	0.7502		0.8942	
		Small	-	0.6912	+5.68	0.8171	+7.52
			H-TRAPL	0.7480		0.8923	
		Tiny	-	0.6947	+5.21	0.8092	+8.22
			H-TRAPL	0.7468		0.8914	
ViT	UPerNet	Base	-	0.7168	+2.32	0.8622	+2.18
			F-TRAPL	0.7400		0.8840	
		Small	-	0.7376	+1.11	0.8824	+1.06
			F-TRAPL	0.7487		0.8930	
		Tiny	-	0.7325	+0.88	0.8782	+0.84
			F-TRAPL	0.7413		0.8866	
Swin	UPerNet	Base	-	0.7641	+0.60	0.9060	+0.51
			H-TRAPL	0.7701		0.9111	
		Small	-	0.7597	+0.38	0.9018	+0.42
			H-TRAPL	0.7635		0.906	
		Tiny	-	0.7585	+0.48	0.9008	+0.55
			H-TRAPL	0.7633		0.9063	
	DC	Base	-	0.7436	+2.71	0.8865	+2.45
			H-TRAPL	0.7707		0.9110	
		Small	-	0.7526	+0.93	0.8959	+0.84
			H-TRAPL	0.7619		0.9043	
		Tiny	-	0.7374	+2.48	0.8798	+2.48
			H-TRAPL	0.7622		0.9046	

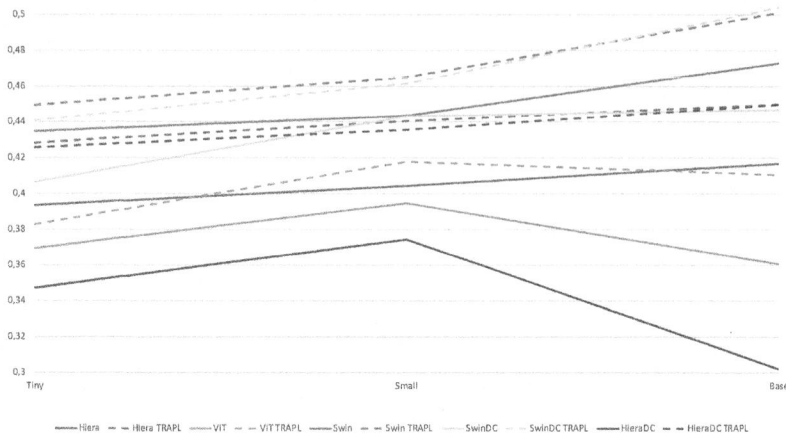

Fig. 5. A visualization of the validation IoU for all models and model sizes evaluated on the ADE20K dataset. Each color represents a model, where the solid lines represent the baseline version, and the dotted lines represent the TRAPL-enhanced models. All of the TRAPL-enhanced models outperform their respective baseline models.

5   Discussion

Our proposed method represents a significant advancement in Transformer-based semantic segmentation, consistently delivering performance enhancements across various architectures and datasets. Our approach's universal applicability stands out, effectively boosting the capabilities of all models in the experiments. For instance, our comprehensive evaluations reveal that the enhancements are especially pronounced when employing the DC decoder with the ADE20K dataset. The TRAPL-enhanced models using the DC decoder not only show marked improvements in IoU scores but also exhibit a notable stabilization of the training process, underscoring the method's potential for real-world application robustness.

By focusing on precise patch-class distribution estimation, our method offers substantial improvements in semantic accuracy, as evidenced by marked gains in IoU metrics. This positions our approach as a vital enhancement to the state-of-the-art, underlining its potential as a universal upgrade for semantic segmentation tasks.

While our method may not set new benchmarks in terms of absolute performance metrics, the enhancements it brings to transformer-based semantic segmentation are significant and cannot be overlooked. It's imperative to understand that many of the top-performing methods, particularly those backed by large-scale industry players, are often reinforced by enormous computational resources and infrastructure that are not readily available to all research entities. The scale of their computational capacity has the potential to train their models and achieve record-breaking evaluation metrics. However, the merit of a method should not be judged solely by its peak performance but also by its ability to demonstrate relative improvements under consistent conditions, which our method exhibits.

A vital aspect of our method's efficiency is its design philosophy. During training, TRAPL introduces a minimal increase in parameters. Additionally, an auxiliary objective is incorporated, which has a slight impact on the training speed. In contrast, during inference, there's no computational overhead. This ensures that the models remain fast and efficient in real-world applications.

Furthermore, the efficacy of our approach on small- and medium-scale models provides a promising indication of its scalability. If it can boost performance metrics on a limited number of parameters, there is a compelling argument to be made that, given sufficient computational resources akin to those available to the aforementioned large-scale players, it could very well replicate or even amplify these improvements on larger models. In essence, the relative improvements in small-to-medium models demonstrate consistent, scalable, and, most importantly, replicable enhancements in performance across a spectrum of models and datasets.

6   Conclusion

In this paper, we have introduced TRAPL, an end-to-end approach that significantly enhances semantic representations in transformer-based segmentation models, demonstrating remarkable improvements across various datasets and marking a notable advancement in the field. TRAPL's wide applicability and robustness underscore its potential to advance semantic segmentation techniques. Although TRAPL has not achieved absolute state-of-the-art results, its consistent relative improvements on multiple models and datasets indicate its effectiveness. Our findings pave the way for future research and applications in semantic segmentation, suggesting that continued exploration and refinement of patch-level semantic integration could yield even more significant advancements.

6.1   Future Work

As we look into the future, the potential for scaling and further optimization is apparent. The promise shown on smaller scales indicates that, with more substantial resources, TRAPL could potentially challenge or even surpass current benchmarks. We hope our contributions invigorate further research in this area, pushing the boundaries of what's possible with transformer architectures in computer vision.

Further exploration in the scaling of TRAPL for larger datasets and more intricate scenarios is a promising direction. Investigating how TRAPL adapts to increased data variability and its performance in diverse, real-world applications could provide deeper insights into its scalability and robustness. Additionally, future work could focus on algorithmic enhancements to TRAPL. Optimizing the transformer architecture for increased efficiency and integrating advanced learning techniques may lead to significant performance improvements. Lastly, a crucial area of future research is examining the robustness and generalization capabilities of TRAPL. Further, exploring how well TRAPL generalizes across various visual styles and unstructured environments could significantly broaden its application scope and utility in real-world scenarios.

References

1. Alonso, I., Sabater, A., Ferstl, D., Montesano, L., Murillo, A.C.: Semi-supervised semantic segmentation with pixel-level contrastive learning from a class-wise memory bank. In: Proceedings of the IEEE/CVF International Conference on Computer Vision (ICCV), pp. 8219–8228 (2021)
2. Cordts, M., et al.: The cityscapes dataset for semantic urban scene understanding. In: Proceedings of the IEEE Conference on Computer Vision and Pattern Recognition, pp. 3213–3223 (2016). https://doi.org/10.1109/CVPR.2016.350
3. Dosovitskiy, A., et al.: An image is worth 16x16 words: transformers for image recognition at scale. In: Proceedings of the 9th International Conference on Learning Representations (ICLR), pp. 1–21 (2021). https://doi.org/10.48550/arxiv.2010.11929
4. Duman Keles, F., Mahesakya Wijewardena, P., Hegde, C., Agrawal, S., Orabona, F.: On the computational complexity of self-attention. In: Proceedings of Machine Learning Research, vol. 201, pp. 597–619 (2023)
5. He, K., Chen, X., Xie, S., Li, Y., Dollár, P., Girshick, R.: Masked autoencoders are scalable vision learners. In: Proceedings of the IEEE/CVF Conference on Computer Vision and Pattern Recognition (CVPR), pp. 16000–16009 (2022)
6. Huang, L., et al.: A two-stage contrastive learning framework for imbalanced aerial scene recognition. In: ICASSP, IEEE International Conference on Acoustics, Speech and Signal Processing - Proceedings, pp. 3518–3522 (2022). https://doi.org/10.1109/ICASSP43922.2022.9746248
7. International Society for Photogrammetry and Remote Sensing: 2D Semantic Labeling Contest - Potsdam
8. Jain, J., Li, J., Chiu, M.T., Hassani, A., Orlov, N., Shi, H.: OneFormer: one transformer to rule universal image segmentation. In: Proceedings of the IEEE/CVF Conference on Computer Vision and Pattern Recognition (CVPR), pp. 2989–2998 (2023)
9. Jyhne, S., et al.: MapAI: precision in building segmentation. Nordic Mach. Intell. **2**(3), 1–3 (2022). https://doi.org/10.5617/NMI.9849
10. Jyhne, S., Jacobsen, J.R., Goodwin, M., Andersen, P.A.: DeNISE: deep networks for improved segmentation edges. In: Artificial Intelligence Applications and Innovations, pp. 81–89 (2023). https://doi.org/10.1007/978-3-031-34111-3_8
11. Jyhne, S.R., Andersen, P.A., Goodwin, M., Oveland, I.: A contrastive learning scheme with transformer innate patches. In: Bramer, M., Stahl, F. (eds.) SGAI 2023. LNCS, vol. 14381, pp. 103–114. Springer, Cham (2023). https://doi.org/10.1007/978-3-031-47994-6_8
12. Li, T., Roy, S., Zhou, H., Lu, H., Lathuilière, S.: Contrast, stylize and adapt: unsupervised contrastive learning framework for domain adaptive semantic segmentation. In: Proceedings of the IEEE/CVF Conference on Computer Vision and Pattern Recognition (CVPR) Workshops, pp. 4869–4879 (2023)
13. Liu, B., Ravikumar, P., Risteski, A.: Contrastive learning of strong-mixing continuous-time stochastic processes. In: International Conference on Artificial Intelligence and Statistics (2021)

14. Liu, S., Zhi, S., Johns, E., Davison, A.J.: Bootstrapping semantic segmentation with regional contrast. In: International Conference on Learning Representations (2022). https://doi.org/10.48550/arxiv.2104.04465

15. Liu, X., Peng, H., Zheng, N., Yang, Y., Hu, H., Yuan, Y.: EfficientViT: memory efficient vision transformer with cascaded group attention. In: Proceedings of the IEEE/CVF Conference on Computer Vision and Pattern Recognition (CVPR), pp. 14420–14430 (2023)

16. Liu, Z., et al.: Swin transformer V2: scaling up capacity and resolution. In: Proceedings of the IEEE/CVF Conference on Computer Vision and Pattern Recognition (CVPR), pp. 12009–12019 (2022)

17. Ryali, C., et al.: Hiera: a hierarchical vision transformer without the bells-and-whistles. In: ICML (2023)

18. Teichmann, M., Weber, M., Zöllner, M., Cipolla, R., Urtasun, R.: MultiNet: real-time joint semantic reasoning for autonomous driving. In: 2018 IEEE Intelligent Vehicles Symposium (IV), pp. 1013–1020 (2018). https://doi.org/10.1109/IVS.2018.8500504

19. Wang, L., Li, R., Duan, C., Zhang, C., Meng, X., Fang, S.: A novel transformer based semantic segmentation scheme for fine-resolution remote sensing images. IEEE Geosci. Remote Sens. Lett. **19** (2022). https://doi.org/10.1109/LGRS.2022.3143368

20. Wang, W., Zhou, T., Yu, F., Dai, J., Konukoglu, E., Van Gool, L.: Exploring cross-image pixel contrast for semantic segmentation. In: Proceedings of the IEEE/CVF International Conference on Computer Vision (ICCV), pp. 7303–7313 (2021)

21. Wei, Y., et al.: Contrastive Learning Rivals Masked Image Modeling in Fine-tuning via Feature Distillation. arXiv (2022). https://doi.org/10.48550/arxiv.2205.14141

22. Xia, Z., Pan, X., Song, S., Li, L.E., Huang, G.: Vision transformer with deformable attention. In: Proceedings of the IEEE/CVF Conference on Computer Vision and Pattern Recognition (CVPR), pp. 4794–4803 (2022)

23. Xiao, T., Liu, Y., Zhou, B., Jiang, Y., Sun, J.: Unified perceptual parsing for scene understanding. Lecture Notes in Computer Science, vol. 11209, pp. 432–448 (2018). https://doi.org/10.1007/978-3-030-01228-1_26

24. Zhang, F., Torr, P., Ranftl, R., Richter, S.R.: Looking beyond single images for contrastive semantic segmentation learning. Adv. Neural. Inf. Process. Syst. **34**, 3285–3297 (2021)

25. Zhao, X., et al.: Contrastive Learning for Label Efficient Semantic Segmentation (2021)

26. Zhou, B., Zhao, H., Puig, X., Fidler, S., Barriuso, A., Torralba, A.: Scene parsing through ADE20K dataset. In: Proceedings of the IEEE Conference on Computer Vision and Pattern Recognition (CVPR) (2017)

DATE: Derivative Alignment Training for Extrapolation with Neural Networks

Enrico Lopedoto$^{(\boxtimes)}$, Tillman Weyde, and Kizito Salako

Department of Computer Science, City, University of London, Northampton Square, London, UK
{enrico.lopedoto,t.e.weyde,k.o.salako}@city.ac.uk

Abstract. In this work we introduce *DATE* (Derivative Alignment Training for Extrapolation), a method to improve the extrapolation behaviour of neural networks (NN) with Rectified Linear Unit activation (ReLU) on univariate regression tasks. ReLU NNs naturally lend themselves to linear extrapolation beyond the training data range. However, there are two known limitations of extrapolation properties of trained ReLU NNs, that we address in this paper. When minimising the error of the prediction, the derivative of the NN model function can still show high variation, which can cause variable extrapolation. Non-linearities of the model function outside the training data range can lead to inconsistent extrapolation behaviour. In prior work, the extrapolation issue has been addressed with a set of regularisation functions, called *ReLEx*. To improve extrapolation and interpolation, we introduce two new regularisation terms: $D1$-loss and IR-loss. The $D1$-loss directly penalises the deviation of the model derivative from a target derivative as estimated from the data by interpolating between neighbouring data points. The IR-loss penalises positions of the non-linearities of the ReLU units outside a given range. Optimising the combination of $D1$ with IR loss and/or some of the *ReLEx* functions constitutes the *DATE* method. We evaluate *DATE* on regression tasks with noiseless data generated from analytic functions. We test different *DATE* configurations and find that training with *DATE* can reduce the variability of the model slope, prevent non-linearities outside the training data range, and improve extrapolation consistency as measured by different metrics. The most effective *DATE* variants also have reduced complexity compared to *ReLEx*.

Keywords: Extrapolation · Regression · Neural Networks · Derivative

1 Introduction

In supervised machine learning the immediate objective is to fit the model function to the training data by minimising a loss function. This loss function is typically defined in terms of the values of the data and the model, and for regression the error metric is typically the mean squared error (MSE). The most popular machine learning models in recent years have been neural networks

M. Bramer and F. Stahl (Eds.): SGAI 2024, LNAI 15446, pp. 130–143, 2025.
https://doi.org/10.1007/978-3-031-77915-2_10

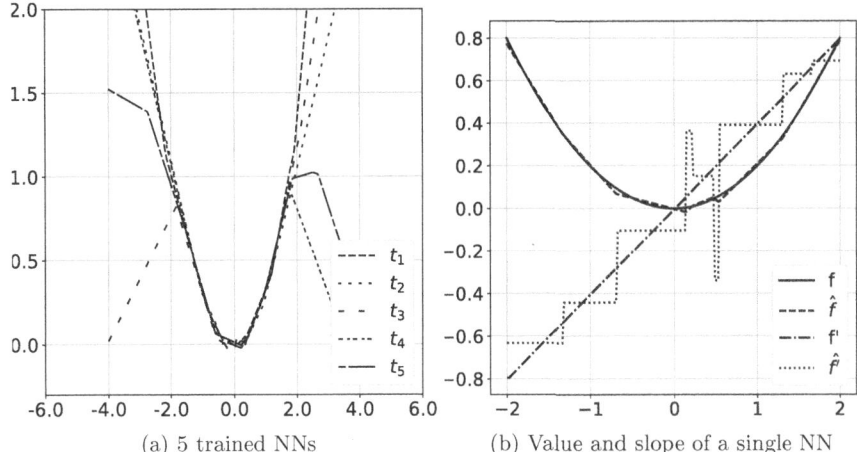

(a) 5 trained NNs   (b) Value and slope of a single NN

Fig. 1. (a) Extrapolation in the range $[-4,4]$ of a quadratic function with data trained in the range $[-2,2]$ with a ReLU NN trained with MSE loss only. b) we display the interpolation range $[-2,2]$ true function (solid), the model function (dashed), the slope of the target function (dashdotted) and the slope of the model function (dotted).

(NN). In particular, NNs with rectified linear unit (ReLU) activation have desirable properties in terms of computational efficiency and conceptual simplicity so that ReLU has become the standard activation function [6].

Here, we are concerned with the extrapolation of the model beyond the range of the training data. We explore specifically linear extrapolation behaviour, which is made possible by the ReLU activation function as opposed to previously more common sigmoid functions (logistic function and tanh). When training ReLU NNs to minimise the MSE, there are two problems that can be observed in Fig. 1: (a) shows predictions inside and outside of the training data range $[-2,2]$ of five separately trained NNs with one hidden layer of 10 neurons, and we observe a wide variation of behaviour outside the training data range, at least for some models; (b) shows the value and slope of the model vs the target function in the training data range, where the slope of the model function deviates in some places far from the true slope value. A solution to the extrapolation problem (a) has been proposed in the *ReLEx* method [10], which, however, increases the computational complexity of the training and exacerbates the derivative deviations (b).

The goal of this work is extend and improve over *ReLEx* with a method that achieves desirable linear extrapolation as well as interpolation behaviour in standard ReLU neural networks more effectively, more efficiently and with fewer changes compared to standard neural network learning.

Our contributions are as follows: 1) we introduce improved extrapolation of NN models through derivative alignment; 2) we propose *DATE*, a new method to improve extrapolation in regression task with ReLU neural networks including two new regularisation terms, $\mathcal{L}_{D1}$ and $\mathcal{L}_{IR}$; and 3) we provide an implementation of $DATE$ in PyTorch and an evaluation of learning five different target functions with simple NNs using $DATE$.

2   Related Work

In supervised machine learning, over the last decade, neural networks (NN) have been adopted for many machine learning problems [4,6]. However, neural networks display differences in behaviour when predicting a function between data points and predicting a function for points outside the range of the training data. We refer to prediction in the training data range as *interpolation* and outside the training data range as *extrapolation*, (see, e.g., [1]). Some methods to address the extrapolation problems for mathematical functions have been proposed by [15] and [12], who introduce non-standard NN models with activation functions such as identity and multiplication functions and achieve improved extrapolation.

A lack of extrapolation has also been observed in the context of linguistic structures, where rules are not generalised between different words or syllables [7,8,14,16], or when we need to extrapolate from even to odd numbers [13], or when extrapolating Dyck language recognition to long sequences [3].

2.1   Extrapolation with ReLU NNs

The rectified linear unit ($ReLU$) function is the most popular activation function in modern neural networks [6], firstly introduced by [5] to the best of our knowledge. The ReLU activation offers the possibility of performing unbounded linear extrapolation that is not possible with bounded activation function like the logistic sigmoid or $tanh$ functions. However, NNs trained with MSE using ReLU show high variability in the extrapolation, as illustrated above.

There is no single ideal extrapolation behaviour in the absence of a known function outside the training data range. As we have decided to limit ourselves to linear extrapolation, a possible target is the tangent line at the data point or points. In addition, there are considerations with respect to the learning process of NNs, where we adopt the desiderata from [10]:

- the NN should learn how to extrapolate from the training data;
- the NN should adapt the learning process making as little changes to the network structure, activation functions and training process as possible;
- the method and implementation should be easy for practitioners to replicate and use.

We also adopt the design decision of [10] to address the problem by changing only the loss functions and not the structure of the NN itself.

2.2   Simple ReLU NNs and *dying ReLUs*

From here on, we consider a simple feed-forward ReLU neural network with a single input, a single hidden layer (comprising H neurons), and a single output that calculates the function $f(x, \beta) = b_o + \sum_{h=1}^{H} w_{ho} \cdot ReLU(w_h x + b_h)$, where w_h and b_h are the weight and bias value of hidden neuron h, respectively. The weight between hidden neuron h and the output neuron is w_{ho}, while b_o is the bias of the output neuron. All these weights and biases make up the vector β. We will also write $\hat{y}$ in short for $f(x, \beta)$.

The ReLU function, $ReLU : \mathbb{R} \to \mathbb{R} = max(x, 0)$, has two parts, for negative arguments the output is constant 0, we call this the *constant part* of the ReLU. For positive inputs x, the output is x and we call this the *linear part* of the ReLU. At input 0, the ReLU is not differentiable, this is often referred to as the *non-linearity* of the ReLU or the *0-point* as defined below.

A known problem in NN learning is a *dying ReLU*, as described in [2, 11]. This refers to a situation where all training data points lead to a negative input to the ReLU function, so that it operates only in its constant part, where its output is 0 and its derivative is 0. In this situation, the input weights of that neuron will not be changed during learning by gradient descent. The linear part of that neuron will therefore not depend on the data but only on the initialisation of the weights. Examples of this are the observed variation of slopes outside the data range in Fig. 1(a), where we plot the output over the range $[-8, 8]$ of the 5 NN training runs with different random initialisation. The specifics of the data, networks and training are described below in Sect. 4. In (b), we plot the output value and slope of a single trained NN and of the target function.

2.3   *ReLEx* and *0-Points*

ReLEx, introduced in [10], is a method that aims to control extrapolation behaviour by introducing additional loss functions, which mainly control the position and orientation of the ReLU function in the hidden neurons. The results show that the usage of the proposed loss functions improves the extrapolation behaviour, but the method has limitations and requires tuning of several parameters. In addition, these loss terms increase the computational complexity compared to training with MSE alone.

The *ReLEx* method, is focused on *0-points*, i.e., the points in the input space where the ReLU's constant and linear parts meet and where the ReLU function is non-linear. Formally, the *0-points* are the input values x_{h0} that lead to input 0 for a hidden neuron h: $0 = w_h \cdot x_{h0} + b_h$, so that the *0-point* for hidden neuron h is $x_{h0} = -b_h/w_h$.

The *ReLEx* regularisation introduces four individual loss terms $\mathcal{L}_l$ with associated scaling parameters θ_l. They serve different purposes which we describe here briefly. The formal definitions are listed in Table 1. The **Centripetal** loss ($\mathcal{L}_{CP}$) pulls all the *0-points* inside the training data range; the **Mutually Repellent** loss ($\mathcal{L}_{MR}$) is responsible for counter balancing the $\mathcal{L}_{CP}$ force by distributing the *0-points* inside the training data range; the **Weight Orientation** loss ($\mathcal{L}_{WO}$) moves the *0-point* for each ReLU so that the constant part covers most of the data points and only data points close to the margins of the training data range determine the slope of the extrapolation; lastly, the **Weight Sign** loss ($\mathcal{L}_{WS}$) recovers from the degenerate case when all the weights have

Table 1. The loss terms used in ReLEx improve extrapolation. K is the number of data points. H is the number of hidden neurons. x_{h0} is the *0-point* of hidden neuron h (dependent only on the network weights w_h and b_h). $\bar{x}$ is the average of the training data. The complexity refers to a single calculation of the loss value.

Loss Name	Symbol	Definition	Complexity
Centripetal	$\mathcal{L}_{CP}$	$\sum_{h=1}^{H} \sum_{k=1}^{K} (x_{h0} - x_k)^2$	$O(HK)$
Mutually Repellent	$\mathcal{L}_{MR}$	$\sum_{h=1}^{H} \sum_{j>i}^{H} \frac{1}{(x_{h0}-x_{j0})^2+\varepsilon}$	$O(H^2)$
Weight Orientation	$\mathcal{L}_{WO}$	$-\sum_{h=1}^{H} ReLU((x_{h0} - \bar{x}) \cdot w_h + \varepsilon)$	$O(H)$
Weight Sign	$\mathcal{L}_{WS}$	$(\sum_{h=1}^{H} w_h)^2$	$O(H)$

the same sign (occurring on average only in 1 out of 2^{H-1} random initialisation of a network with H hidden neurons).

3 *DATE*—Derivative Alignment Training for Extrapolation

In this work, we explore a new approach to improve extrapolation, which involves directly controlling the slope of the model function, and also a new approach to avoid *0-points* outside the data range. This helps to solve the two issues of NNs for extrapolation illustrated previously (Fig. 1). To avoid the 0-points outside the training data range, i.e. *dying ReLUs*, as shown in 1(a), we introduce a new efficient loss term $\mathcal{L}_{IR}$. To improve the alignment of the slope of the target and model, as shown in 1(b), we introduce a new loss term $\mathcal{L}_{D1}$. Optimising the combination of $D1$ and IR losses constitute the *DATE* method.

3.1 $\mathcal{L}_{D1}$

The concept of derivative alignment has been introduced in [9] with a special regularisation term, the *DLoss*. Here, we introduce $D1$-loss – $\mathcal{L}_{D1}$ – a univariate version of *DLoss*. Like *DLoss*, $\mathcal{L}_{D1}$, penalises the deviation of the model's derivative from the target function derivative estimated from the training data points. More formally, it is the sum of the squared differences between the model derivative $\hat{f}'$ – the first derivative of the model function $\hat{f}$ – and an estimate of the target derivative y', based on the training data.

While *DLoss* uses sampling in the multi-dimensional case, there is a total order of the input data in the univariate real case, so we can define the data vector $XY = [(x_1, y_1), \ldots, (x_K, y_K)]$ ordered by the values of x.

Then, we estimate the first derivative of the target function y' at $k-1$ points x' as the vector of pairs

$$XY' := [(x_1', y_1',), \ldots, (x_{k-1}', y_{k-1}')] \tag{1}$$

where

$$(x'_k, y'_k) = \left((x_{k+1} + x_k)/2, (y_{k+1} - y_k)/(x_{k+1} - x_k)\right), \tag{2}$$

i.e., we take y'_k, the slope of the line between two data consecutive points, as the derivative value for argument x'_k, the mid-point between two consecutive x-values.

Without additional assumptions, we do not know anything about the true target function except for the provided data and, thus, cannot give any guarantees on how far the estimated derivative y' may be from the true derivative. However, if the true function f is differentiable, we do know that y'_{k+1} is the derivative value $f'(x)$ for some $x \in [x_k, x_{k+1}]$ by the mean value theorem.

We calculate the model derivative $\hat{f}'$ using the finite difference method with a parameter ε as

$$\hat{f}'(x) = \frac{\hat{f}(x + \varepsilon) - \hat{f}(x - \varepsilon)}{2\varepsilon}. \tag{3}$$

We use $\varepsilon = 0.05$ as it is large enough to avoid numerical issues and suitable for the curvature of the functions that we use in our experiments here. $\mathcal{L}_{D1}$ is then defined as

$$\mathcal{L}_{D1} = \sum_{(x',y') \in XY'} \left(y' - \hat{f}'(x')\right)^2 \tag{4}$$

and with it we are able to approximate the local slope of the model function to the local slope of the data with complexity of $O(HK)$.

3.2 $\mathcal{L}_{IR}$

In Fig. 1(a) we saw undesired behaviour outside the data range. We are interested in making sure that at least two data points are covered by the linear part of every ReLU, so that the slope of the model in the extrapolation range will be determined by the data.

To do so, in *ReLEx*, $\mathcal{L}_{CP}$ tries to pull the 0-points inside the training range. For higher θ_{CP} values, however, we have observed that all 0-points cluster around the data mean. To counterbalance this effect $\mathcal{L}_{MR}$ was introduced to equally distribute the 0-points over the range.

To avoid *0-points* outside the training data range, we introduce the Internal Range loss $\mathcal{L}_{IR}$ defined as:

$$\mathcal{L}_{IR} = \sum_{k=1}^{K} \left(ReLU(-x_{k0} + L - \tau) + ReLU(x_{k0} - R + \tau)\right)^2, \tag{5}$$

where K is the number of hidden neurons, L and R are the most left point and right point of the training data range respectively and τ defines the margin from where data points within the training data range are covered. This loss pulls the 0-points outside the training data range toward the inside with margin τ.

Only hidden neurons where the 0-points fall outside of the training data range with a margin τ are affected by $\mathcal{L}_{IR}$ as opposed to $\mathcal{L}_{CP}$, where stronger weight drives 0-points toward the mean of the data set and $\mathcal{L}_{MR}$ distributes them, making the calibration of their relative weights necessary.

Another benefit of using $\mathcal{L}_{IR}$ is that it has computational complexity $O(K)$. It fulfils the same function as $\mathcal{L}_{CP}$ combined with $\mathcal{L}_{MR}$ complexity is $O(H^2)$. While the $O(HK)$ complexity of $\mathcal{L}_{CP}$ could be reduced to $O(H)$ by using the mean of the data instead of the individual points), $\mathcal{L}_{MR}$ has complexity $O(H^2)$ that cannot be reduced directly.

4   Experiments

We evaluate the effect of three different $DATE$ configurations by training a small ReLU NN on data sampled from analytical functions. The baselines are standard NNs with $MSE = \frac{1}{n}\sum_{y\in Y}(y-\hat{y})^2$ and $ReLEx$ losses (as described above). We run different experiments with settings described below.

Method. We chose ReLU-based NN with a single input, single output, and one hidden linear layer with 10 neurons. To train it we use the Adam optimiser.

Data Generation. For this paper, we only consider noise-free data points sampled from a specific mathematical function $f(x)$. The training data range of the input x is $[-2, 2]$ with a fixed grid of 200 equidistant points. We use five different functions $lin\ f(x) = x$, $abs\ f(x) = |x|)$, $pow\ f(x) = \frac{1}{5}x^2$, $sigm$ $f(x) = 1/(1 + e^{-x}))$, and $(sin\ f(x) = \sin(x))$.

Hyper-Parameters. We use the following hyper-parameters for the training: learning rate $\epsilon = 0.007$; momentum $\nu = 0.9$; and 700 epochs with mini-batch size 20. These parameters have shown in preliminary experiments to reliably achieve convergence without major instabilities during the training process. We varied $\theta_{D1} = \{0.1, 0.3, 0.5, 0.7, 0.9\}$ to explore the effect of $DATE$. For the other losses the parameters that we use in the experiments are those found in [10] to work well, specifically $\theta_{CP} = 0.3$, $\theta_{MR} = 10$, $\theta_{WO} = 0.3$, $\theta_{WS} = 0.1$ and $\theta_{IR} = 5$.

4.1   Evaluation Metrics

We use two types of metrics: interpolation and extrapolation metrics.

Interpolation metrics are calculated on the training data range $[-2,2]$ where we use 200 equidistant samples:

- MSE_{int}: MSE of prediction against true value on a 200 feature points sampled from a uniform distribution in the training data range;
- MSE_{D1}: MSE of model derivative against y' on a 200 feature points sampled from a uniform distribution in the training data range.

Extrapolation metrics are calculated on the *extrapolation set*, which consists of 200 points, 100 sampled from a uniform distribution in the left $[-10, -2]$ and 100 from the right $[2, 10]$ extrapolation range. We calculate these metrics individually for the right and left extrapolation set and their average.

The ranges of values the margins that determine the interpolation can make a difference both for the extrapolation and the measurement. We can use a wider range from the margin or use more local information. Less local extrapolations will be more robust against noise in the data, but further away from the tangent at the last data point. Therefore we use a spectrum of targets to measure the precision of extrapolation. This is reflected in the different metrics calculated on the extrapolation data range:

- Tan_{ex}: MSE of prediction against the tangent lines to the target function at the margins of the training data range.
- WLR_{ex}: MSE of the model prediction against a weighted linear regression (WLR) over the data points near the margin. In the WLR, we over-weight data closer to the margins of the training data range. The weighting scheme used is as per [10] Sect. 5.1, defined by a exponential function which allocates weights rising exponentially toward the margin L and R of the training data range. The weights are normalised to sum up to 1.
- $D1_{ex}$: MSE of the model prediction against the line of the last two point with slopes y'_1 for and y'_{k-1}.

The metrics reported are the average values obtained from 10 runs for each experiment. In addition, we measure extrapolation consistency with the standard deviation of the slope of the linear regression over the $(x, \hat{y})$ points in the extrapolation set. We do this, as before, separately on the negative and positive extrapolation ranges.

- σ_S: is the extrapolation variability over 10 runs. It is calculated as the standard deviation of the slope resulting from the linear fitting over the predicted values in the portion S of the extrapolation range, i.e. $[-10, -2]$ for left and $[2, 10]$ for right.

4.2 *DATE* Configurations

We compare different configurations of *DATE* in order to evaluate the effects of $\mathcal{L}_{D1}$ and $\mathcal{L}_{IR}$. We test MSE and *ReLEx* and three other different variants of *DATE*. Below we describe each configuration.

$DATE_1$: **Full *ReLEx* + $\mathcal{L}_{D1}$**. Here, we add $\mathcal{L}_{D1}$ to all *ReLEx* loss terms. We hypothesise that $\mathcal{L}_{D1}$ will improve the derivative alignment and, thus, lead to better extrapolation. The total loss function $\mathcal{L}$ is defined as:

$$\mathcal{L} = ReLEx + \theta_{D1}\, \mathcal{L}_{D1} + MSE \qquad (6)$$

$DATE_2$: $\mathcal{L}_{WO} + \mathcal{L}_{WS} + \mathcal{L}_{IR} + \mathcal{L}_{D1}$. In this loss configuration, we replace the $\mathcal{L}_{CP}$ and $\mathcal{L}_{MR}$ terms that are part of *ReLEx* with $\mathcal{L}_{IR}$. We hypothesise that this configuration should improve the adaptability within the training data range compared to the $ReLEx$ and $DATE_1$. The total loss function $\mathcal{L}$ is defined as:

$$\mathcal{L} = \theta_{WO}\,\mathcal{L}_{WO} + \theta_{WS}\,\mathcal{L}_{WS} + \theta_{IR}\,\mathcal{L}_{IR} + \theta_{D1}\,\mathcal{L}_{D1} + MSE \qquad (7)$$

$DATE_3$: $\mathcal{L}_{WS} + \mathcal{L}_{IR} + \mathcal{L}_{D1}$. We hypothesise that $\mathcal{L}_{WO}$ might not be needed, as we do not have a strong theoretical justification for it. The total loss function $\mathcal{L}$ is defined as:

$$\mathcal{L} = \theta_{WS}\,\mathcal{L}_{WS} + \theta_{IR}\,\mathcal{L}_{IR} + \theta_{D1}\,\mathcal{L}_{D1} + MSE \qquad (8)$$

While $DATE_1$ includes $\mathcal{L}_{MR}$, its complexity is quadratic in terms of H, $O(H^2)$, $DATE_2$ and $DATE_3$ use only $\mathcal{L}_{IR}$, with complexity $O(K)$, i.e., lower than the complexity of standard back-propagation (greater than $O(HK)$), so that the overall complexity of $DATE_1$ is reduced compared to $DATE_2$ and $DATE_3$.

5   Results

We report the metrics as explained in previous section when applying different loss configurations in Table 2. We show how each individual analytical function behaves with the best parameters in Table 3.

In Table 2, we report results depending on different θ_{D1} for $\mathcal{L}_{D1}$. $DATE_2$ is the configuration which offers the best results (in bold) for MSE_{int} and majority of the extrapolation metrics. Using $DATE_1$ provides the best result w.r.t. WLR_{ex} and $DATE_3$ provide the best MSE_{D1} result.

In Table 3 we report results for each individual function obtained with the best θ_{D1} configuration for each function – selected to achieve the lowest MSE_{D1} and make all the 0-points are inside the data range. We observe how linear function lin and abs achieve best results across the interpolation metrics and Tan_{ex} and $D1_{ex}$ with $DATE_1$. For pow, $sigm$ and sin the best results for interpolation, Tan_{ex} and $D1_{ex}$ are obtained with $DATE_2$ and $DATE_3$. WLR_{ex} remains the metric to be minimised by $ReLEx$.

6   Discussion

With the $DATE$ approach, MSE_{int} is in most cases improved. In $DATE_2$ and $DATE_3$, $\mathcal{L}_{IR}$ is responsible for pulling 0-points toward the margins of the training data range. We observe that using $\mathcal{L}_{IR}$ is at least as effective as using $\mathcal{L}_{CP} + \mathcal{L}_{MR}$. In $DATE_2$, the $\mathcal{L}_{WO}$ is apparently still useful because its results show less variable extrapolation than $DATE_3$.

Depending on the portion of the data range close to the margins that we consider local, we can arbitrarily decide how much locally determined the extrapolation target is. The Tan_{ex} and WLR_{ex} metrics for $DATE_{1,2,3}$ are lower than MSE and $ReLEx$ training for all functions considered. We expect Tan_{ex} to be

Table 2. Results with all θ_{D1} settings as average across all analytic functions by loss configuration. We report MSE_{int}, MSE_{D1} and Tan_{ex}, WLR_{ex}, $D1_{ex}$ metrics for interpolation and extrapolation respectively. Results as average across all the functions *lin, pow, abs, sigm, sin.*

Loss	θ_{D1}	MSE_{int}	MSE_{D1}	Tan_{ex}	WLR_{ex}	$D1_{ex}$
MSE	0.0	0.026	0.330	8.641	7.797	8.641
$ReLEx$	0.0	0.013	0.501	0.636	0.170	0.630
$DATE_1$	0.1	0.009	0.192	0.583	0.166	0.578
	0.3	0.008	0.141	0.548	**0.164**	0.544
	0.5	0.008	0.126	0.507	0.179	0.503
	0.7	0.011	0.127	0.497	0.172	0.494
	0.9	0.011	0.128	0.483	0.187	0.479
$DATE_2$	0.1	0.010	0.072	0.106	0.719	0.107
	0.3	0.016	0.071	0.185	0.832	0.186
	0.5	0.010	0.088	**0.036**	0.816	**0.035**
	0.7	0.008	0.081	0.056	0.747	0.055
	0.9	**0.005**	0.059	0.074	0.755	0.074
$DATE_3$	0.1	0.014	0.118	0.782	1.263	0.782
	0.3	0.020	0.065	0.195	0.737	0.190
	0.5	0.020	0.081	0.183	0.755	0.182
	0.7	0.011	**0.053**	0.114	0.806	0.114
	0.9	0.012	0.068	0.101	0.748	0.100

lower for $DATE_2$ and $DATE_3$, because the slope modelled with these methods will match more closely the one at the marginal of the data range. This is indeed the case as shown in Table 2.

Figure 2 shows the convergence of the predicted function to the true function in the range $[-2, 2]$ on 5 runs $DATE_1$, $DATE_2$ and $DATE_3$. These are obtained with each of the models trained over 700 epochs with batch size of 20 and Adam optimiser. In Fig. 2 we note that the slope of the model prediction in the training data range for $DATE_1$ (subfigure a) is not matching the slope of the target function as well as to $DATE_2$ and $DATE_3$ (subfigures b and c).

Lastly, Fig. 3 shows the learning curves for $DATE_1$, $DATE_2$ and $DATE_3$. Compared to $DATE_1$, MSE_{D1} seems to reduce faster and be less variable across multiple runs for $DATE_2$ and $DATE_3$. With $DATE_1$ we have a more stable metrics toward the ends of the training, but at higher loss levels. With $DATE_2$ and $DATE_3$, we observe more fluctuations toward the end of training for MSE_{int}, but at lower error levels. We also observe that the Tan_{ex} error is more controlled at earlier stages for $DATE_1$ but reaches lower error with $DATE_2$ and $DATE_3$.

Limitations. One of the fundamental assumption in $DATE$ method is the continuation of the local linear trend at the boundary regions. The linear extrap-

Table 3. Results with the best model parameters for each function. We report results with MSE_{int} and MSE_{D1} metrics for interpolation: MSE on training set and $D1$-Loss, respectively. We report results with Tan_{ex}, WLR_{ex} and $D1_{ex}$ metrics for extrapolation with respect to tangent, weighted linear regression and slope respectively. We display σ_R and σ_L, the extrapolation variability on the left and right side, separately because certain functions are not symmetric. θ_{D1} reported is the one which minimises the MSE_{D1}.

$f(x)$	Loss	θ_{D1}	σ_R	σ_L	MSE_{int}	MSE_{D1}	Tan_{ex}	WLR_{ex}	$D1_{ex}$
abs	MSE	-	0.047	0.134	0.004	0.347	2.268	2.341	2.282
	$ReLEx$	-	0.004	0.001	0.020	1.389	0.021	0.599	0.016
	$DATE_1$	0.5	0.000	0.001	**0.001**	**0.080**	**0.001**	0.432	**0.000**
	$DATE_2$	0.5	0.002	0.003	0.007	0.115	0.005	**0.417**	0.004
	$DATE_3$	0.5	0.004	0.010	0.023	0.100	0.016	0.417	0.016
lin	MSE	-	0.399	0.745	0.019	0.138	13.219	13.227	13.227
	$ReLEx$	-	0.003	0.003	0.002	0.152	0.005	0.002	0.002
	$DATE_1$	0.7	0.002	0.002	**0.001**	**0.002**	**0.002**	**0.001**	**0.001**
	$DATE_2$	0.7	0.002	0.003	0.004	0.073	0.007	0.007	0.007
	$DATE_3$	0.7	0.005	0.027	0.009	0.019	0.053	0.055	0.055
pow	MSE	-	0.490	0.459	0.081	0.808	8.974	5.317	8.958
	$ReLEx$	-	0.004	0.024	0.036	0.673	2.970	**0.244**	2.955
	$DATE_1$	0.5	0.027	0.008	0.038	0.511	2.376	0.460	2.362
	$DATE_2$	0.5	0.021	0.022	**0.007**	0.108	**0.141**	3.463	**0.138**
	$DATE_3$	0.7	0.055	0.024	0.011	**0.097**	0.206	3.272	0.202
sigm	MSE	-	1.873	1.527	0.006	0.219	5.522	4.874	5.511
	$ReLEx$	-	0.052	0.142	0.005	0.137	0.180	**0.002**	0.175
	$DATE_1$	0.3	0.014	0.045	0.002	0.034	0.154	0.003	0.149
	$DATE_2$	0.7	0.088	0.246	**0.002**	**0.006**	**0.005**	0.152	**0.005**
	$DATE_3$	0.7	0.074	1.527	0.017	0.021	0.020	0.139	0.019
sin	MSE	-	1.895	0.511	0.096	4.040	22.916	34.459	23.270
	$ReLEx$	-	0.016	0.010	0.499	8.972	0.605	**14.676**	0.879
	$DATE_1$	0.5	0.004	0.007	0.184	3.633	**0.313**	25.968	**0.170**
	$DATE_2$	0.7	0.004	0.034	**0.023**	**0.796**	2.924	37.808	2.448
	$DATE_3$	0.7	0.095	0.024	0.031	0.874	1.050	28.014	0.857

olation is a popular choice in many applications because of its simplicity. The choice of loss function would need to be reconsidered under a non-linear assumption. This would involve using non-linear activation functions and higher order derivatives. The $DATE$ method is so far only defined for univariate situation and only for a single hidden layer. These are obviously severe limitation in practice and will need to be addressed. However, as the goal extrapolation is already not uniquely defined in the univariate case, in the multi-dimensional feature space,

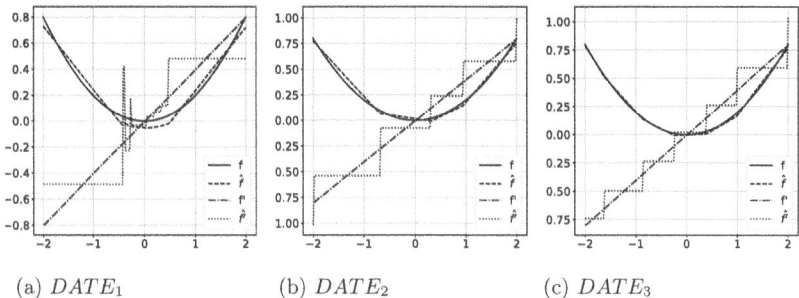

(a) $DATE_1$ (b) $DATE_2$ (c) $DATE_3$

Fig. 2. Various models trained with *DATE* variations in (a)–(c) to approximate a quadratic function. For presentation purposes, only the output range $[-1, 1]$ is accounted for.

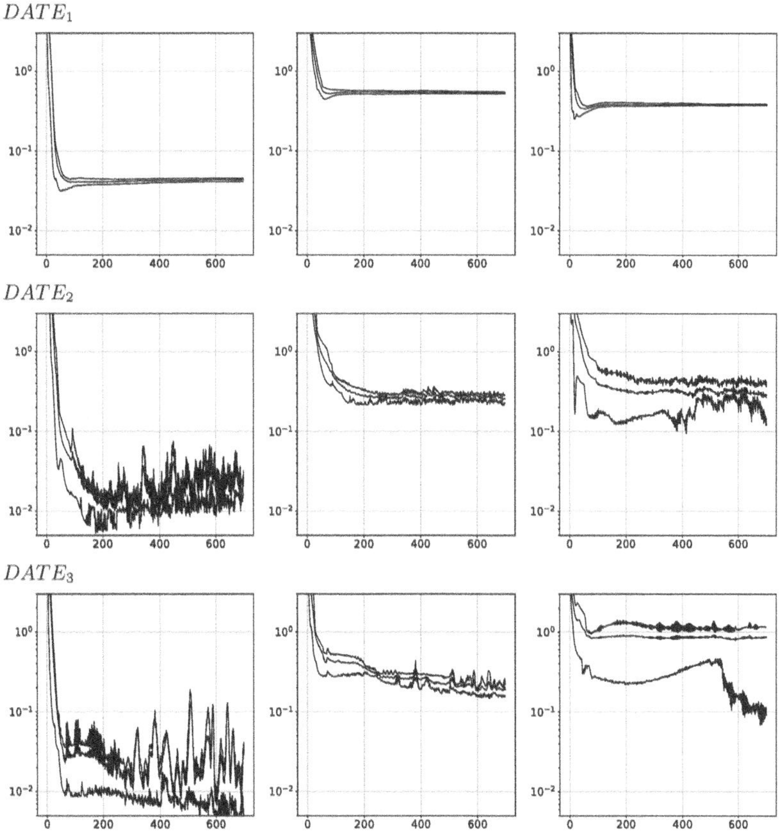

$DATE_1$

$DATE_2$

$DATE_3$

(a) MSE_{int} (b) MSE_{D1} (c) Tan_{ex}

Fig. 3. Learning curves from training on scaled quadratic function for $DATE_1$, $DATE_2$ and $DATE_3$ respectively. The learning represented is the average over 5 runs with 700 epochs, batch size 20. The solid black line represents the average and the dotted lines represents the percentile interval $[20, 80]$.

both, appropriate loss functions and metrics will be even more complex. The $DATE$ method assumes that the slope at the margins of the data range is most important for the extrapolation. The reliance on slope at the margins will need more attention in the case of real data, as is may amplify noise.

7 Conclusions

We propose $DATE$, a method which introduces two new loss terms to regularise the behaviour of a ReLU network, such that it produces desirable linear extrapolations beyond the margins of the training data range. We have implemented $DATE$ in PyTorch and we have applied it to a network with a single hidden layer of 10 neurons, single input, and single output. We have proposed different metrics to measure the extrapolation, as well as interpolation, performance.

In $ReLEx$ we observed that better extrapolation results were coming at the cost of higher interpolation instability. We observe now with $DATE$ how, in general, consistent linear extrapolations paired with low interpolation error is achieved. $DATE$ has shown some preliminary benefits in the NN case and we expect that $DATE$ can be extended to other regression methods.

Although with $DATE$ we have improved the complexity of the regularisation, we have still some limitations to overcome with future work. Future work will include the formulation of higher order derivative, extrapolation applied to multiple dimensions, different network structures and/or other regression methods as well as working with classification problems.

References

1. Abiodun, O.I., Jantan, A., Omolara, A.E., Dada, K.V., Mohamed, N.A., Arshad, H.: State-of-the-art in artificial neural network applications: a survey. Heliyon **4**(11), e00938 (2018)
2. Douglas, S.C., Yu, J.: Why relu units sometimes die: analysis of single-unit error backpropagation in neural networks. In: 2018 52nd Asilomar Conference on Signals, Systems, and Computers, pp. 864–868. IEEE (2018)
3. El-Naggar, N., Madhyastha, P.S., Weyde, T.: Theoretical conditions and empirical failure of bracket counting on long sequences with linear recurrent networks. In: Conference of the European Chapter of the Association for Computational Linguistics (2023)
4. Fan, J., Ma, C., Zhong, Y.: A selective overview of deep learning. Stat. Sci. A Rev. J. Inst. Math. Stat. **36**(2), 264–290 (2019)
5. Fukushima, K.: Cognitron: a self-organizing multilayer neural network. Biol. Cybern. **20**, 121–136 (1975)
6. Goodfellow, I., Bengio, Y., Courville, A.: Deep Learning. MIT Press, Cambridge (2016)
7. Lake, B., Baroni, M.: Generalization without systematicity: on the compositional skills of sequence-to-sequence recurrent networks. In: International Conference on Machine Learning, pp. 2873–2882. PMLR (2018)
8. Li, D., Yang, Y., Song, Y.Z., Hospedales, T.: Learning to generalize: meta-learning for domain generalization. In: AAAI Conference on Artificial Intelligence (2018)

9. Lopedoto, E., Shekhunov, M., Aksenov, V., Salako, K., Weyde, T.: Derivative-based regularization for regression (2024)
10. Lopedoto, E., Weyde, T.: ReLEx: regularisation for linear extrapolation in neural networks with rectified linear units. In: Bramer, M., Ellis, R. (eds.) SGAI 2020. LNCS (LNAI), vol. 12498, pp. 159–165. Springer, Cham (2020). https://doi.org/10.1007/978-3-030-63799-6_13
11. Lu, L., YeonjongSu, Y., Em Karniadakis, G.: Dying relu and initialization: theory and numerical examples. Commun. Comput. Phys. **28**(5), 1671–1706 (2020)
12. Madsen, A., Johansen, A.R.: Neural arithmetic units. In: International Conference on Learning Representations (2020)
13. Marcus, G.F., Vijayan, S., Rao, S.B., Vishton, P.M.: Rule learning in 7-month-old infants. Science **283**, 77–80 (1999)
14. Mitchell, J., Stenetorp, P., Minervini, P., Riedel, S.: Extrapolation in NLP. In: Bisk, Y., Levy, O., Yatskar, M. (eds.) Proceedings of the Workshop on Generalization in the Age of Deep Learning, New Orleans, Louisiana, pp. 28–33. Association for Computational Linguistics (2018)
15. Sahoo, S., Lampert, C., Martius, G.: Learning equations for extrapolation and control. volume 80 of. Proceedings of Machine Learning Research, pp. 4442–4450
16. Suzgun, M., Belinkov, Y., Shieber, S.M.: On evaluating the generalization of LSTM models in formal languages. In: Jarosz, G., Nelson, M., O'Connor, B., Pater, J. (eds.) Proceedings of the Society for Computation in Linguistics (SCiL) 2019, pp. 277–286 (2019)

Interactive Simulator Framework for XAI Applications in Aquatic Environments

Ahmed H. Elsayed[1]([✉]) [iD], Tarek A. El-Mihoub[1] [iD], Christoph Manss[1] [iD],
Andre Miedtank[1] [iD], Lars Nolle[1,2], and Frederic Stahl[1] [iD]

[1] German Research Center for Artificial Intelligence GmbH (DFKI),
26129 Oldenburg, Lower Saxony, Germany
ahmed.elsayed@dfki.de
[2] Department of Engineering Science, Jade University of Applied Sciences,
Wilhelmshaven, Germany

Abstract. Trust in Artificial Intelligence (AI) systems is essential for their lasting success, and methods for understanding and justifying their results are of paramount importance. This paper addresses this need by presenting a simulation framework, where an interacting user is prompted through an interface to describe and explain their actions depending on different situations. This simulation framework can generate a dataset annotated with explanations for training explainable AI models for mission planning. Firstly, This paper presents the development of a simulator built with Unity3D. The simulator recreates an aquatic use case that involves aquatic vessel mission planning for lake maintenance. Therefore, the simulator randomises environmental conditions and simulates various interactions with simulated boats on the lake. Secondly, the paper introduces an annotation interface integrated into the simulator to collect textual actions and their explanations. Here, a skipper of a boat in the lake can describe and explain actions, which are then captured together with the boat camera's current view. In addition to the captured image, instance and semantic segmentation of the boat's current view can be recorded as ground truth, along with bounding box annotations of the objects in the simulator. The dataset is then used to pinpoint these explanations in a visual context, i.e. generate grounding visual explanations, through a multi-modal object detector, i.e. MDETR or YOLO-World. The source code and the dataset for explaining the skipper's actions collected using the simulator is available at github.com/dfki-ni/aqua-sim-xai.

Keywords: XAI · Textual Explanation · Interactive Simulator · Unity3D

1 Introduction

In high-stakes domains, Artificial Intelligence (AI) models must provide reliable estimations; otherwise, human end-users might make decisions based on inaccurate or wrong predictions. Aquatic navigation is one of these domains, where AI

M. Bramer and F. Stahl (Eds.): SGAI 2024, LNAI 15446, pp. 144–157, 2025.
https://doi.org/10.1007/978-3-031-77915-2_11

models are being utilised [30]. Even though there are AI systems, which offer explainability by design, e.g. rule-based AI systems [1], others operate as black boxes, where reasoning is complicated [11]. 0Therefore, the prevalent black box models have to be developed and aligned with methods for explainability such that they eventually might transform into glass box models. Moreover, explainability helps end-users to gain trust in the developed AI models.

Here, simulations might be of help. Simulations can mimic real-world scenarios, especially in high-cost/less safe environments such as aquatic environments. For example, in a simulator, visual reasoning of outputs of an AI model can help build trust in a developed system. Additionally, visual reasoning provides better comprehension for end-users who are less familiar with technical concepts of the used models and algorithms [8]. Domain experts can also use these visual aids to verify whether the outputs of the AI models are reasonable and helpful. Thus, simulators can serve as a visualisation tool of aquatic environments that enable the rapid development of applications and help verify complex algorithms' outputs. The use of synthetic datasets to train AI models is becoming more common in the industry [28]. For instance, synthetic datasets are employed in the autonomous car industry to train models and validate developed algorithms [29]. The paper contributes in two interconnected aspects:

1. A simulator framework is developed in Unity 3D to replicate a real-world lake environment. First, this simulator provides a testing and evaluation environment for AI models and algorithms. Moreover, this framework can be used to explain the behaviour of AI algorithms in the aquatic environment by visualising the different actions and decisions in various situations. Furthermore, the simulator enables exploring the behaviour of various aquatic vehicles under different conditions and scenarios. This framework can therefore help build trust in the developed algorithms in a controlled environment before real-world deployment.

2. The developed simulator also provides an interface for collecting textual explanations, which function as ground truth explanations for future algorithms [15]. The paper presents how a textual dataset can be generated, and applied to train AI models to be explainable. In the end, an example scenario is presented, where a human user manually steers a boat in the simulation or can switch to autonomous navigation, and pauses to provide action justifications through this interface to generate a dataset. The generated dataset compares two multi-modal object detectors and grounds the textual explanations visually using these detectors.

The paper is structured as follows. Section 2 shows related work with a focus on textual explanations. Section 3 presents the developed simulator with the functionality of domain randomisation. Section 4 explains how datasets for textual annotations can be generated. Section 5 evaluates the collected dataset with two open-world models for grounded explanations. Section 6 concludes the paper and shows the future work.

2 Related Work

In the context of eXplainable AI (XAI), the idea of explainability embodies a flexible philosophical notion of 'satisfying the subjective curiosity for causal information' [20]. The essence of explainability lies in facilitating comprehension of the comprehensive attributes and limitations of AI models, thereby enabling the anticipation of their behaviours and implementing corrective measures [32]. XAI often shares a common goal, which is making AI models' behaviours understandable for users. It is broadly conceived as encompassing various techniques aimed at enhancing the understandability of AI, including direct interpretability, the generation of explanations or justifications, provision of transparency information, behaviour visualisation, and more [21]. XAI has diverse techniques that depend on the end-user's level of expertise [9].

Visualisation techniques have been employed to reason decision processes in AI models. Instead of presenting complex algorithms or abstract representations, visual explanations can provide instant and interpretable insights into the decision process. Heatmaps and attention maps are the most common forms of visual interpretations [6]. Through visualising the interactions between AI models and their environment, understanding of their functionality can be enhanced, enabling the prediction of their behaviours.

For example, visualising the optimal path within a search environment can serve as a good means of interpretation to justify different decisions taken during path optimisation to achieve diverse objectives within the search constraints, e.g. time constraints, fuel consumption, etc.

The combination of simulation and visualisation can help to provide counterfactual explanations [7] and conduct what-if-analysis in visual forms. This can help to build trust in AI models by revealing reasons for their estimations. Also, it can help in acquiring deeper knowledge about the problem domain, which in turn contributes to the development of more efficient and effective AI models. Thus, visual simulation is a technique that can be considered as an approach towards more interpretability for deep learning algorithms.

Visual simulation has been utilised for AI task planning explanation [26]. AI, particularly Deep Reinforcement Learning (DRL), has been utilised in path planning for various case scenarios. In the domain of autonomous ship docking, DRL with different XAI approaches was conducted [23]. However, these explanations were found to be shallow, because they focus only on the technical aspects such as the forces and the torques exerted by the ship's thrusters, rather than providing descriptive textual explanation. For example, in [12], an explainable DRL algorithm has been developed for navigating an Unmanned Aerial Vehicle (UAV) autonomously. This DRL algorithm generates both visual and textual explanations to justify the actions of the UAV. Its visual explanation method relies on feature attribution [27]. The textual explanations justify the UAV's actions by analysing the differences between the UAV's current and previous states.

Textual explainability has been investigated in the context of self-driving cars as a method to increase trust and reliability by justifying the AI model's decisions

[18]. Several datasets were created and annotated to provide textual justification of a car driver's actions built on top of Berkely Deep Drive (BDD) datasets such as [15] and [33]. These datasets served as ground truth for training an AI model to generate textual explanations to explicitly explain its output [5,33].

For creating a textual explanation dataset for AI models, simulators can be used to save time and cost by utilising synthetic data. To build realistic simulators for the robotics industry, Game engines, such as Unreal Engine and Unity 3D can be utilised. Marine robotics is an example of using realistic simulators such as HoloOcean [25] and Marus [22] for simulating harsh marine environments. These engines, originally designed for creating immersive game worlds and utilised for enhanced graphical experience, are proving to be adaptable to real-world applications. Since game engines are optimized for games and realistic scene creation, their physics engines are reliable for achieving complex physics simulations. On the other side, there are simulators such as Gazebo, which offers better integration with robotics systems and a more capable physics engine but lacks realistic visualisation when compared to game engines [4]. In this paper, we leverage the capabilities of game engines to develop a simulator that recreates an aquatic case scenario for testing and evaluating AI models in the following section.

3   Framework Overview

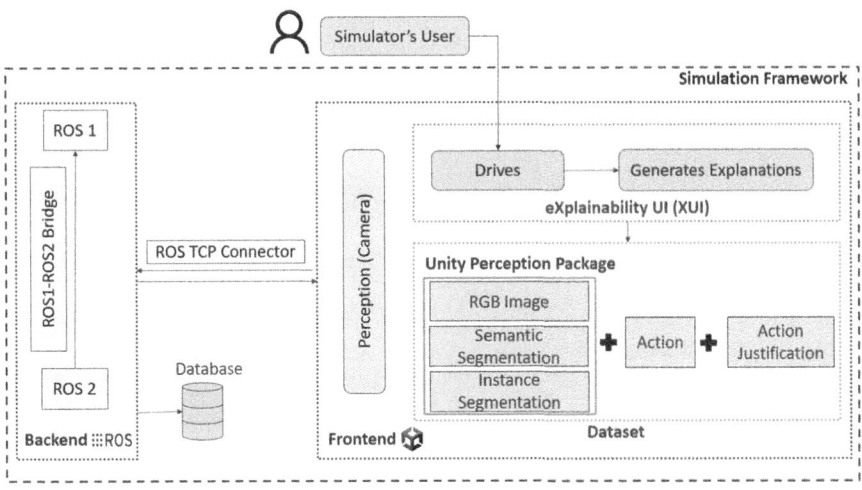

Fig. 1. System overview of the explainable simulation framework.

The interactive explainable framework, illustrated in Fig. 1, can be separated into the backend and the frontend. The backend utilises the Robot Operating System

(ROS) 2 framework as middleware for communication. The frontend consists of a Unity3D simulator with an eXplainability User Interface (XUI) integrated.[1]

In the simulation environment, an operator controls an integrated aquatic vehicle. The operator can generate textual annotations detailing the actions performed. Additionally, explanations for these actions can be provided. These annotations and explanations are captured across various navigation scenarios using the XUI. They are stored in a database to serve later as a dataset, which comprises an **image**, an **action**, and an **action justification**.

The following sections provide a more detailed description of the frontend and the backend together with their key features. This is followed by a description of the domain randomisation and how the dataset is generated through this simulation.

(a)   (b)

Fig. 2. Lake Maschsee in a) Open Street Maps, and b) the simulation in Unity3D.

(a)   (b)

Fig. 3. a) Berky Weed Harvester in operation at Lake Maschsee. b) Simulation of the Berky weed harvester in a virtual Lake Maschsee environment.

---

[1] https://www.unity.com, accessed on: 19-06-2024.

3.1   Frontend: Unity3D

The simulator is implemented in the Unity3D game engine, selected for its ease of use and the availability of open-source packages for integration with ROS. The simulator replicates the lake Maschsee in Hanover, Germany, with the coordinates from Open Street Maps[2] (see Fig. 2). The simulator models the water maintenance scene scenario using a weed harvester from Berky[3] as shown in Fig. 3. Leveraging Unity's High Definition Render Pipeline (HDRP), high-fidelity rendering of water features is achieved, providing a realistic simulation environment. The simulator's modularity enables modifying obstacles' location and environmental conditions, such as weather, to evaluate diverse scenarios. Additionally, the simulator includes dynamic obstacles, such as moving boats on the lake, providing a means to demonstrate the credibility and reliability necessary for aquatic surface vehicles to operate under various conditions.

3.2   Backend: Robot Operating System

The backend features a connection to the simulation through ROS 2, a meta-framework where software, denoted as nodes, communicates through messages. This makes ROS 2 programming language agnostic. Moreover, many algorithms and sensors provide a ROS 2 interface, which facilitates the development and users can test their algorithms without the need for extensive coding. ROS 2 is selected over ROS 1 as the main middleware for Unity3D, as ROS 2 can be used in distributed real-time applications due to the Data Distributed Service (DDS) [24]. Moreover, ROS 2 has a better Quality of Service (QoS), which allows for more reliable messages. Compatibility with ROS 1 is achieved via a ROS 1/2 bridge, which enables seamless integration between these two versions. The communication between the frontend and the backend is carried out through a ROS TCP connector.[4] This way, Machine Learning (ML) algorithms and AI models can be tested, implemented, and observed in the Unity3D simulator while using the ROS 2 environment.

3.3   Domain Randomisation

To address the reality gap between synthetic data generated from the presented simulator and the real-world data, domain randomisation is utilised to create variability in the output data [31]. This requires the simulator to incorporate different scenarios, e.g. different weather conditions as illustrated in Fig. 4. Additionally, users can adjust the visibility of the lake directly within the simulator settings.

---

[2] https://www.openstreetmap.org, accessed on: 19-06-2024.
[3] https://www.berky.de/en/mowing-boats-and-weed-harvester, accessed on: 19-06-2024.
[4] https://github.com/Unity-Technologies/ROS-TCP-Endpoint, accessed on: 19-06-2024.

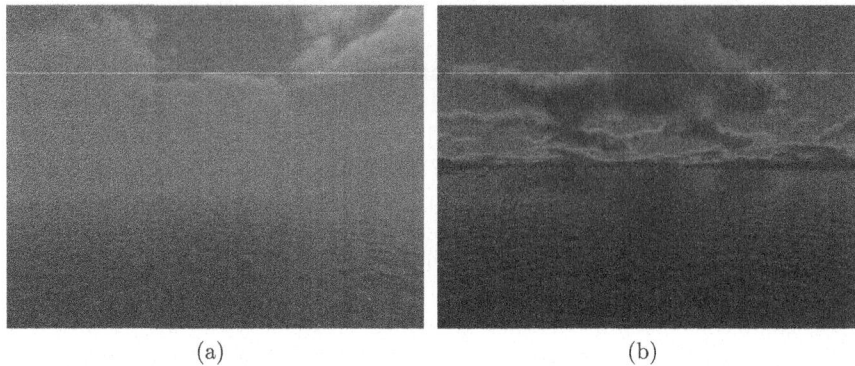

| (a) | (b) |

Fig. 4. Example of different weather conditions in the simulator [a] Foggy night [b] Full moon night.

To mimic real-world scenarios and enhance domain randomisation, various situations can be introduced within the simulated environment. For instance, autonomous patrol boats equipped with collision avoidance systems could navigate the lake using the Unity AI Navigation package.[5] These patrol boats dynamically avoid collisions with other vehicles, leading to unpredictable scenarios. Some of these autonomous boats deliberately operate without collision avoidance, forcing the simulator's user to react to potential collisions. This approach ensures a diverse dataset with a range of challenging situations.

4   Dataset Generation

This section presents the workflow of the annotation process as well as the resulting dataset. The dataset is aimed at textual explainability of the aquatic vehicle's actions.

 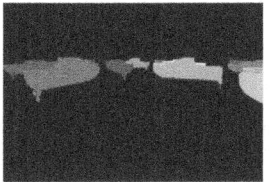 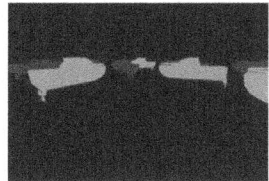

Fig. 5. Simulation output using Unity Perception Package. Images from left to right: original, instance segmentation, and semantic segmentation.

---

[5] https://docs.unity3d.com/Packages/com.unity.ai.navigation@2.0, accessed on: 19-06-2024.

4.1 Annotation Process

The open-source Unity perception package (see Fig. 1) is used for extracting ground truth data from the simulation environment [2]. The ground truth images dataset consists of Instance Segmentation, Semantic Segmentation, and the original image as shown in Fig. 5. Semantic segmentation classifies the image pixels and assigns them to the object class (category). Instance Segmentation assigns each pixel in the image to the specific object it belongs, aiming to delineate individual objects [10]. Combining information about object categories and individual object instances from panoptic segmentation [16]. All these segmentation techniques aim to aid computer vision techniques for better scene understanding.

To generate a dataset, an operator controls an aquatic vehicle and can add justifications for the action taken through an interface - the XUI. The XUI is overlaid on top of the running simulation, as visualised in Fig. 6.

Fig. 6. eXplainability User Interface (XUI) in Unity, where users can type the action and the justification in the corresponding fields, see on the right of the figure.

To provide more freedom and ease of use of the simulator to the operator, two modes are implemented. In the first mode, **Free Roaming**, the operator controls the aquatic vessel and roams freely through the simulation. Here, the operator can pause the simulation and annotate the current view with actions and justifications for their decisions. The second mode is **Autonomous Navigation**, where the vehicle navigates autonomously, utilising the Unity AI Navigation system. This mode saves the operator's effort to navigate and annotate. Thus, this eliminates the need for manual navigation. The operator may leave the autonomous option set to 'ON', pause the simulation, and annotate at their convenience. To narrow down the options for the user, 7 actions, 7 justifications, and 3 weather conditions are predefined, as shown in Table 1. This approach is adopted due to the possibility of multiple ways to describe the same scenario.

Table 1. Predefined list of actions and justifications with weather conditions

Justification	Action	Weather Condition
To avoid collision with underwater rocks	Forward (F)	Day
To avoid the boat coming from the northeast	Right (R)	Night
To avoid the boat coming from the northwest	Left (L)	Fog
To avoid collision with crossing boat(s)	Stop (S)	-
Shore on the left	Move (R, L, F)	-
Shore on the right	Move (R, F)	-
Nothing in the way	Move (L, F)	-

Table 2. Sample of the resulting dataset

ID	Image	Action	Justification	Weather
0		Left, Right or Forward	Nothing in the way	Day
174		Left or Forward	Shore on the right	Night
223		Right or Forward	Shore on the Left	Fog
325		Stop	Collision with crossing boats	Day

4.2   The Resulting Dataset

To assess the outcomes of the textual ground truth dataset generation, a qualitative methodology was employed (see Sect. 5). Exemplary pairings of image, action, and justification were used for evaluation. These pairings include various scenarios and diverse weather conditions, contributing to a comprehensive analysis. Given the complexity of AI systems, it is beneficial for these systems to describe their actions in a human-understandable way. Explanations can be provided through methods like question answering [19] or situation descriptions [15]. There are already some datasets that aim at textual explanations, but often they are not for aquatic use cases [15,33]. This work provides a possibility to generate a dataset for textual explanation in aquatic environments. This dataset could build the foundation for systems that explain the behaviour of an AI path planning. Table 2 shows a sample of the resulting dataset. Each entry includes an image identifier, the image path, the corresponding action taken, the justification for that action, and the weather conditions during the scenario.

5   Dataset Evaluation for XAI Applications

The collected dataset can be used as an example for grounding visual explanations for the current situation [13]. For instance, an AI multi-modal object detector can be trained to provide useful justifications to the end-users for their actions. The dataset used in this context is evaluated by using YOLO-World [3] and MDETR [14]. YOLO-World is a real-time open-vocabulary object detector, that we utilise to ground visual explanations based on the collected dataset. MDETR is a deep learning model that processes both text and image data simultaneously, allowing it to relate descriptions in the text to corresponding elements in the image. Both object detectors use the information from the text input to guide the detection process. Through this, the detectors focus on objects relevant to the text to improve their accuracy. They effectively combine and analyse the information from the image and the text. These algorithms are valuable tools for tasks that require understanding the interplay between language and vision.

In this work, multi-modal object detectors are used as referring expression comprehension models to detect the objects mentioned in justifying the action taken. To assess the accuracy and reliability of these models in grounding visual explanations, a subset of 68 images were selected from the dataset, providing each model with text justifications corresponding to the actions depicted in the images. MDETR achieved a higher Precision of 91.25% and Recall of 89.02%, outperforming YOLO-World, which achieved 57.14% and 51.28%, respectively. Table 3 presents qualitative results comparing MDETR and YOLO-World to assess the visually grounded explanations.

Our evaluation shows that both models can pinpoint the justifications that explain the actions to different degrees. For instance, YOLO-World can detect weather conditions, unlike MDETR. On the other hand, MDETR's pre-trained model cannot detect instances of 'nothing in the way', as it is not trained on negative samples, unlike YOLO-World. Moreover, YOLO-World provides a comprehensive explanation of the action, while MDETR highlights part of the explanation. Notably, MDETR pre-trained model confidence scores may not reliably indicate detection accuracy; for instance, it mistakenly identifies a lake with underwater rocks with 99% confidence. This means we cannot rely on the confidence score of the MDETR pre-trained model to judge the correctness of the detection. In the case of 'Collision with crossing boats', YOLO-World detected only two boats, while MDETR detected six boats. However, not all the detected boats might pose a collision risk. These findings show that these multi-modal object detectors can serve as preliminary verification tools for evaluating the correctness of the collected dataset. However, we cannot completely rely on them; a human would need to approve these verifications and select the main cause of the action's justification.

Table 3. Grounded Visual Explanations for the resulting dataset using MDETR and YOLO-World

YOLO-World	MDETR

Action: Turn Left
Weather Condition: Day
Textual Explanation: Collision with underwater rocks

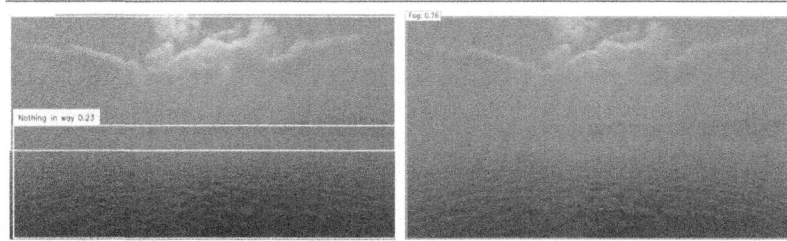

Action: Turn Left, Right or go Forward
Weather Condition: Fog
Textual Explanation: Nothing in the way

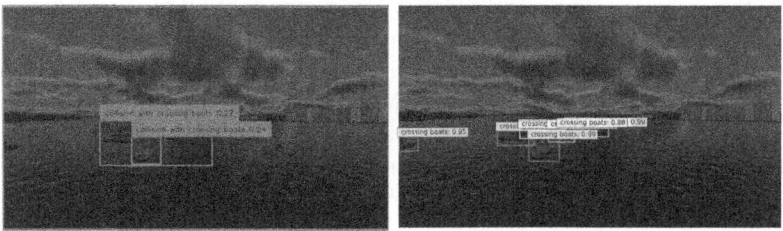

Action: Stop
Weather Condition: Night
Textual Explanation: Collision with crossing boats

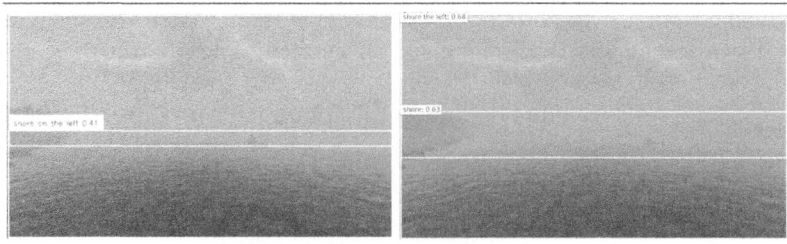

Action: Turn Right or go Forward
Weather Condition: Fog
Textual Explanation: Shore on the Left

6   Conclusion and Future Work

This paper presented an interactive simulator framework based on Unity3D, which recreates an aquatic scenario of a real lake. Users can drive a boat and provide textual justifications for their driving actions. This way, the users generate a synthetic dataset consisting of images, actions, and actions' justification. The resulting dataset is evaluated through a qualitative analysis using multimodal object detectors such as MDETR and YOLO-World. Without further training on our dataset, these models provided grounded visual explanations, allowing for a comparison.

While the simulator is currently operational, further refinement is necessary to enhance its user interface. Future enhancements include adding diverse scenarios for different lakes and open seas. Additionally, integrating microphone input will enable real-time audio explanations, reducing user interruptions compared to typed input [17]. An important feature for future development is to ground the explanations visually using bounding boxes and pinpoint the justification to that bounding box. For instance, if a crossing boat is the cause of why the boat has stopped, then, in the ground truth dataset in addition to the image, a bounding box is drawn around that specific crossing boat. This will facilitate deeper comparisons between different multi-modal detectors that provide a grounded explanation.

This framework could serve as a benchmark for explainability in larger ship vessels, addressing real-world scenarios and enhancing trust in AI-driven autopilot systems. The generated dataset will be used to develop the HAI-X system, focusing on explainability in path planning for weeding boats on Lake Maschsee to gain trust in the developed AI models.

Acknowledgments. This work is done within the HAI-x project, which is funded by the BMBF (Funding number: 01IW23003). We acknowledge the creators of the 'Rock and Boulders 2' (https://assetstore.unity.com/packages/3d/props/exterior/rock-and-boulders-2-6947, accessed on: 19-06-2024) and 'Boats Polypack' (https://assetstore.unity.com/packages/3d/vehicles/sea/boats-polypack-189866, accessed on: 19-06-2024) free asset packs from the Unity Asset Store for their 3D models that we used in creating the simulator and collecting the synthetic dataset in this research.

References

1. Almutairi, M., Stahl, F., Bramer, M.: Reg-rules: an explainable rule-based ensemble learner for classification. IEEE Access **9**, 52015–52035 (2021)
2. Borkman, S., et al.: Unity perception: generate synthetic data for computer vision. arXiv preprint arXiv:2107.04259 (2021)
3. Cheng, T., Song, L., Ge, Y., Liu, W., Wang, X., Shan, Y.: Yolo-world: real-time open-vocabulary object detection. arXiv preprint arXiv:2401.17270 (2024)
4. De Melo, M.S.P., da Silva Neto, J.G., Da Silva, P.J.L., Teixeira, J.M.X.N., Teichrieb, V.: Analysis and comparison of robotics 3d simulators. In: 2019 21st Symposium on Virtual and Augmented Reality (SVR), pp. 242–251. IEEE (2019)

5. Dong, J., Chen, S., Miralinaghi, M., Chen, T., Labi, S.: Development and testing of an image transformer for explainable autonomous driving systems. J. Intell. Connected Veh. **5**(3), 235–249 (2022)
6. El-Mihoub, T.A., El Gadi, A., Nolle, L., Stahl, F.: On object detection and explainability with sonar imagery. In: 2024 IEEE 4th International Maghreb Meeting of the Conference on Sciences and Techniques of Automatic Control and Computer Engineering (MI-STA), pp. 779–786. IEEE (2024)
7. El-Mihoub, T.A., Nolle, L., Stahl, F.: Explainable boosting machines for network intrusion detection with features reduction. In: Bramer, M., Stahl, F. (eds.) SGAI-AI 2022. LNCS, vol. 13652, pp. 280–294. Springer, Cham (2022). https://doi.org/10.1007/978-3-031-21441-7_20
8. Feldkamp, N., Strassburger, S.: From explainable AI to explainable simulation: using machine learning and XAI to understand system robustness. In: Proceedings of the 2023 ACM SIGSIM Conference on Principles of Advanced Discrete Simulation, pp. 96–106 (2023)
9. Gunning, D., Vorm, E., Wang, Y., Turek, M.: Darpa's explainable AI (XAI) program: a retrospective. Authorea Preprints (2021)
10. Hafiz, A.M., Bhat, G.M.: A survey on instance segmentation: state of the art. Int. J. Multimedia Inf. Retrieval **9**(3), 171–189 (2020)
11. Hassija, V., et al.: Interpreting black-box models: a review on explainable artificial intelligence. Cogn. Comput. **16**(1), 45–74 (2024)
12. He, L., Aouf, N., Song, B.: Explainable deep reinforcement learning for UAV autonomous path planning. Aerosp. Sci. Technol. **118**, 107052 (2021)
13. Hendricks, L.A., Hu, R., Darrell, T., Akata, Z.: Grounding visual explanations. In: Proceedings of the European Conference on Computer Vision (ECCV), pp. 264–279 (2018)
14. Kamath, A., Singh, M., LeCun, Y., Synnaeve, G., Misra, I., Carion, N.: MDETR-modulated detection for end-to-end multi-modal understanding. In: Proceedings of the IEEE/CVF International Conference on Computer Vision, pp. 1780–1790 (2021)
15. Kim, J., Rohrbach, A., Darrell, T., Canny, J., Akata, Z.: Textual explanations for self-driving vehicles. In: Proceedings of the European Conference on Computer Vision (ECCV) (2018)
16. Kirillov, A., He, K., Girshick, R., Rother, C., Dollár, P.: Panoptic segmentation. In: Proceedings of the IEEE/CVF Conference on Computer Vision and Pattern Recognition, pp. 9404–9413 (2019)
17. Kühn, M.A., Omeiza, D., Kunze, L.: Textual explanations for automated commentary driving. In: 2023 IEEE Intelligent Vehicles Symposium (IV), pp. 1–6. IEEE (2023)
18. Kuznietsov, A., Gyevnar, B., Wang, C., Peters, S., Albrecht, S.V.: Explainable AI for safe and trustworthy autonomous driving: a systematic review. arXiv preprint arXiv:2402.10086 (2024)
19. Lanchantin, J., Sukhbaatar, S., Synnaeve, G., Sun, Y., Srinet, K., Szlam, A.: A data source for reasoning embodied agents (2023)
20. Li, X.H., et al.: A survey of data-driven and knowledge-aware explainable AI. IEEE Trans. Knowl. Data Eng. **34**(1), 29–49 (2022). https://doi.org/10.1109/TKDE.2020.2983930
21. Liao, Q.V., Varshney, K.R.: Human-centered explainable AI (XAI): from algorithms to user experiences (2022)
22. Lončar, I., et al.: MARUS-a marine robotics simulator. In: OCEANS 2022, Hampton Roads, pp. 1–7. IEEE (2022)

23. Løver, J., Gjærum, V.B., Lekkas, A.M.: Explainable AI methods on a deep reinforcement learning agent for automatic docking. IFAC-PapersOnLine **54**(16), 146–152 (2021)
24. Maruyama, Y., Kato, S., Azumi, T.: Exploring the performance of ROS2. In: Proceedings of the 13th International Conference on Embedded Software, pp. 1–10 (2016)
25. Potokar, E., Ashford, S., Kaess, M., Mangelson, J.G.: Holoocean: an underwater robotics simulator. In: 2022 International Conference on Robotics and Automation (ICRA), pp. 3040–3046. IEEE (2022)
26. Roberts, J.O., Mastorakis, G., Lazaruk, B., Franco, S., Stokes, A.A., Bernardini, S.: vPlanSim: an open source graphical interface for the visualisation and simulation of AI systems. In: Proceedings of the International Conference on Automated Planning and Scheduling, vol. 31, pp. 486–490 (2021)
27. Shrikumar, A., Greenside, P., Kundaje, A.: Learning important features through propagating activation differences. In: International Conference on Machine Learning, pp. 3145–3153. PMLR (2017)
28. Song, Z., et al.: Synthetic datasets for autonomous driving: a survey. IEEE Trans. Intell. Veh. (2023)
29. Talwar, D., Guruswamy, S., Ravipati, N., Eirinaki, M.: Evaluating validity of synthetic data in perception tasks for autonomous vehicles. In: 2020 IEEE International Conference on Artificial Intelligence Testing (AITest), pp. 73–80. IEEE (2020)
30. Thombre, S., et al.: Sensors and AI techniques for situational awareness in autonomous ships: a review. IEEE Trans. Intell. Transp. Syst. **23**(1), 64–83 (2020)
31. Tobin, J., Fong, R., Ray, A., Schneider, J., Zaremba, W., Abbeel, P.: Domain randomization for transferring deep neural networks from simulation to the real world. In: 2017 IEEE/RSJ International Conference on Intelligent Robots and Systems (IROS), pp. 23–30. IEEE (2017)
32. Viseras, A., Wiedemann, T., Manss, C., Karolj, V., Juan Marchal, D.S.: Beehiveinspired information gathering with a swarm of autonomous drones. Sensors **19**(19), E4349 (2019). https://doi.org/10.3390/s19194349. https://europepmc.org/articles/PMC6806085
33. Xu, Y., et al.: Explainable object-induced action decision for autonomous vehicles. In: Proceedings of the IEEE/CVF Conference on Computer Vision and Pattern Recognition, pp. 9523–9532 (2020)

Detection of Vascular Leukoencephalopathy in CT Images

Zuzana Cernekova$^{(\boxtimes)}$ (iD), Viktor Sisik, and Fatana Jafari (iD)

Faculty of Mathematics Physics and Informatics, Comenius University Bratislava,
Bratislava, Slovakia
{zuzana.cernekova,sisik1,fatana.jafari}@uniba.sk

Abstract. Artificial intelligence (AI) has seen a significant surge in popularity, particularly in its application to medicine. This study explores AI's role in diagnosing leukoencephalopathy, a small vessel disease of the brain, and a leading cause of vascular dementia and hemorrhagic strokes. We utilized a dataset of approximately 1200 patients with axial brain CT scans to train convolutional neural networks (CNNs) for binary disease classification. Addressing the challenge of varying scan dimensions due to different patient physiologies, we processed the data to a uniform size and applied three preprocessing methods to improve model accuracy. We compared four neural network architectures: ResNet50, ResNet50 3D, ConvNext, and Densenet. The ConvNext model achieved the highest accuracy of 98.5% without any preprocessing, outperforming models with 3D convolutions. To gain insights into model decision-making, we implemented Grad-CAM heatmaps, which highlighted the focus areas of the models on the scans. Our results demonstrate that AI, particularly the ConvNext architecture, can significantly enhance diagnostic accuracy for leukoencephalopathy. This study underscores AI's potential in advancing diagnostic methodologies for brain diseases and highlights the effectiveness of CNNs in medical imaging applications.

Keywords: CNN · Leukoencephalopathy · CT scans · Grad-CAM

1 Introduction

The rapid advancement and integration of artificial intelligence (AI) in various fields have notably impacted medicine. AI technologies are transforming diagnostic approaches and patient care, offering new insights into complex medical conditions. One such condition is leukoencephalopathy, a disease of small brain vessels also known as cerebral microangiopathy. This condition is the most common cause of vascular dementia and a major contributor to hemorrhagic strokes, necessitating effective diagnostic tools. Figure 1 illustrates two CT brain scans: one with marked leukoencephalopathy and a comparative slice without it.

Current diagnostic methods for leukoencephalopathy rely heavily on brain imaging techniques such as computed tomography (CT) scans. However, the

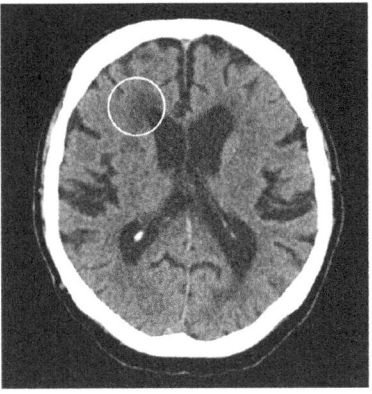 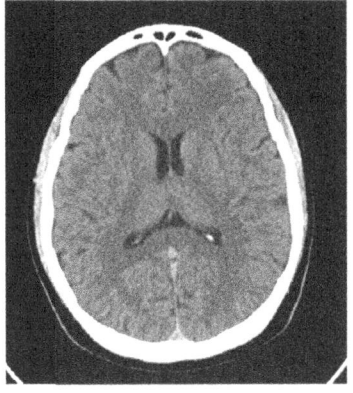

Fig. 1. Leukoencephalopathy on a CT scan - the left image shows a brain slice with leukoencephalopathy marked in a white circle; the right image shows a brain slice without leukoencephalopathy

interpretation of these scans requires significant expertise and can be time-consuming. AI, particularly convolutional neural networks (CNNs), offers a promising solution by automating and potentially improving the accuracy of such diagnoses.

In this study, we leverage a dataset of approximately 1200 patients with axial brain CT scans to train CNN models for the binary classification of leukoencephalopathy. We address challenges such as varying scan dimensions due to different patient physiologies by preprocessing the data to a uniform size. Furthermore, we employ three different preprocessing methods to enhance model accuracy and compare the performance of four neural network architectures: ResNet50 [8], ResNet50 3D, ConvNext [11], and Densenet [9].

Our findings indicate that the ConvNext architecture achieved the highest classification accuracy of 98.6% without any preprocessing. We also utilized Grad-CAM to generate heatmaps, providing insights into the regions of the scans that the models focused on during classification. This research underscores the potential of AI in advancing diagnostic methodologies for brain diseases, particularly leukoencephalopathy, and sets the stage for further exploration and refinement of AI-driven diagnostic tools in clinical settings.

2   Related Work

Leukoencephalopathy is an active research area. Recent 2024 studies include neurosurgical perspectives on cerebral calcifications and cysts [16], atypical MRI features in progressive multifocal leukoencephalopathy, and advanced imaging techniques for chemoradiotherapy-induced leukoencephalopathy [4].

2.1   Medical Image Processing

In this section, we review previous approaches and studies in the field of artificial intelligence that have influenced our work. The article [6] addresses the classification of brain CT scans into hemorrhagic, ischemic, and normal categories. It tackles two main areas: image preprocessing and image classification using neural networks.

The proposed approach for medical image preprocessing (CT slices) focuses on removing contrast abnormalities to improve classification accuracy. This involves creating two copies of input images, performing contrast adjustments for better visualization on the first copy, and applying average filtering on the second. The preprocessed images are then merged together to form a single image.

Regarding model architectures, the article introduces a newly proposed architecture of convolutional neural networks called P_CNN. Unlike other deep learning architectures, P_CNN can process CT scan images without resizing them, which is crucial for preserving image quality. The architecture includes the use of 96 filters in the second layer, convolution with the input layer, ReLU activation, and max pooling. The article also compares P_CNN with other CNN architectures such as AlexNet and ResNet50.

Overall, this approach involves a detailed algorithm for image preprocessing and the use of the P_CNN framework for image classification.

In article [17], the authors described a model for lung cancer classification trained on CT scans. They outlined the process of working with CT scans in DICOM format and their conversion into Hounsfield units.

Article [15] focuses on developing deep convolutional neural networks for detecting COVID-19 from medical images, proposing a single architecture for both CT scans and X-ray images simultaneously. The authors discuss the importance of rapid and reliable COVID-19 detection, emphasizing the need for effective tools for the diagnosis and monitoring of this disease. They highlight the significance of comparing COVID-19 with other coronavirus diseases to better understand its characteristics and spread. The article describes a proposed deep neural network, experimentation methods, and achieved results, focusing on optimizing parameters for the best model performance.

The proposed neural network in the article consists of 3 alternating convolutional and pooling layers. The convolutional layers had 32, 16, and 8 filters with sizes of 5×5, 4×4, and 3×3, respectively, using ReLU activation.

Within the article, the authors compared their proposed model with other architectures like InceptionV3, MobileNet, and ResNet, where their model outperformed all others with an accuracy of 96.28%. Additionally, their proposed model had significantly fewer parameters compared to other model architectures.

In further research [19], a convolutional neural network was proposed for the binary classification of chest CT scans into COVID-19 positive and negative cases. The dataset used in the article consisted of 746 CT scans collected from 216 patients, including 349 images from COVID-19-infected patients and 397 from non-infected patients. The images varied in dimensions, with heights ranging from 153 to 1853 and widths from 153 to 1485. These images were collected by a radiologist in Wuhan during the COVID-19 outbreak from January to April 2020 and are publicly available for research.

For model training, all images were resized to a uniform size of 150×150 pixels and labeled according to classes 0 (negative) and 1 (positive). The entire dataset was then split into a training subset comprising 80% of the total dataset and a testing subset comprising 20%. Both divided datasets were normalized between values of 0–1.

The authors employed algorithms for binary classification using CNNs with hyperparameters to achieve higher accuracy in detecting COVID-19. The algorithm involved tuning hyperparameters such as different numbers of epochs, batch sizes, and various optimizers. The trained model with the best parameters achieved an accuracy of 86.9%.

3   Dataset

We have acquired a dataset of CT scans from the hospital of St. Cyril and Methodius in Bratislava. The dataset consisted of 1244 folders, each named with a numerical identifier (ID) representing anonymized patients. Each patient's folder contained .DCM (DICOM) files for individual scan slices and a .json file with the same numerical identifier, which included metadata such as medical findings, examination number, and the doctor's name. This study focused exclusively on brain slices in a specific plane, filtering out other body parts or planes.

Medical imaging data, particularly CT scans, are usually stored in DICOM (Digital Imaging and Communications in Medicine) format. This standard is widely used in modern medical imaging devices due to its ease of integration and continuous development. DICOM files, represented as ".dcm", consist of a header and image data encapsulated in one file. The header contains patient demographics, acquisition parameters, image dimensions, and intensity data necessary for proper image display. This encapsulation ensures that image data cannot be separated from the header, maintaining the integrity and context of the image.

CT scan data are expressed in Hounsfield Units (HU), which are linear transformations of measured X-ray absorption coefficients relative to water. These units serve as gray levels in the voxels of CT images. A voxel, or volumetric pixel, is a data point on a three-dimensional grid. In CT imaging, voxels represent the varying densities within the scanned volume, providing a detailed three-dimensional representation of the scanned area. Bones appear lighter on CT images due to their higher density and greater radiation absorption, while water and air appear darker. The standard conversion formula for calculating HU for any material is:

$$HU = \frac{\mu - \mu_{water}}{\mu_{water} - \mu_{air}} \times 1000 \tag{1}$$

where μ is the absorption coefficient of the examined region.

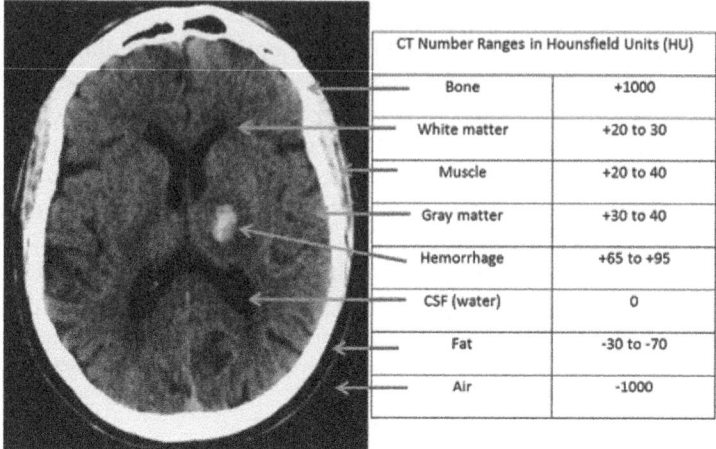

CT Number Ranges in Hounsfield Units (HU)	
Bone	+1000
White matter	+20 to 30
Muscle	+20 to 40
Gray matter	+30 to 40
Hemorrhage	+65 to +95
CSF (water)	0
Fat	-30 to -70
Air	-1000

Fig. 2. Example of Hounsfield Unit values in different brain regions. From top to bottom, the values are for bone, white matter, muscle, gray matter, hemorrhage, water, fat, and air [10].

4   CNN Architectures

Convolutional Neural Networks (CNNs) are the cornerstone of many successful applications in image processing. Among the most well-known architectures are *ResNet50*, *DenseNet*, *VGGNet*, and *ConvNeXt*, all of which have significantly advanced the field of computer vision. Below, we briefly describe the architectures utilized in this work.

ResNet50 is a foundational CNN architecture that employs residual blocks to enhance the efficiency of deep learning. This architecture includes 50 layers, comprising convolutional and fully connected layers. Residual blocks enable information to be transmitted through multiple layers of the network without loss or learning difficulties. This approach helps address the vanishing gradient problem in deep neural networks, where adding more layers can lead to poorer performance due to learning issues [7].

DenseNet is another prominent CNN architecture consisting of transition layers and dense blocks. Each convolutional layer in a dense block is connected to all other layers within the block. This unique mechanism enhances the network's learning capacity by repeatedly leveraging features and reducing parameter requirements, thereby improving gradient flow during training [20].

ConvNeXt (Convolutional Neural Network eXtended) represents an innovative architecture that significantly pushes the boundaries of CNNs. ConvNeXt combines CNNs and transformers to leverage the strengths of both architectures. It employs bottleneck layers inspired by transformer architecture, where the number of elements is downsampled and upsampled, along with deep convolutions and residual blocks. Unlike traditional CNNs that heavily use Rectified Linear Units (ReLU), ConvNeXt replaces ReLU with Gaussian Error Linear

Units (GeLU). The hybrid nature of ConvNeXt allows it to achieve superior results in various computer vision tasks [2,12].

These architectures represent a fundamental part of the rich spectrum of CNNs that have a significant impact on the field of computer vision. Each has unique features and advantages tailored to different tasks and application needs in image processing.

All the mentioned architectures are typically designed with *2D* convolutional layers; however, in our work, we also explored their *3D* convolutional counterparts. CNN architectures may have specific requirements for minimum image size due to their configuration and filter schemes, which are critical for their efficiency and performance. Filtering local parts of an image with small kernels in convolutional layers can be more challenging with smaller dimensions, potentially degrading the network's ability to capture relevant patterns [1].

5   Data Preprocessing

In this session, we will describe data preprocessing done before training the CNN model. Data preprocessing is essential in preparing medical imaging data for machine learning models. This process ensures that the data is standardized and optimized for effective model training and analysis. In our study, we adopted several preprocessing steps to enhance the quality and consistency of the input data.

5.1   Depth Normalization

Initially, all brain images of each patient were standardized to a uniform *depth*, which represents the number of stacked 2D slices in the final 3D image. The variation in depth is due to differences in head sizes among patients and variations in the determination of scan start/end points by technicians before each CT scan (initial images typically show only air-black).

The central slice and the surrounding slices were chosen based on the *depth* and *center_position* parameters as follows: We set the *center_position* of the new volume to $\frac{3}{5}$ of the total number of slices n from the start of the skull to the neck. Therefore, the central p-th slice is calculated as $p = n \times center\_position$. We then select $p \pm \frac{depth}{2}$ slices from this central slice. In our settings, *depth* was set to 30 slices.

5.2   Resizing Scans

Then we resize the images to ensure uniform dimensions, a crucial step for machine learning models requiring fixed-size inputs. In our study, most patient scan slices had dimensions of $512 \times 512 \times depth$, with depth varying per patient due to physiological differences. However, we encountered instances where scan dimensions were $512 \times \mathbf{600} \times depth$. These outliers needed to be resized to match the majority dimension to facilitate their inclusion in tensors for further processing.

Beyond ensuring uniform dimensions, resizing images is crucial for computational efficiency. Reducing the size of large images can significantly decrease the computational resources required for training and inference in machine learning models. Smaller images typically lead to faster training times and lower memory consumption, which is especially beneficial when working with large datasets. Therefore, we reduced the image size to 256×256, optimizing for consistency and computational efficiency.

5.3   Pixel Value Rescaling

We selected only the pixel values (x) from the interval $< 0, 100 >$ and normalized them to the range $< 0, 1 >$ using the formula

$$x = \begin{cases} 1 & \text{if } x >= 100 \\ 0 & \text{if } x < 0 \\ x/100 & \text{else} \end{cases} \tag{2}$$

5.4   Preprocessing A

In our study, we utilized different combinations of preprocessing methods. In the first approach, we applied only the common preprocessing steps mentioned above.

5.5   Preprocessing B - with Filtering and Morphological Operations

In the second approach, we added the following image processing steps in addition to the common preprocessing steps:

– Filtering: We removed pixels that represented calcifications, skull, and water, following the formula:

$$x = \begin{cases} 0 & \text{if } x \geq 0.8 \\ 0 & \text{if } x \leq 0.18 \\ x & \text{otherwise} \end{cases} \tag{3}$$

– Morphological operation: We applied the morphological opening operation with a structuring element of size 4×4. This operation helps reduce noise by performing erosion followed by dilation, thus enhancing the target areas.

5.6   Preprocessing C - with Mean Filtering and Contrast Adjustment

In the third approach, we applied mean filtering and contrast adjustment in addition to the common preprocessing steps.

– Mean filtering: We applied a mean filter with a kernel size of 3×3 to reduce noise and smooth the images.
– Contrast adjustment: We adjusted the image contrast by stretching the intensity range between the darker regions (pixel values around $low = 0.15$) and the lighter regions (pixel values around $high = 0.65$). This technique, inspired by *skimage's* rescale intensity function, enhances the visibility of critical structures within the scans.
– Filtering: We removed all pixels with a value of $x = 1$ to eliminate irrelevant areas such as the skull.

5.7   Data Augmentation

Data augmentation is a crucial technique in training convolutional neural networks (CNNs), which are known for their high data requirements. It involves applying diverse transformations to existing images to enhance the diversity of the training dataset. This helps CNNs generalize better to different variations in input data and improves their performance on unseen test data. Augmentation is especially beneficial when the training dataset is limited in size, effectively increasing its size and reducing overfitting. Common augmentations include rotation, scaling, flipping, and adding noise [5,13].

In our study, we applied rotation to simulate variations in patient positioning during scans, ensuring our models learn robust features. We also used horizontal flipping to account for the absence of statistically dominant findings of leukoencephalopathy on a specific side of the brain. These augmentations aimed to enhance the model's ability to generalize across different orientations and conditions encountered in medical imaging analysis.

6   Training Details and Obtained Results

We divided the data into three subsets without further modifications: training, validation, and testing in the ratios 70 : 15 : 15. Class balance was maintained naturally as the dataset contained a near 1:1 ratio of patients with leukoencephalopathy (633) and without (611). No additional class weighting was applied during training, but we ensured an equal distribution across the training, validation, and test sets.

The architectures we compared were ResNet50, ResNet50 3D, ConvNext DenseNet. For training **2D models**, we identified the following optimal hyperparameters: a learning rate of 10^{-5}, the Adam optimizer, a batch size of 64, and 50 epochs.

For training the **3D model**, the optimal hyperparameters were a learning rate of 10^{-5}, the Adam optimizer, a batch size of 2, and 50 epochs.

During each training session, we utilized *early stopping* when the model's performance ceased to improve after several epochs.

For our training, we used pre-trained models with weights from the *ImageNet* dataset, which consists of color images with 3 channels. To match this format, we replicated our grayscale data three times to create the necessary number of channels.

A significant issue encountered was *overfitting* during the training of 3D models. Approximately 1000 data samples were used for training, and the model struggled to generalize well on new data.

6.1   Evaluation

In this section, we evaluate the performance of model architectures on the pre-processed data. We used binary accuracy as our accuracy metric, which measures how often the predicted values y_{pred} match the actual values y_{true}. Mathematically, it is defined as:

$$binary_{accuracy} = \frac{count(y_{pred} == y_{true})}{n} \tag{4}$$

where n is the total number of elements in the test set. We used binary cross-entropy (BCE) as the loss function, which is commonly used in binary classification problems. BCE measures the dissimilarity between the true classes and the predicted ones.

It is important to note that we evaluated the classification accuracy of the models on individual slices in the case of 2D models and on selected slices for the 3D models. The slice selection method is described in Sect. 5.1. This means we did not evaluate the accuracy of classifying individual patients based on their CT scans.

It is important to clarify that our evaluation focused on the classification accuracy of individual CT slices rather than entire patient scans. For 2D models, we assessed accuracy on each slice separately, while for 3D models, only a selected subset of slices was evaluated, as described in Sect. 5.1. This approach means that patients could be represented by multiple slices, potentially leading to multiple evaluations for a single patient. Thus, the reported accuracy reflects slice-level performance, not patient-level diagnosis.

The results of training various model architectures using data preprocessing type A, B, and C are shown in Table 1.

Table 1. Results on validation data set preprocessed using methods A, B and C

	Model	ResNet50	ResNet50 3D	ConvNeXt	DenseNet
preprocessing A	AVG	92.5%	75.7%	95.9%	93.3%
	BEST	95.7%	79.0%	**98.6%**	94.5%
preprocessing B	AVG	85.5%	74.4%	87.3%	84.0%
	BEST	86.0%	79.0%	88.2%	85.9%
preprocessing C	AVG	90.9%	74.4%	86.4%	89.4%
	BEST	92.5%	76.6%	89.6%	90.3%

The recorded results were obtained from the classification accuracy on the validation set, which matched the accuracy on the test data within a deviation of ±3%. The evaluation of the models consisted of more than 8 trained models in each case, meaning that the AVG row in the tables represents the average accuracy results of the models on the validation data from more than 8 different training sessions of the same model and training parameters. The BEST row indicates the best results among these training sessions.

Table 2. Results on test data set preprocessed using methods A, B and C

	Model	ResNet50	ResNet50 3D	ConvNeXt
preprocessing A	AVG	94.1%	71.7%	92.6%
	BEST	94,7%	77.6%	**98.5%**
preprocessing B	AVG	88.8%	75.2%	87.3%
	BEST	91.4%	75.8%	88.1%
preprocessing C	AVG	87.2%	74.8%	87.2%
	BEST	88.2%	78.3%	89.3%

The results on the test set are shown in Table 2. Models of all architectures achieved the best results without any data preprocessing. The overall best-performing model, with an accuracy of 98.5% on the test set, was the ConvNeXt architecture.

A few words on model accuracy. The trained models aim not to replace doctors but to provide an objective tool for aiding diagnosis. Therefore, the model should ideally have as few false negatives as possible, even at the cost of higher false positives, which a doctor can then review. The problem arises when the model fails to identify a patient who should be classified as positive.

6.2   Discussion

The main issue in this study was the small dataset specific to the problem. Training models with architectures using 3D convolutional layers often led to overfitting, even with increased regularization or data augmentation.

Another significant challenge was the selection of slices (images) for training the neural network. Only a few slices from the entire scan contain areas of leukoencephalopathy. Finding a general rule for selecting these slices is difficult due to different brain physiologies and associated conditions (e.g., brain atrophy). Strict rules often eliminate useful slices, resulting in a very small trained set. Looser rules included slices without leukoencephalopathy, potentially skewing model accuracy.

In 2D models, a voting system could be introduced to determine the final classification of a patient, mitigating the issue of "poorly" selected slices mentioned above. The voting would involve dividing the entire CT scan into k 2D slices, classifying each, and setting a threshold $t \in\ <1, k>$. If the number of positively classified slices p exceeds t, the patient would be classified as positive.

7   Grad-CAM

Grad-CAM, short for Gradient-weighted Class Activation Mapping, is a technique used to visualize which parts of an image are most important for a convolutional neural network (CNN) to make predictions about the class. Grad-CAM operates by computing gradients of the score (the network assigns a score to each class - a probability) concerning the last convolutional layer. These gradients are then used to generate a *heatmap* that highlights the regions of the image contributing the most to the prediction of a specific class. In other words, it projects a heatmap onto the image indicating where the model is "looking" when making its prediction.

Grad-CAM is used to enhance the interpretability of CNN models by helping understand the decisions made by the model during prediction through the visualization of regions of interest.

In medical practice, the advantages of Grad-CAM can provide an objective tool to obtain a second opinion on medical data. It assists doctors in highlighting important areas, thereby increasing diagnostic accuracy. Moreover, it supports medical education by illustrating how CNNs analyze images, aiding students in understanding diagnostic thinking [3,14,18].

In the case of leukoencephalopathy, the model must focus primarily on the areas of the brain's ventricles, where the problem is located, rather than on the periphery of the brain. This is because an estimated 80–90% of patients exhibit associated brain atrophy alongside leukoencephalopathy. By utilizing Grad-CAM, it is possible to evaluate the model more comprehensively from a different perspective beyond just classification accuracy on test data. In Figs. 3 and 4 we can observe that the networks focus on the regions where leukoencephalopathy typically appears.

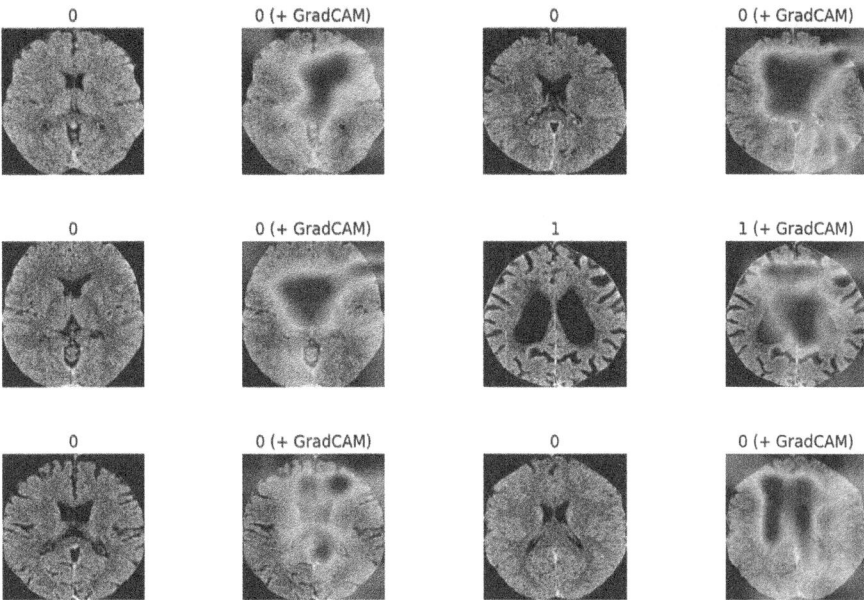

Fig. 3. Grad-CAM on test data for a ConvNeXt model trained on preprocessed Type C data is visualized in four columns. The first column displays the test data with their respective classes in the header (0 - negative, 1 - positive). The second column overlays the image with a heatmap (darker areas indicate higher attention), highlighting the regions the model focuses on. The header of this column states the predicted class of the image by the trained network. The same format applies to the third and fourth columns.

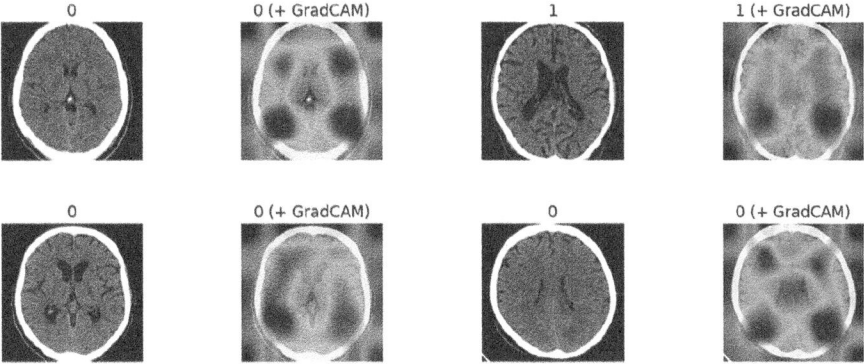

Fig. 4. Grad-CAM on test data for a ResNet50 model trained on preprocessed Type A data is visualized in four columns. The first column displays the test data with their respective classes in the header (0 - negative, 1 - positive). The second column overlays the image with a heatmap (darker areas indicate higher attention), highlighting the regions the model focuses on. The header of this column states the predicted class of the image by the trained network. The same format applies to the third and fourth columns.

8   Conclusion and Future Work

This study aimed to explore methods for processing medical data, specifically CT scans, and to train an AI model capable of accurately classifying CT slices containing leukoencephalopathy. Developing well-annotated datasets is crucial for training models that can effectively integrate AI into daily medical practice, potentially saving time for healthcare professionals and improving patient outcomes.

We tested three different preprocessing approaches for CT scans, finding that the approach with minimal preprocessing was the most effective. We employed four different model architectures: ResNet50, DenseNet, ConvNeXt, and ResNet50 with 3D convolutional layers. ConvNeXt achieved the highest accuracy of 98.5% on the test set. Although several trained models demonstrated satisfactory accuracy, the limited dataset size was a constraint, particularly for models with 3D convolutional layers, which frequently encountered overfitting issues. The ResNet50 variant with 3D layers showed lower accuracy, but it holds the potential for better capturing the deeper connections between CT scan slices with further data and refinement.

In our dataset, an estimated 80–90% of patients had comorbid brain atrophy, visible on CT scans as dark protrusions around the brain's perimeter. We used Grad-CAM heatmaps to highlight the regions where the model focused during classification, providing an additional layer of verification for the model's accuracy.

Future research should focus on expanding the dataset to improve the robustness and generalizability of the models, particularly those utilizing 3D convolutional layers. Investigating advanced preprocessing techniques and their impact on model performance will be essential. Additionally, developing methods for better slice selection and classification, including the use of ensemble techniques and voting mechanisms, could enhance model accuracy and reliability.

Acknowledgments. This publication was supported by projects: the TERAIS project, Horizon-Wider-2021 programme of the European Union under grant agreement number 101079338, project APVV-23-0250, and student project UK/3190/2024.

Disclosure of Interests. The authors have no competing interests to declare that are relevant to the content of this article.

References

1. Adaloglou, N.: Understanding the receptive field of deep convolutional networks (2020). https://theaisummer.com/. https://theaisummer.com/receptive-field/
2. Ahmadian, A., Liu, L.S., Fei, Y., Plataniotis, K.N., Hosseini, M.S.: Pseudo-inverted bottleneck convolution for darts search space. In: 2023 IEEE International Conference on Acoustics, Speech and Signal Processing (ICASSP 2023), pp. 1–5. IEEE (2023)

3. Aravinda, C., Lin, M., Udaya Kumar Reddy, K., Amar Prabhu, G.: 23 - a demystifying convolutional neural networks using grad-cam for prediction of coronavirus disease (covid-19) on x-ray images. In: Kose, U., Gupta, D., de Albuquerque, V.H.C., Khanna, A. (eds.) Data Science for COVID-19, pp. 429–450. Academic Press (2021). https://doi.org/10.1016/B978-0-12-824536-1.00037-X
4. Celardo, G., et al.: Case report: exploring chemoradiotherapy-induced leukoencephalopathy with 7t imaging and quantitative susceptibility mapping. Front. Neurol. **15**, 1362704 (2024). https://doi.org/10.3389/fneur.2024.1362704
5. Cirillo, M.D., Abramian, D., Eklund, A.: What is the best data augmentation for 3D brain tumor segmentation? In: 2021 IEEE International Conference on Image Processing (ICIP), pp. 36–40 (2021). https://doi.org/10.1109/ICIP42928.2021.9506328
6. Gautam, A., Raman, B.: Towards effective classification of brain hemorrhagic and ischemic stroke using CNN. Biomed. Signal Process. Control **63**, 102178 (2021)
7. He, K., Zhang, X., Ren, S., Sun, J.: Deep residual learning for image recognition (2015). https://arxiv.org/abs/1512.03385
8. He, K., Zhang, X., Ren, S., Sun, J.: Deep residual learning for image recognition. In: 2016 IEEE Conference on Computer Vision and Pattern Recognition (CVPR), pp. 770–778 (2016). https://doi.org/10.1109/CVPR.2016.90
9. Huang, G., Liu, Z., Van Der Maaten, L., Weinberger, K.Q.: Densely connected convolutional networks. In: 2017 IEEE Conference on Computer Vision and Pattern Recognition (CVPR), pp. 2261–2269 (2017). https://doi.org/10.1109/CVPR.2017.243
10. Kamalian, S., Lev, M.H., Gupta, R.: Chapter 1 - Computed tomography imaging and angiography – principles. In: Handbook of Clinical Neurology, vol. 135. Elsevier (2016). https://doi.org/10.1016/B978-0-444-53485-9.00001-5. https://www.sciencedirect.com/science/article/pii/B9780444534859000015
11. Liu, Z., Mao, H., Wu, C.Y., Feichtenhofer, C., Darrell, T., Xie, S.: A convnet for the 2020s. In: 2022 IEEE/CVF Conference on Computer Vision and Pattern Recognition (CVPR), pp. 11966–11976 (2022). https://doi.org/10.1109/CVPR52688.2022.01167
12. Liu, Z., Mao, H., Wu, C.Y., Feichtenhofer, C., Darrell, T., Xie, S.: A convnet for the 2020s. In: Proceedings of the IEEE/CVF Conference on Computer Vision and Pattern Recognition, pp. 11976–11986 (2022)
13. Michelucci, U.: Advanced Applied Deep Learning: Convolutional Neural Networks and Object Detection. Apress (2019). https://books.google.sk/books?id=hJyyDwAAQBAJ
14. Moujahid, H., et al.: Combining CNN and grad-cam for covid-19 disease prediction and visual explanation. Intell. Autom. Soft Comput. **32**(2), 723–745 (2022). https://doi.org/10.32604/iasc.2022.022179
15. Mukherjee, H., Ghosh, S., Dhar, A., Obaidullah, S.M., Santosh, K., Roy, K.: Deep neural network to detect covid-19: one architecture for both CT scans and chest X-rays. Appl. Intell. **51**, 2777–2789 (2021)
16. Novegno, F., Iaquinandi, A., Ruggiero, F., Salvati, M.: Leukoencephalopathy with cerebral calcifications and cysts: the neurosurgical perspective. literature review. World Neurosurg. **190**, 99–112 (2024)
17. Polat, H., Danaei Mehr, H.: Classification of pulmonary CT images by using hybrid 3D-deep convolutional neural network architecture. Appl. Sci. **9**(5), 940 (2019)
18. Selvaraju, R.R., Cogswell, M., Das, A., Vedantam, R., Parikh, D., Batra, D.: Grad-cam: visual explanations from deep networks via gradient-based localization. Int.

J. Comput. Vision **128**(2), 336–359 (2019). https://doi.org/10.1007/s11263-019-01228-7

19. Shambhu, S., Koundal, D., Das, P., Sharma, C.: Binary classification of covid-19 CT images using CNN: covid diagnosis using CT. Int. J. E-Health Med. Commun. (IJEHMC) **13**(2), 1–13 (2021)
20. Yilmaz, F., Kose, O., Demir, A.: Comparison of two different deep learning architectures on breast cancer. In: 2019 Medical Technologies Congress (TIPTEKNO), pp. 1–4 (2019). https://doi.org/10.1109/TIPTEKNO47231.2019.8972042

Large Language Models

PlanBERT: From Messy Zonal Plans to Informative Vector Embeddings

Henrik Brådland[1,2](✉) 🆔, Morten Goodwin[1] 🆔, Per-Arne Andersen[1] 🆔,
and Alexander S. Nossum[2] 🆔

[1] Centre for Artificial Intelligence Research, University of Agder, Kristiansand,
Norway
henbra@norkart.no
[2] Norkart AS, Oslo, Norway

Abstract. Text embedding models trained on vast web-scraped corpus generalize well to daily language. However, they often fall short when applied in specialized domains that require precise language and foreign terms, like law and medicine. This gap highlights the necessity for data-efficient methodologies to fine-tune these models for narrow-domain applications. This paper introduces PlanBERT, a new approach for enabling data-efficient domain adaptation and fine-tuning of embedding models. The approach builds on self-supervised contrastive pre-training, synthetic training data generated by large language models (LLMs), and decorrelation of embedding features. The paper also introduces the term "informative vector embeddings" to adjust the training objectives to incentivise more analytics-friendly embeddings and demonstrate that PlanBERT can learn the domain language of zonal plans and outperform larger and more complex state-of-the-art models in challenging real-world zonal plan tasks.

Keywords: Text embedding · Feature decorrelation ·
Domain-adaptation

1 Introduction

In 2022, Norwegian municipalities faced the challenge of processing over 69,000 building permit applications, with each application taking an average of 28 days, [16] largely due to caseworker overload. This inefficiency not only strains public resources but also causes significant delays and economic repercussions for citizens awaiting permit approvals. The long process times are related to finding and reading zonal plans, which are a substantial part of the legal basis for building permits. The zonal plans, often outdated, contradictory, and inconsistently digitized, require historical knowledge, leading to distractions and sub-optimal workflows for caseworkers.

Recent advances in natural language processing (NLP) with the usage of large transformer architectures have led to language models with great contextual understanding [31]. This has resulted in significant improvements in

M. Bramer and F. Stahl (Eds.): SGAI 2024, LNAI 15446, pp. 175–188, 2025.
https://doi.org/10.1007/978-3-031-77915-2_13

text embedding [7,18] and text retrieval [32] thus making traditional domain-adaptable methods like TF-IDF and word2vec outdated [18]. The models produced by recent research are developed for broad domains and are tested on a wide variety of downstream tasks on large benchmarks like MTEB [14]. These benchmarks are feasible for pushing the state-of-the-art but do not accurately measure the performance of narrow domains like law, medicine, building applications and others that contain precise terms not found in daily language. These narrow domains often lack the vast data sources needed to train customized language models. There is, therefore, a need to develop methods for the efficient adoption of embedding models to work on narrow domains, as this will enable the usage of popular technologies like retrieval-augmented generation and complex domain-specific semantic information retrieval tasks. Embedding vectors that represent real-world concepts are useful for downstream analysis tasks and the term "informative vector embeddings" is therefore introduced. This work lays the foundation for future efforts in computationally processing zonal plans and developing tools for more efficient case handling as part of the KartAi project[1].

Key Contributions. This paper presents a new approach for training domain-adapted text embedding models to work on narrow domains where annotated training data is scarce. The proposed methodology utilizes the concepts of self-supervised learning and synthetic data generation to overcome the lack of annotated data. Early results show significant improvements in downstream tasks within the zonal plan domain.

Article Outline. Section 2 provides an insight into terminology and related work that forms the basis for the proposed approach, which is described in detail in Sect. 3, including design choices and architecture. In Sect. 4, the data foundation and test results are presented, and in Sect. 5, the results are discussed, and the proposed method is evaluated. The findings and future work are then summarized in Sect. 6 and 7, respectively.

2   Related Work

The field of natural language processing has seen significant advancements in recent years, primarily driven by the development and broader impact of large language models [31]. These advancements have transformed the way text embedding models are constructed and trained, leading to substantial improvements in performance across various downstream NLP tasks [18]. This section reviews the progress in text embedding models, the challenges of dimensional collapse, the utilization of synthetic training data, and the current state of Norwegian pre-trained language models, concluding with strategies for domain adaptation.

---

[1] The KartAi project page: https://kartai.no/. Co-funded by the Research Council of Norway project 341319.

2.1   Text Embedding

Embedding models produce low-dimensional vector representations of data while minimizing the loss of semantic information. In a vector space, each data point x_i is represented with a corresponding m-dimensional vector $z_i \in \mathbb{R}^m$, represents semantic similarity by some distance metric $\sigma(\cdot)$, commonly the cosine distance[2]. If x_0 and x_1 have similar semantic meanings, then $\sigma(z_0, z_1)$ will yield a small value. The formation of text embeddings is a well-studied area [7] as it has been an essential component in the field of information retrieval.

It becomes more challenging to incorporate semantic relations for long texts like paragraphs and documents as these can be far apart in the text. Pre-trained language models have shown great abilities in capturing longer contextual relations in text [31] and are therefore often used when producing document embeddings [27]. LSTM-based language models pre-trained on machine translation have been a popular way to acquire context-aware embedding models [18], but these fall short when compared to the transformer-based language models [18]. With their attention mechanism, the transformer-based language models have allowed for even greater contextual representations and are the current standard for text embedding [18]. The BERT model [3] and its variants have seen wide adoption in text embedding [18], but recent studies have seen the adoption of LLMs for producing text embeddings [1,27], with the Mistral-7B [8] model being a prominent choice for the base model.

Dimensional collapse is a phenomenon in self-supervised representation learning where the embedding vectors disproportionately utilize certain dimensions of the embedding space. The collapsed dimensions can potentially lead to collapsed solutions or constant features [6], which are shown to negatively affect the performance of downstream tasks [25]. Additionally, feature collapse and feature decorrelation are closely related to the "alignment" and "uniformity" of the embedding space which is also shown to correlate with performance on downstream tasks [4,29].

Correlated embedding features are the cause of dimensional collapses, thus providing an incentive for enforcing feature decorrelation [6]. He & Ozay proposed the NESum [5] (normalized eigenvalue sum) metric that compares the eigenvalues λ in the covariance matrix $M \in \mathbb{R}^{m \times m}$ for a sample of n embeddings vectors $Z \in \mathbb{R}^{m \times n} = (z_0, z_1, ..., z_{n-1})$ as shown in Eq. 1.

$$NESum(M) = \sum_{i=1}^{m} \frac{\lambda_i}{\lambda_1}, \qquad M = cov(Z) \tag{1}$$

The NESum metric produces values in the interval $\langle 0, m]$ where a value approaching 0 indicates a total collapse of all dimensions (also referred to as complete collapse [6]), and a value of m corresponds to complete feature decorrelation, addressed as whitened features by the original authors [5]. The NESum metric correlates better with performance on downstream tasks when

---

[2] Vector space is also referred to as latent space or embedding space in literature.

compared to other metrics for evaluating the quality of embedding models trained in unsupervised fashion [25].

2.2 Synthetic Training Data

Acquiring sufficient training data is often a challenge due to scarcity, cost, or ethical issues [10]. Synthetic data can replace real data in such cases [12]. Tang et al. [24] show that synthetic data from LLMs improves NLP task performance and that accurate prompts are crucial. Wang et al. [27] use GPT-4 [17] to create synthetic document-query pairs for training text embedding models, demonstrating the effectiveness of this approach with a Mistral-7B model [8].

2.3 Norwegian Pre-trained Language Models

The zonal plans and related questions are formulated in Norwegian, thus the underlying language model should be developed for the Norwegian language. This includes a tokenizer that produces tokens in line with the structures found in the Norwegian language and a language model pre-training on a corpus consisting primarily of sources in Norwegian. There are few language models fully pre-trained on a Norwegian corpus due to the extensive data and computational infrastructure required. In addition, multi-

Table 1. An overview of architectures with one or more language models pre-trained from scratch on Norwegian text.

Architecture	Parameters	Self-attention
BERT [3]	15 - 323M	Bi-directional
Mistral [8]	7B	Directions
T5 [19]	32 - 808M	Bi-directional
BLOOM [2]	7B	Directional

lingual LLMs have a respectful level when working in Norwegian, thus reducing the need for Norwegian-based language models. Nevertheless, two main initiatives have trained Norwegian-based language models: The NORA.LLM project[3] developed BERT [3], T5 [15], Mistral-7B [8] and BLOOM-7B [2] models. And the NorwAI project[4] developed Mistral-7B [8] models.

2.4 Domain Adaptation of Language Models

Domain adaptations enhance language models' performance in specific tasks. Ling et al. [11] classify these into three types based on access to the model: "External Augmentation" (limited access via interfaces), "Prompt Crafting" (modifiable prompts via API), and "Model Fine-tuning" (full access to model weights). External augmentation offers minimal adaptation. Prompt crafting involves using task-specific prompts to guide model responses. Model fine-tuning adapts pre-trained models to specific domains by training on relevant data [31].

---

[3] The project details can be found at https://hf.co/norallm.
[4] The project details can be found at https://hf.co/NorwAI.

3 Approach

We introduce the concept of "informative vector embeddings," which refers to embedding vectors that are rich in information and accurately reflect the real-world properties of the original data. Unlike traditional embeddings, which often optimize abstract axes for data separation, informative vector embeddings aim to retain meaningful attributes that can be directly utilized in downstream analysis tasks. These embeddings are characterized by a broader distribution of attributes, enhancing the interpretability and utility of the embedding space. In a conventional embedding space correlated attributes in the data points will be represented with the same embedding feature, while informative vector embeddings attempt to decorrelate the attributes to make them easier to tell apart in the vector space.

To address data scarcity and domain adaptation challenges, we present Plan-BERT, an approach for domain-adapting text embedding models to create informative vector embeddings. PlanBERT focuses on not requiring annotated data due to annotation costs and lack of labelled data in narrow domains. Previous approaches include weakly supervised contrastive learning [4,15,26] and supervised training on synthetic data [1,27]. PlanBERT employs a two-step training process: contrastive pre-training with a feature decorrelation regulator to create an information-rich embedding space, followed by fine-tuning with synthetic data in a dual-encoder setup as seen in Fig. 1. Detailed steps are discussed in Subsects. 3.2 and 3.3.

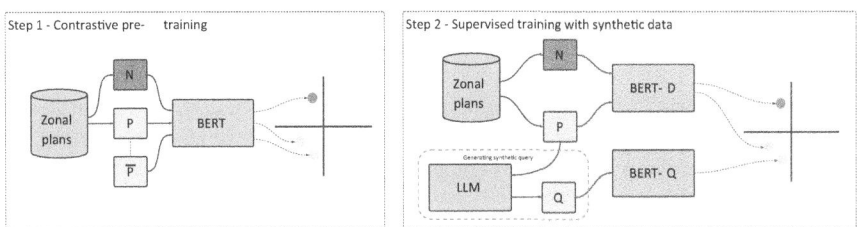

Fig. 1. An illustration of the workings of the two training steps. "N" and "P" refer to negative and positive samples, while "Q" refers to queries generated from positive samples.

3.1 Base Model and Embedding Construction

Due to the success of transformer-based language models pre-trained on NLP tasks in text embedding applications, PlanBERT should follow a similar architecture. When comparing the options listed in Table 1, BERT is selected as the base model due to its wide adaptation within the field and bi-directional attention mechanism. Nevertheless, larger language models will likely yield better results based on their dominance on the MTEB benchmark [14], especially the Mistral model. However, these larger languages are more data-hungry due to their need for extensive pre-training to convert to bi-directional attention [1] and their severe increase in the number of parameters. Additionally, Ghader et al. [1] show that their proposed training method, which has similarities to the one proposed in this paper, has a positive effect on both the BERT and Mistral models. Therefore, It is assumed that this paper's findings will be transferable to a Mistral architecture.

NorBERT3 [22], the newest Norwegian pre-trained BERT model, is distributed in four different sizes NorBERT3$_{xs}$ (15M), NorBERT3$_{small}$ (40M), NorBERT3$_{base}$ (123M) and NorBERT3$_{large}$ (323M). The NorBERT3$_{large}$ version is chosen due to being the best-performing model when tested on a variety of Norwegian language modelling tasks [22], although none of the tested tasks is retrieval-based.

As a part of the BERT architecture, a dedicated class token $[cls]$ is always the first in the sequence of input tokens. This class token of the BERT architecture can serve as the text representation, as suggested by Devlin et al. [21], because of the bi-directional attention mechanisms in BERT that allow the vector representation of the class token to be influenced by the rest of the input tokens. The alternative is a mean pooling of all output tokens as done by Ghader et al. [1]. However, since PlanBERT is based on the BERT architecture, it is apparent to utilize the in-built class token for text representation since this approach has previously proven to work well [4,21].

3.2   Contrastive Pre-training (Step 1)

A model pre-trained on general language will have a vector space optimized for distinguishing a varied set of concepts where only a smaller subset is relevant for the narrow target domain (zonal plans). As shown in Fig. 1, the first step of PlanBERT, therefore, intends to adapt to domain language by having the models gradually adjust the axis of the embedding space to incorporate domain-specific terms. Self-supervised contrastive training is consequently applied as the first step to adapt the model to the domain language, and to learn ways to best separate data.

How to augment a data point d to from a data pair $\{d, \bar{d}\}$ is an important factor in contrastive learning. Regardless of modality, the applied augmentation must only work on the noise, not the information, as the intent is to learn the distinction between essential and excessive features in the data. It is more straightforward for image applications as camera properties like expositor and colour balance can be altered during training with simple matrix operations. It is less obvious how to augment text data, especially in a self-supervised fashion. Modern LLMs and their recent popularity as components in a training loop [13,27] would be feasible for augmentation. An LLM like GPT-4 [17] can rewrite text by altering words and changing the sentence structure. As PlanBERT is meant for domain-specific text with precise wording, this is viewed as too error-pruned as LLMs do not have a clear understanding of the underlying domain, and essential terms could, therefore, be incorrectly translated, and the essence of the text would then be altered. In addition, in an LLM-based rewriting augmentation strategy, the level of augmentation is given by the prompting, making it difficult to scale the intensity of augmentation and acquire an appropriate dissimilarity.

Gao et al. [4] proposed to utilize the dropout functionality of neural networks to perform the necessary augmentation of the input data. The data is then augmented during the forward pass as the affected dropout nodes are changed between the first and second forward passes. The level of augmentation is then regulated by the dropout probability parameter α.

Loss Function. The triplet loss function (Eq. 2) and variant are extensively used in training of embedding models [1,4,21,23,27]. The challenge is to form good triplets where the models have difficulty distinguishing the anchor a from the positive sample p and the negative sample n. The margin δ is added to prevent a collapsed solution.

$$\mathcal{L}_{triplet}(a,p,n) = max\Big(\sigma(a,p) - \sigma(a,n) + \delta, 0\Big) \tag{2}$$

In the earlier stages, the samples can be more random as the model will focus on separating different topics, but for later stages, the text should optimally be more semantically alike. An adequate sampling strategy that progressively samples harder negative samples is therefore important to acquire strong results. GISTEmbed [23] use a pre-trained embedding model to sample the in-batch hardest negatives for the triplet loss.

Similar to GISTEmbed, PlanBERT also uses a "model-in-the-loop" approach to acquire hard triplets. PlanBERT generates an in-memory vector database for the entire training set used for sampling hard negatives by conducting similarity searches at runtime. The database is updated at regular intervals to incorporate the new knowledge of the model and ensure that the negative samples always stay relevant to the knowledge gap of the model.

Feature Decorrelation. INES, short for Inverse-exponential Normalized Eigenvalue Sum, is introduced as a complementary loss function to regulate the features correlation of the embedding vectors Z, thus creating more informative vector embeddings. As shown in Eq. 3, INES build upon the NESum metric (Eq. 1) to work directly on the covariance of the embedding features. The regulator operates on a batch level, thus providing the optimizer with a secondary objective, namely to even out the eigenvalues of the in-batch covariance matrix.

$$\mathcal{L}_{INES}(Z) = \gamma \cdot e^{-\tau\big(NESum(M)\big)}, \quad M = cov(Z) \tag{3}$$

The scale factor γ is introduced to adjust the impact of INES compared to the main objective, while the exponent τ regulates how aggressively INES punishes correlated features. INES optimizes for in-batch embedding space, thus its effect is tied to the batch size and the data shuffling in the same way as gradient descent [9]. A small batch size or poor data shuffling, thus large varieties between the batches, will make the regularization term useless since the covariance for each batch should be a good approximation of the overall covariance of the training set.

3.3 Supervised Training (Step 2)

The text embedding model is duplicated to form a dual encoder architecture with a dedicated model for document chunks (BERT-D) and queries (BERT-Q) as shown in Fig. 1. Both models work towards the same embedding space and are trained by the same optimizer, thus forming a symbiosis where each model can focus on a separate aspect of the data while still guiding each other during training by having a shared optimizer. The loss function from step 1 (Subsect. 3.2) is used, but the anchor is now a query q, thus the forming triplets of $\{q_i, c_i, c_j\}$ where $j = \underset{x,\, x\neq i}{\operatorname{argmin}}\ \sigma(c_i, c_x)$.

Synthetic Data Generation. Data pairs $\{q_i, c_i\}$ are acquired by an LLM generating a query q_i that can be answered with the content of a randomly sampled chunk c_i. The chunk and query are semantically linked as the LLM is instructed to generate queries that can only be answered with the chunk content. These data pairs serve as a replacement for or a complement to real-world training data, as the model learns their semantic relations.

Zero-shot data generation fails to generate high-quality data, thus promoting strategies with examples is essential for acquiring good results [12,13,24]. A prompt template containing examples ensures high-quality and relevant questions. Inspired by the "Persona" prompt pattern by White et al. [30], the Plan-BERT template samples a role from a pre-defined collection to account for the linguistic difference between users of downstream applications. The LLM is also instructed to use synonyms and paraphrases, and only produce questions relevant to the provided chunk.

4   Results

4.1   Data

The data foundation consists of 70.000 publicly available zonal plans[5] from the past four decades collected from various geographically spread Norwegian municipalities, thus representing the diversity in language across the nation and throughout time. Only the textual descriptions of the plans were used, while the geographical information was neglected for PlanBERT's training. Nevertheless, the textual contents are often outdated, lack formal structure, and are inconsistently digitized, similar to legal documents like juristic contacts and medical records. The zonal plans were further split into 500.000 document chunks that form the data points used in contrastive pertaining (step 1, see Subsect. 3.2).

---

[5] Zonal plans are collected from https://arealplaner.no.

The KartAi project gathegray an expert-annotated test set[6] of 91 retrieval pairs (q, D_q) with a query q and a collection $D_q = \{d_q^0, d_q^1, ...\}$ consisting of one to four document chunks d_q. These expert-annotated pairs alone form the test set used to calculate metrics for both training steps (see Subsects. 3.2 and 3.3).

The synthetic data generation yielded 150.000 unique data points that alone form the training and validation sets for the second training step (see Subsect. 3.3). The GPT-4 model [17] was chosen as the LLM for the data generation because of the model's good performance in diverse tasks across several languages. 46 hand-crafted instructions were created to reflect the identity of different user groups like citizens, case workers, and politicians when generating the data (see examples in the box below). GPT-4's temperature parameter is set to 1.0 to acquire a wider variety of wording in the generated questions. This combination of a high value for the temperature parameter and injection of randomly sampled roles into the system prompt ensures diversity in the generated synthetic data.

Hand-crafted instructions

```
6: Du er en politisk aktiv innbygger som har engasjert deg i
planarbeidet. Formuler sp{\o}rsm{\aa}lene med politisk vinkling.

21: Du er en milj{\o}konsulenter som skal lage en milj{\o}rapport.
Formuler sp{\o}rsm{\aa}lene med fokus p{\aa} milj{\o}. Bruk faguttrykk.
```

4.2   Training Output

Various variants of PlanBERT are trained to isolate and evaluate the effect of the proposed architectural components. The first training step (described in Subsect. 3.2), denoted PlanBERT$_{Contrastive}$, is trained with and without the INES regulator. For the second training step (described in Subsect. 3.3), both the usage of a single (PlanBERT$_{Single}$) or dual (PlanBERT$_{Dual}$) encoder are tested with NorBERT weights, weights from PlanBERT$_{Contrastive}$ and with the INES regulator. All training was done using the Adams optimizer, a batch size of 256, and the triplet-loss margin set to $\delta = 0.5$. The learning rates used are all in the magnitude of 10^{-4} to 10^{-3}, and the models are trained for one epoch. For the INES regulator the exponent is set to $\tau = 0.05$ and the scaling factor to $\gamma = 20$. All versions of PlanBERT and other selected models are tested on the expert-annotated dataset. Information retrieval and retrieval-augmented generation (RAG) are the most imminent applications for a domain-adapted embedding model, thus, the retriever-related metrics nDCG and Recall were chosen for model comparison. The nDCG and Recall are calculated from the test set and are shown in Table 2 for all variants of PlanBERT. The relation between the nDCG and Recall metrics and the NESum (see Subsect. 2.1) value for the models is plotted in Fig. 2.

---

[6] The test set is published at https://hf.co/datasets/kartai/NorPlanQA.

Table 2. Test results for variants of PlanBERT compagray to the results of selected generally-purpose pre-trained multi-lingual models and the TF-IDF algorithm on the expert annotated test dataset. The parameter k indicates the number of retrieved elements.

Model	nDCG			Recall			NESum
	$k=1$	$k=5$	$k=10$	$k=1$	$k=5$	$k=10$	
PlanBERT$_{Contrastive}$	0.24	0.32	0.40	0.19	0.41	0.64	11.46
+ INES	0.24	0.34	0.42	0.22	0.43	0.68	57.73
PlanBERT$_{Dual}$	0.33	0.52	0.57	0.26	0.70	0.84	8.17
+ INES	0.34	0.49	0.57	0.27	0.63	0.84	22.58
+ Contrastive pre-training	0.46	**0.59**	0.63	0.38	**0.72**	0.84	26.75
PlanBERT$_{Single}$	0.38	0.52	0.57	0.29	0.68	0.80	9.06
+ INES	0.42	0.57	0.63	0.36	0.71	0.87	29.96
+ Contrastive pre-training	0.45	**0.59**	**0.64**	0.36	**0.72**	0.87	36.76
text-embedding-ada-002[a]	0.37	0.53	0.61	0.26	0.67	**0.88**	-
distiluse-base-multilingual-cased-v2[b]	0.24	0.39	0.46	0.18	0.52	0.72	-
multilingual-e5-large[c]	**0.47**	0.57	**0.64**	**0.39**	0.67	0.86	-
TF-IDF	0.33	0.46	0.52	0.23	0.60	0.76	-

[a] https://openai.com/index/new-and-improved-embedding-model/
[b] https://hf.co/sentence-transformers/distiluse-base-multilingual-cased-v2
[c] https://hf.co/intfloat/multilingual-e5-large

5 Discussion

Three selected multi-lingual general-purpose models are also tested on the test set to form a test reference. Although the reference models are not domain-specific, they are still trained on extensive amounts of data and are all multi-lingual, thus they are expected to perform well. The TF-IDF [20] is included to compare results with those of a naive approach. All the results for the reference models and TF-IDF are added to Table 2.

Feature Decorrelation as Secondary Objective. The secondary training objective provided by the INES regulator shows a significant gain in NESum values for pre-training and fine-tuning without negatively affecting the primary objective as shown in Table 2. The INES regulator appears to be more impactful for the contrastive pre-training as the NESum values have five folded, while the single-encoder fine-tuning benefits the most from the secondary objective as all metrics have a significant gain. As visualized in Fig. 2 there is a positive correlation between the NESum values and metrics, especially nDCG, for all tested values of k, thus further supporting feature decorrelation as a useful secondary objective in the training of embedding models. By increasing the NESum values, the vector embeddings utilize more of the vector space, thus they are more in line with the

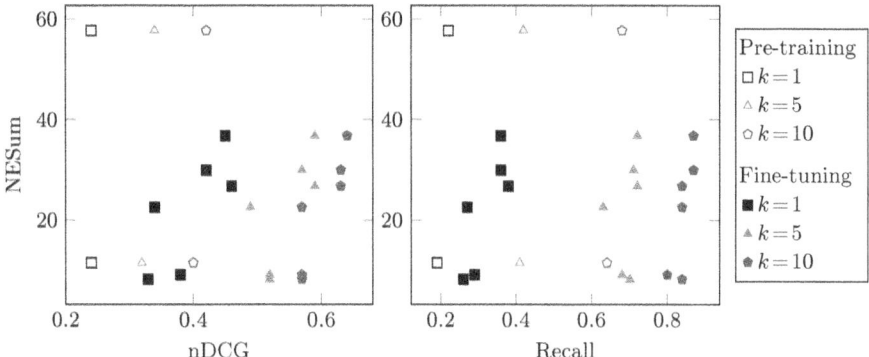

Fig. 2. The relation between the NESum and the performance metrics nDCG and Recall for the PlanBERT models presented in Table 2. The k-values indicate the number of retrieved elements used when calculating the metrics. Markers without fill result from the contrastive pre-training, while filled markers result from fine-tuning on synthetic data.

definition of informative vector embeddings in Sect. 3. In other words, the INES regulator is the first step in forming more informative vector embeddings.

Dual vs Single Encoder. Based on the results presented in Table 2 there is no evident effect on the downstream performance when training a dual encoder network versus a single encoder network. This indicates that the performance limitations are unaffected by the horizontal scaling of the model as both setups appear to have learned equally good data representations although the dual setup

Table 3. Comparison of prerequisites for PlanBERT and mE5 (`multilingual-e5-large` [28]).

	PlanBERT	mE5
Model parameters	323M	560M
Contrastive data	500K	1B
Fine-tuning data	150K	1.6M

has twice the amount of parameters as the single setup. On the other hand, the single encoder utilizes the embedding space better than the dual encoder as indicated by the roughly 35% larger NESum values. This is likely caused by the single encoder being exposed to both queries and chunks, thus more varied inputs, compared to the encoders in the dual setup. In another way, the dual encoder learns a more compact information flow by relying on fewer vector elements to reach the same embedding quality as the single encoder. This is likely also why the performance gained by introducing the INES regulator is significantly higher for the single encoder compared to the dual encoder. These differences in utilization of the embedding space indicate that implicit information, like whether a data point is a query or a chunk, is not learned for the dual encoder, thus supporting the original claim that the dual encoder allows each encoder to learn specific aspects of the data.

The Value of Synthetic Data. The results show that training on synthetic data generated with simple prompting strategies can, without including any real-world data, push the performance of BERT models beyond that of the industry-wise widely adopted `text-embedding-ada-002` model. PlanBERT also performs comparably to the multilingual model `multilingual-e5-large` [28] (Table 2) although PlanBERT has significantly fewer parameters and is trained on a vastly smaller corpus as shown in Table 3. These results strengthen the findings of others [1,27] claiming that training on synthetic data yields strong embedding qualities, but also demonstrates that strong domain-specific embedding models can be trained without the need for annotated data. Nevertheless, PlanBERT's synthetic data-generating approach assumes that there is a one-to-one mapping from query to document chunk, while in reality, there are often several document chunks that are relevant. This assumption can explain why results stagnate as a maximal *recall@5* of 0.72 is insufficient for some applications. Also, the true semantics of the chunks are not intrinsic properties as the content of a chunk at the start of a document can affect the meaning of later chunks.

6   Conclusion

In this study, we proposed PlanBERT for domain adaptation of text embedding models based on recent trends within the field. The test results show that PlanBERT performs well when compared with larger proprietor models trained on vast datasets like OpenAI's Ada model and the *mutlilingual − e5 − large* model. PlanBERT also demonstrates that efficient embedding models can be developed for narrow domains without costly annotated data simply by using a combination of contrastive pre-training and fine-tuning on fully synthetic data. The study also highlights the importance of feature decorrelation and shows how the INES regulator positively affects the embedding quality when used as a secondary training objective.

7   Future Work

The chunking strategy is not focused on in PlanBERT but is likely essential in reaching more informative vector embeddings for the zonal plans domain. The naive chunking strategy in PlanBERT does not allow for optimal embedding as the semantics of chunks are not guaranteed to be intrinsic properties. Also, the map part of the zonal plans is excluded in PlanBERT, although it carries essential information for understanding the written part. We therefore intend to continue the research by exploring new ways of chunking zonal plans where the semantics of a chunk becomes an intrinsic property and where the geospatial information from the map is included in the embedding process. In addition, there is a need to develop better metrics for scoring the "informativeness" of vector embeddings concerning the definition carried out in this paper.

References

1. Behnam Ghader, P., Adlakha, V., Mosbach, M., Bahdanau, D., Chapados, N., Reddy, S.: LLM2Vec: Large Language Models Are Secretly Powerful Text Encoders, pp. 1–27 (2024)
2. BigScience: BigScience Language Open-science Open-access Multilingual (BLOOM) Language Model (2022)
3. Devlin, J., Chang, M.W., Lee, K., Toutanova, K.: BERT: pre-training of deep bidirectional transformers for language understanding. Technical report (2019). https://doi.org/10.18653/v1/N19-1423
4. Gao, T., Yao, X., Chen, D.: SimCSE: simple contrastive learning of sentence embeddings. In: EMNLP 2021 - 2021 Conference on Empirical Methods in Natural Language Processing, Proceedings, pp. 6894–6910 (2021). https://doi.org/10.18653/v1/2021.emnlp-main.552
5. He, B., Ozay, M.: Exploring the gap between collapsed & whitened features in self-supervised learning. Proc. Mach. Learn. Res. **162**, 8613–8634 (2022)
6. Hua, T., Wang, W., Xue, Z., Ren, S., Wang, Y., Zhao, H.: On feature decorrelation in self-supervised learning. In: Proceedings of the IEEE International Conference on Computer Vision, pp. 9578–9588 (2021). https://doi.org/10.1109/ICCV48922.2021.00946
7. Incitti, F., Urli, F., Snidaro, L.: Beyond word embeddings: a survey (2023)
8. Jiang, A.Q., et al.: Mistral 7B, pp. 1–9 (2023)
9. LeCun, Y.A., Bottou, L., Orr, G.B., Müller, K.-R.: Efficient BackProp. In: Montavon, G., Orr, G.B., Müller, K.-R. (eds.) Neural Networks: Tricks of the Trade. LNCS, vol. 7700, pp. 9–48. Springer, Heidelberg (2012). https://doi.org/10.1007/978-3-642-35289-8_3
10. Lien, H., Biermann, D., Palumbo, F., Goodwin, M.: An exploration of semi-supervised text classification. In: Iliadis, L., Jayne, C., Tefas, A., Pimenidis, E. (eds.) EANN 2022. CCIS, vol. 1600, pp. 477–488. Springer, Cham (2022). https://doi.org/10.1007/978-3-031-08223-8_39
11. Ling, C., et al.: Domain Specialization as the Key to Make Large Language Models Disruptive: A Comprehensive Survey (2024)
12. Liu, R., et al.: Best Practices and Lessons Learned on Synthetic Data for Language Models, pp. 1–26 (2024)
13. Mitra, A., et al.: Orca 2: Teaching Small Language Models How to Reason (2023)
14. Muennighoff, N., Tazi, N., Magne, L., Reimers, N.: MTEB: massive text embedding benchmark. In: EACL 2023 - 17th Conference of the European Chapter of the Association for Computational Linguistics, Proceedings of the Conference, pp. 2006–2029 (2023). https://doi.org/10.18653/v1/2023.eacl-main.148
15. Neelakantan, A., et al.: Text and Code Embeddings by Contrastive Pre-Training (2022)
16. Norwegian statistics authorities (SSB): Table 13434 - Municipal management of planning and building applications
17. OpenAI: GPT-4 Technical Report, vol. 4, pp. 1–100 (2023)
18. Patil, R., Boit, S., Gudivada, V., Nandigam, J.: A survey of text representation and embedding techniques in NLP. IEEE Access **11**, 36120–36146 (2023). https://doi.org/10.1109/ACCESS.2023.3266377
19. Raffel, C., et al.: Exploring the limits of transfer learning with a unified text-to-text transformer. J. Mach. Learn. Res. **21**, 1–67 (2020)

20. Ramos, J., et al.: Using TF-IDF to determine word relevance in document queries. In: Proceedings of the First Instructional Conference on Machine Learning, vol. 242, pp. 29–48. Citeseer (2003)
21. Reimers, N., Gurevych, I.: Sentence-BERT: Sentence Embeddings using Siamese BERT-Networks (2019)
22. Samuel, D., et al.: NorBench – A Benchmark for Norwegian Language Models (2023)
23. Solatorio, A.V.: GISTEmbed: Guided In-sample Selection of Training Negatives for Text Embedding Fine-tuning (2024)
24. Tang, R., Han, X., Jiang, X., Hu, X.: Does Synthetic Data Generation of LLMs Help Clinical Text Mining? (2023)
25. Tsitsulin, A., Munkhoeva, M., Perozzi, B.: Unsupervised embedding quality evaluation. Proc. Mach. Learn. Res. **221**, 169–188 (2023)
26. Wang, L., et al.: Text Embeddings by Weakly-Supervised Contrastive Pre-training, pp. 1–17 (2022)
27. Wang, L., Yang, N., Huang, X., Yang, L., Majumder, R., Wei, F.: Improving Text Embeddings with Large Language Models (2023)
28. Wang, L., Yang, N., Huang, X., Yang, L., Majumder, R., Wei, F.: Multilingual E5 Text Embeddings: A Technical Report (2024)
29. Wang, T., Isola, P.: Understanding contrastive representation learning through alignment and uniformity on the hypersphere. In: 37th International Conference on Machine Learning, ICML 2020, PartF16814, pp. 9871–9881 (2020)
30. White, J., et al.: A Prompt Pattern Catalog to Enhance Prompt Engineering with ChatGPT (2023)
31. Zhao, W.X., et al.: A Survey of Large Language Models (2023)
32. Zhu, Y., et al.: Large Language Models for Information Retrieval: A Survey (2023)

ArgueMapper Assistant: Interactive Argument Mining Using Generative Language Models

Mirko Lenz[1,2(✉)] and Ralph Bergmann[1,2]

[1] Trier University, Universitätsring 15, 54296 Trier, Germany
info@mirko-lenz.de, bergmann@uni-trier.de
[2] Branch Trier University, German Research Center for Artificial Intelligence (DFKI), Behringstraße 21, 54296 Trier, Germany
{mirko.lenz,ralph.bergmann}@dfki.de

Abstract. Structured arguments are a valuable resource for analyzing and understanding complex topics. However, manual annotation is time-consuming and often not feasible for large datasets, and automated approaches are less accurate. To address this issue, we propose an interactive argument mining system that takes advantage of generative language models to support humans in the creation of argument graphs. We present the open source ArgueMapper Assistant featuring two prompting strategies and evaluate it on a real-world news dataset. The resulting corpus containing 88 argument graphs is publicly available as well. With generative models, the annotation time is reduced by about 20% while the number of errors is slightly increased (mostly due to missing argumentative units and wrong relation types). A survey provides insights into the usefulness and reliability of the assistant features and shows that participants prefer to use the assistant in the future.

Keywords: Argument Mining · Argument Graphs · Large Language Models · Interactive Systems · Data Annotation

1 Introduction

Argumentation is available in many forms and plays a crucial role in various domains such as law, politics, and science. A common way to represent it is using natural language texts—for instance, in the form of news articles or scientific papers. Although these texts contain valuable information that can be understood by humans, they are not directly usable by machines. To bridge this gap, Argument Mining (AM) [16] aims to extract structured argumentative elements from natural language text. This may be done manually by trained annotators—leading to high-quality structures—or automatically—which is often less accurate. Consequently, a major challenge in AM is the time-consuming nature of manual annotation, leading to the lack of high-quality datasets for many topics/domains. Research in this field typically focuses on improving automated

M. Bramer and F. Stahl (Eds.): SGAI 2024, LNAI 15446, pp. 189–203, 2025.
https://doi.org/10.1007/978-3-031-77915-2_14

approaches or interfaces for manual annotation, but to the best of our knowledge, no work has been done to bring together both worlds.

In this paper, our aim is to bridge this gap through an *interactive* argument mining system that *assists* human annotators in the process of converting plain text arguments to a structured graph-based representation. With recent advances in Natural Language Processing (NLP) [2], AM has seen a shift toward the use of transformer-based language models—either in the form of end-to-end models [15] or as part of a pipeline [18]. Although these supervised approaches reach State of the Art (SOTA) performance, large amounts of labeled data is needed for training—which is scarce for certain domains—and their predictions cannot be adjusted on the fly. In contrast, Large Language Models (LLMs) work in an unsupervised manner and can easily be adjusted to the user's needs through prompting. We leverage this capability to create an interactive system that allows human annotators to hand over parts of the annotation process to the model, reducing the manual effort. Consequently, we seek to answer the following research question: *How to decrease the manual annotation time of argument graphs while maintaining the output quality through LLM-based assistance?* We make the following contributions to answer this question: (i) Two prompting strategies to convert plain text arguments to graphs via LLMs, (ii) a ready-to-use and open-source application enabling interactive argument mining (see Fig. 1), (iii) a qualitative evaluation of the system on a real-world news dataset, and (iv) a publicly available corpus containing 88 argument graphs for future research.

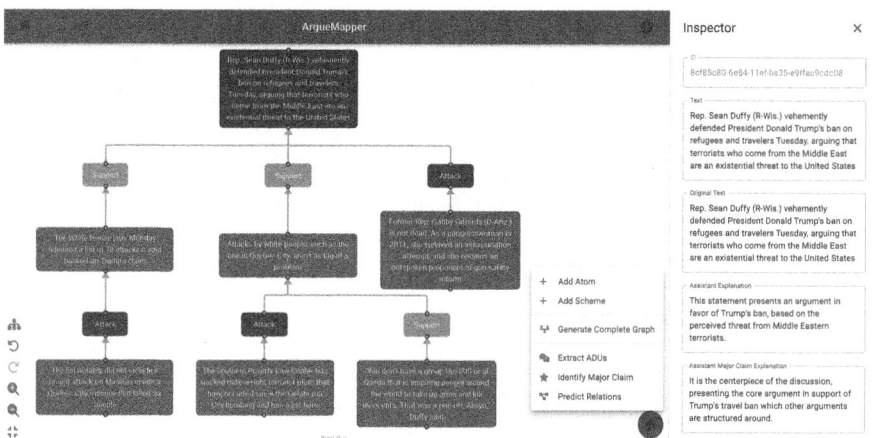

Fig. 1. Screenshot of the interactive mining system with a graph excerpt from the *News Articles* dataset [8]. The assistant button (lightning bolt) contains the actions and the inspector (right sidebar) the explanations.

2   Foundations

In the following section, we first provide an overview of Computational Argumentation (CA) with a focus on AM, followed by a brief introduction to LLMs.

Computational Argumentation. A structured *argument* typically consists of one claim and a set of premises that either *support* or *attack* the claim [22]. Being the smallest units of argumentation, they are also commonly called Argumentative Discourse Units (ADUs) [20]. Claims may also be used as premises in other arguments, enabling the creation of complex argumentative structures. Such chains of arguments often have one central conclusion, the major claim. A common way to represent these structures is to use a directed graph $G = (V, E)$ with the set of nodes V and the set of edges E. The Argument Interchange Format (AIF) [7] defines two types of nodes: (i) *Information* or *atom nodes* being the ADUs, and (ii) *scheme nodes* being the relationships between the ADUs. An example of this format is shown in the screenshot of our annotation tool in Fig. 1. Multiple argumentation microstructures have been proposed to represent the relationships between ADUs in a graph, such as serial, linked, and convergent arguments [23]. This distinction has been subject to discussion in the literature—for instance, Goddu [14] argues that there "is no good reason to bother making the distinction" between linked and convergent arguments. Consequently, we focus on linked arguments in our work—that is, a scheme node may only have one premise and one conclusion. AM is concerned with extracting these argumentative elements from natural language text. The term AM comprises a variety of tasks, including (but not limited to) ADU extraction, claim/premise classification, and relation prediction [5]. They may be combined to form a pipeline, allowing the extraction of complete argumentative structures, including argument graphs [18,19]. We refer the interested reader to the study conducted by Lawrence and Reed [16] for a complete overview of the available approaches.

Large Language Models. Arguments are expressed mainly in natural language, which means that there is a strong connection between AM and NLP. Providing a proper introduction to the topic is beyond the scope of this paper, but we briefly introduce the concept of LLMs. They are based on the transformer architecture and its *attention* mechanism, allowing the model to consider the entire input sequence at once [24]. OpenAI's Generative Pre-trained Transformer (GPT) family of LLMs popularized by ChatGPT uses a decoder-only variant that predicts the next token given only the previous sequence as input. Instead of fine-tuning the model for a specific task, *prompting* can be used to guide the model towards the desired output via *few-shot learning* (i.e., giving examples of user input and the desired model output) or even *zero-shot learning* (i.e., providing only user input without output samples) [4].

3 Related Work

To the best of our knowledge, there is no prior work combining manual and automated approaches to AM. In Sect. 5, we analyze several existing software tools to manually create argument graphs, while in this section we focus on the use of LLMs in text annotation and AM tasks.

Text Annotation with LLMs. ChatGPT has been used in various annotation tasks in the field of NLP. For stance and topic detection, it has been found to outperform humans by 25% while being about 30 times cheaper than crowd-sourced labor [13]. In another study, the model has been used to reproduce human labels for sentiment analysis and stance detection tasks, achieving an average accuracy of 0.6 [26]. In addition, ChatGPT has been proposed as an annotation metric for Natural Language Generation (NLG) tasks, showing competitive performance with human ratings [25].

Argument Mining with LLMs. AM tasks have also been investigated with LLMs. When applied for common tasks such as claim detection and summarization, ChatGPT achieved average accuracy values of 0.6 for binary classification and 0.5 for multi-class classification with performance varying depending on the number of shots used for prompting [6]. Another study investigated two prompt settings for AM tasks with GPT-4, achieving F metrics of up to 0.7 for ADU detection and 0.5 for relation detection [10]. Compared to a specialized model, GPT-4 was found to be competitive in predicting discourse markers in argumentative texts, even exceeding the specialized model in one metric [21]. Unlike these results, small domain-specific models have been found to outperform GPT-4 for ADU classification in the legal domain—possibly due to its structural complexity [1]. AM has also been treated as an end-to-end text generation task where ADUs and their relations are generated in a single step [9,15].

4 Mining Argument Graphs Using Prompts

Through our literature review in the previous section, we know that LLMs like ChatGPT are capable of performing AM tasks with a certain degree of accuracy, sometimes even outperforming specialized models. Anticipating the use of our strategy in an interactive setting, we developed (i) an *end-to-end* approach and (ii) a *pipeline-based* one. While the former makes the annotation rather straightforward by returning a complete graph, the latter allows the annotator to fix wrong predictions and/or add missing elements. The pipeline has the additional advantage of letting the annotator decide which subtasks to perform—for instance, they may choose to identify ADUs manually and let the model predict the relations afterwards. In both scenarios, the model is asked for its reasoning in the form of a *textual explanation*, allowing the annotator to better understand the model's decision when reviewing the results. To ensure reproducibility, we provide the prompt template along with each task.

Prompting Strategy. A critical aspect in designing the prompts is the balance between *zero-shot* and *few-shot* learning. The creation of argument graphs is a rather subjective task where multiple different solutions may be equally correct [12], so few-shot learning may lead to a situation where the model leans towards a different annotation style than the human. To mitigate the issue of unpredictable output when using zero-shot learning, we use *function calling* as offered by OpenAI's recent ChatGPT models. The core idea is to express a function and its parameters as a JSON-Schema object, pass this information to a model specifically trained, and execute some function locally using the generated arguments. JSON-Schema allows the definition of complex structures: for each parameter, it may include additional information such as a description, expected data types, and constraints. As its name suggests, this feature was originally built to call functions, but we found it to work equally well to extract structured data such as ADUs from a free-form text.

Implementation. In addition to the interactive system, we provide a Python implementation[1] of the pipeline-based approach to allow batch processing of large datasets. It contains a server component to easily integrate the LLM-based mining to existing systems and an example client to demonstrate its usage.

4.1 Pipeline-Based Graph Generation

Our approach is loosely based on the pipeline described by Lenz et al. [18], consisting of four main steps: (i) Argument extraction, (ii) relation type classification, (iii) major claim detection, and (iv) graph construction. When developing our interactive system, we found steps (ii) and (iv) to be closely related and therefore merged them into a single step to simplify the process. Step (iii) could also be merged into this step (i.e., by inferring the most important claim from the predicted relations), but we decided to keep it separate to allow for more flexibility and control. The three remaining steps are described below.

ADU Detection. Given the original text of the resource to be annotated, the model is prompted to extract all ADUs to be used as atom nodes. We do not differentiate between claims and premises here since a claim may also play a double role as a premise in another argument in graphs. The LLM is instructed to extract only ADUs and not modify the text in the process—otherwise, it will not be possible to locate ADUs in the original text. For the time being, we ignore any kind of *reconstruction*—for instance, replacing pronouns with the correct entities—and leave this to the annotator.

> *Prompt:* The user will provide a long text that contains a set of arguments. Your task is to identify all argumentative discourse units (ADUs) in the text. They will subsequently be used to construct a graph. The user will have the chance to correct the graph, so DO NOT change any text during this step. You shall only EXTRACT the ADUs from the text.

---

[1] https://github.com/recap-utr/arg-services-llm.

Major Claim Identification. Given the ADUs extracted from the original text and their IDs, the model is prompted to identify the major claim among them. In case a non-existent ID is returned by the LLM, the response is discarded, and the annotator will either need to retry or manually select the major claim. In this step, we assume that the major claim is part of the ADUs sent to the model. If it is not part of the original text—and thus not automatically extracted—the annotator may choose to add it manually before executing this step.

> *Prompt:* The user will provide a list of argumentative discourse units (ADUs). Your task is to identify the major claim/conclusion of the argument. This node will subsequently be used as the root node of an argument graph. Please provide the ID of the ADU that you consider to be the major claim.

Relation Prediction. Given the extracted ADUs and the major claim, the model is prompted to predict relations and their type (i.e., support or attack) between them. Each relation is used as a scheme node in the graph with edges connecting it to the source and target ADUs. As in the previous step, the LLM shall return the IDs of the source and target ADUs. If one of them is not part of the ADU set, the predicted relation is discarded. To simplify the graph construction process, we treat the major claim as the root node of the graph—an assumption that has been made in previous work as well [18].

> *Prompt:* The user will provide a list of argumentative discourse units (ADUs) and the ID of the major claim. Your task is to predict sensible relations in the form of support/attack between them. You shall produce a valid argument graph with the major claim being the root node. You shall create a hierarchical graph with the major claim being the root node (i.e., it should have no outgoing relations, only incoming ones). Flat graphs (i.e., all ADUs directly connected to the major claim directly) are discouraged. There should be no cycles in the graph and no orphaned ADUs.

4.2   End-to-End Graph Generation

The overall goal of this strategy is to perform all three tasks in a single step and thus better utilize the large context window of recent LLMs such as GPT-4 Turbo. Bundling them together should make the generation faster due to the reduced number of requests—we only need one request instead of three. At the same time, the costs should also be lower, since we do not need to feed the output of the model back into the system multiple times. As with the pipeline-based approach, here is the procedure: Given the original text of the resource to be annotated, the model is prompted to perform all three tasks simultaneously and return the complete argument graph.

> *Prompt:* The user will provide a long text that contains a set of arguments. Your task is to generate a complete argument graph containing all ADUs, the major claim, and the relations between the ADUs. ADUs shall only be

EXTRACTED from the text, not changed. Relations can either be of type support or attack. You shall create a hierarchical graph with the major claim being the root node (i.e., it should have no outgoing relations, only incoming ones). Flat graphs (i.e., all ADUs directly connected to the major claim directly) are discouraged. There should be no cycles in the graph and no orphaned ADUs.

5 Interactive Argument Mining System

With the prompting strategy for the AM tasks in place, we now discuss their integration into a user-friendly annotation interface. Instead of writing a new tool from scratch, we decided to build on an existing tool to manually build argument graphs from a plain text source. When investigating the available options, we set the following three constraints: (i) The tool should be open-source so that our extensions can be used by other researchers, (ii) its graph representation should be compatible with AIF, and (iii) it should be well-maintained to avoid building on abandoned software. Among options such as Online Visualization of Arguments (OVA) [3] and MonkeyPuzzle [11], we settled on ArgueMapper [17] as the foundation for our AM system. While OVA has a larger user base and is capable of dealing with dialogical arguments, ArgueMapper was easier to extend due to its modern technology stack—for instance, it uses React for state management and TypeScript for type safety. The Argument Buffers (Arguebuf) [17] format used by ArgueMapper is also compatible with AIF, allowing easy integration with existing tools and datasets.

The following modifications were made to ArgueMapper: (i) The *Plus* button to create new elements is replaced with an *Assistant* button allowing the annotator to invoke the four prompts described in Sect. 4. Clicking on one of them opens a dialog where the user can add custom instructions to the built-in prompt (e.g., to specify the ADU segmentation level). (ii) A field for nodes containing the textual explanation generated by the model. (iii) Settings to provide an API key, select the model (GPT-3.5 Turbo or GPT-4 Turbo), and specify a custom endpoint. (iv) In case an error occurs during the generation, a bottom bar with details for the user (since the model output is probabilistic, the annotator is encouraged to try it again and/or modify the custom instructions). All changes have been merged into the upstream project[2] under the same MIT license to ensure that the community can benefit from them.

Like the rest of ArgueMapper, our assistant features do not require running a backend component on a server—instead, all requests to the LLM are sent directly from the browser. By setting a custom API endpoint, the assistant features can be used with any LLM that offers an OpenAI compatible API (e.g., using `ollama.com`). As such, our system is compatible not only with proprietary ChatGPT, but also with open models such as Llama.

---

[2] https://github.com/recap-utr/arguemapper.

6   User Study

Having presented both our prompting strategy and its integration in ArgueMapper, in the following we evaluate the feasibility of LLM assisted AM through a user study. Returning to our research question formulated in Sect. 1, there are two main dimensions that we investigate by formulating two hypotheses: speed (H1) and quality (H2). While the former can be evaluated using quantitative measures, the latter one is more difficult to assess because of the inherent subjectivity—two completely different graphs may be of equal quality. We therefore combine quantitative and qualitative measures to check H2.

H1 (Annotation Time): When given access to the ArgueMapper assistant, annotators are faster than not having access to LLM-based generations.

H2 (Annotation Quality): The availability of an LLM assistant does not cause a decrease in the quality of the resulting argument graphs.

6.1   Experimental Setup

The following section highlights the dataset, the annotation procedure, and the evaluation metrics used in our study. We focus on the pipeline-based approach described in Sect. 4.1, leaving the end-to-end approach for future work.

Dataset Selection. We refrained from re-annotating an existing argument graph corpus, since that could lead the annotators to look up the "reference" solutions and thus biasing the results. Instead, we decided to annotate a new one from scratch. We settled on the *News Articles* dataset compiled by [8] and released under the public domain license CC0 1.0. It consists of 3,824 texts collected between December 2016 and March 2017 from multiple media sources without a specific focus on certain topics. Due to the broad coverage, annotators were not required to have prior knowledge about the dataset. The articles differed greatly w.r.t. the overall length and the dataset exhibited encoding issues with Chinese characters—we therefore removed all articles from "China Daily". To ensure a consistent annotation process covering arguments of comparable length, we also filtered out articles with fewer than 1000 or more than 5000 characters, leaving us with a total of 2335 candidates for annotation.

Annotation Procedure. To perform the annotation, we relied on three male computer science students who were familiar with CA and had prior experience in annotating argument graphs using tools such as the aforementioned OVA and ArgueMapper. They had a regular contract with our institution and received a salary above the minimum wage. To get them on the same page about this annotation task, we provided them with guidelines developed by Dumani et al. [12] for a similar type of dataset. Each student annotated a total of 15 articles without the LLMs assistant and 15 with it, selected at random from the preprocessed dataset. Each of them worked with the regular ArgueMapper application for the first 15 articles and only was given access to the assistant for the remaining 15. Two of the students were then asked to identify and fix any errors in the graphs not created by themselves (the articles of the third student were randomly split between the other two), meaning that for each article, two graphs are available in the final corpus. Theoretically, one could compute the Inter-Annotator Agreement (IAA) between the annotators, but the values would be meaningless since the annotators fixed each other's errors instead of creating distinct graphs. Also, computing IAA values for graphs is challenging due to potential differences in the graph structure and potential propagation of errors—for example, if two annotators do not identify the same set of ADUs, the set of relations that can be compared is different as well.

Evaluation Methodology. To assess H1, we measure the time from the start of the annotation—that is, loading the article into the tool—to the last edit made to any element of the graph. Furthermore, each annotator recorded the time needed for the annotations in an effort to verify the scores obtained from ArgueMapper. To verify H2, we compare the number of errors identified in the second phase of the annotation. We already pointed to the subjective nature of the task, so our initial assumption is that the number of errors does not increase when using the assistant. To further investigate the quality of the annotations, we conducted a survey to gather the annotators' feedback on the assistant features. Among other questions, they were asked to rate *usefulness* and *reliability* of the assistant features on a three-point scale. While the former tries to estimate whether the features were considered helpful in general, the latter assesses the trustworthiness of the results—which, given the tendency of LLMs to confabulate/hallucinate, is a critical aspect. In this context, an example would be the model predicting ADUs that are not present in the original text. They should also assess *perceived impact* of the assistant on speed/quality, the observed response latency, and the preferred ChatGPT model. Lastly, they could provide *free-form feedback* and choose whether they would *prefer using the assistant* in the future or not. After completing the survey individually, we organized a virtual meeting with all annotators to discuss their feedback together.

6.2   Results and Discussion

We now present the results obtained through our user study, starting with the analysis of H1 and then moving on to the evaluation of H2. As part of the process, the annotators identified two articles that did not contain any argumentative information and were therefore not annotated: a list of Grammy winners and a list of Donald Trump's most memorable lines. The corpus containing the remaining 88 argument graphs is publicly available[3] under the attribution license CC BY 4.0 for future research. On average, the graphs created manually contain 9.61 atom nodes and 8.64 scheme nodes, while the assistant-based ones contain 9.93 and 8.93, respectively. Combined, the published corpus contains a total of

---

[3] https://github.com/recap-utr/news-articles-corpus.

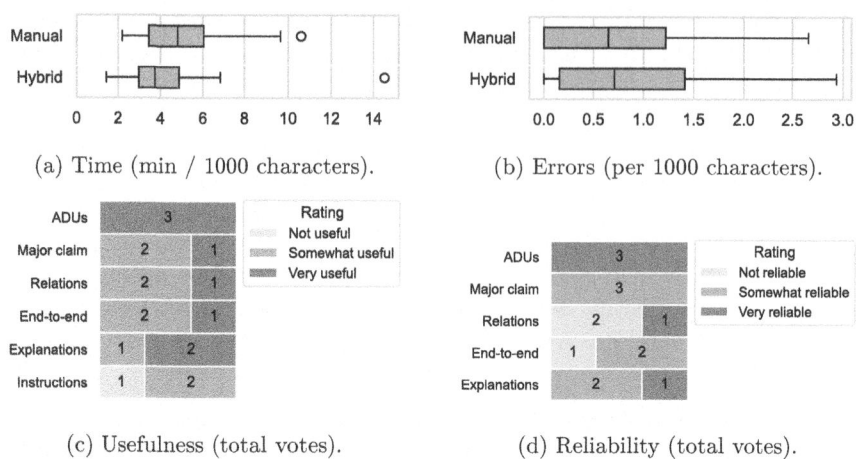

(a) Time (min / 1000 characters).

(b) Errors (per 1000 characters).

(c) Usefulness (total votes).

(d) Reliability (total votes).

Fig. 2. Results of the user study, color scheme uses dark shades for favorable and light shades for unfavorable results.

860 atom nodes and 773 scheme nodes. The annotator names have been redacted from the published version and replaced with unique identifiers to ensure their privacy. We also make available versions of the graphs with the errors identified and corrected by the annotators in the second phase of the annotation.

Annotation Time. Using the created/edited timestamps of the graphs proved to be unreliable: If an annotator paused the annotation and resumed it later, the break would count towards the total time. We therefore used the manually recorded times for our analysis. Since each annotator worked on a different set of articles, we computed the required time per 1,000 characters to allow for a fair comparison. Analyzing the average duration as shown in Fig. 2a, we find that the annotators were indeed faster when using the assistant: The mean duration decreased from five to four minutes—a reduction of $\sim 20\%$. In case of the assistant-based approach, there is one outlier that took more than 14 min per 1,000 characters, while the remaining cases took less than 8 min per 1,000 characters. The annotator did not provide any additional information about the outlier, but possible reasons include difficulties in understanding the article and/or unwanted predictions by the LLM that needed to be corrected.

Given the ability to test both GPT-3.5 Turbo and GPT-4 Turbo, all three students preferred the latter. Although the more advanced model was found to be slower, the additional time was worth it due to the better results. The two models also differ in terms of costs: GPT-4 Turbo is about 20 times more expensive than GPT-3.5 Turbo. With most requests using GPT-4 Turbo, the total cost for the 45 cases was ~ 4.50 USD (or ~ 0.10 USD per article).

In addition to the raw times, we also asked the annotators about the *perceived impact* of the assistant on the annotation speed: All three reported feeling faster when using the LLM functionality. They also unanimously replied that the observed latency of the responses was fast enough for interactive use. Given that both quantitative and qualitative results support H1, we conclude that the assistant-based approach is indeed faster than the manual one.

Annotation Quality. To assess H2, we need to verify that the availability of the LLM features had no negative impact on the quality of the annotated argument graphs. An indicator of quality is the number of errors identified by the annotators in the second phase of the annotation—shown in Fig. 2b. We find that the average number of errors per 1,000 characters increased from 0.79 to 0.90 (about 14%). In both cases, we observe less than one error per 1,000 characters, which we consider to be a good result given the complexity of the task. There are no outliers in both boxplots and the maximum number of errors only increased slightly from 2.7 to 2.9. Closer investigation revealed that most errors were related to missing ADUs and wrong relation types.

Additional insights can be gained from the user study shown in Figs. 2c and 2d. The *ADU extraction* was rated both as "useful" and as "reliable" by the three annotators. The *major claim identification* and *relation prediction* were rated at least "somewhat useful", but differed in terms of reliability. The former was found to be "somewhat reliable" by all participants, but the latter was rated as "not reliable" by two of them. Since these features are successive steps in a pipeline, we conclude that the more complex the task, the less reliable the results. This interpretation is consistent with the feedback received for the *end-to-end graph generation*: They found it to be at least "somewhat useful", but one student rated it as "not reliable" and the others as "somewhat reliable". The explanations generated by the LLM were found to be "useful" by most annotators, but were considered "not/somewhat reliable". *Custom instructions* were the only feature not found to be "useful" by at least one participant, there was even a vote for "not useful". We did not measure its reliability of the feature as it changes the behavior of the LLM and does not generate any output on its own.

Overall, the assistant features are mostly considered to be useful. Reliability ratings are more mixed, with the relation prediction and end-to-end approach being the most problematic. When asked about the assistant's *perceived impact* on the quality of the argument graphs, two annotators reported no change, while one even found that the assistant had a positive impact. Although there were some issues with the assistant, they found it to be a valuable tool for the annotation of argument graphs, especially when dealing with long texts, and would prefer to use it again in the future. Although the results of the user study suggest that the assistant features do not negatively impact the quality of the annotated argument graphs, the error analysis shows that the number of errors increased slightly. We therefore reject H2, but note that the increase in errors may be mitigated in the future with improvements in the LLM technology, optimized prompts that better guide the model towards the desired result, and special training of the annotators to better understand the model's behavior.

Free-Form Feedback. Besides answering multiple questions, the annotators also provided free-form feedback. We summarize the main points in the following, starting with general aspects. The participants reported multiple instances where the LLM response could not be parsed properly by the application, meaning that they had to try again and wait for a new response. Such errors may occur if invalid JSON objects are generated by the LLM, meaning that OpenAI does not strictly enforce the provided schema in all cases. The probabilistic nature of the assistant was received with mixed feelings: It allowed the annotators to obtain different results by running the same generation twice (as anticipated), but these inconsistent results also led to some confusion as to which one to keep. Finally, the annotators wanted to have a best-practice guide on how to use the assistant features effectively.

The discussion of individual features mainly confirmed the findings obtained from Figs. 2c and 2d. The *ADU extraction* was praised by all participants and even helped one of them better understand the structure of the text. They also reported that this step should rather extract too much than too little, as it is easier to remove unwanted ADUs than adding missing ones. A problem of this step was that the model sometimes rephrased ADUs—requiring the human to fix the text manually. The *major claim identification* was found to be useful if the text actually contained a statement that could be considered the main conclusion. As an improvement, they suggested adding a feature to automatically synthesize a major claim from the original text—for instance, through summarization. The *relation prediction* was found to be more effective in shorter texts and less so in longer ones. The annotators reported multiple instances of isolated subgraphs and/or circular relations. The generation of graphs using the *end-to-end* approach was not extensively used, and instead the annotators preferred to fix issues between the individual steps manually. The *explanations* were found to be consistent with the generated predictions; their usefulness, however, was somewhat limited: ADU that were deemed non-argumentative by the annotator often provided contained a summary of its content instead of proper reasoning—indicating that the model should not have extracted them in the first place. *Custom instructions* were seldom used: In cases where the model output was not satisfactory, it was faster for them to do it manually instead of trying to fix the assistant's behavior. Instead, participants wished to modify the temperature of the model so that they could decide between more creative and more conservative responses depending on the current article.

Limitations. Using LLMs for the graph construction task may introduce biases towards certain structures which the annotators may accept without question. The assistant tends to generate more hierarchical graphs than annotators would manually create in certain cases. In addition, predicting relations and/or complete graphs may lead to semantically invalid results, which the annotator has to fix manually (e.g., circular relations). LLMs are probabilistic models with results that vary greatly in different runs even when using the same input—potentially leading to confusion for the annotator. At the same time, this variation allows us to incorporate the notion of subjectivity into our interactive use case: The annotator may choose to run the same generation twice to obtain different results and decide which one to keep based on their own judgement.

Our qualitative results are based on feedback from three annotators and one dataset, which may not be representative of real-world scenarios. The students also likely knew what we were trying to show, which may have influenced their votes on the usefulness and reliability of the assistant features. To determine the speed improvement, we analyzed the annotation time for the entire graph creation process without breaking it down into individual tasks. Consequently, it may be the case that the speedup is caused by one of the tasks, whereas others may actually be slower.

7   Conclusion and Future Work

In this paper, we have presented an interactive system for the annotation of argument graphs that integrates LLMs to support the annotators. Our prompting strategy covers both an end-to-end technique and a pipeline-based one, allowing annotators to choose the most suitable approach for the task at hand. Our user study demonstrated that the modified version of ArgueMapper in fact decreases the annotation time of the argument graphs, while only having a slight impact on the resulting quality. In addition to making our ArgueMapper assistant publicly available, we also release the argument graph corpus created as part of our study. The speed improvements of the interactive system may contribute to the availability of more argument graph corpora, which in turn could positively affect the retrieval of arguments.

In future work, we plan to extend the functionality offered by the assistant— for instance, by adding a way to synthesize a major claim from the original text. Furthermore, we see the potential of using the LLM features to onboard new annotators: In addition to written guidelines with a static selection of examples, they could utilize LLM predictions to receive dynamic feedback for their task.

Acknowledgments. This work has been funded by *German Academic Scholarship Foundation (Studienstiftung des deutschen Volkes)*.

Disclosure of Interests. The authors have no competing interests to declare that are relevant to the content of this article.

References

1. Al Zubaer, A., Granitzer, M., Mitrović, J.: Performance analysis of large language models in the domain of legal argument mining. Front. Artif. Intell. (2023)
2. Allen, J.F.: Natural language processing. In: Encyclopedia of Computer Science, pp. 1218–1222. Wiley (2003)
3. Bex, F., Lawrence, J., Snaith, M., Reed, C.: Implementing the argument web. Commun. ACM 66–73 (2013)

4. Brown, T., et al.: Language models are few-shot learners. In: Advances in Neural Information Processing Systems, pp. 1877–1901. Curran Associates, Inc. (2020)

5. Cabrio, E., Villata, S.: Five years of argument mining: a data-driven analysis. In: Proceedings of the 27th International Joint Conference on Artificial Intelligence, pp. 5427–5433. AAAI Press (2018)

6. Chen, G., Cheng, L., Tuan, L.A., Bing, L.: Exploring the Potential of Large Language Models in Computational Argumentation (2023)

7. Cheñevar, C.I., et al.: Towards an argument interchange format. Knowl. Eng. Rev. 293 (2006)

8. Dai, T.: News Articles (2017). https://doi.org/10.7910/DVN/GMFCTR

9. Das, N., Choudhary, V., Saradhi, V.V., Anand, A.: End-to-End Argument Mining as Augmented Natural Language Generation (2024)

10. de Wynter, A., Yuan, T.: I'd Like to Have an Argument, Please. Argumentative Reasoning in Large Language Models (2024)

11. Douglas, J., Wells, S.: Monkeypuzzle - towards next generation, free & open-source, argument analysis tools. In: CMNA@ICAIL (2017)

12. Dumani, L., et al.: The ReCAP corpus: a corpus of complex argument graphs on German education politics. In: IEEE Proceedings of the 15th International Conference on Semantic Computing (ICSC), pp. 248–255 (2021)

13. Gilardi, F., Alizadeh, M., Kubli, M.: ChatGPT outperforms crowd workers for text-annotation tasks. Proc. Natl. Acad. Sci. e2305016120 (2023)

14. Goddu, G.C.: Against making the linked-convergent distinction. In: van Eemeren, F.H., Garssen, B. (eds.) Pondering on Problems of Argumentation: Twenty Essays on Theoretical Issues, pp. 181–189. Springer, Dordrecht (2009). https://doi.org/10.1007/978-1-4020-9165-0_13

15. Kawarada, M., Hirao, T., Uchida, W., Nagata, M.: Argument mining as a text-to-text generation task. In: Proceedings of the 18th Conference of the European Chapter of the Association for Computational Linguistics (Volume 1: Long Papers), pp. 2002–2014. Association for Computational Linguistics (2024)

16. Lawrence, J., Reed, C.: Argument mining: a survey. Comput. Linguist. 765–818 (2019)

17. Lenz, M., Bergmann, R.: User-centric argument mining with ArgueMapper and Arguebuf. In: Computational Models of Argument, pp. 367–368. IOS Press (2022)

18. Lenz, M., et al.: Towards an argument mining pipeline transforming texts to argument graphs. In: Proceedings of the 8th International Conference on Computational Models of Argument, pp. 263–270. IOS Press (2020)

19. Nguyen, H.V., Litman, D.J.: Argument mining for improving the automated scoring of persuasive essays. In: Thirty-Second AAAI Conference on Artificial Intelligence (2018)

20. Peldszus, A., Stede, M.: From argument diagrams to argumentation mining in texts - a survey. IJCINI 1–31 (2013)

21. Rocha, G., Lopes Cardoso, H., Belouadi, J., Eger, S.: Cross-genre argument mining: can language models automatically fill in missing discourse markers? Argument Comput. 1–41 (2024)

22. Stab, C., Gurevych, I.: Identifying argumentative discourse structures in persuasive essays. In: Proceedings of the 2014 Conference on Empirical Methods in Natural Language Processing (EMNLP), pp. 46–56. Association for Computational Linguistics (2014)

23. Stab, C., Gurevych, I.: Parsing argumentation structures in persuasive essays. Comput. Linguist. 619–659 (2017)

24. Vaswani, A., et al.: Attention is all you need. In: Advances in Neural Information Processing Systems. Curran Associates, Inc. (2017)
25. Wang, J., et al.: Is ChatGPT a good NLG evaluator? A preliminary study. In: Proceedings of the 4th New Frontiers in Summarization Workshop, pp. 1–11. Association for Computational Linguistics (2023)
26. Zhu, Y., Zhang, P., Haq, E.U., Hui, P., Tyson, G.: Can ChatGPT Reproduce Human-Generated Labels? A Study of Social Computing Tasks (2023)

Machine Learning

Contextual Transformers for Goal-Oriented Reinforcement Learning

Oliver Dippel[1,2]([✉])[ID], Alexei Lisitsa[1][ID], and Bei Peng[1][ID]

[1] University of Liverpool, Liverpool, UK
{oliver.dippel,lisitsa,bei.peng}@liverpool.ac.uk
[2] Centre for Doctoral Training in Distributed Algorithms, Liverpool, UK

Abstract. Transformer architectures have become popular across deep-learning disciplines due to their capability of efficiently integrating information across extensive temporal spans and handling large datasets. Recently, this property of transformer models has also been utilized for reinforcement learning (RL) by learning in-context. In in-context learning for decision-making problems, i.e., RL, a transformer model is usually pre-trained on an offline dataset and is tasked to predict the most likely action given a context. Such a model is able to make inference on the fly without parameter updates. Despite great success, the use of transformer architectures for RL is still in its infancy. In this paper, we further investigate the in-context learning abilities of transformer-based goal-oriented RL. We introduce *Goal-Focused Transformer* (GFT), a transformer meta-agent for goal-oriented RL. Building upon the Decision-Pretrained Transformer (DPT), GFT incorporates a function which distills goal information from the context, which we refer to as "goal-controller" (gc) and facilitates task inference during evaluation. By learning to distil useful information from context about the goal states, GFT enhances the exploration-exploitation dynamics and achieves superior performance and stability compared to DPT in environments with sparse rewards. Our contributions highlight GFT's efficacy in increasing average return, enhancing data efficiency, and providing a valuable mechanism for operating in dynamic environments while consistently striving to achieve predefined objectives.

Keywords: Goal-Oriented Reinforcement Learning · In-Context Reinforcement Learning · Transformer-Based Reinforcement Learning

1 Introduction

Self-attention transformer architectures have emerged in natural language processing (NLP) due to their remarkable ability to seamlessly integrate information across extensive temporal spans and handle large datasets [30]. Supervised learned at scale, transformer models have demonstrated remarkable capabilities in generalizing to unseen tasks when provided with input contexts [5,34].

© The Author(s), under exclusive license to Springer Nature Switzerland AG 2025
M. Bramer and F. Stahl (Eds.): SGAI 2024, LNAI 15446, pp. 207–220, 2025.
https://doi.org/10.1007/978-3-031-77915-2_15

This ability can be understood as a form of meta-learning and commonly phrased as in-context learning [2]. In-context learning refers to the ability to learn algorithms, e.g., SGD, or infer tasks from contexts. When transformer agents are used for in-context learning in the framework of RL, RL reduces to a prediction problem that can be solved via supervised learning [25].

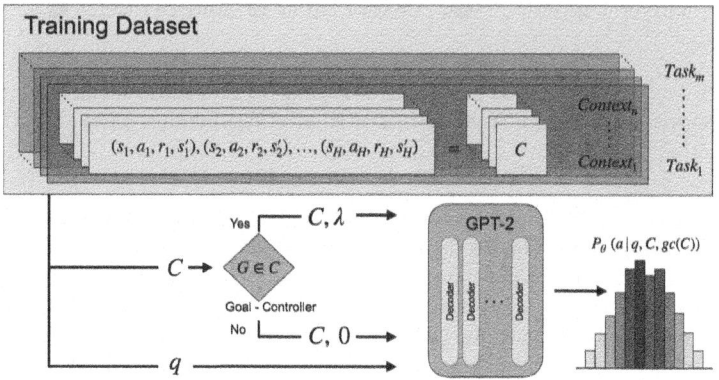

Fig. 1. Goal-Focused Transformer (GFT) outputs the distribution over actions conditioned on a query state and context. During training, GFT learns via supervised learning to predict optimal actions given a manifold of query states, contexts, and the output of the *goal-controller* (*gc*), which is a function that distills goal information from the context.

Among the first frameworks of in-context learning using a transformer model in RL, [4] uses a "reward-on-the-go" mechanism. At test time, a target reward is provided as conditional information to be achieved during rollout. Following approaches [13,15,17,18,20,22] rather rely purely on, e.g., learning policy improvements, achieving great success in offline RL using a transformer model. In this paper, we aim to build upon these accomplishments by further exploring transformer-based models for goal-oriented RL. We leverage the task generalization capabilities of the transformer model, navigating through uncertainty about the ground truth task, and seamlessly transitioning to exploitation as uncertainty diminishes. In goal-oriented RL, agents are trained to achieve predefined objectives or goals within a given environment. This subfield of RL has emerged to be a practical framework for robotic manipulation tasks, in which an agent is required to reach a certain goal defined by a function on the state space [27]. Key challenges include efficiently exploring the environment and making decisions that lead to the successful attainment of the specified goal while maintaining it over time. Successful agents need to learn an efficient exploration strategy and switch to exploitation once the goal is sufficiently certain. Although there has been rapid development in transformer-based RL, there is little literature [12] on utilizing its great potential for goal-oriented RL.

In this paper, we aim to further investigate transformer-based in-context learning for goal-oriented RL. Our work builds upon the Decision-Pretrained Transformer (DPT) [18] and augments the algorithm by introducing a function to distill goal information from the context. DPT first traverses through a supervised pertaining phase, where it takes in a dataset of interactions and can be queried with a forward pass for predictions of the optimal action via inputting a query state and an in-context dataset of interactions. Like most in-context learning agents based on transformer models, DPT changes behaviour based solely on the observed context. DPT has proven superior task generalization performance compared to other in-context transformer-based RL algorithms, e.g., Algorithm Distillation (AD) [17], and performs in-context posterior sampling under certain conditions.

Building upon DPT, we introduce *Goal-Focused Transformer* (GFT), a transformer meta-agent trained on an offline in-context dataset of interactions, a query state, and a function for distilling goal information from the context, which we refer to as the *goal-controller*. The in-context dataset of interactions consists of <state, action, reward, next state> tuples of environment transitions. Figure 1 shows a visualization of the model. The agent learns to infer tasks based on the context originating from a common Markov Decision Process (MDP). The query state provides information about the current agent location in the environment. As the agent traverses through the environment, they collect past transitions as context. Based on the collected context transitions, the *goal-controller* distills information about the goal location. Once the goal is observed in the context, the *goal-controller* emphasises exploitation and strengthens the belief in the underlying task. If the goal is unobserved, the agent maintains its exploration behaviour. The *goal-controller* distinguishes GFT from DPT, resulting in overall performance improvements, while being more data-efficient for goal-oriented environments with sparse rewards. We use the valuable properties of in-context and meta RL for goal-oriented RL to quickly adapt to new unseen tasks, transfer knowledge of seen tasks, and ensure robustness to task variability, while enabling an efficient mechanism to switch from exploration to exploitation.

In summary, our main contribution in this work is the introduction of GFT, a new transformer-based in-context learning method for goal-oriented RL. GFT can quickly adapt to new unseen tasks in goal-oriented environments - by learning to distill useful information from the context. We evaluate GFT in Dark Room [17,18,35], a discrete action environment with sparse rewards that requires targeted exploration. Our experimental results show that, compared to DPT, GFT can 1) achieve better performance and 2) be more data-efficient in terms of the number of tasks and examples per task required to reach the same level or superior performance.

2   Related Work

Inspired by the great success of [30] for large language models, transformer models have been used for decision-making in offline reinforcement learning. By supervised learning from offline data, transformer models are capable of conducting sequential decision-making directly [19]. Commonly in RL, transformers autoregressively predict actions based on a context. Resulting algorithms can learn the policy directly and apply it or infer the task from sequences of trajectories. Hence, some transformer models can be seen as meta RL agents [21] that quickly adapt their policies to new unseen tasks.

Meta-Learning focuses on quickly adapting to new unseen tasks. In RL, this often refers to learning a function which outputs the policy instead of learning a policy for a specific task [1]. A versatile solution involves integrating the entire learning algorithm within a neural network, enabling the network to acquire the ability of learning-to-learn through context [2,9,11,14,29,31].

In-context learning refers to the ability to learn algorithms, e.g., SGD, or infer tasks from contexts. Previous work demonstrates that neural networks can meta-learn in context [11,23,28,29]. Recently, more work focuses on using large language models (LLMs) and transformer for in-context learning [3,10,16]. The works in [2,26] apply large language models (LLMs) for text completion following prompts. In-context learning within the framework of RL has been successfully applied, as demonstrated in [9,31]. In later approaches the context usually takes the form of trajectories of past transition tuples [4,21,32,33].

Goal-oriented RL focuses on training agents to achieve pre-defined goals within an environment. Commonly, goal-oriented RL is applied in areas such as robotics and recommendation systems. Deep RL is used for goal-oriented obstacle avoidance in [6] and later applied for goal-driven autonomous exploration in the work of [7].

Transformer models introduce a novel architecture based on self-attention mechanisms, helping to retain information in long sequences. First introduced in [30], transformer relies on multi-head attention mechanisms and positional encodings to capture long-range dependencies in sequential data without recurrent connections. Once successfully trained, transformer-based agents can learn fully in context for decision-making due to context dynamics without parameter updates. Despite the great success of the transformer architecture, its application in the RL setting is still an open challenge [23,24].

The Decision Transformer (DT) [4] is among the first to successfully use a transformer model for action prediction by framing reinforcement learning (RL) as an autoregressive generation problem with a "reward-on-the-go" mechanism. By conditioning on a target return, DT can learn without relying on explicit temporal difference (TD) learning. The work in [13] repurposes beam search as a planning tool, combining it with a transformer model for imitation learning, goal-conditioned reinforcement learning, and offline reinforcement learning. A method described in [17] learns policy improvements of source RL algorithms by analyzing episode trajectories spanning entire learning processes. In [15], the next action is autoregressively predicted based on transition tuples, with training performed on tuples of increasing performance generated by a Proximal Policy Optimization (PPO) algorithm. Meanwhile, the approach in [12] employs a Vision Transformer backbone [8] for autonomous navigation.

Among existing work using transformer models in the RL setting, the Decision-Pretrained Transformer (DPT) approach by [18] is most similar to the algorithm presented in this paper. DPT uses a transformer to predict the distribution over optimal actions based on a query state and context transition tuples for task inference. We further develop this approach for goal-oriented RL by augmenting the transformer model with a goal information feature, distilling goal information from the context. The so-developed algorithm achieves stable high cumulative rewards while being data efficient.

3 Model

3.1 Preliminaries

We define a Markov decision process (MDP) as a tuple of $\mathcal{M} = \langle \mathcal{S}, \mathcal{A}, \mathcal{R}, \mathcal{T}, \mathcal{H}, \gamma, \rangle$, where $\mathcal{S}$ defines the states space, $\mathcal{A}$ represents the action space, $\mathcal{R}(r_{t+1}|s_t, a_t, s_{t+1})$ is the reward function, $\mathcal{T}(s_{t+1}|s_t, a_t)$ is the state transition function including the initial state distribution $\mathcal{T}_0(s_0)$, $\mathcal{H}$ is the finite horizon, and γ is the discount factor. A task is characterized by a distinct MDP $\mathcal{M}_i$. We follow a standard meta-learning setup in which we have a distribution over possible tasks $p(\mathcal{M})$. While generating the offline training dataset, we repeatedly sample from $\mathcal{M}_i \sim p(\mathcal{M})$ defined by a tuple $\mathcal{M}_i = \langle \mathcal{S}, \mathcal{A}, \mathcal{R}_i, \mathcal{T}_i, \mathcal{H}, \gamma, \rangle$. Each index i represents a task description with alternating reward functions and/or transition functions, e.g., varying goal locations and/or state transitions. For each $\mathcal{M}_i$, we generate N examples of transition contexts $\{\mathcal{C}_{n,i} := \{\tau_h := (s_h, a_h, r_h, s'_h)_{h=1}^{\mathcal{H}}\}\}_{n=1}^{N}$ following $\mathcal{R}_i$ and $\mathcal{T}_i$.

An agent interacts with the environment by observing $s \sim \mathcal{S}$ and executing $a \sim \pi(s)$ according to its internal policy, observing the new state situation $s' \sim \mathcal{T}(\cdot|s, a)$ and receiving a reward of $r \sim \mathcal{R}(\cdot|s, a)$ until the episode ends after $\mathcal{H}$ timesteps. A policy $\pi(a|s)$ maps state observations to distributions over actions and is used to interact with $\mathcal{M}$. A policy π_M^* is optimal for tasks $\mathcal{M}$ if it maximizes the value function $V(\pi_M^*) := max_\pi \mathbb{E}_\pi \sum_{h=1}^{\mathcal{H}} \gamma^h r_h$. We assume that each $\mathcal{M}_i$ has one particular goal location $\mathcal{G}_i$ which is determined by $\mathcal{R}_i$. To maximize the cumulative reward (reach the goal and maintain it) in an unseen MDP, we train the agent to first efficiently explore the state space $\mathcal{S}$ and then switch to exploiting the goal information once $\mathcal{G}$ has been observed.

3.2 Goal-Focused Transformer

Training. We sample batches of $\mathcal{C}_{n,i} := \{\tau_h := (s_h, a_h, r_h, s'_h)_{h=1}^{\mathcal{H}}\}_{n=1}^{N}$ providing contextual information for inference about $\mathcal{M}$. Based on $\mathcal{C}$, we sample a query state $q \sim \mathcal{S}$ from the state space and an optimal action $a^* \sim \pi^*(\cdot|q)$. While transition tuples τ in $\mathcal{C}$ can come from various sources, e.g., expert demonstrations, random interactions with $\mathcal{M}$, and rollouts of a source algorithm, the optimal actions a^* need to come from an expert source. The query state q and the context $\mathcal{C}$, likewise to the in-context dataset of DPT [18], are used as inputs to a causal GPT-2 transformer model P_θ parameterized by θ. We define a function $gc(\mathcal{C})$, which we refer to as *goal-controller* (gc), either outputting information about $\mathcal{G}$ if $\mathcal{C}$ contains $\mathcal{G}$, or a non-informative zero vector $\mathbf{0}$ otherwise, as specified in (1). This output is then appended to the input of P_θ.

$$gc(\mathcal{C}) = \begin{cases} \lambda, & \text{if } \mathcal{G} \in \mathcal{C} \\ \mathbf{0}, & \text{otherwise} \end{cases} \tag{1}$$

Note λ is environment specific. In this work, we set $\lambda = \mathcal{G}$. However, other information criteria might be possible and more suitable for other domains. We leave that for future work. Consequently, P_θ is trained via supervised learning to predict the distribution over actions using a negative log-likelihood (NLL) loss:

$$\mathcal{L}(\theta) := - \sum_{m=1}^{M} \sum_{n=1}^{N} \sum_{h=1}^{\mathcal{H}} log \, P_\theta(a_{mn}^* | q_{mn}, \mathcal{C}_{mn}, gc(\mathcal{C}_{mn})), \tag{2}$$

with M being the amount of training tasks $\mathcal{M}_{train} \subseteq \mathcal{M}$, N being the number of training examples per task, and $\mathcal{H}$ being the finite horizon. A training dataset $\mathcal{D}_{train}$ consists of the following[1]:

$$\mathcal{D}_{train} :=$$
$$\left\{ \left\{ \left(a^*, q, \mathcal{C} := \{\tau_j := (s_j, a_j, r_j, s_j')_{j \in [\mathcal{H}]}\}, gc(\mathcal{C}) \right) \right\}_{n=1}^{N} \sim p(\mathcal{M}_{train}) \right\}_{m=1}^{M}. \tag{3}$$

While both continuous and discrete actions are possible, we concentrate on the latter using a softmax parameterization. Since transformer models are inherently good at classification tasks, we treat the problem as such. We refer to our method of predicting the action distribution from query states, contexts, and goal location information from a goal-controller as *Goal-Focused Transformer* (GFT).

Architecture. Let $\mathcal{S}$ and $\mathcal{A}$ be subsets of $\mathbb{R}^{d_S}$ and $\mathbb{R}^{d_A}$, respectively. From the training tasks $\mathcal{M}_{train} \subseteq \mathcal{M}$, we generate a training dataset $\mathcal{D}_{train}$. Each consists of $\mathcal{H}$ transition tuples providing the context $\mathcal{C}$, a query state q, an optimal action a^*, and a goal location information from $gc(\mathcal{C})$. During training, we sample from $\mathcal{D}_{train}$, building an embedding input $\mathcal{E}(X)$ for the backbone GPT-2 transformer model, with X being an input array of stacked query states q, contexts $\mathcal{C}$, and the output of $gc(\mathcal{C})$. We form the input array $X := (v_1, v_2, \mathcal{C})$, over batches $\mathcal{B}$, for the embedding $\mathcal{E}$ by concatenating $v_1 := (q, \mathbf{0})$, $v_2 := (gc(\mathcal{C}), \mathbf{0})$, and $\mathcal{C}$, with $\mathbf{0}$ being a zero vector, equaling the length of all vectors to be $d_v = 2d_S + d_A + 1$ resulting in $\mathcal{X}$ being of dimensions $d_X = (\mathcal{H} + 2) \times d_v \times \mathcal{B}$. We add no positional encoding on top of X in cases where the order of $\mathcal{C}$ does not matter. The embedding $\mathcal{E}(X)$ is passed to the transformer model outputting a

---

[1] For clarity in notation, we have omitted the subscripts; for instance, $\mathcal{C}$ may be interpreted as $\mathcal{C}_{mn}$.

sequence $Y = \{(\hat{y}_{1,1}, \hat{y}_{1,2}, \ldots, \hat{y}_{1,j}), \ldots, (\hat{y}_{b,1}, \hat{y}_{b,2}, \ldots, \hat{y}_{b,j})\}_{b \in [\mathcal{B}], j \in [\mathcal{H}]}$ of predictions for the corresponding optimal actions $\{a_b^*\}_{b \in [\mathcal{B}]}$. The entries of Y are used as logits and are converted to a distribution over actions in $\mathcal{A}$ by computing the action probabilities as $\hat{p}_{bj} = softmax(\hat{y}_{bj})$, measuring the loss of the training per batch $\mathcal{B}$:

$$\mathcal{L}(\mathcal{B}) = -\sum_{b=1}^{\mathcal{B}} \sum_{j=1}^{\mathcal{H}} log \ \hat{p}_{bj}(a_b^*). \tag{4}$$

Evaluation. First, GFT is trained in a supervised manner on the offline training dataset $\mathcal{D}_{train}$ to minimize the cross entropy loss as specified in (4). Second, during evaluation, we deploy GFT online in the environment on the holdout tasks $\mathcal{M}_{eval} = \mathcal{M} \setminus \mathcal{M}_{train}$ for 40 episodes. When evaluating online, at the very beginning, the context $\mathcal{C}$ is empty and GFT acts purely based on the query state q provided by the environment. Hence, the predicted action can be seen as a prior given no contextual information. While the agent is interacting with the environment, the context $\mathcal{C}$ is filling up until the maximum capacity of $\mathcal{H}$ transition is reached. Thereafter, new transition rollouts replace the oldest in $\mathcal{C}$ according to the paradigm of "first in, first out" (FIFO). Note that during the evaluation phase, no parameter updates are required. Differences in the action selection of GFT's policy $a \sim \pi_\theta(\cdot|q, \mathcal{C}, gc(\mathcal{C}))$ for the same query states q originate from the dynamic nature of $\mathcal{C}$. While the agent explores the sparse reward environment, the context $\mathcal{C}$ is constantly checked for goal location information based on the reward payout during the rollout. Once the goal has been observed in the context, the *goal-controller* distills this information and prompts it to the agent. GFT switches from exploration to exploitation based on the information provided by $gc(\mathcal{C})$. GFT aims to maximize the cumulative reward in goal-oriented (dynamic) environments to optimally trade-off exploration and exploitation to maintain a predefined goal. Note, a goal location in the considered environment is indicated by a reward payout of $+1$ and 0 otherwise. While this payout holds true for the used environment, other environments may differ in this regard. To generalize over environments, the *goal-controller* needs the ability to adapt and process various reward functions including continuous spaces. We leave that for future work.

4   Experiments

In this section, we investigate GFT's properties of task-solving in an environment that requires targeted exploration. We compare the performance of GFT against Decision-Pretrained Transformer (DPT) [18], in terms of generalization to new tasks, data efficiency, and stability. We observe that GFT shows superior generalization ability across seeds compared to DPT, while being up to one order of magnitude more data efficient to reach the same level of performance. GFT autonomously switches from exploration to exploitation while being robust against false prompts from external sources, i.e., provided false goal location information. During the online evaluation, action selection relies on a greedy policy, which entails choosing the most probable action from the output action distribution. Experimental details and hyperparameters can be found in the Appendix.

4.1   Environment

We test our agent in an environment that requires targeted exploration. Once the goal has been found, the agent switches to exploitation to solve the task and collect the maximum cumulative reward. The chosen environment is Dark Room [17,18,35], a 2D discrete action environment, in which an overall goal exists - finding an unknown goal location. The agent navigates a 10×10 grid with a predefined timesteps horizon of $H = 100$. The agent's observation is its xy-position and its previous transitions. Actions are left, right, up, down, and stay with deterministic transitions. A reward of $+1$ is awarded while the agent is at the goal location, and 0 otherwise. During evaluation, the agent starts at $(x = 0, y = 0)$ and transits through the grid world by interacting with it based on its learned policy. Training and evaluation tasks are drawn randomly without replacement from the 100 possible grid goal locations. Testing for generalization is executed on different percentages of training and holdout tasks, with a ratio of $(80/20, 60/40, 40/60, 20/80)$, respectively.

4.2   Dark Room Online Evaluation

Both algorithms GFT and DPT are trained on the same offline training dataset $\mathcal{D}_{train}$ with four different ratios between training and holdout tasks, e.g., $80/20$ refers to 80% training goal locations $\mathcal{M}_{train}$ and 20% holdout goal locations $\mathcal{M}_{eval}$. During the evaluation, GFT and DPT act online in the environment on the holdout goal locations $\mathcal{M}_{eval}$ for 40 episodes. Per training task $\mathcal{M}_{train}$, we use $N = 1000$ contexts $\mathcal{C}$. Note that fewer training tasks refer to fewer examples during training, i.e., $80/20$ equals 80,000 seen training examples, while $20/80$ equals only 20,000 seen different training examples. Hence, a lower training-to-holdout goal location ratio refers to a higher difficulty in terms of generalization. Figure 2 shows the average return of GFT compared to DPT in the online setting across 5 seeds on the same dataset $\mathcal{D}_{train}$[2]. The standard errors are calculated from the individual performances over the holdout tasks and seeds. Both methods are trained for 1000 epochs. In this setting, we compare the performance stability. For the extreme cases $80/20$ and $20/80$, GFT outperforms DPT in terms of cumulative reward across seeds, both in terms of absolute performance and learning speed. For the other two train-evaluation ratios, the performance differences between GFT and DPG are not clearly differentiable.

Next, we compare GFT and DPT in terms of data efficiency and generalization potential. For that, we handpick the best-performing seed for the baseline

---

[2] To showcase the performance, we use identical metrics (mean and standard error) as detailed in [18].

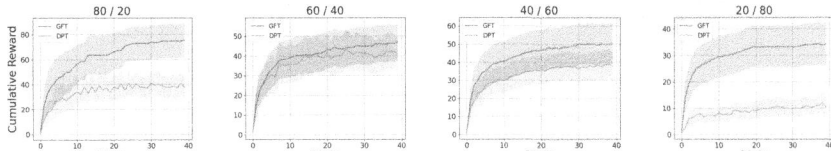

Fig. 2. Mean cumulative online reward (solid line) ± standard error (shaded area) across 5 seeds for different ratios of training and holdouts tasks. Both methods GFT and DPT are trained for 1000 epochs.

DPT and use the same seed for GFT on a *80/20* train-evaluation ratio, thereby giving DPT an advantage[3]. While the across seed performance is relatively stable for GFT, we choose the best performing (average return) seed for DPT and match the seed for GFT. Figure 3 shows the average return after 100, 200, 500 and 1000 training epochs for GFT and DPT. After 1000 epochs, the performance of both algorithms is comparable, however, after only 100 epochs of training, GFT already learns to generalize to new, unseen tasks, while DPT hardly learns to generalize at all. We argue that in terms of generalization, DPT heavily relies on an informative and versatile context during training. While this holds true for GFT, too, we believe GFT can process rare reward occurrences in the context more efficiently and consequently enables faster learning, speeding up training by up to one order of magnitude. Note that GFT is neither provided with goal location information during evaluation nor are the holdout tasks included in the training dataset. GFT successfully and quickly learns to adapt to new unseen tasks by distilling useful information from the context.

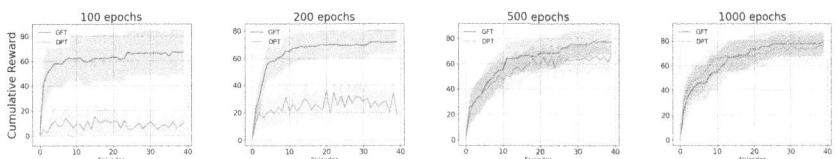

Fig. 3. Mean cumulative online reward (solid line) ± standard error (shaded area) for one handpicked seed after a certain amount of training epochs. The selection is based on the best-performing seed for DPT and matched for GFT (same seed for both algorithms) on a *80/20* train-evaluation ratio.

We also aim to analyze GFT's capability to efficiently transit from exploration to exploitation. To achieve this, we assess the individual performances of both GFT and DPT across *each* holdout task, employing the same training dataset seed combination as previously. Illustrated in Fig. 4a, the cumulative reward per task for both GFT and DPT is depicted. Notably, as soon as GFT

---

[3] See Appendix B for additional performances across seeds.

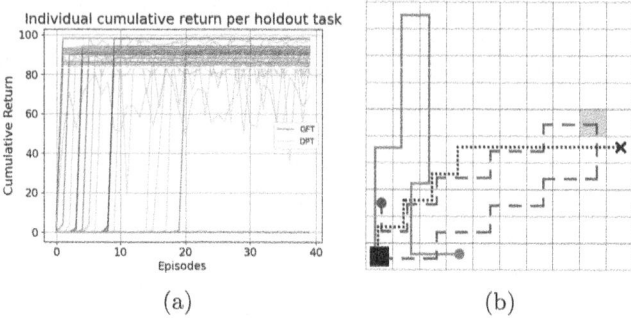

Fig. 4. (a) Each learning curve represents the cumulative online reward per holdout task. (b) Behavior of GFT in the Darkroom environment with different goal prompts provided. The agent starts at the bottom left (black square) and has to navigate to an unknown goal location (cross). (—) Exploration behavior of GFT with an empty goal prompt. (····) Goal prompt consist of the true goal location. (- -) A false goal information (shaded square) was prompted to GFT.

"discovers" evidence of the goal location within the context, the algorithm automatically shifts from exploration to exploitation, indicated by a constant cumulative return over time. While DPT achieves commendable cumulative rewards, the algorithm struggles to stabilize the overall performance, exhibiting volatile returns over time. This demonstrates GFT's superior ability to task identification.

Next, we aim to evaluate GFT's ability to handle externally provided prompts for a selected holdout task in the Dark Room environment and test GFT's robustness against potential false goal information prompts. Figure 4b illustrates three distinct exploration behaviors of GFT after 1000 epochs of training. When no goal prompt is provided (—), when the true goal location is prompted (····), and when false goal information is provided (- -). The agent begins at the bottom left (black square) and must navigate toward an unknown goal (cross) while maintaining it. In the absence of a goal prompt, GFT follows its learned default strategy (—) while the context accumulates past trajectories. After initial timesteps, GFT leaves out a blind spot in the upper left corner of the grid world - even when explored later on the exploration behavior may not be optimal. We argue that this is a result of little to no goal-locations in the upper left corner during training. When provided with a prompt providing the true goal location (····), GFT swiftly navigates to the goal and maintains it thereafter, showcasing the preferred behavior. In the event of a false goal prompt (- -), GFT initially adheres to the provided task information. However, once it reaches the supposed goal location (shaded square), GFT reverts to its default strategy. This behavior is attributed to GFT's continuous monitoring of the context by the *goal-controller*, rendering it resilient to false goal information.

5 Conclusion

In this paper, we explored in-context learning for goal-oriented RL using a transformer model. To achieve this, we extended DPT and introduced GFT, a meta-transformer agent trained through supervised learning on offline data to predict optimal actions based on a combined input of query states, contexts, and a goal controller output. Through online evaluation on holdout tasks in the Darkroom environment, we demonstrated strong generalization capabilities and data efficiency of our method in a goal-oriented context. With external goal prompts, we observed improved exploration-exploitation behavior, while the goal controller effectively prevented false information from corrupting the agent's policy. These findings underscore the potential of transformer models with in-context decision-making abilities in the goal-oriented RL setting.

Limitations. Despite the strong capabilities of GFT in goal-oriented RL, we contend that its generalization abilities heavily depend on the distribution of training tasks and the size of the state space in the training dataset. GFT is susceptible to "blind spots" in its exploration behavior, which may result in poor generalization for unseen tasks. Another drawback is GFT's reliance on expert actions during training, which poses additional challenges.

Future Work. The limitations of GFT also serve as a roadmap for future research. There is significant potential in expanding the diversity of the training task distribution, such as through data augmentation techniques or leveraging distributional source agents to generate training data. This approach can enhance the model's generalization capabilities to new, unseen tasks. Additionally, further refinements of the *goal-controller* for continuous state and action spaces is warranted, while ensuring compatibility with more complex goal-oriented environments with sparse rewards.

A Hyperparameters

We used the PyTorch framework fand seeds 1–5 during training. The handpicked seed for the best DPT performance is 4.

Hyperparameters for GFT and DPT are listed below, are equal for both, and are based on the findings of [18]. We use an embedding size of 32, a horizon $\mathcal{H}$ of length 100, 4 hidden layers, 1 attention head and no residual/embedding/attention dropout. We use the AdamW optimizer with weight decay 1e−4, learning rate 1e−4 and a batch size of 64.

B Additional Experimental Results

In the following, we display the performance after 100, 200, 500 and 1000 epochs of training for DPT and GFT across 5 different seeds - for all train-evaluation ratios (*80/20, 60/40, 40/60, 20/80*). Displayed are the mean cumulative online rewards (solid line) ± standard error (shaded area).

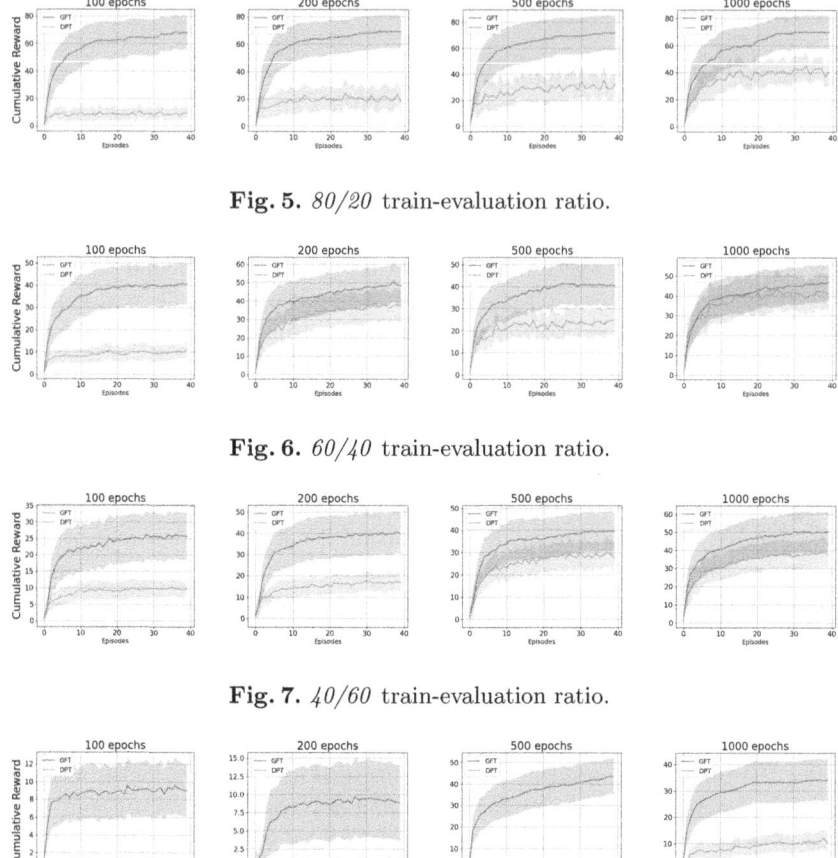

Fig. 5. *80/20* train-evaluation ratio.

Fig. 6. *60/40* train-evaluation ratio.

Fig. 7. *40/60* train-evaluation ratio.

Fig. 8. *20/80* train-evaluation ratio.

References

1. Beck, J., et al.: A survey of meta-reinforcement learning. arXiv preprint arXiv:2301.08028 (2023)
2. Brown, T., et al.: Language models are few-shot learners. Adv. Neural. Inf. Process. Syst. **33**, 1877–1901 (2020)
3. Chan, S., et al.: Data distributional properties drive emergent in-context learning in transformers. Adv. Neural. Inf. Process. Syst. **35**, 18878–18891 (2022)
4. Chen, L., et al.: Decision transformer: reinforcement learning via sequence modeling. Adv. Neural. Inf. Process. Syst. **34**, 15084–15097 (2021)
5. Chen, Y., Wang, X.: Transformers as meta-learners for implicit neural representations. In: Avidan, S., Brostow, G., Cissé, M., Farinella, G.M., Hassner, T. (eds.) ECCV 2022. LNCS, vol. 13677, pp. 170–187. Springer, Cham (2022). https://doi.org/10.1007/978-3-031-19790-1_11

6. Cimurs, R., Lee, J.H., Suh, I.H.: Goal-oriented obstacle avoidance with deep reinforcement learning in continuous action space. Electronics **9**(3), 411 (2020)
7. Cimurs, R., Suh, I.H., Lee, J.H.: Goal-driven autonomous exploration through deep reinforcement learning. IEEE Robot. Autom. Lett. **7**(2), 730–737 (2021)
8. Dosovitskiy, A., et al.: An image is worth 16x16 words: transformers for image recognition at scale. arXiv preprint arXiv:2010.11929 (2020)
9. Duan, Y., Schulman, J., Chen, X., Bartlett, P.L., Sutskever, I., Abbeel, P.: Rl ^{2}: fast reinforcement learning via slow reinforcement learning. arXiv preprint arXiv:1611.02779 (2016)
10. Garg, S., Tsipras, D., Liang, P.S., Valiant, G.: What can transformers learn in-context? A case study of simple function classes. Adv. Neural. Inf. Process. Syst. **35**, 30583–30598 (2022)
11. Hochreiter, S., Younger, A.S., Conwell, P.R.: Learning to learn using gradient descent. In: Dorffner, G., Bischof, H., Hornik, K. (eds.) ICANN 2001. LNCS, vol. 2130, pp. 87–94. Springer, Heidelberg (2001). https://doi.org/10.1007/3-540-44668-0_13
12. Huang, W., Zhou, Y., He, X., Lv, C.: Goal-guided transformer-enabled reinforcement learning for efficient autonomous navigation. arXiv preprint arXiv:2301.00362 (2023)
13. Janner, M., Li, Q., Levine, S.: Offline reinforcement learning as one big sequence modeling problem. Adv. Neural. Inf. Process. Syst. **34**, 1273–1286 (2021)
14. Kirsch, L., Flennerhag, S., van Hasselt, H., Friesen, A., Oh, J., Chen, Y.: Introducing symmetries to black box meta reinforcement learning. In: Proceedings of the AAAI Conference on Artificial Intelligence, vol. 36, pp. 7202–7210 (2022)
15. Kirsch, L., Harrison, J., Freeman, C.D., Sohl-Dickstein, J., Schmidhuber, J.: Towards general-purpose in-context learning agents. In: NeurIPS 2023 Workshop on Distribution Shifts: New Frontiers with Foundation Models (2023)
16. Kirsch, L., Harrison, J., Sohl-Dickstein, J., Metz, L.: General-purpose in-context learning by meta-learning transformers. arXiv preprint arXiv:2212.04458 (2022)
17. Laskin, M., et al.: In-context reinforcement learning with algorithm distillation. arXiv preprint arXiv:2210.14215 (2022)
18. Lee, J.N., et al.: Supervised pretraining can learn in-context reinforcement learning. arXiv preprint arXiv:2306.14892 (2023)
19. Li, W., Luo, H., Lin, Z., Zhang, C., Lu, Z., Ye, D.: A survey on transformers in reinforcement learning. arXiv preprint arXiv:2301.03044 (2023)
20. Li, Y., Ildiz, M.E., Papailiopoulos, D., Oymak, S.: Transformers as algorithms: generalization and stability in in-context learning. In: International Conference on Machine Learning, pp. 19565–19594. PMLR (2023)
21. Melo, L.C.: Transformers are meta-reinforcement learners. In: International Conference on Machine Learning, pp. 15340–15359. PMLR (2022)
22. Mirchandani, S., et al.: Large language models as general pattern machines. arXiv preprint arXiv:2307.04721 (2023)
23. Mishra, N., Rohaninejad, M., Chen, X., Abbeel, P.: A simple neural attentive meta-learner. arXiv preprint arXiv:1707.03141 (2017)
24. Parisotto, E., et al.: Stabilizing transformers for reinforcement learning. In: International Conference on Machine Learning, pp. 7487–7498. PMLR (2020)
25. Paster, K., McIlraith, S., Ba, J.: You can't count on luck: why decision transformers and RVS fail in stochastic environments. Adv. Neural. Inf. Process. Syst. **35**, 38966–38979 (2022)
26. Rae, J.W., et al.: Scaling language models: methods, analysis & insights from training gopher. arXiv preprint arXiv:2112.11446 (2021)

27. Ren, Z., Dong, K., Zhou, Y., Liu, Q., Peng, J.: Exploration via hindsight goal generation. In: Advances in Neural Information Processing Systems, vol. 32 (2019)
28. Santoro, A., Bartunov, S., Botvinick, M., Wierstra, D., Lillicrap, T.: Meta-learning with memory-augmented neural networks. In: International Conference on Machine Learning, pp. 1842–1850. PMLR (2016)
29. Schmidhuber, J.: A 'self-referential' weight matrix. In: Gielen, S., Kappen, B. (eds.) ICANN 1993, pp. 446–450. Springer, London (1993). https://doi.org/10.1007/978-1-4471-2063-6_107
30. Vaswani, A., et al.: Attention is all you need. In: Advances in Neural Information Processing Systems, vol. 30 (2017)
31. Wang, J.X., et al.: Learning to reinforcement learn. arXiv preprint arXiv:1611.05763 (2016)
32. Xu, M., Lu, Y., Shen, Y., Zhang, S., Zhao, D., Gan, C.: Hyper-decision transformer for efficient online policy adaptation. arXiv preprint arXiv:2304.08487 (2023)
33. Xu, M., et al.: Prompting decision transformer for few-shot policy generalization. In: International Conference on Machine Learning, pp. 24631–24645. PMLR (2022)
34. Zhang, Y., et al.: Meta-transformer: a unified framework for multimodal learning. arXiv preprint arXiv:2307.10802 (2023)
35. Zintgraf, L., et al.: Varibad: a very good method for bayes-adaptive deep RL via meta-learning. arXiv preprint arXiv:1910.08348 (2019)

Localized Affinity-Based Reinforcement Learning for Interpretable State-Specific Decision-Making

Ajay Vishwanath[✉][iD] and Christian Omlin[iD]

Centre for Artificial Intelligence Research (CAIR), University of Agder,
4872 Grimstad, Norway
{ajay.vishwanath,christian.omlin}@uia.no

Abstract. Designing a reward function that elicits the desired behavior poses a significant challenge in the field of reinforcement learning (RL). Existing techniques such as constrained RL, safe RL, and reward shaping, while effective, still depend on the transformation of the reward function, potentially complicating interpretability. Recently, policy regularization methods have been employed to achieve the desired behavior. One such method, known as affinity-based RL, has found applications in domains such as finance and machine ethics. In this paper, we introduce a variant called localized affinity-based RL (LAb-RL), which is versatile in state-specific decision-making. Our experiments show that agents can exhibit desired behaviors, and their actions in a given state can be interpreted through their localized affinities. We conclude by advocating the extension of this algorithm to other problems that necessitate state-specific and interpretable decision-making.

Keywords: Affinity-based Reinforcement Learning · Policy Regularization · Interpretability

1 Introduction

Reinforcement learning (RL) is a powerful tool which uses a reward-based mechanism to learn the optimal actions an agent commits in an environment [16]. It has widespread use in our daily lives, such as in transportation [20], robotics [5], and healthcare [14] applications. Typically, in RL, an agent must navigate an environment with states and commit actions. However, in many cases, designing a reward function to ensure that the agent behaves appropriately is a difficult problem and makes it challenging to explain the agent's behavior, even with the help of domain experts [4]. Although reward shaping [10] can help encourage agents to learn the intentions of an expert, it adds to the problem of a lack of algorithmic transparency. This often amplifies issues such as reward hacking

---

Supported by University of Agder, Norway.

M. Bramer and F. Stahl (Eds.): SGAI 2024, LNAI 15446, pp. 221–234, 2025.
https://doi.org/10.1007/978-3-031-77915-2_16

[15]. Whereas, paradigms such as constrained RL, which aims at avoiding certain actions, can further complicate the reward function [3,6]. Others, such as preference-based learning replace the reward function with action preferences, which require human intervention [21].

Another technique known as policy regularization has been used, where recent work [17] has imprinted desired behavior in the agent's policy rather than rewards. A variant of policy regularization known as affinity-based RL (ab-RL) encourages agents to learn strategies that are partially decoupled from reward functions [8]. It aims at (1) a simple, yet surprisingly effective method based on a regularization of the objective function with a distinct action distribution that encourages RL agents ("prototypes") to globally choose preferred actions based on desired agent traits, (2) an inherent RL interpretability which overcomes the obfuscation of opaque RL models that rely on post-hoc explanations and interpretations, and (3) the creation of mixed strategy agents through fuzzy time-variant superpositions of prototypical policies with hierarchical RL, each interpretable by its action affinities, that are globally interpretable.

Ab-RL was first demonstrated in a Manhattan Pizza Delivery environment where the agent's goal was to navigate a grid from a starting point to a destination location, and right turns were preferred [7]. This approach was further applied [8] to a financial investment problem, where based on the personality profile and age of the customer, the agent recommended a customized investment strategy. Other researchers [18,19] have explored the use of affinity-based RL to encourage an agent to perform virtuous actions in Papers, Please environment. Here, the agent, being an immigration agent, is faced with a moral dilemma between taking a bribe from illegal entrants and being honest on the job, and it was shown that the agent can be made to prefer honest actions. However, in these scenarios, the agent acts honestly regardless of the state, and it remains to be seen whether it can result in desired behavior depending on the state.

To pursue this goal, we introduce localized affinity-based RL (LAb-RL), where depending on the state, an agent behaves so that it prefers certain actions in those states. For example, in the Manhattan Pizza Delivery scenario, where the agent prefers right turns in some regions of the grid while preferring to go straight in other parts, this novel algorithm aims to demonstrate that it is possible to achieve desired behavior localized in a state, thus making it interpretable. We believe that this research direction has promise in applications beyond grid-world problems, financial advisors, and machine ethics.

Our research contributions are as follows:

1. A novel interpretable method to incentivize an agent with preferences as a function of the agent's state.
2. An evaluation metric to measure how well an agent has achieved its affinities.
3. An extension of ab-RL which trains RL agent policy by combining state-dependent prototypical agents.

The rest of this paper is organized as follows, beginning with Sect. 2 which discusses state-of-the-art research on regularization in RL. Next, we describe the methods employed to implement LAb-RL, the evaluation metric and experimentation (Sect. 3), followed by a section outlining our results (Sect. 4). Finally, we discuss our results and motivate future work in Sect. 5.

2   Related Works

In this section, recent research on imprinting desired behavior in RL along with alternatives such as constrained RL and preference-based RL is discussed. This is followed by recent developments in ab-RL and relevant information about its mathematical definition.

2.1   Reinforcement Learning and Desired Behavior

Recently, the problem of training an RL agent to optimize a reward function while also imprinting desired behavior patterns has garnered increasing attention. For instance, Constrained RL, which steers clear of unwanted states and actions, is being employed for applications that are critical to safety [1,3]. The task of assigning costs to each state-action pair, which might occur infrequently but could lead to severe outcomes, and can be quite daunting, particularly for extensive state-action spaces. Overall, reward functions often encapsulate complex expert domain knowledge, and crafting an appropriate one can be notoriously challenging. This complexity is further intensified by practices like reward shaping [10], which introduce intricate modifications to the reward function to guide agents towards learning an expert's intentions. This practice also exacerbates issues such as reward hacking [15], where agents learn the exact reward function rather than generalizing the expert's intention. Preference-based RL leverages the knowledge of domain experts to enforce preferences for actions based on states [21]. However, a significant limitation is the requirement for a comprehensive set of preferences or preference functions for continuous problems, as it is impractical to simulate human input for preferences for the actual reward function.

While RL excels at learning in situations with sparse and delayed rewards, it often faces a dilemma known as the exploration/exploitation trade-off [16], which involves choosing between exploiting known effective solutions or exploring potentially better unknown solutions. A more advanced approach involves using intrinsic motivation with policy regularization in deep RL, which allows agents to learn strategies that are somewhat independent of the anticipated rewards [8]. This approach accelerates the learning process by guiding policy selection, such as from a uniform action distribution, thereby promoting exploration. It eliminates the need for complex objective functions while ensuring that agents act as intended. Therefore, it is plausible that regularization could also be employed to instill desirable behaviors specific to the domain. For example, it has been used in offline RL with dataset constraint to overcome the value overestimation issue with a bounded performance gap, as exemplified in navigation and locomotion tasks [12].

The concept of using priors to instill a specific behavior in RL agents through policy regularization has been suggested, where models of probabilistic trajectories encapsulate the preferred behavior patterns [17]. These priors, which introduce an inductive bias, are learned collectively, proving beneficial for multi-task and transfer learning scenarios, as well as applications where safety is paramount. A recent proposal introduced a method to enhance an RL agent with legibility [11]. This method regularizes the agent's policy post-training, eliminating the need to alter its learning algorithm. It fosters an observer model, where a pair of Bayesian networks, representing the agent and observer respectively, encompass a previously learned set of policies, thereby enhancing the distinction between the agent's actual policy and other potential policies. Other researchers [9], used policy regularization for smooth control of action policies in a continuous scenario. The agent is penalized if the action taken in the next state is significantly dissimilar from the action taken in the current state, and further policy smoothening to mitigate noise.

2.2   Affinity-Based Reinforcement Learning

Recently, a universal framework known as affinity-based RL has instilled globally preferred behavior patterns [8]. Similar to entropy-based RL [22], its objective function comprises the sum of the anticipated cumulative rewards and a regularization term. The primary goal of policy regularization was to enhance convergence, with a guarantee of no negative impacts. Essentially, its implicit and unspoken purpose is to exert control over the learning process. Affinity-based RL governs the learning process by employing a specific probabilistic action distribution as the regularization term. This adjustment shifts the balance between exploration and exploitation, causing the policy to observe an overall action probability distribution. It ingrains an inherent preference for certain actions while deterring the selection of others.

Formally, in the equation below, the objective function is given by:

$$J(\theta) = E_{S,A \sim D}[R(S,A)] - \lambda L \tag{1}$$

$$L = \frac{1}{M} \sum_{j=0}^{M} [E_{S,A \sim \pi_\theta}[a_j] - (a_j | \pi_0(A))]^2 \tag{2}$$

The regularizing term L is the mean-squared error of the expected action and a specified prior distribution of actions π_0, which the agent aims to emulate. a_j is the jth action from a set of M actions and π_θ is the policy from which an action probability is sampled. λ is the regularization strength of L. Because of its interpretable nature, one can persuade an agent to commit actions based on π_0. In this manuscript we tailor L to target action preferences as a function of state. In the next section, we define our algorithm and environment.

3   Methodology

In this section, we begin by briefly discussing the environment used to train RL agents. Next, we discuss affinity-based RL which is implemented using the proximal policy optimization (PPO) algorithm [13]. Finally, we describe some practical parameters involved in the training of ab-RL agents.

3.1   Environment

Manhattan Pizza Delivery is a 6×6 grid world environment which simulates a pizza delivery scenario, where the kitchen is located at (3, 0) and the delivery locations appear in elsewhere in the grid (Fig. 1a). The goal is to deliver the pizza via the shortest path. The states are given in Table 1 where *heading* refers to the direction of the agent ranging from 0 to 3, i.e., North, East, South and West respectively.

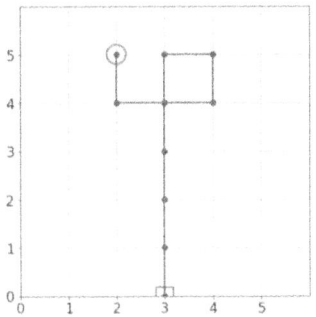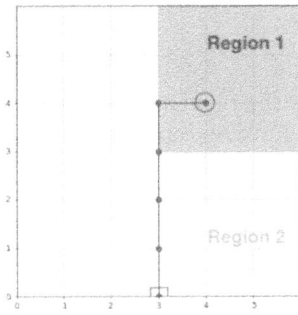

(a) Without Region 1 and Region 2 distinctions.

(b) With Region 1 and Region 2 distinctions.

Fig. 1. Shown here are different Manhattan Pizza Delivery environments: a) the original environment used by [7] with an agent's preference to turn right with a prior action distribution of [0.0, 0.4, 0.6], and b) the environment used for this work to demonstrate LAb-RL.

Since this work aims to exhibit different behaviors in different regions of the environment, we have included two additional observation variables denoted by 'x region 1 start' and 'y region 1 start'. In Fig. 1b Region 1 starts at (3, 3). Here, the borders [(3, 3), (3, 6), and (3, 3),(6, 3)] are included as a part of Region 1.

3.2   Localized Affinity-Based Reinforcement Learning

In Sect. 2, we defined ab-RL as a technique to incentivize an agent to prefer some actions over the others. In the Manhattan scenario, if the prior probabilities of

Table 1. State space in Manhattan Pizza Delivery including the two additional observation variables specifying the start of Region 1 shown *italicized*.

State	Value range	Example		State	Value range	Example
x distance to goal	$[-6, 6]$	1		y location	$[0, 6]$	3
y distance to goal	$[-6, 6]$	-4		*x region 1 start*	$[0, 6]$	5
heading	$[0, 3]$	2		*y region 1 start*	$[0, 6]$	1
x location	$[0, 6]$	-2				

action are defined as $[0.0, 0.4, 0.6]$, i.e., a preference for turning right, it is possible to train this agent to prefer right turns as shown in Fig. 1a.

Based on ab-RL, we introduce a more focused and customizable method known as *localized affinity-based reinforcement learning* (LAb-RL) which is based on action probabilities defined for each state in the environment. Hence, we replace L in Eq. 1 with L_s, which is the localized regularization loss. Hence, the objective function can be defined as:

$$J(\theta) = E_{S,A \sim D}[R(S, A)] - \lambda L_s \tag{3}$$

where λ is the regularization strength similar to Eq. 1. L_s is calculated similarly to L from Eq. 2, except that the prior probability is now a function of the agent's state. The regularization loss is calculated as follows:

$$L_s = \frac{1}{M} \sum_{j=0}^{M} [E_{S,A \sim \pi_\theta}[a_j] - (a_j | \pi_{0i}(S, A))]^2 \tag{4}$$

Here, L_s is the mean-squared error of the expected action and the prior π_{0i}, which is a function of the agent's state and action.

3.3 Experimental Parameters

The Proximal Policy Optimization (PPO) algorithm is preferred in RL because of its simplicity, computational efficiency, and consistent performance. By permitting multiple epochs of mini-batch updates, PPO circumvents the intricate constrained optimization process characteristic of Trust Region Policy Optimization (TRPO), thereby increasing sample efficiency [13]. Additionally, it incorporates a clipping mechanism to maintain stability in policy updates. PPO exhibits versatility, demonstrating effective performance across both discrete and continuous action spaces, and consistently attains state-of-the-art results across various benchmark tasks. Furthermore, the direct policy update approach and its compatibility with continuous action spaces render PPO more effective than deep Q-Networks (DQN) in complex environments [16]. In our version, training is terminated after 2000 episodes and the hyperparameters used to train the model are shown in Table 2.

Table 2. Hyperparameters used in training the PPO algorithm with LAb-RL

Hyperparameter	Value	Hyperparameter	Value
Actor Layers	(1024, 1024)	Batch size	16
Critic Layers	(1024, 1024)	Epochs	10
Input size	7	γ	0.99
Actor Learning rate	$3e^{-4}$	Max iterations	2000
Critic Learning rate	$1e^{-3}$		

3.4   Evaluation Metric: Affinity Error

Affinity error is a metric to estimate the divergence from the prior probabilities. It is given by the mean squared error between number of actions in specific states t and the prior probabilities π_0. The affinity error is given by:

$$\pi_{err} = 1/N \sum_{i=1}^{N} (\tilde{t}_i - \pi_{0i})^2$$

where $\tilde{t}_i$ and π_{0i} are the normalized number of actions and prior probability in state i out of N possible states, respectively. For example, the prior probability could be $\pi_0 = [[0.8, 0.1, 0.1], [0.1, 0.8, 0.1]]$. If the number of turns in each state $t_i = [[2, 4, 2], [1, 2, 3]]$, normalizing t yields: $\tilde{t}_i = [[0.25, 0.5, 0.25], [0.167, 0.33, 0.5]]$. Thus, the affinity error for each state is: $\pi_{err} = [0.162, 0.127]$. The ideal result would be if $\pi_{err} = [0.0, 0.0]$.

4   Results

In this section, we first show the impact of LAb-RL and then analyze the extent to which the regularization strength, λ, influences learning and agent preferences. Next we study the impact of Region 1 location, followed by the regularization probability distribution π_0.

4.1   LAb-RL Training

We trained the PPO model using policy regularization shown in Eq. 2 and the relevant hyperparameters. Here, we present the results of training the LAb-RL algorithm and visualize the reward function and loss function (Fig. 2). We can observe that depending on the regularization strength, λ, the convergence varies. In other words, higher the value of λ, slower the convergence.

We further analyzed the loss function based on the regularization terms, i.e., the reward loss and Region 1 loss. This helps us understand which losses the model prioritizes and how they are balanced during training. Figure 3 shows that λ plays a similar role in convergence and that a higher λ results in slower convergence. Another interesting trend is that Region 1 and Region 2 losses are minimized faster than Reward loss; hence, regardless of λ, they are minimized in fewer episodes of training.

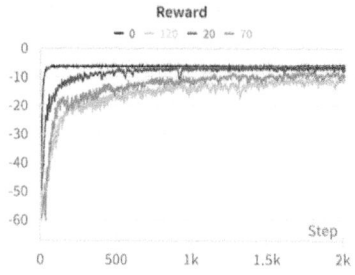
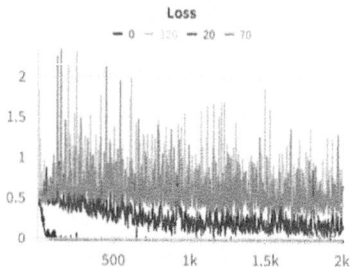

Fig. 2. Reward and Loss functions for our LAb-RL agents varied by regularization strength for each training episode.

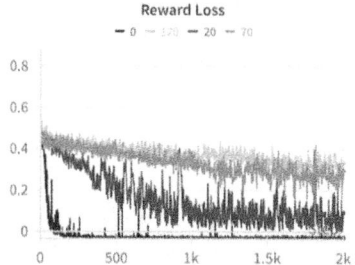
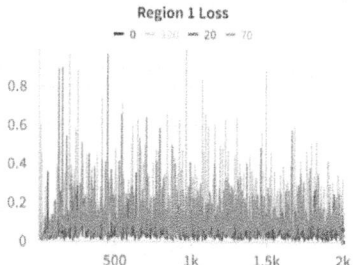

Fig. 3. Reward and Region 1 losses incurred by LAb-RL agents varied by regularization strength, λ, for 2000 episodes.

4.2 Impact of Regularization Strength (λ)

To further understand the impact of λ, we use our previously defined evaluation metric, affinity error (π_{err}). We varied λ between 0 and 140 in steps of 10, and trained our model for 2000 episodes. We observe an overall decline of π_{err} with $\lambda = 0$ yielding the highest reward and highest π_{err}. Figure 4 illustrates this decline of π_{err} with increasing λ.

The dark gray and light gray bars in Fig. 4 represent Region 1 and Region 2 respectively, where Region 1 is the region in Fig. 1b shaded dark gray. While the black bars show the decreasing reward with increasing λ. The starting location of Region 1 in this experiment is (3, 3) for 80 tests. In the next subsection, we show the impact of starting location of Region 1 on our results (Fig. 5).

4.3 Impact of Region 1 Location on Affinity Error

Previous observations indicate that the value of π_{err} decreases as the parameter λ increases. This study aims to demonstrate that a comparable trend is observable for locations in Region 1, specifically at coordinates (1, 1), (2, 2), and (3, 3) in Fig. 7. Conversely, for the location (4, 4), the decrease in π_{err} appears to be less uniform. This inconsistency can be attributed to the low probability of this location serving as the agent's delivery target. Extending the training

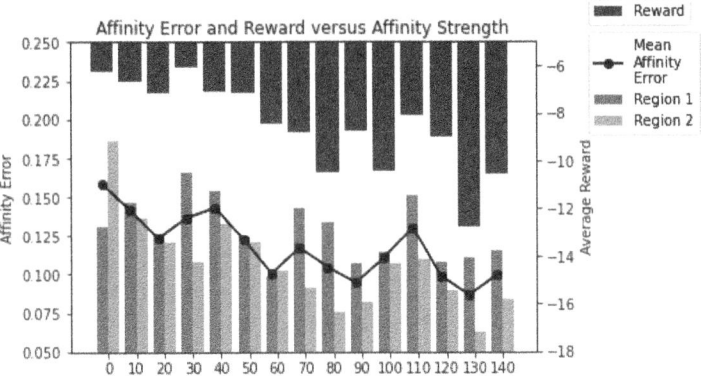

Fig. 4. Average reward and affinity error versus regularization strength for 80 test runs and Region 1 location at $(3, 3)$.

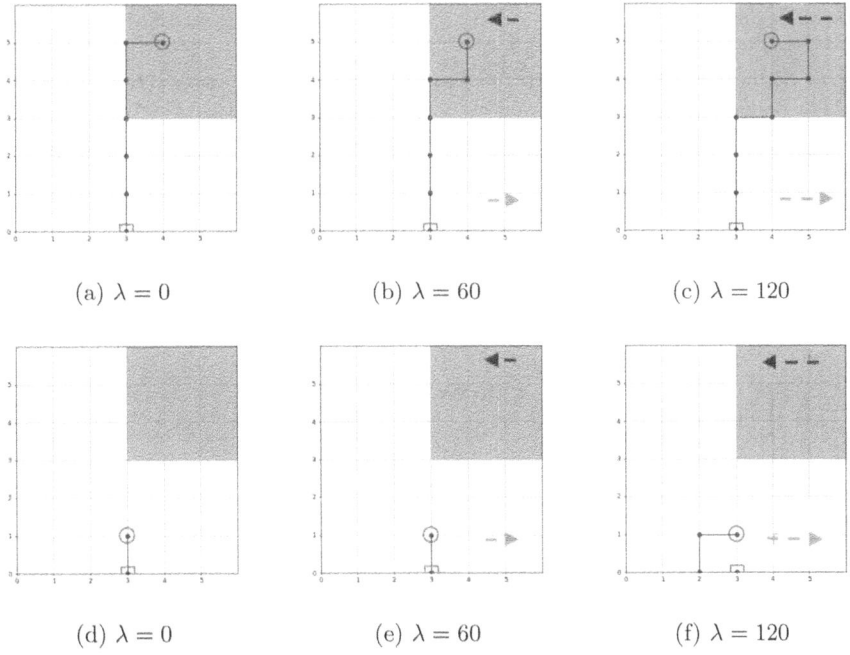

(a) $\lambda = 0$ (b) $\lambda = 60$ (c) $\lambda = 120$

(d) $\lambda = 0$ (e) $\lambda = 60$ (f) $\lambda = 120$

Fig. 5. Impact of regularization strength (λ) on affinity error. Higher the λ, more the affinities towards certain actions. The black arrow denotes the affinity in Region 1 while the gray arrow indicates affinity in Region 2. π_0 for this experiment was $[[0.8, 0.2, 0.0], [0.0, 0.2, 0.8]]$.

duration of the model and incorporating additional data points from this region is anticipated to generate a more uniform trend for the coordinates $(4, 4)$ and $(5, 5)$. In Figs. 6a and 6b, it is observed that agents exhibit a higher affinity error in Region 2 and Region 1, respectively. Furthermore, the frequency of visits to these minority regions by the agents varies-frequent for Region 2 and infrequent for Region 1-subsequently influencing the value of π_{err}.

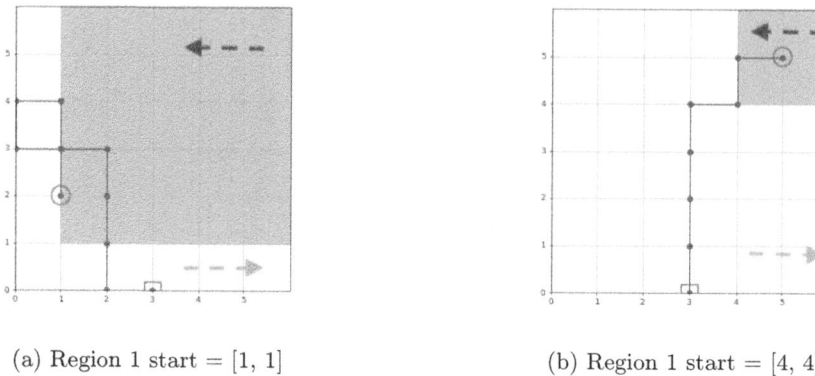

(a) Region 1 start = [1, 1]   (b) Region 1 start = [4, 4]

Fig. 6. Examples of Region 1 start location of (1, 1) and (4, 4) respectively. These are for high regularization strengths and $\pi_0 = [[0.6, 0.3, 0.1], [0.1, 0.3, 0.6]]$.

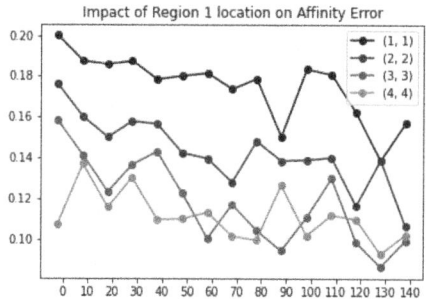

Fig. 7. Impact of Region 1 location on affinity error across 80 test episodes. The x-axis represents λ, while the y-axis is π_{err}

4.4 Impact of Prior Probability on Affinity Error

To understand the impact of the localized prior probabilities, we generated 15 random probabilities based on a Dirichlet distribution, which is a continuous distribution defined on the a generalization of the range of possible values for probability distributions. In Fig. 8, we can visualize each of the 15 distributions, for each region in the Pizza Delivery grid. Region 1 lies between (3, 0) and (6, 6), while Region 2 lies between (0, 0) and (2, 6).

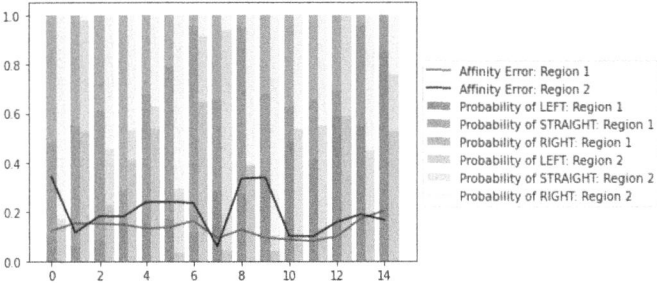

Fig. 8. Impact of regularization parameters on affinity error. The y-axis represents π_{err} and x-axis is the trial with the faded bars being the respective prior probabilities. The black and gray lines denote π_{err} for Region 2 and Region 1 respectively.

Upon training the LAb-RL agent based on these distributions, we observe the affinity errors, π_{err}. For Region 1, π_{err} is between 0.1 and 0.2, while Region 2 sees more fluctuations. When we explore why the values are high (Fig. 9) we see that the prior probability, π_0, of turning right is very high (0.8 to 0.9). An explanation for these higher values, is due to the location of Region 2. In Region 2, there is a higher probability that an agent goes straight from its starting point (3, 0) to reach its destination.

5   Discussion and Future Work

Affinity-based RL has been previously shown to exhibit interpretable preferred behavior in grid-world problems [7], investment planning based on personality [8] and virtuous behavior [19]. In this paper, we develop this research direction further by building an RL agent's policy by combining state-dependent prototypical agents. Our results show that it is possible to customize an agent's behavior by optimizing hyperparameters in the objective function rather than handcrafting a reward function (which is often a tedious task), thus making an agent's behavior interpretable. For instance, in Fig. 4 we show that it is possible to optimize a reward function and an agent's affinities in specific regions of an environment using LAb-RL. Future work could focus on any of the following directions:

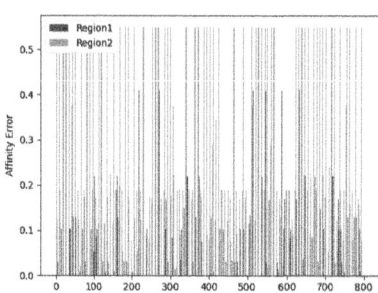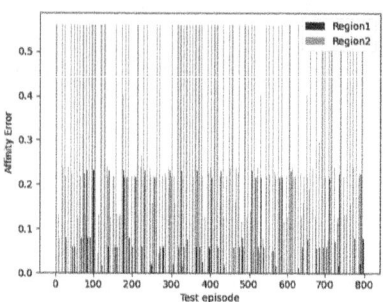

Fig. 9. Episode-wise affinity errors for Region 2 affinities of $[0.14, 0.03, 0.83]$ and $[0.03, 0.07, 0.90]$. It can be seen that Region 2 incurs a high cost compared to Region 1.

Multiple regions: Currently, we demonstrate that it is possible to train an agent to behave differently in two different regions. We could instead adopt the same approach for more regions. Figure 10 illustrates that behaviours could be customized for different parts of the Manhattan Pizza Delivery grid.

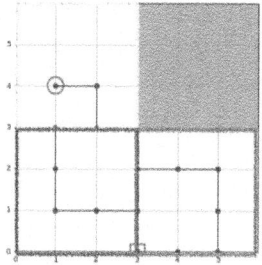

Fig. 10. LAb-RL applied to more than two regions.

Continuous action spaces: So far, our objective function has been defined for discrete state and action spaces based on the mean squared error. Instead, we might be able to experiment in continuous action spaces with an equation such as Eq. 5. Here, we calculate the mean integrated squared error using the prior probability distribution π_0 which is a true density function of state and action, and $E_{S,A\sim\pi_\theta}(a)$ is the estimated density function.

$$L_s = \lim_{M \to \infty} \frac{1}{M} \int_{-\infty}^{\infty} (E_{S,A\sim\pi_\theta}(a) - (a|\pi_0(s,a)))^2 da \tag{5}$$

Benchmarking: There are many benchmark environments such as Frozen Lake, Breakout, etc. [2]. The successful application of LAb-RL in these environments would significantly advance our understanding of behaviors derived from prototypical agents. This would serve as a substantial contribution to the field.

Interpretation of complex agent behavior: Since ab-RL learns a superposition of prototypical agents in the form of their linear combination, it is conceivable that parameter estimation from action observations of complex agent behavior could serve as a tool for the interpretation of global complex agent behavior in terms of the global behavior of prototype agents. This would fill an important knowledge gap: current RL interpretation techniques typically use inverse RL to arrive at an opaque model, and the explanations are typically restricted to either single actions or, at best, specific action sequences.

In conclusion, we have introduced an interpretable RL algorithm called LAb-RL to incentivize an agent to prefer certain actions in certain states in an environment. We used a modified Manhattan Pizza delivery environment where the agent has state-based preferences, and our algorithm exhibited these affinities, which was empirically verified using our performance metric known as affinity error. Finally, we have provided a compelling rationale for future research endeavors in the field of ab-RL. We have also highlighted several promising directions that this line of inquiry could potentially explore. This underscores the dynamic and evolving nature of this research direction.

References

1. Achiam, J., Held, D., Tamar, A., Abbeel, P.: Constrained policy optimization. In: International Conference on Machine Learning, pp. 22–31. PMLR (2017)
2. Brockman, G., et al.: Openai gym. arXiv preprint arXiv:1606.01540 (2016)
3. Garcıa, J., Fernández, F.: A comprehensive survey on safe reinforcement learning. J. Mach. Learn. Res. **16**(1), 1437–1480 (2015)
4. Gupta, A., Pacchiano, A., Zhai, Y., Kakade, S., Levine, S.: Unpacking reward shaping: understanding the benefits of reward engineering on sample complexity. Adv. Neural. Inf. Process. Syst. **35**, 15281–15295 (2022)
5. Kober, J., Bagnell, J.A., Peters, J.: Reinforcement learning in robotics: a survey. Int. J. Rob. Res. **32**(11), 1238–1274 (2013)
6. Liu, Y., Halev, A., Liu, X.: Policy learning with constraints in model-free reinforcement learning: a survey. In: The 30th International Joint Conference on Artificial Intelligence (IJCAI) (2021)
7. Maree, C., Omlin, C.: Reinforcement learning your way: agent characterization through policy regularization. AI **3**(2), 250–259 (2022)
8. Maree, C., Omlin, C.W.: Can interpretable reinforcement learning manage prosperity your way? AI **3**(2), 526–537 (2022)
9. Mysore, S., Mabsout, B., Mancuso, R., Saenko, K.: Regularizing action policies for smooth control with reinforcement learning. In: 2021 IEEE International Conference on Robotics and Automation (ICRA), pp. 1810–1816. IEEE (2021)
10. Ng, A.Y., Harada, D., Russell, S.: Policy invariance under reward transformations: theory and application to reward shaping. In: ICML, vol. 99, pp. 278–287. Citeseer (1999)
11. Persiani, M., Hellström, T.: Policy regularization for legible behavior. Neural Comput. Appl. 1–10 (2022)

12. Ran, Y., Li, Y.C., Zhang, F., Zhang, Z., Yu, Y.: Policy regularization with dataset constraint for offline reinforcement learning. In: International Conference on Machine Learning, pp. 28701–28717. PMLR (2023)
13. Schulman, J., Wolski, F., Dhariwal, P., Radford, A., Klimov, O.: Proximal policy optimization algorithms (2017). https://arxiv.org/abs/1707.06347
14. Shortreed, S.M., Laber, E., Scott Stroup, T., Pineau, J., Murphy, S.A.: A multiple imputation strategy for sequential multiple assignment randomized trials. Stat. Med. **33**(24), 4202–4214 (2014)
15. Skalse, J., Howe, N.H.R., Krasheninnikov, D., Krueger, D.: Defining and characterizing reward hacking. In: Proceedings of the 36th International Conference on Neural Information Processing Systems. NIPS 2022. Curran Associates Inc., Red Hook (2024)
16. Sutton, R.S., Barto, A.G.: Reinforcement Learning: An Introduction, 2nd edn. The MIT Press, Cambridge (2018)
17. Tirumala, D., et al.: Behavior priors for efficient reinforcement learning. J. Mach. Learn. Res. **23**(1), 9989–10056 (2022)
18. Vishwanath, A., Bøhn, E.D., Granmo, O.C., Maree, C., Omlin, C.: Towards artificial virtuous agents: games, dilemmas and machine learning. AI Ethics (2022). https://doi.org/10.1007/s43681-022-00251-8
19. Vishwanath, A., Omlin, C.: Exploring affinity-based reinforcement learning for designing artificial virtuous agents in stochastic environments. In: Farmanbar, M., Tzamtzi, M., Verma, A.K., Chakravorty, A. (eds.) FAIEMA 2023, pp. 25–38. Springer, Singapore (2024). https://doi.org/10.1007/978-981-99-9836-4_3
20. Wiering, M.: Multi-agent reinforcement learning for traffic light control. In: ICML, pp. 1151–1158 (2000)
21. Wirth, C., Akrour, R., Neumann, G., Fürnkranz, J., et al.: A survey of preference-based reinforcement learning methods. J. Mach. Learn. Res. **18**(136), 1–46 (2017)
22. Yin, P.Y.: Maximum entropy-based optimal threshold selection using deterministic reinforcement learning with controlled randomization. Signal Process. **82**(7), 993–1006 (2002)

Navigating the Landscape of Case Fidelity and Competence in Case-Based Reasoning

Adwait P. Parsodkar[1(✉)], Deepak P.[1,2], and Sutanu Chakraborti[1]

[1] Indian Institute of Technology Madras, Chennai, India
{cs20d404,sutanuc}@cse.iitm.ac.in, deepaksp@acm.org
[2] Queen's University Belfast, Belfast, UK

Abstract. In this paper, we survey measures aimed at quantifying the intrinsic quality of cases' contents, which we collectively refer to as case *fidelity*, and measures that capture their *competence* within the Case-Based Reasoning literature. We discuss how insights from the Truth Discovery and Item Response Theory literature can respectively inform advancements in estimating case fidelity and competence. Additionally, we highlight novel research directions that emerge from a deeper examination of case fidelity and competence.

Keywords: Case-Based Reasoning · Case Base Maintenance · Case Competence

1 Introduction

Case-Based Reasoning (CBR) [7] is a problem-solving paradigm that involves solving an input problem by first retrieving cases (problem-solution pairs) similar to it from a repository called the case base. The solutions proposed by these neighboring cases are then modified using the adaptation knowledge to suit the particular needs of the problem in question. If the proposed solution proves effective for the problem at hand, this problem-solution pair is optionally retained in the case base. This reasoning ability of the case-based reasoner is attributed to the four knowledge containers, namely the vocabulary (the case representation strategy), case base, similarity, and adaptation [23].

It is known that, over time, one or more of these knowledge containers may accumulate invalid or outdated knowledge. To address this, the broader framework of Case-Based Reasoner Maintenance [31] was proposed and involves the maintenance of the four knowledge containers. In that, the maintenance of the case bases, referred to as Case Base Maintenance (CBM) [5], which typically involves the removal of *poor quality* cases from the case base, has garnered significant attention. This evaluation of case quality often encompasses various criteria, such as whether the solution present in a case is suitable for its corresponding problem, the contribution of the case in preserving the problem-solving ability of the reasoner, etc. In addition, recent developments have also highlighted the necessity to account for the contribution of cases in making unfair decisions, such as in [17].

In this work, we provide what we believe is the first of its kind, a unified view of the approaches in the CBR literature that attempt to quantify case *fidelity*—a term we use to collectively refer to measures that capture the intrinsic quality of a case's contents—and its *predictive competence*—the criticality of a case in preserving the problem-solving ability of the reasoner. It is to be noted that our study does not center on methodologies for maintaining case bases. Readers interested in exploring recent advancements in CBM methodologies are encouraged to consult the comprehensive survey provided in [5]. Additionally, our analysis of case competence is confined to the predictive performance of cases, excluding notions such as *explanatory competence*, which pertains to explanation aspects as outlined in [6]. Henceforth, we will refer to predictive competence simply as competence.

We further explore methodologies beyond the confines of CBR to identify frameworks that may inspire novel approaches for quantifying the fidelity and competence of cases. Furthermore, our study of case fidelity and competence unveils several open research directions that include the necessity for the fidelity and competence measure to interact and the imperative need to widen the scope of maintenance to other knowledge containers as well.

The organization of our work is summarized as follows. In Sect. 2, we survey methodologies proposed in the literature for quantifying the fidelity and competence of cases. Section 3 explores literature beyond the realm of CBR that may offer potential insights into advancing methodologies for quantifying case fidelity and competence. Finally, in Sect. 4, we highlight key directions for research that spawn from a deeper inspection of case fidelity and competence.

2   Literature Review

In this section, we provide background into two classes of measures used to quantify the goodness of cases, namely, their fidelity and competence. We review the existing approaches in the literature that attempt to capture these properties. As we shall see, the demarcation between these two facets appears somewhat blurry in the literature. We finally illustrate, using a synthetic example, that although these properties may be perceived as indicators of the goodness of a case, they need not necessarily have a bearing on one another.

2.1   Understanding Fidelity and Competence

The Merriam-Webster dictionary defines the term fidelity as 'accuracy in details'[1]. In the context of CBR, the *true* fidelity of a case would refer to how

---

[1] https://www.merriam-webster.com/dictionary/fidelity.

well a domain expert perceives its solution component appropriate for the problem description (or conversely). In this work, we refer to a case with high (low) fidelity as *faithful* (*unfaithful*).

In practice, however, obtaining expert feedback may not always be feasible or timely [9], thereby making it difficult to acquire true fidelity scores. The CBR community has proposed multiple approaches over the years to arrive at a proxy to the true fidelity estimates of cases in the case base via bottom-up means. As would be surveyed in Sect. 2.2, these methods largely rely on arriving at fidelity estimates of cases by inspecting the extent to which they comply with the foundational assumption in CBR that *similar problems have similar solutions*.

It is important to note that the estimates arrived at by such approaches need not necessarily conform with human assessments. Specifically, a case could be attributed a high fidelity score by an expert but not by bottom-up measures due to the presence of poor similarity and/or adaptation knowledge.

The competence of a case, on the other hand, can be defined as the *criticality* of the case in preserving the problem-solving ability of the reasoner. A case that plays an indispensable role by heavily contributing to the problem-solving ability of the reasoner is regarded as competent, while a case whose contribution is subsumed by other cases is deemed redundant.

Since it is not possible to envisage all possible problems that the reasoner may encounter in the future, the *true* competence of cases in the case base cannot be estimated. The measures proposed for estimating the competence of a case, therefore, assume that the case base serves as a good representative of the problems that the reasoner might encounter in the future [27]. Thus, the criticality of a case in preserving the problem-solving ability over its cases is used as a proxy for its true competence.

A distinguishing feature between fidelity and competence concerns with their implications on the effectiveness and efficiency of the reasoner. In particular, the deletion or undermining of cases with low fidelity is associated with an improvement in the prediction quality of the reasoner. Competence, on the other hand, has predominantly been used for the compaction of case base, thereby leading to efficiency enhancements. While an improvement in efficiency need not necessarily result in effectiveness gains, experiments in [13] have shown some improvements in average accuracy scores upon removal of redundant cases.

It is crucial to emphasize at this point that although fidelity and competence scores may appear to associate exclusively with the cases in the case base, they cannot be determined in isolation from other knowledge containers. For instance, the neighborhood information necessitates the similarity knowledge container, while the *solves* function also incorporates adaptation. In all the approaches that follow, the fidelity and competence estimates are considered to be implicitly conditioned on one or more of the knowledge containers.

2.2 Approaches for Estimating Case Fidelity

The literature on estimating case fidelity has proposed a multitude of approaches. These approaches operate under an implicit assumption that the unfaithfulness of cases stems from their solution components. A predominant theme observed in quantifying the fidelity of cases involves inspecting the extent to which a case is *well aligned* with its neighborhood. In this section, we briefly review these measures.

Alignment-Based Approaches. The *cohesion* measure [8], one of the first case fidelity measures, captures the extent of overlap between the problem-side and solution-side neighbors of a case.

$$cohesion(c) = \frac{|\mathcal{N}_c^{Prob} \cap \mathcal{N}_c^{Sol}|}{|\mathcal{N}_c^{Prob} \cup \mathcal{N}_c^{Sol}|} \tag{1}$$

where $\mathcal{N}_c^{Prob}$ and $\mathcal{N}_c^{Sol}$ represent the problem-side and solution-side neighbors of the case c, respectively. A high cohesion value is assigned to a case if its problem-side neighbors tend to have similar solutions *and* the solution-side neighbors have similar problem parts.

A significant limitation of the cohesion measure arises from the observation that, while it is necessary in CBR for problem-side neighbors to have similar solutions, the converse is not essential. Consequently, a case may be unjustly penalized by the cohesion measure if its solution-side neighbors do not exhibit similar problem-side attribute values. In contrast, the *alignment* measure proposed in [15] addresses this issue by assigning higher scores to cases whose problem-side neighbors have similar solutions while disregarding the converse. The alignment of a case c with its problem-side neighbors $\mathcal{N}_c$ is given by,

$$alignment(c) = \frac{\sum_{c' \in \mathcal{N}_c} s_{cc'}^{Prob} \times s_{cc'}^{Sol}}{\sum_{c' \in \mathcal{N}_c} s_{cc'}^{Prob}} \tag{2}$$

where $s_{cc'}^{Prob}$ and $s_{cc'}^{Sol}$ indicate respectively the problem-side and solution-side similarity[2] between c and c'. Furthermore, the formulation allows a closer problem-side neighbor to exert more influence on the alignment score than a distant one.

It is important to note that the applicability of cohesion and alignment measures extends beyond regression and classification settings. An empirical comparison of these measures in the context of Textual CBR can be found in [22].

While it is a common practice to use the $k-$nearest neighbors, denoted here by $\mathcal{N}_c^k$ for the case c, Eq. 2 was further extended in [2] where a higher-order neighborhood $\mathcal{N}_c^{k^n}$ was considered. For instance, $\mathcal{N}_c^{k^2}$ refers to the second-order neighbors of c and contains the k-nearest neighbors of the cases in $\mathcal{N}_c^k$.

---

[2] It is important to recognize that estimating solution-side similarity is often a non-trivial task in various settings. We point the readers to [21] for relevant discussions in the context of Textual CBR (TCBR).

Another approach that accounts for a wider neighborhood is the *Complexity* measure [13]. Proposed in a classification setting, it captures the proportion of neighbors of c that belong to a class different from that of c as the neighborhood size increases. The complexity within the neighborhood of c is given by,

$$complexity(c) = 1 - \frac{1}{K} \sum_{k=1}^{K} P_{l_c}(\mathcal{N}_c^k) \tag{3}$$

where $P_{l_c}(\mathcal{N}_c^k)$ denotes the proportion of neighbors in $\mathcal{N}_c^k$ that belong to l_c, the class label of c. A case c with complexity greater than a predefined threshold is considered unfaithful.

The *heterogeneity* score proposed in [29] and Reputation-Based Maintenance [18], much like complexity, also account for the distribution of the neighboring cases to the different classes in the set of classes $\mathcal{L}$. The heterogeneity score associated with a case c is given by,

$$heterogeneity(c) = \sum_{l \in \mathcal{L}} P_l(\mathcal{N}_c \cup \{c\})^2 \tag{4}$$

The *reputation* of a case c is the difference between the number of neighbors with the same class as c and the number of those belonging to a different class.

$$reputation(c) = \sum_{c' \in \mathcal{N}_c^k} \mathbb{I}(v_c = v_{c'}) - \sum_{c' \in \mathcal{N}_c^k} \mathbb{I}(v_c \neq v_{c'})$$
$$= |\mathcal{N}_c^k| \times \left(P_{l_c}(\mathcal{N}_c^k) - P_{\mathcal{L}-l_c}(\mathcal{N}_c^k) \right) \tag{5}$$

where $\mathbb{I}(p)$ is the identity function that returns 1 if p evaluates to `true`, 0 otherwise. This approach regards a case as unfaithful if it has a negative reputation.

The *Friend-to-Enemy* ratio $(F : E)$ [14], in contrast to the class distribution-based approaches, makes use of the average distance of the case c to its $k-$nearest like neighbors $\mathcal{N}_c^{k(+)}$ and that to its $k-$nearest unlike neighbors $\mathcal{N}_c^{k(-)}$.

$$F : E(c) = \frac{\sum_{c' \in \mathcal{N}_c^{k(+)}} d(c, c')}{\sum_{c' \in \mathcal{N}_c^{k(-)}} d(c, c')} \tag{6}$$

where $d(c, c')$ is the distance between the problem parts of c and c'. Consequently, c is regarded unfaithful if it is closer to its enemies $(\mathcal{N}_c^{k(-)})$ than its friends $(\mathcal{N}_c^{k(+)})$.

The methods discussed thus far implicitly assume that the neighboring cases of a given case provide a sound basis for assessing its fidelity. In particular, they regard all the cases within $\mathcal{N}_c$ as uniformly faithful when estimating the fidelity of c. This may result in erroneous conclusions in the presence of truly unfaithful neighbors. Specifically,

1. Consider a case c that is truly faithful but has a neighborhood predominantly comprising unfaithful cases. Since a large proportion of the cases similar to c have dissimilar solutions, c would be falsely assigned low fidelity by the measures discussed this far.

2. On the other hand, if c is a truly unfaithful case situated in a neighborhood of predominantly unfaithful cases, the problems similar to c can potentially have similar solutions. Thus, c may be falsely regarded as faithful by virtue of its agreement with its unfaithful neighbors.

That is, the fidelity of the neighboring cases in $\mathcal{N}_c$ should be accounted for while estimating the fidelity of c in order to discount the influence of unfaithful neighbors. RelCBR, proposed in [19], uses a circular definition to quantify the *reliability* of cases in the case base. It considers *a case to be reliable if it is well aligned with its reliable neighbors*. The reliability vector $r^* = \{r_c^*\}_{c \in \mathcal{C}}$ is given by

$$r^* = \underset{\{r_c\}_{c \in \mathcal{C}}}{\operatorname{argmin}} \sum_{c \in \mathcal{C}} r_c \times d^{Sol}(v_c, v_c^e)^2 \tag{7}$$

where r_c is the reliability score assigned to the case c, v_c^e denotes the reliability-weighted solution proposed by cases in $\mathcal{N}_c$ for c, and $d^{Sol}(v_c, v_c^e)$ captures the discrepancy between v_c^e and the solution mentioned in c. The details associated with the optimization procedure can be found in [19].

A notable distinguishing trait of reliability, compared to other fidelity estimation approaches discussed previously, is its ability to account for the adaptation knowledge when computing the solution proposed for cases ($\{v_c^e\}_c$) using the solution of their neighbors.

We would also like to emphasize that the above circular formulation lends RelCBR visibility to a wider neighborhood. Specifically, the reliability of a case c is determined by examining the reliability of cases in $\mathcal{N}_c^k$. However, the reliability of each neighbor within $\mathcal{N}_c^k$ is itself dependent on the reliability of their own neighbors, collectively denoted by $\mathcal{N}_c^{k^2}$, and so forth. Therefore, r_c is effectively dependent on the reliability of cases in its higher-order neighborhood.

Finally, we present a comparative analysis of the fidelity estimation approaches in Table 1.

Table 1. A comparison of fidelity estimation approaches.

	Cohesion	Alignment	Higher-order Alignment	Complexity	Heterogeneity	Reputation	F:E	Reliability
Need for solution-side similarity/neighbors?	Y	Y	Y	N	N	N	N	Y
Local (L) or Extended (E) Visibility?	L	L	E	E	L	L	E	E
Applicable beyond Classification settings?	Y	Y	Y	N	N	N	N	Y
Accounts for adaptation knowledge?	N	N	N	N	N	N	N	Y
Agnostic to the presence of unfaithful neighbors?	Y	Y	Y	Y	Y	Y	Y	N

Provenance-Based Approach. The alignment-based approaches have been largely employed to estimate the fidelity of cases within a static snapshot of the case base. However, the provenance-based approach introduced in [9] offers a temporal perspective, aiming to identify potentially unfaithful cases by considering the growth of the case base over time. This approach operates under the assumption that the case base comprises faithful cases during the onset of the reasoner, with the accumulation of unfaithful cases occurring due to the retention of unverified cases. The claim is that a case whose parent case is itself unverified is more likely to be unfaithful compared to another with a verified parent case. In general, the unfaithfulness of a case is captured by the length of the path to its nearest verified ancestor.

2.3   Approaches for Estimating Case Competence

The competence of a case denotes its *criticality* in preserving the problem-solving ability of the reasoner. In other words, a case with low competence may be deemed *redundant* to the reasoner's problem-solving ability. An accurate estimate of the competence of the cases in the case base would require assessing the cases over all possible scenarios that the reasoner may encounter. However, since this information is not known apriori, it is commonplace to assume that the case base denotes a representative sample of the future target problems [27]. Consequently, the competence of a case c is measured in terms of its criticality in solving the other cases from the case base.

The most rudimentary measure of competence of a case c is given by the cardinality of its *Coverage Set* [28], the cases which are *solved* by c.

$$CoverageSet(c) = \{ \ c' \mid c' \ \in \ \mathcal{C} \ , \ c \ solves \ c' \ \} \tag{8}$$

where c *solves* $c' = \mathtt{true}$ indicates that c is retrieved for c' and the solution of c can be adapted to arrive at the solution of c'.

The *Competence Measure (CM)* proposed in [1] regards a case to be competent if it solves multiple cases but is solved by few cases, and is given by

$$CompetenceMeasure(c) = \frac{\mid CoverageSet(c) \mid}{\mid ReachabilitySet(c) \mid} \tag{9}$$

where *ReachabilitySet(c)* denotes the set of cases in the case base that solve c.

These measures regard the number of cases solved by a case as a key indicator of its competence. However, it is recognized that a case with large coverage need not necessarily be competent by virtue of the possibility of its coverage being subsumed by other cases. In contrast, a case may be regarded as competent despite having a small coverage set comprising of cases that are not solved by other cases in the case base.

The *Relative Coverage* [27] attempts to address this issue by rewarding a case for solving cases that are not solved by many cases.

$$RelativeCoverage(c) = \sum_{c' \in CoverageSet(c)} \frac{1}{\mid ReachabilitySet(c') \mid} \tag{10}$$

This measure of case competence is also used to identify the *representative* cases in each competence group using the footprint algorithm [27]. Other approaches to identify representative cases make use of clustering techniques, such as in [26].

The Relative Coverage provides yet another perspective in the context of CBM. Heuristically, it denotes the likelihood of a case being retained in the case base post CBM. This interpretation of case competence is explored in the *Retention Score* measure [16]. It further addresses a key limitation of the Relative Coverage measure by allowing Compositional Adaptation [30].

$$RS(c) = \sum_{c' \ \in \ CoveredCases(c)} RS(c') \sum_{\mathbb{C} \ \in \ SupportCases(c,c')} \min_{c' \in \mathbb{C}} \frac{RS(c')}{|\ \mathbb{C}\ |} \qquad (11)$$

In essence, a case c is assigned a high retention score if (i). c participates in solving multiple cases (captured by *Covered Cases*) that have high Retention Score, (ii). c requires support from a few cases to solve $c' \in CoveredCases(c)$ (captured by each $\mathbb{C} \in$ *Support Cases*), and (iii). These supporting cases are likely to be retained.

2.4   Relation Between Fidelity and Competence

Since fidelity and competence capture the goodness of the cases in the case base, a natural question in this context is whether these characteristics have a bearing on one another. Specifically, if information regarding a case's fidelity is available, can we infer anything about its competence, or vice versa?

Consider a case-based reasoner that predicts the class of a test instance as that of its nearest neighbor (i.e., null adaptation) based on the Euclidean distance measure from its case base depicted in Fig. 1. In such a setting, it may be seen that the cases within the case base may be categorized as both faithful and competent (such as c_1 and c_2 that can collectively preserve the problem-solving ability of the reasoner to a large extent), unfaithful and redundant (c_3), and faithful but redundant (c_6). However, there is also a possibility of a case being perceived as unfaithful but competent. Cases c_4 and c_5 may be considered unfaithful but can be regarded as competent by virtue of them exclusively solving each other, thereby preserving the problem-solving ability of the reasoner over its cases. It is important to note that the notion of competence does not inherently account for the fidelity of cases, and as a result, c_4 and c_5, although likely unfaithful, are attributed high competence.

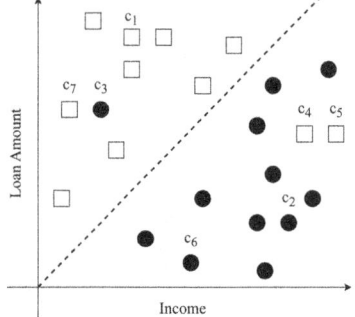

Fig. 1. A sample case base in the Loan Application domain. Each case has two attributes *Income* and *Loan Amount* in its problem part, while the solution is either *Approved* (denoted by ●) or *Rejected* (denoted by □).

This example illustrates that it is possible for a case to have high or low fidelity irrespective of its competence, and vice versa. This underscores the inadequacy of any atomic measure - one that cannot be broken down into two or more parts - to simultaneously capture both the fidelity and competence of cases within the case base. This, in our opinion, demands a reassessment in the literature, where approaches such as complexity (Eq. 3) and reputation (Eq. 5) claim to capture both aspects simultaneously.

3 Literature Beyond CBR for Estimating Fidelity and Competence

In this section, we highlight relevant literature outside the CBR context that may inspire further development in estimating the fidelity and competence of cases in the case base. We also highlight why these may not be trivially applicable in the CBR context by bringing out how they fundamentally differ from CBR. The following discussion also motivates the necessity to propose novel circularity-aware approaches [20] for estimating case fidelity and competence.

3.1 Truth Discovery

Truth Discovery [11] deals with a set of *sources* that provide potentially conflicting *answers* to *questions* from a set of questions. Within this framework, the objective is to estimate the *reliability* of the sources and *trustworthy* answers to the questions. In contrast to assigning uniform reliability to the sources and considering the majority voted answer as trustworthy, Truth Discovery advocates for a nuanced reliability-weighted aggregation.

The overarching theme for estimating the two sets of parameters - reliability of sources and the trustworthy answers to the questions - is captured in the following circular statement:

A source is considered reliable if it provides trustworthy answers. An answer is deemed trustworthy if it is supported by multiple reliable sources.

Although mapping this setting to the CBR context might appear trivial, there are complexities involved. We highlight the key differences here. For an input query (question) q, the similarity function dictates an eligibility criterion that permits only a few cases to participate in answering q. Further, the solution proposed by each of the eligible cases c is not directly projected as a proposed solution for q but is instead passed through an adaptation function. In addition, cases may be allowed to collaborate by means of compositional adaptation, unlike the typical independent source assumption in Truth Discovery. In effect, the reliability score thus obtained is a commentary not only on a case in isolation but also accounts for the similarity function and adaptation rule employed.

One approach, motivated by Truth Discovery, is proposed in [19] with a focus on regression and classification tasks. Further extensions could explore settings beyond classification and regression, examine the algorithm's convergence guarantees, and incorporate aspects such as fine-grained source reliability [11].

3.2   Item Response Theory

The Item Response Theory (IRT) [4] is widely employed in the context of Psychometrics for assessing the latent *abilities* of the respondents and the *difficulty* of the question[3] presented to the respondents. The use of IRT in the evaluation of high-stakes examinations such as the Scholastic Assessment Test (SAT) and Graduate Record Examinations (GRE) underscores its substantive influence. IRT has also recently garnered attention in the context of Natural Language Processing [24] and more broadly in Machine Learning [12].

IRT allows discrimination between two participants even though they correctly answer the exact same number of questions in a questionnaire when the correct responses by one are attributed to a set of simpler questions while the other correctly answers more difficult ones.

Note the departure from the Truth Discovery setting in that each question is marked with a ground truth solution, but the difficulty annotations are unavailable. The two properties - respondent ability and item difficulty - are intertwined:

A respondent who answers multiple difficult questions, in addition to the simpler ones, will be assigned a higher competence, while questions answered primarily by competent respondents are regarded as difficult.

In the context of CBR, competence estimation approaches based on *CoverageSet* (Eq. 8 and 9) account solely for the number of cases (questions) solved. Relative Coverage (Eq. 10), on the other hand, considers a slightly nuanced perspective. It models an aspect similar to the difficulty of q, the case being solved, by means of the $1/ \mid ReachabilitySet(q) \mid$ term. That is, a case is deemed difficult if it is solved by fewer (competent or otherwise) cases.

It is important to note that the Relative Coverage measure persists to have setbacks despite its significant resemblance to the IRT framework. Firstly, the difficulty measure used in Relative Coverage remains competence agnostic, unlike the circular statement employed in IRT. Further, its applicability is restricted to reasoners that employ $1-$nearest neighbor.

4   Potential Research Directions

In this section, we enumerate some research directions that emerge from our discussions thus far. In particular, the significant deficit of the consideration of adaptation knowledge while computing case fidelity can be traced down to how the problem-solution regularity [10] is defined in the literature. We propose the need for a reassessment of this in the light of adaptation knowledge. Secondly, insights from Sect. 2.4 motivate the need for interaction between fidelity and competence. Lastly, we advocate for extending the focus of maintenance efforts to include not only the case base but also other knowledge containers.

---

[3] Technically, referred to as *items* in IRT.

4.1   An Adaptation-Aware Definition of Problem-Solution Regularity

Validating the applicability of CBR in a given problem domain involves verifying whether the foundational assumption that similar problems yield similar solutions largely holds [13]. Measures such as cohesion (Eq. 1) and alignment (Eq. 2) have been used in the literature to quantify this problem-solution regularity within the local neighborhood of a case. An average of these across all the cases in the case base gives an estimate of the problem-solution regularity across the entire case base. If this global regularity measure falls below a predefined threshold, it often suggests that CBR may not be suitable for the task. Additionally, the regularity measures can also support authoring case-based reasoners [8] by assisting in making a choice between different configurations of knowledge containers.

While measures like cohesion and alignment have been employed in designing case-based reasoners, their limitations have been acknowledged in the literature. As noted by the authors in [3], measures such as cohesion and alignment fail to account for adaptation. However, experimental results in [3] indicate that incorporating adaptation into the computation of global problem-solution regularity results in better correlation with generalization accuracy compared to adaptation-agnostic measures.

This motivates the need for a shift in perspective from viewing problem-solution regularity as merely similar problems having similar solutions. Instead, we suggest an adaptation-aware viewpoint by accounting for all four knowledge containers.

A case c is well-aligned with its neighbors when the solutions of the neighbors can be adapted to solve c.

This definition of problem-solution regularity offers two key benefits: firstly, it can allow for more informed decision-making on the suitability of CBR for a given problem setting and can assist in authoring CBR systems. Secondly, it can serve as a sound basis for further advancements in case fidelity estimation techniques that encompass adaptation knowledge.

4.2   Interaction Between Fidelity and Competence Computation

In the CBR literature, fidelity and competence computation are typically viewed as non-interacting steps. However, the case of c_4 and c_5 from Fig. 1 being deemed competent while potentially being unfaithful motivates the need for an interaction between the two measures of case quality. Potential strategies for such an interaction involve (i). performing fidelity assessment followed by a fidelity-aware competence computation, (ii). computing competence scores and incorporating them into the fidelity assessment, or (iii). iteratively cycling through fidelity and competence computations.

The experiments in [13] propose discarding unfaithful cases before computing the competence of cases (akin to strategy (i) noted above) to prevent assigning high competence scores to cases that have noisy class labels. While this suggests that fidelity assessment is a useful precursor for competence computation, the exploration of other strategies remains open in the literature.

We note that the deletion of unfaithful cases prior to estimating competence in [13] disregards the fact that cases exhibit varying degrees of fidelity rather than being strictly faithful or unfaithful. This may lead to the loss of potentially useful information. An alternate strategy might be to incorporate fidelity awareness in the estimation of the competence of cases. A similar extension - competence-aware fidelity - may be proposed for the other potential interaction strategy.

4.3   Extending Maintenance to Other Knowledge Containers

One central bottleneck in effective CBR maintenance is the availability of expert knowledge. In the spirit of active learning, it makes sense to selectively seek expert intervention in a way that can potentially have the highest impact on the problem-solving ability of the reasoner. This suggests that the order in which we present cases or other knowledge containers to an expert to seek their feedback can play an important role in minimizing the overall knowledge acquisition effort.

While CBM has received much attention in the context of the maintenance of case-based reasoners, the maintenance of knowledge containers may warrant closer inspection as well. For instance, a lack of problem-solution regularity between cases in a certain locality can be attributed to deficiencies in the way vocabulary, similarity (or adaptation[4]) knowledge have been encoded – and fixing one of these problems can avoid examination of several cases in isolation.

From a cognitive standpoint, the issue of CBM opens up many interesting frontiers of exploration. For a start, a case that has a solution component very different from other cases in its neighborhood appears to be an outlier and may be considered as a candidate for deletion. However, as humans, any experience that is strikingly different from the norm often paves the way for learning. Of particular mention is the classical model of human reminding proposed by Roger Schank in his seminal work Dynamic Memory [25] that was instrumental in paving the way for a large class of computational models of human memory and their applied counterparts, such as Case-Based Reasoning. According to Schank's model, humans generate expectations based on generalized representations of memory, and when these expectations fail, they are curious and seek explanations for such failures. These explanations, in turn, lead to further generalizations. Thus, according to Schank's model, a case that is not well-aligned with its neighborhood could be potentially very interesting since it could trigger expert intervention in meaningful ways to bring about changes in either the case representation itself or in associated vocabulary, similarity, or adaptation knowledge. One of Schank's examples is the case where one visits a restaurant where one has to pay before they eat – this is strikingly different from his past experiences where people pay only after eating. Accommodating such *outliers*

---

[4] In the extended notion of alignment presented in this paper where adaptation knowledge is integrated.

may necessitate revisiting the underlying vocabulary, the language in which cases are expressed and indexed. For instance, adding more attributes can help better discriminate between classes – interestingly, this is also the philosophy behind bottom-up approaches such as Support Vector Machines. In the context of CBR, attributes may be drawn from more involved types, such as trees/hierarchies or graphs, to bring about richer representations of the underlying domain knowledge.

5   Conclusion

In this work, we have presented a survey of approaches in the CBR literature aimed at quantifying the fidelity and competence of cases. We highlight how insights from Truth Discovery and Item Response Theory can serve as potential inspirations for proposing circularity-aware approaches that attempt to estimate the fidelity and competence of cases. We finally identify three key research directions emerging from a closer examination of these measures. First, we advocate for a reassessment of how problem-solution regularity is defined in the literature. Second, we emphasize the need for an interaction between fidelity and competence measures. Finally, we underscore the need for further study on the maintenance of the other knowledge containers for effective CBR maintenance.

References

1. Chebel-Morello, B., Haouchine, M.K., Zerhouni, N.: Case-based maintenance: structuring and incrementing the case base. Knowl.-Based Syst. **88**, 165–183 (2015)
2. Dileep, K., Chakraborti, S.: Towards higher order complexity measures for text classification
3. Ganesan, D., Chakraborti, S.: A reachability-based complexity measure for case-based reasoners. In: The Thirty-Second International Flairs Conference (2019)
4. Hambleton, R.K., Swaminathan, H.: Item Response Theory: Principles and Applications. Springer, Dordrecht (2013). https://doi.org/10.1007/978-94-017-1988-9
5. Juarez, J.M., Craw, S., Lopez-Delgado, J.R., Campos, M.: Maintenance of case bases: current algorithms after fifty years. In: IJCAI International Joint Conferences on Artificial Intelligence Organization (2018)
6. Keane, M.T., Smyth, B.: Good counterfactuals and where to find them: a case-based technique for generating counterfactuals for explainable AI (XAI). In: Watson, I., Weber, R. (eds.) ICCBR 2020. LNCS (LNAI), vol. 12311, pp. 163–178. Springer, Cham (2020). https://doi.org/10.1007/978-3-030-58342-2_11
7. Kolodner, J.L.: An introduction to case-based reasoning. Artif. Intell. Rev. **6**(1), 3–34 (1992)
8. Lamontagne, L.: Textual CBR authoring using case cohesion. In: Proceedings of 3rd Textual Case-Based Reasoning Workshop at the 8th European Conference on CBR, pp. 33–43 (2006)
9. Leake, D., Whitehead, M.: Case provenance: the value of remembering case sources. In: Weber, R.O., Richter, M.M. (eds.) ICCBR 2007. LNCS (LNAI), vol. 4626, pp. 194–208. Springer, Heidelberg (2007). https://doi.org/10.1007/978-3-540-74141-1_14

10. Leake, D.B., Wilson, D.C.: When experience is wrong: examining CBR for changing tasks and environments. In: Althoff, K.-D., Bergmann, R., Branting, L.K. (eds.) ICCBR 1999. LNCS, vol. 1650, pp. 218–232. Springer, Heidelberg (1999). https://doi.org/10.1007/3-540-48508-2_16

11. Li, Y., et al.: A survey on truth discovery. ACM SIGKDD Explorations Newsl. **17**(2), 1–16 (2016)

12. Martínez-Plumed, F., Prudêncio, R.B., Martínez-Usó, A., Hernández-Orallo, J.: Making sense of item response theory in machine learning. In: ECAI 2016, pp. 1140–1148. IOS Press (2016)

13. Massie, S., Craw, S., Wiratunga, N.: Complexity profiling for informed case-base editing. In: Roth-Berghofer, T.R., Göker, M.H., Güvenir, H.A. (eds.) ECCBR 2006. LNCS (LNAI), vol. 4106, pp. 325–339. Springer, Heidelberg (2006). https://doi.org/10.1007/11805816_25

14. Massie, S., Craw, S., Wiratunga, N.: When similar problems don't have similar solutions. In: Weber, R.O., Richter, M.M. (eds.) ICCBR 2007. LNCS (LNAI), vol. 4626, pp. 92–106. Springer, Heidelberg (2007). https://doi.org/10.1007/978-3-540-74141-1_7

15. Massie, S., Wiratunga, N., Craw, S., Donati, A., Vicari, E.: From anomaly reports to cases. In: Weber, R.O., Richter, M.M. (eds.) ICCBR 2007. LNCS (LNAI), vol. 4626, pp. 359–373. Springer, Heidelberg (2007). https://doi.org/10.1007/978-3-540-74141-1_25

16. Mathew, D., Chakraborti, S.: A generalized case competence model for case base maintenance. AI Commun. **30**(3–4), 295–309 (2017)

17. Mitra, S., Mathew, D., Deepak, P., Chakraborti, S.: Group fairness in case-based reasoning. In: Massie, S., Chakraborti, S. (eds.) ICCBR 2023. LNCS, vol. 14141, pp. 217–232. Springer, Cham (2023). https://doi.org/10.1007/978-3-031-40177-0_14

18. Nakhjiri, N., Salamó, M., Sànchez-Marrè, M.: Reputation-based maintenance in case-based reasoning. Knowl.-Based Syst. **193**, 105283 (2020)

19. Parsodkar, A.P., Deepak, P., Chakraborti, S.: Never judge a case by its (unreliable) neighbors: estimating case reliability for CBR. In: Keane, M.T., Wiratunga, N. (eds.) ICCBR 2022. LNCS, vol. 13405, pp. 256–270. Springer, Cham (2022). https://doi.org/10.1007/978-3-031-14923-8_17

20. Parsodkar, A.P., Deepak, P., Chakraborti, S.: The case for circularities in case-based reasoning. In: Massie, S., Chakraborti, S. (eds.) ICCBR 2023. LNCS, vol. 14141, pp. 85–101. Springer, Cham (2023). https://doi.org/10.1007/978-3-031-40177-0_6

21. Raghunandan, M.A., Chakraborti, S., Khemani, D.: Robust measures of complexity in TCBR. In: McGinty, L., Wilson, D.C. (eds.) ICCBR 2009. LNCS (LNAI), vol. 5650, pp. 270–284. Springer, Heidelberg (2009). https://doi.org/10.1007/978-3-642-02998-1_20

22. Raghunandan, M.A., Wiratunga, N., Chakraborti, S., Massie, S., Khemani, D.: Evaluation measures for TCBR systems. In: Althoff, K.-D., Bergmann, R., Minor, M., Hanft, A. (eds.) ECCBR 2008. LNCS (LNAI), vol. 5239, pp. 444–458. Springer, Heidelberg (2008). https://doi.org/10.1007/978-3-540-85502-6_30

23. Richter, M.M.: The knowledge contained in similarity measures. Invited Talk at the First International Conference on Case-Based Reasoning, ICCBR 1995, Sesimbra, Portugal (1995)

24. Rodriguez, P., Barrow, J., Hoyle, A.M., Lalor, J.P., Jia, R., Boyd-Graber, J.: Evaluation examples are not equally informative: how should that change NLP leaderboards? In: Proceedings of the 59th Annual Meeting of the Association for

Computational Linguistics and the 11th International Joint Conference on Natural Language Processing (Volume 1: Long Papers), pp. 4486–4503 (2021)

25. Schank, R.C.: Dynamic Memory: A Theory of Reminding and Learning in Computers and People. Cambridge University Press, Cambridge (1983)

26. Smiti, A., Elouedi, Z.: WCOID-DG: an approach for case base maintenance based on weighting, clustering, outliers, internal detection and Dbsan-Gmeans. J. Comput. Syst. Sci. **80**(1), 27–38 (2014)

27. Smyt, B., McKenna, E.: Footprint-based retrieval. In: Althoff, K.-D., Bergmann, R., Branting, L.K. (eds.) ICCBR 1999. LNCS, vol. 1650, pp. 343–357. Springer, Heidelberg (1999). https://doi.org/10.1007/3-540-48508-2_25

28. Smyth, B., McKenna, E.: Modelling the competence of case-bases. In: Smyth, B., Cunningham, P. (eds.) EWCBR 1998. LNCS, vol. 1488, pp. 208–220. Springer, Heidelberg (1998). https://doi.org/10.1007/BFb0056334

29. Wang, K., Liu, J.N., Ma, W.M.: A study on the reliability of case-based reasoning systems. In: 2008 IEEE International Conference on Data Mining Workshops, pp. 60–68. IEEE (2008)

30. Wilke, W., Bergmann, R.: Techniques and knowledge used for adaptation during case-based problem solving. In: Pasqual del Pobil, A., Mira, J., Ali, M. (eds.) IEA/AIE 1998. LNCS, vol. 1416, pp. 497–506. Springer, Heidelberg (1998). https://doi.org/10.1007/3-540-64574-8_435

31. Wilson, D.C., Leake, D.B.: Maintaining case-based reasoners: dimensions and directions. Comput. Intell. **17**(2), 196–213 (2001)

Evolutionary and Genetic Algorithms

Tree-Based Genetic Programming for Evolutionary Analog Circuit with Approximate Shapley Value

Xinming Shi[1]($\boxtimes$)(iD), Leandro L. Minku[2](iD), and Xin Yao[2,3](iD)

[1] School of Electronics, Electrical Engineering and Computer Science, Queen's University Belfast, Belfast, UK
x.shi@qub.ac.uk
[2] School of Computer Science, University of Birmingham, Birmingham, UK
l.l.minku@bham.ac.uk
[3] School of Data Science, Lingnan University, Hong Kong, China
xinyao@ln.edu.hk

Abstract. The automated design of analog circuits presents a significant challenge due to the complexity of circuit topology and parameter selection. Traditional evolutionary algorithms, such as Genetic Programming (GP), have shown potential in this domain but are often hindered by inefficient search processes and the large design space. Furthermore, fitness evaluation in the evolutionary design of circuits is often computationally very expensive. In this paper, we introduce a novel evolutionary framework that leverages approximate Shapley values to guide the optimization process in tree-based genetic programming for analog circuit design. Our approach addresses the computational challenges associated with computing Shapley values by introducing a two-stage evolutionary framework that includes a Shapley Value Library (SV_{lib}) and a KNN-based prediction for efficient estimation of Shapley values. Our proposed work not only enhances the search efficiency by focusing on the most beneficial sub-circuits but also leads to more compact and efficient circuit designs. Furthermore, fitness evaluation in the evolutionary design of circuits is often computationally very expensive experiments, we verify that our framework accelerates evolutionary convergence and outperforms traditional methods in terms of circuit optimization.

Keywords: Tree-based genetic programming · Evolvable hardware · Shapley Value · KNN · Analog circuit design

1 Introduction

The design of analog circuits is a critical yet challenging task in electronics, where achieving optimal configurations is essential for performance and efficiency. Traditional methods often struggle with the complexity of analog circuit design [17], making evolutionary algorithms, particularly Genetic Programming (GP) [13],

M. Bramer and F. Stahl (Eds.): SGAI 2024, LNAI 15446, pp. 253–267, 2025.
https://doi.org/10.1007/978-3-031-77915-2_18

a promising alternative for automating this process. However, the efficiency of these algorithms is hampered by the vast search space and the intricate interplay between circuit topology and parameters.

In evolutionary analog circuit design, genetic operators like crossover and mutation play a pivotal role, yet their efficacy is often constrained by the choice of circuit representation. Typically, these operators are applied to genes selected at random, a strategy that can inadvertently discard valuable sub-circuits, thereby diminishing search efficiency. Additionally, the evolution process might be plagued by the bloat phenomenon [14], where circuits become unnecessarily large due to components that contribute nothing to the overall functionality.

The crux of enhancing search efficiency lies in the ability to discern which parts of a sub-circuit are truly instrumental in driving evolutionary progress. Current methods such as the Leave-One-Out (LOO) approach [7], while useful in other contexts, fall short in circuit design as they fail to account for the intricate interdependencies among circuit elements. Consequently, there is a pressing need for a more apt metric that can accurately assess the significance of each gene within the circuit's framework, thereby refining the evolutionary process. In recent years, Shapley values, derived from cooperative game theory, have gained prominence as a robust tool for interpreting machine learning models, especially tree-based models. By attributing quantified contributions to each feature, SHAP values offer a transparent and consistent approach to model interpretation. Despite their theoretical appeal, the computation of SHAP values is notoriously resource-intensive, posing a significant challenge for large datasets or complex models such as deep tree structures [26]. This issue is particularly acute in evolutionary analog circuit design, where efficiently assessing the contribution of circuit components is crucial for guiding the evolutionary process toward optimal designs.

Motivated by the computational challenges associated with SHAP values and the need for a more efficient method in the context of analog circuit design, we propose an evolutionary framework that leverages approximate Shapley values to guide the optimization process. Our approach aims to enhance the search efficiency and circuit quality by retaining and exploiting beneficial sub-circuits, thereby addressing the limitations of traditional genetic operators that often operate randomly and may discard useful circuit components.

Our key contributions are as follows:

1. **Shapley Value Library Creation for Circuit Trees:** We establish a novel methodology for the computation of Shapley values in circuit tree individuals, laying the groundwork for a Shapley Value Library (SV_{lib}). This library represents a comprehensive collection of real Shapley values for nodes in circuit trees, providing a crucial reference for evolutionary operations.

2. **Two-Stage Evolutionary Framework with Accelerated Computation:** We introduce a two-stage evolutionary framework that leverages the SV_{lib}. The first stage involves the creation of this library by calculating the real Shapley values of nodes in circuit tree individuals. In the second stage, we utilize KNN-based prediction to rapidly estimate the Shapley values of nodes

in new individuals. This accelerated computation significantly enhances the efficiency of the evolutionary process.

3. **Guided Evolution of Circuit Trees Using Approximated Shapley Values:** Within our evolutionary framework, we employ the predicted Shapley values to guide the crossover and mutation processes. This approach ensures that evolutionary operations are informed by a node's importance, directing the evolution of analog circuits towards more promising regions of the search space.

4. **Experimental Studies to Show Enhanced Evolutionary Efficiency and Circuit Optimization:** Experiments shows that our approach accelerates evolutionary convergence and produces more efficient circuit designs. This verifies the effectiveness of integrating Shapley value computation with tree-based genetic programming in circuit evolution.

The rest of this paper is structured as follows. Section 2 introduces the related work. Section 3 proposes a novel genetic programming approach for evolving analog circuits. Section 4 describes the experimental studies for verifying our proposed method. The conclusions of our work are presented in Sect. 5.

2   Related Work

2.1   Preliminary Knowledge of Shapley Value

In Cooperative Game Theory (CGT) [3], a set of N players are interconnected through a score function $V : 2^N \rightarrow \mathbb{R}$, where $V(S)$ represents the performance of the model after setting the elements in $N \setminus S$ to zero. To distribute the collective reward among the players equitably, the Shapley value [25] is introduced. It quantifies the contribution of player i to the coalition by defining the marginal contribution $\Delta_V(i, S)$ as the additional value generated by including i in S:

$$\Delta_V(i, S) = V(S \cup i) - V(S) \tag{1}$$

The Shapley value is essentially the average of the marginal contributions across all possible subsets of players, considering the permutations where a particular ordering of S immediately precedes player i:

$$u_i = \frac{1}{|N|} \sum_{S \subseteq N \setminus i} \frac{\Delta_V(i, S)}{\binom{|N|-1}{|S|}} \tag{2}$$

This formulation accounts for interactions between players, capturing scenarios where the performance improvement is contingent on the presence or absence of specific players.

Shapley values have found applications beyond traditional game theory, such as in feature attributions for machine learning models, where they offer insights consistent with human intuition [19]. They have also been used to evaluate the importance of training samples [8,12] and to assess the contribution of individual elements within a model, such as neurons in a neural network [28]. These applications underscore the versatility and relevance of Shapley values in various domains.

2.2   Evolutionary Design of Analog Circuits

In the realm of automated circuit design, evolutionary algorithms have emerged as a powerful tool, with a plethora of approaches being explored [4,10,13,16]. One notable example is the work of Kruiskamp et al. [15], who leveraged Genetic Algorithms (GA) to tackle the synthesis of CMOS operational amplifiers (opamps). In their approach, each individual in the population represented a potential circuit design encoded as a multi-gene chromosome, which could be decoded into an actual circuit. In a different way, Grimbleby et al. [9] utilized GA for the automated synthesis of analog networks, focusing on configuring the circuit structure. However, this approach necessitated numerical optimization to ascertain the values of the circuit components, adding a layer of complexity to the design process.

Moreover, approaches based on Genetic Programming (GP) have shown the ability to evolve circuit netlists that encompass both topology and device values, offering a more integrated solution. While some researchers have used GA to encode circuit topology and parameter values as strings, this often results in limited circuit diversity and a cumbersome decoding process [6,18]. In contrast, GP-based methods enable a richer variety of circuit designs and a more streamlined decoding process, making them a promising avenue for advancing the field of analog circuit design.

2.3   Knowledge-Driven Evolutionary Operators

In standard Genetic Programming (GP), crossover and mutation operators play a crucial role in generating offspring. However, the random selection of genes for these evolutionary operations may hinder search efficiency by overlooking potentially valuable sub-circuits [11]. Additionally, the presence of devices with zero contribution can lead to bloat, resulting in larger evolved circuits [11]. To overcome these limitations, researchers have explored more sophisticated approaches that incorporate semantic information to enhance the exploration of the search space [5,21,24]. For instance, Beadle et al. [2] utilized semantic information to guide GP crossover in Boolean problem domains, while Krawiec et al. [15] defined the semantics of an individual as a vector of outputs for corresponding input fitness cases. Nguyen et al. [23] proposed a semantic crossover approach for real-value domains. However, these advanced operations are tailored for Boolean or real-value problem domains and are not directly applicable to analog circuit design, where circuit validity is a crucial consideration [30].

In the context of evolutionary analog circuit design, it is essential to account for the dependencies among sub-circuits and assign appropriate importance measures. Moreover, the concept of equivalent circuits, which refers to circuits with identical input-output characteristics as the original circuit [1], should be integrated into the design process. While there has been an attempt to evaluate the importance of sub-circuits using the LOO strategy [11], this approach neglects the dependencies among different sub-circuits/devices and their combinations, and it has been limited to digital circuits. Analogue circuits handle continuous signals, while digital circuits use binary signals. To the best of our knowledge, there is no existing work in evolutionary analog circuit design that comprehensively addresses these two perspectives. As discussed in Sect. 2.1, the Shapley value offers a promising solution for measuring the importance of sub-circuits/devices while considering their dependencies.

3   Our Method

We introduce a novel genetic programming approach for evolving analog circuits, utilizing an approximated Shapley Value for enhanced efficiency.

The algorithm commences with a population of circuit trees, a Shapley Value Library, and an archive for individual records. It operates in two stages: initially, it calculates real Shapley values for nodes in each circuit tree, updating the library and archive. Beyond a certain threshold, it employs KNN to predict Shapley values using historical data, guiding the genetic operations of crossover and mutation. This process iterates until a set number of iterations are reached, yielding a refined population of circuit trees. This method innovatively integrates Shapley values into circuit evolution, streamlining the search process and improving design outcomes. The specific description of our proposed approach is presented as Algorithm 1.

In this section, we introduce the overarching goal of the algorithm: to efficiently compute the Shapley values of nodes within circuit tree individuals, which represent potential solutions to a given circuit design problem. The initialization process is crucial as it sets up the initial population of circuit tree individuals, denoted as P_t Each individual is a tree-like structure where nodes represent different circuit components, and the connections between nodes define the circuit's topology.

Additionally, the Shapley Value Library (SV_{lib}) is established. This library is a vital component of the algorithm, as it stores the Shapley values of nodes, providing a measure of their importance or contribution to the overall performance of the circuit. An archive is also set up to store individuals alongside their computed Shapley values, creating a historical record that will be instrumental in predictive modeling during later stages of the algorithm.

3.1   Tree-Based Hierarchical Circuit Encoding Method

In evolutionary analog circuit design, it is crucial to consider both the evolution of circuit topology and the optimization of device values. Our approach represents circuits using a multi-tree structure, T, where the set of all nodes in the tree is denoted as M_T. The internal nodes, or function nodes, are represented by the set N_F. Each function node consists of two parts: the device type and a value tree. The value tree is a binary tree that represents the numeric value of the circuit device, with internal nodes for arithmetic operations and leaf nodes for numeric values. For devices that do not require a value, the value tree is null.

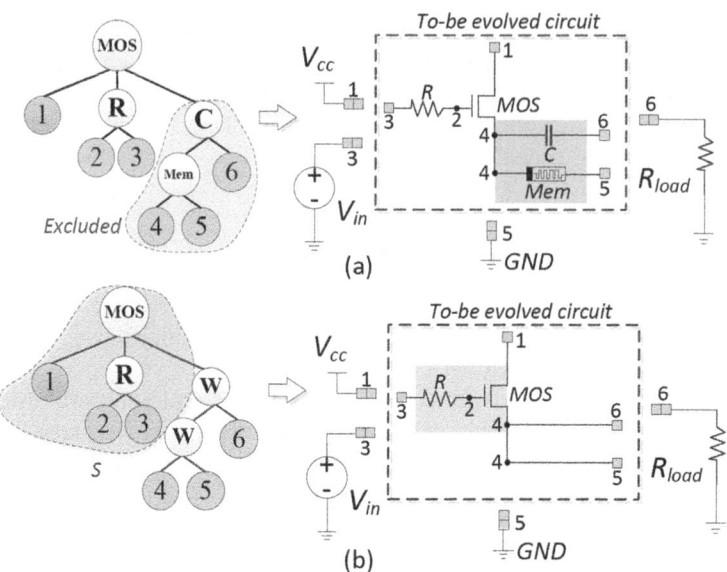

Fig. 1. (a) An example of tree encoding method for a circuit. (b) Equivalent sub-circuit during Shaley value calculation.

The leaf nodes, or terminal nodes, are denoted by the set N_T. Each terminal node represents the position of one device port in the circuit netlist. The arity of a function node, which is the number of child nodes, is determined by the number of device ports. We define $Ch_k(node_i)$ as the k-th child of function node $node_i$. To enhance flexibility in circuit representation, devices with polarity are represented by different function nodes, allowing for any-connection circuits.

To transform the tree-based circuit representation into circuit netlists, each function node is assigned a netlist position number, determined by the left-most terminal nodes corresponding to all its children. For example, consider a circuit with function nodes MOS, R, C, and Mem, and terminal nodes $\{1,2,3,4,5,6\}$. The hierarchy formed by these nodes defines the circuit connection, with the position of each node given by a function $U(H(node_i))$, where $H(node_i)$ is defined based on whether the node is a terminal or function node.

To ensure circuit feasibility, three strategies are applied: avoiding dangling terminals in the embryo circuit, preventing dangling terminals in the evolved circuit, and restricting tree depth. An embryo circuit is a basic initial circuit that needs to be connected to the evolved circuit to form a complete circuit loop. The evolved circuit must ensure that each terminal node is used at least twice to prevent dangling terminals. Finally, a maximum depth limit is imposed on the tree to prevent tree bloat, with any nodes exceeding this limit replaced by their left terminal node. More details of tree-based hierarchy circuit encoding and decoding methods could be found in work [27].

3.2   Shapley Value-Based Evaluation of Sub-Circuits to Guide Genetic Operators

In order to evaluate the contribution of the function node to the whole circuit tree representation, several desirable proprieties to evaluate the circuit device should be taken into the consideration. We list these properties below:

- **Zero contribution:** One decision to make is how to handle circuit devices/blocks that have no contribution. We say that a function node i has no contribution if $\forall S \subseteq N \setminus \{i\} : V(S \cup \{i\}) = V(S)$. This means that it does not change the performance when added to any subtree in of the whole tree. For such null function node, the valuation should be 0.
- **Symmetric elements:** If two nodes contribute exactly the same to any subset of the rest of function nodes, they will have the same values by definition. Mathematically, if $\forall S \subseteq N \setminus \{i\} : V(S \cup \{i\}) = 0$.
- **Additivity in Performance Metric:** As for a circuit device and circuit evolution task, there are two or more performance metrics $V_1, V_2, \ldots$ for an evolved circuit. For example V_1 measures it's performance on output accuracy and V_2 is its performance on circuit area. A natural way to measure the overall performance of the model is having a linear combination of such metrics $e.g. : V = V_1 + V_2$. The additivity in our context is an optional property, since the circuit performance of output accuracy is more dominated compared with other metrics due to its critical impact on reliability and effectiveness in applications.

The Shapley Value-based importance u_{node_i} of a function node $node_i$ can be calculated using the following formula, which uniquely satisfies all these properties:

$$u_{node_i} = \frac{1}{|N_F|} \sum_{S \subseteq N_F - \{i\}} \frac{V(SubTree_{S \cup node_i}) - V(SubTree_S)}{\binom{|N_F| - 1}{|S|}} \tag{3}$$

where $V(S)$ denotes the performance of subtree S. To evaluate the fitness $V(s)$ of subtrees, we consider two scenarios:

(1) If the subtree π_j has overlapping nodes with the subtrees $\pi_i \in \pi, i < j$, the fitness is calculated based on the differences between the voltages on the input and output terminals of the subtree and the target voltage.
(2) If the subtree π_j has no overlapping nodes with the subtrees $\pi_i \in \pi, i < j$, its fitness is calculated based on the maximum fitness of the previous subtrees or the fitness of π_j itself.

Figure 1(b) illustrates the example of evaluating the Shapley value within the context of a circuit. To ascertain the contribution of a specific function node, it is temporarily omitted from the circuit and substituted with a distinct node, denoted by W. This node W signifies a wire connection, effectively short-circuiting the circuit element whose contribution is under evaluation. By comparing the circuit's performance, before and after this substitution, we can discern the impact of the excluded node, thereby quantifying its individual contribution to the overall circuit functionality. This process enables a precise calculation of each element's Shapley value based on the variance in fitness it induces.

This Shapley Value-based approach provides an equitable assignment of values to nodes, enabling the evaluation of the contribution of sub-circuits in a circuit-plausible way. As in [26], crossover will swap the subtree rooted by the function node whose Shapley value is the highest in the one parent with the one whose Shapley value is the lowest in the other parent. Mutation will delete or replace the function node with the lowest Shappley value by a new randomly generated one.

3.3   Two-Stage Based Evolutionary Framework

In the initial stage, the focus is on populating the Shapley Value Library SV_{lib} with real Shapley values. For each individual i the population P_t, the algorithm computes the real Shapley value for each node, reflecting its contribution to the individual's overall performance. These calculated Shapley values are then used to update SV_{lib}, ensuring that it contains the most recent and accurate information. Concurrently, the individual i and its node Shapley values are stored in the archive, providing a rich dataset for future predictions.

The second stage of the algorithm highlights our novel methodology. As the iteration count t surpasses the predefined threshold T_1, the algorithm transitions to using a KNN (K-Nearest Neighbors) based approach for predicting the Shapley values of nodes in new individuals.

3.4   KNN-Based Approximation of Shapley Values

Once the iteration count exceeds the predefined threshold T_1, our proposed approach uses KNN to predict the Shapley values of nodes in new individuals, leveraging historical data from the archive for quick estimation of node importance. The predicted values then guide genetic operations such as crossover and mutation, instead of the Shappley values themselves. This enables the algorithm to focus on nodes with higher importance to create offspring with improved performance, while avoiding the computational cost of computing the Shapley values. After these operations, the population P_t is updated with the new, evaluated individuals.

The integration of KNN-based predictions with genetic operations is a key feature, enabling efficient exploration of the solution space. As the algorithm reaches the maximum number of iterations ($maxiter$), it concludes with a final refined population P_t. The innovative use of KNN for predicting Shapley values, combined with strategic genetic operations, makes the algorithm a powerful tool for circuit design optimization.

The algorithm effectively integrates the concept of Shapley values into the evolutionary process of circuit trees, utilizing a two-stage approach to enhance efficiency. The first stage is dedicated to building a comprehensive Shapley Value

---

Algorithm 1. Shapley Value Approximation Using KNN for Circuit Tree Evolution

---

1: **Input:** Circuit tree individuals, target
2: **Output:** Individuals after crossover and mutation based on importance
3: Initialize population P_t, Shapley Value Library SV_{lib}, and archive $Archive$
4: **while** $t < maxiter$ **do**   ▷ Iterate until max number of iterations is reached
5: **if** $t < T_1$ **then**   ▷ First Stage: Shapley Value Library Creation
6:    **for** each individual i in P_t **do**
7:      Calculate real Shapley value of each node in i
8:      Update SV_{lib} with real Shapley values
9:      Store individual i and its node Shapley values in $Archive$
10:   **end for**
11: **else**   ▷ Second Stage: Accelerated Computation with KNN Prediction
12:    Use KNN to predict Shapley values of nodes in new individuals using $Archive$
13:    **for** each new individual i in P_t **do**
14:      Predict importance of nodes in i using KNN with $Archive$
15:      Perform crossover and mutation on i guided by predicted importance
16:    **end for**
17:    Evaluate new individuals and integrate into the population
18: **end if**
19: **end while**
20: **Return** P_t

Library, while the second stage accelerates the computation by predicting Shapley values using KNN, thereby guiding the evolutionary operations more effectively.

4   Experimental Studies

The main loop of our evolutionary framework is developed in Python, while the performance evaluation of the circuits is conducted through simulations in NGSPICE [29], a tool derived from Spice3 [22].

The experimental study encompasses three distinct types of circuit evolution tasks, focusing on the evaluation of the proposed method across three circuits: a voltage reference circuit, a temperature sensor circuit, and a Gaussian function generator. These circuits are commonly utilized in assessing the efficacy of evolutionary analog circuit design methods and are referenced extensively in the literature [4,14,20], demonstrating their relevance and applicability to this field. Parameter setting is given in Table 1.

Reference Voltage Circuit. In this task, the objective is to design and refine a reference voltage circuit that consistently delivers a fixed output of $2V$. To assess the circuit's performance across a range of temperatures, the output voltage is measured at various points for each temperature condition. These measurements

Table 1. Parameter setting

Algorithm Parameter	Value
Population Size (Pop_Size)	100
Tournament Size (Tou_Size)	20
Maximum Iterations (Max_Iteration)	500
Crossover Probability (P_{cross})	0.8
Mutation Probability (P_{mutation})	0.2
K Value (K)	10
Threshold (T_1)	50
Crossover Value Probability ($P_{\mathrm{valuecross}}$)	0.2

are compared against predetermined ideal values to evaluate circuit accuracy. The effectiveness of a given design is quantified by a fitness function, which is a summation of the squared deviations between the measured and target voltages, adjusted for a margin of error. Only deviations exceeding a threshold of $0.01V$ are considered, reflecting the precision goal of the circuit design [14]. The embryo circuit setting of reference voltage circuit is presented in our previous work [27]. The fitness function is given as the following equation [14]:

$$fitness = -\sum_{i,j} \varepsilon_{ij}, \tag{4}$$

where ε_{ij} is:

$$\varepsilon_{ij} = \begin{cases} \left(V_{outi,j} - V_{outi,j}^*\right)^2, & \text{if } |V_{outi,j} - V_{outi,j}^*| \geq 0.01V \\ 0, & \text{if } |V_{outi,j} - V_{outi,j}^*| < 0.01V. \end{cases} \tag{5}$$

At various circuit temperatures T_i, each measured output voltage point $V_{outi,j}$ corresponds to a target value $V_{outi,j}^*$. i represents the i-th circuit temperature, and j represents the sampled output voltage points.

Temperature Sensing Circuit. The challenge involves developing a circuit capable of sensing temperature changes, as reflected by variations in its output voltage. The output voltage linearly correlates with temperature. The linear relationship is characterized by a constant, ensuring output voltage directly corresponds to ambient temperature changes. The circuit's performance is evaluated through a fitness function, which aggregates the squared differences between actual and expected output voltages. This approach allows for precise calibration of the circuit's temperature sensitivity, leveraging genetic algorithms to fine-tune its response characteristics. The embryo circuit setting of temperature sensor is presented in our previous work [27]. The fitness function is defined as following [14]:

$$fitness = -\sum_{i} (V_{outi} - V^*_{outi})^2 . \tag{6}$$

At various circuit temperatures T_i, the output voltage V_{out} changes and will be measured for evaluation. The target value of the output voltage for the i-th temperature, V^*_{outi}, is linearly related to T_i and is defined as $V^*_{outi} = \eta T_i$. Here, η is a constant representing the linear relationship between the circuit temperature and the output voltage.

Gaussian Function Generator. The task focuses on the creation of a Gaussian function generator, where the aim is to produce an output current that fits a Gaussian distribution in relation to the input voltage. The task is to measure the output current for various input voltages and align these measurements with their theoretical Gaussian counterparts. The alignment is measured using a fitness function with a key normalization factor. This factor adjusts for the scale of the current measurements, ensuring the squared differences between expected and actual currents are accurately compared. This process embodies the application of evolutionary algorithms to the intricate task of circuit function generation, following the methodologies proposed by [14]. The embryo circuit setting of Gaussian function generator is given in our previous work [27]. The fitness function is defined as follows [14]:

$$fitness = -10^{14} * \sum_{i} (I_{outi} - I^*_{outi})^2 . \tag{7}$$

During circuit evolution, the output current is measured for evaluation. Different input voltages V_{in1} will correspond to different target values of the output current.

4.1 Ablation Study

Table 2 gives the average fitness under ablation experiments, focusing on the performance of three approaches (*Random*, *TMC SV*, and *KNN SV*) across three different tasks: a voltage reference circuit, a temperature sensor, and a Gaussian function generator. This approach helps identify which parts are essential and how each component influences the overall effectiveness. Random approach refers to the approach where random nodes are selected for crossover and mutation. The *Random* method serves as a baseline, wherein mutation rates, crossover points, and selection mechanisms are randomized, allowing for straightforward comparisons with more sophisticated strategies. *TMC SV* refers to the approach where the Truncated Monte Carlo Shapley Value (*TMC SV*) is applied. This approach simplifies the computational cost of calculating the exact Shapley values by using a truncated Monte-Carlo technique [26], maintaining a balance between computational cost and accuracy. The parameter setting is the same as the work in [26]. *KNN SV* refers to our proposed approach where the KNN model is applied to the predict the Shapley Value. Each task evaluates the best

Table 2. Average fitness under ablation experiments

Tasks	Cases	|BF|	|MBF|
Voltage reference circuit	Random	0.0051	0.0261
	TMC SV	0.0027	0.0183
	KNN SV	0.0012	0.0142
Temperature sensor	Random	0.0189	0.3981
	TMC SV	0.0096	0.1194
	KNN SV	0.0087	0.1048
Gaussian function generator	Random	0.0874	0.4046
	TMC SV	0.0382	0.1988
	KNN SV	0.0396	0.1208

fitness (|BF|) and mean best fitness (|MBF|) achieved by each method. In our study, we employ three distinct methods for guiding genetic operations.

For the voltage reference circuit, the *KNN SV* method outperforms the others, showing the lowest best fitness and mean fitness, indicating a superior capability to optimize circuit parameters effectively. In the temperature sensor task, *KNN SV* again demonstrates its efficacy with the lowest best fitness and a competitive mean fitness, suggesting its robustness and reliability in sensor optimization. Lastly, for the Gaussian function generator, while *KNN SV* does not achieve the lowest best fitness, it offers a significantly lower mean fitness compared to *TMC SV*, highlighting its consistency and effectiveness in generating functions with high fidelity.

Overall, the *KNN SV* method consistently shows promising results across all tasks, proving its potential as a highly effective tool in these specific applications. Its ability to consistently achieve low best and mean fitness values suggests it might be the preferred method for similar tasks, though specific requirements and goals of each experiment should guide the final methodology choice.

4.2   Comparisons with Previous Work

Table 3 presents a comprehensive comparison between our work and three previous studies, applied to the design of reference voltage circuits, temperature sensors, and Gaussian function generators. A key focus is on the number of evaluations, mean best fitness (|MBF|), and the number of components utilized in each approach.

In the reference voltage task, our proposed approach alongside Shi [27] drastically reduces the number of evaluations to just 50,000, a significant decrease from the millions required in earlier works by Koza [14] and Mattiussi [20]. Moreover, our proposed approach achieves the lowest mean best fitness at 0.0142 and uses the fewest components (15), indicating a substantial improvement in circuit optimization efficiency and precision.

Table 3. Comparisons with previous works

Parameters	[14]	[20]	[27]	Ours
Reference voltage				
Evaluations	5.12×10^7	5.6×10^6	5×10^4	$\mathbf{5 \times 10^4}$
$|MBF|$	6.6	2.64	0.0261	**0.0142**
#Components	67	70.2	32	**15**
Temperature sensor				
Evaluations	1.6×10^7	6.5×10^6	5×10^4	$\mathbf{5 \times 10^4}$
$|MBF|$	26.4	1.13	0.3981	0.1048
#Components	54	27.8	22	**19**
Gaussian function				
Evaluations	2.3×10^7	4.3×10^6	5×10^4	$\mathbf{5 \times 10^4}$
$|MBF|$	0.094	0.3	0.4046	**0.1208**
#Components	14	36	24	25
P-value	[14] VS ours: 0.0404; [20] VS ours:0.0404; [27] VS ours: 0.0452			

Similarly, for the temperature sensor application, both the recent study and Shi [27] have again significantly cut down the evaluation count. Our work excels with a mean best fitness of 0.1048, which is the best among all compared studies, and achieves this with fewer components (19), demonstrating an optimized and efficient design.

The Gaussian function generator results mirror these improvements, with all recent studies requiring fewer evaluations. Although our proposed approach does not achieve the lowest historical mean best fitness, it performs significantly better than Shi [27] with a fitness of 0.1208 and uses a moderate number of components (25), balancing complexity and performance efficiency.

Statistically significant improvements in the current methods over previous studies are confirmed by P-values of 0.0404 and 0.0452. These values indicate a significant enhancement in performance across all metrics, validating the effectiveness of the new approaches.

5   Conclusion

In this paper, we focus on the significant challenges of automated analog circuit design due to the complexity of circuit topology and parameter selection. While traditional evolutionary algorithms like Genetic Programming (GP) have shown potential in this field, they often struggle with inefficient search processes and the vast design space. To address these issues, we introduce a novel evolutionary framework that uses approximate Shapley values to guide the optimization process in tree-based genetic programming for analog circuit design. Our approach reduces the computational costs of Shapley values by implementing a two-stage evolutionary framework. This includes the creation of a Shapley Value Library (SV_{lib}) and a KNN-based prediction phase for quickly estimating Shapley values. Our approach improves search efficiency by focusing on the most beneficial sub-circuits, leading to more compact and efficient circuit designs. Through experimental verification, we demonstrate that our approach accelerates evolutionary convergence and surpasses traditional methods of evolving circuits. Our future includes the scalability of our approach to larger analog circuits.

References

1. Allen, P.E., Holberg, D.R.: CMOS analog circuit design. Elsevier (2011)
2. Beadle, L., Johnson, C.G.: Semantically driven crossover in genetic programming. In: 2008 IEEE Congress on Evolutionary Computation (IEEE World Congress on Computational Intelligence), pp. 111–116. IEEE (2008)
3. Branzei, R., Dimitrov, D., Tijs, S.: Models in Cooperative Game Theory, vol. 556. Springer, Heidelberg (2008). https://doi.org/10.1007/978-3-540-77954-4
4. Castejón, F., Carmona, E.J.: Automatic design of analog electronic circuits using grammatical evolution. Appl. Soft Comput. **62**, 1003–1018 (2018)
5. Ffrancon, R., Schoenauer, M.: Memetic semantic genetic programming. In: Proceedings of the 2015 Annual Conference on Genetic and Evolutionary Computation, pp. 1023–1030 (2015)
6. Gan, Z., Yang, Z., Shang, T., Yu, T., Jiang, M.: Automated synthesis of passive analog filters using graph representation. Expert Syst. Appl. **37**(3), 1887–1898 (2010)
7. Gelfand, A.E., Dey, D.K., Chang, H.: Model determination using predictive distributions with implementation via sampling-based methods. Department of Statistics, Stanford University CA, Technical report (1992)
8. Ghorbani, A., Zou, J.: Data shapley: equitable valuation of data for machine learning. In: International Conference on Machine Learning, pp. 2242–2251. PMLR (2019)
9. Grimbleby, J.B.: Automatic analogue network synthesis using genetic algorithms. In: Proceedings of GALESIA 1995, Sheffield, pp. 53–58 (1995)
10. He, J., Yin, J.: Evolutionary design model of passive filter circuit for practical application. Genet. Program Evolvable Mach. **21**(4), 571–604 (2020)
11. Hodan, D., Mrazek, V., Vasicek, Z.: Semantically-oriented mutation operator in cartesian genetic programming for evolutionary circuit design. In: Proceedings of the 2020 Genetic and Evolutionary Computation Conference, pp. 940–948 (2020)
12. Jia, R., et al.: Towards efficient data valuation based on the shapley value. In: The 22nd International Conference on Artificial Intelligence and Statistics, pp. 1167–1176. PMLR (2019)
13. Koza, J.R., Andre, D., Bennett III, F.H., Keane, M.A.: Use of automatically defined functions and architecture-altering operations in automated circuit synthesis with genetic programming. In: Proceedings of 1st Annual Conference on Genetic Programming, Stanford, pp. 132–140 (1996)
14. Koza, J.R., Andre, D., Keane, M.A., Bennett III, F.H.: Genetic Programming III: Darwinian Invention and Problem Solving, vol. 3. Morgan Kaufmann (1999)
15. Krawiec, K., Wieloch, B.: Functional modularity for genetic programming. In: Proceedings of the 11th Annual Conference on Genetic and Evolutionary Computation, pp. 995–1002 (2009)

16. Kruiskamp, W., Leenaerts, D.: Darwin: CMOS opamp synthesis by means of a genetic algorithm. In: Proceedings of 32nd DAC 1995, San Francisco, pp. 433–438 (1995)
17. Liu, B., et al.: Analog circuit optimization system based on hybrid evolutionary algorithms. Integration **42**(2), 137–148 (2009)
18. Lohn, J.D., Colombano, S.P.: A circuit representation technique for automated circuit design. IEEE Trans. Evol. Comput. **3**(3), 205–219 (1999)
19. Lundberg, S.M., Lee, S.I.: A unified approach to interpreting model predictions. In: Proceedings of the 31st International Conference on Neural Information Processing Systems, pp. 4768–4777 (2017)
20. Mattiussi, C., Floreano, D.: Analog genetic encoding for the evolution of circuits and networks. IEEE Trans. Evol. Comput. **11**(5), 596–607 (2007)
21. Moraglio, A., Krawiec, K.: Geometric semantic genetic programming for recursive boolean programs. In: Proceedings of the Genetic and Evolutionary Computation Conference, pp. 993–1000 (2017)
22. Nagel, L., Pederson, D.O.: Spice (simulation program with integrated circuit emphasis) (1973)
23. Nguyen, Q.U., Nguyen, X.H., O'Neill, M.: Semantic aware crossover for genetic programming: the case for real-valued function regression. In: Vanneschi, L., Gustafson, S., Moraglio, A., De Falco, I., Ebner, M. (eds.) EuroGP 2009. LNCS, vol. 5481, pp. 292–302. Springer, Heidelberg (2009). https://doi.org/10.1007/978-3-642-01181-8_25
24. Pawlak, T.P., Krawiec, K.: Competent geometric semantic genetic programming for symbolic regression and boolean function synthesis. Evol. Comput. **26**(2), 177–212 (2018)
25. Roth, A.E.: The Shapley Value: Essays in Honor of Lloyd S. Shapley. Cambridge University Press, Cambridge (1988)
26. Shi, X., Gao, J., Minku, L.L., Yao, X.: Evolving parsimonious circuits through shapley value-based genetic programming. In: Proceedings of the Genetic and Evolutionary Computation Conference Companion, pp. 602–605 (2022)
27. Shi, X., Minku, L.L., Yao, X.: A novel tree-based representation for evolving analog circuits and its application to memristor-based pulse generation circuit. Genet. Program Evolvable Mach. **23**(4), 453–493 (2022)
28. Stier, J., Gianini, G., Granitzer, M., Ziegler, K.: Analysing neural network topologies: a game theoretic approach. Procedia Comput. Sci. **126**, 234–243 (2018)
29. Vogt, H., Hendrix, M., Nenzi, P.: Ngspice user's manual version 31 (describes ngspice release version) (2019)
30. Zhao, Z., Zhang, L.: An automated topology synthesis framework for analog integrated circuits. IEEE Trans. Comput. Aided Des. Integr. Circuits Syst. **39**(12), 4325–4337 (2020)

A Dominance-Based Surrogate Classifier for Multi-objective Evolutionary Algorithms

Tiwonge Msulira Banda[1,2(✉)] and Alexandru-Ciprian Zăvoianu[1,2]

[1] School of Computing, Robert Gordon University, Aberdeen, Scotland, UK
{t.banda,c.zavoianu}@rgu.ac.uk
[2] National Subsea Centre, Aberdeen, Scotland, UK

Abstract. The application of Multi-Objective Evolutionary Algorithms (MOEAs) is often constrained when addressing computationally expensive Multi-Objective Optimisation Problems (MOOPs). To mitigate this, we propose a dominance-based surrogate classifier that can be integrated into a MOEA to steer the algorithm towards viable (potentially non-dominated) solutions, thereby facilitating faster convergence. This surrogate classifier is paired with a simple, yet effective data labelling mechanism, which assigns a label of 1 to non-dominated solutions and a label of 0 to dominated solutions within a generation. Experimental results demonstrate that a surrogate classifier guided NSGA-II achieves faster convergence compared to the standard NSGA-II across 31 well-known benchmark problems.

Keywords: Surrogate models · Surrogate-classifier · NSGA-II · dominance · MOEA

1 Introduction

Many real-world optimisation scenarios involve multiple and often competing objectives. In these scenarios, the goal is to identify solutions that simultaneously achieve optimal or near-optimal performance across all objectives. For instance, an electrical engineer designing an electric motor might seek a design that is both highly efficient and cost-effective in terms of material usage. To achieve this, the design process would involve optimising the motor's geometry and material selection to satisfy these performance requirements [18].

Multi-Objective Evolutionary Algorithms (MOEAs) are often used in tackling these complex Multi-Objective Optimisation Problems (MOOPs). To date, several state-of-the-art MOEAs exist, including NSGA-II [13], SPEA2 [33], GDE3 [19], NSGA-III [12] and MOEA/D [31]. These algorithms offer diverse strategies for handling MOOPs and as a result they are often used in tackling many industrial and research problems. Despite their success, a significant challenge arises when MOEAs are applied to solving MOOPs with objective functions that are computationally expensive to evaluate. These computationally expensive objective functions, often encountered in industrial applications, require substantial computational resources and time to complete. Returning to the previously discussed example of electric motor design optimisation, the objective function relies on finite-element simulations to assess the performance of each design iteration. To identify optimal solutions, a typical MOEA will need to evaluate thousands of candidate solutions, translating to an equivalent number of computationally demanding simulations [4]. This poses a significant limitation to the practical application of MOEAs in computationally expensive MOOPs.

One way to overcome this challenge is the use of surrogate models, which accelerate the optimisation process. Traditionally, this has been achieved by replacing the computationally expensive objective function evaluations with faster, yet accurate, estimations of the objective function values. This approach, called fitness replacement significantly reduces the overall runtime of the optimisation process without compromising the quality of the results. Consequently, surrogate models have become an active area of research, leading to the development and application of various techniques. Some of the most common surrogate modelling techniques include radial basis function (RBF) [15], polynomial regression [25], support vector machines (SVMs) [1], artificial neural networks (ANNs), and Gaussian processes (GPs), also known as Kriging [27]. These techniques are essentially data-driven regression models that aim to predict the values of the expensive objective function. A comprehensive overview of various surrogate modelling techniques can be found in the work of Diaz-Manriquez et al. (2016) [14].

While successful, regression-based fitness replacement surrogate models are not without limitations. Firstly, as the surrogate replaces the actual fitness function, cumulative errors can potentially affect the overall accuracy of the optimisation. Secondly, since a surrogate needs to be constructed for each objective, this potentially increases the amount of required computational resources, especially in many-objective optimisation problems [23,30]. Lastly, the surrogate may not effectively capture non-linear patterns leading to a poor representation of the Pareto front. Consequently, fitness replacement surrogate-guided MOEAs may not be universally applicable to computationally expensive MOOPs.

An alternative to fitness replacement surrogate modelling is called pre-selection, in which promising solutions are selected for evaluation whereas those deemed non-viable (potentially dominated) are discarded. In this way, the limitations outlined earlier are addressed as the promising solutions are evaluated using the true fitness functions. The core principle behind pre-selection surrogate modelling lies in guiding the MOEA towards promising regions of the search space, thereby accelerating convergence. Building on ongoing research in pre-selecting candidate solutions [22,23,26,30], this paper proposes a new dominance-classifier that can be incorporated into a dominance-based MOEA to steer it towards viable (potentially non-dominated) candidate solutions based on their predicted Pareto-domination. Our approach includes a simple, but effective data labelling strategy that assigns the label of 1 to non-dominated solutions and the label 0 to dominated solutions and uses these for training the dominance classifier.

The rest of the paper is organised as follows: In Sect. 2 we describe our proposed modelling approach including the data labelling strategy; in Sect. 3 we describe the experimental design; in Sect. 4 we provide the results and provide our interpretations; and finally in Sect. 5 we conclude and provide areas of further research.

2   Proposed Approach

Before delving into our proposed approach, it is essential to establish the fundamentals in multi-objective optimisation. An unconstrained MOOP with n real-valued variables and m objectives can be formulates as follows:

$$Minimise\ F(x) = (f_1(x), \ldots f_m(x)),\quad m \leq 3 \tag{1}$$

where $x \in \mathbb{R}^n$ represents a candidate solution and is subject to $x_l \leq x \leq x_u$, and f_1 to f_m represent individual objectives. Typically, there are 2 or 3 objectives. Where there are more, the problem is called a many-objective optimisation problem. The goal is either to minimise or maximise the objective functions simultaneously. In our case here we aim to minimise all objective functions.

When solving a MOOP, a standard MOEA progresses through five distinct stages as illustrated on the left hand side of Fig. 1. The phases are: initialisation, evaluation, replacement, selection, and reproduction (note the line from reproduction to evaluation depicting the standard MOEA path). The specific implementation details of these stages contribute to the unique characteristics of various MOEAs that exist today.

- **Initialisation:** During this initial phase, the algorithm generates a population of candidate solutions. These solutions are randomly created within the predefined upper and lower boundaries of the problem space.
- **Evaluation:** Each solution within the population undergoes an evaluation process where its objective functions are assessed. This evaluation determines the fitness of each solution within the current population.
- **Replacement:** Following evaluation, a comparison between solutions occurs to identify the most promising candidates. Many MOEAs leverage ranking techniques, such as non-dominated ranking and strength ranking, to assign fitness scores based on the concept of Pareto dominance. Additionally, operators like crowding distance are employed to maintain solution diversity within the population and prevent clustering around specific regions of the Pareto front. If the pre-defined termination criteria are satisfied at this stage, the algorithm terminates successfully.
- **Selection:** This stage focuses on selecting suitable parent solutions from the existing population. These parents will participate in the reproduction process to generate offspring for the next generation. Binary tournament selection is a commonly used technique for this purpose.

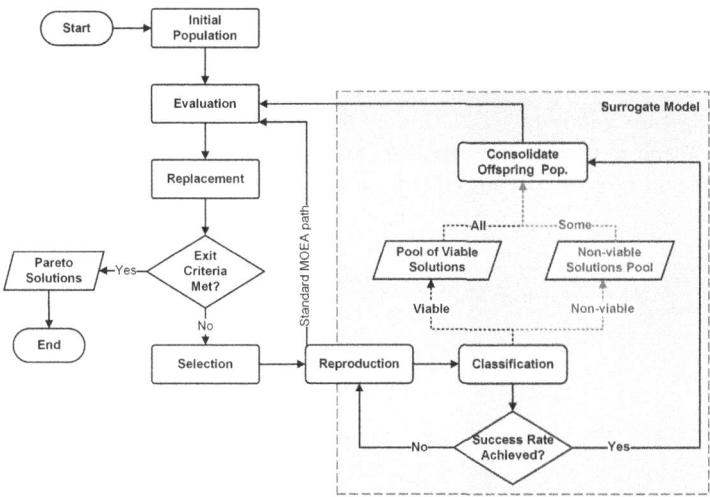

Fig. 1. Flow diagram showing our proposed surrogate model incorporated into a standard MOEA. The left hand side shows the distinct phases of a standard MOEA. On the right is the surrogate model.

- **Reproduction:** The selected parent solutions undergo a process known as reproduction, where genetic operators such as crossover and mutation are applied to generate offspring solutions. These offspring solutions represent the next generation of candidate solutions within the population.

After the reproduction stage, the newly generated offspring solutions are evaluated, and the entire process iterates until a pre-defined termination criterion is met. At the conclusion of each generation (iteration), a standard MOEA typically returns a set of optimal solutions that have been found so far. The optimal solutions dominate all other solutions evaluated by the algorithm, i.e., signifying that their objective function values cannot be simultaneously improved upon [6]. A solution x^1 is said to dominate another solution x^2, if it satisfies two conditions: a) x^1 is strictly superior to x^2 in at least one objective; b) solution x^1 is not poorer than x^2 in any objective [9].

Building on the aforementioned background, we now describe our proposed approach, which is illustrated on the right-hand side of Fig. 1. We posit that a well-trained classifier, equipped with sufficient data from prior generations, can effectively identify non-dominated solutions within a new generation of candidate solutions. We integrate the surrogate model in between the reproduction and evaluation phases of the MOEA framework and leverage on it to filter and discard dominated solutions from the offspring population so that the optimisation process can concentrate its computational resources on evaluating the more promising non-dominated solutions thereby accelerate convergence towards the Pareto front. This targeted approach offers significant potential for enhancing computational efficiency. The surrogate model has two components: a data labelling module and the classifier itself. As the name suggests, the data labeller is responsible for generating training data that maps solution features (input variables) to their corresponding dominance classification (output class, either dominated or non-dominated). The classifier is trained on the data generated by the labeller and is used to classify the candidate solutions. We will delve deeper into the specifics of these components in the following sections.

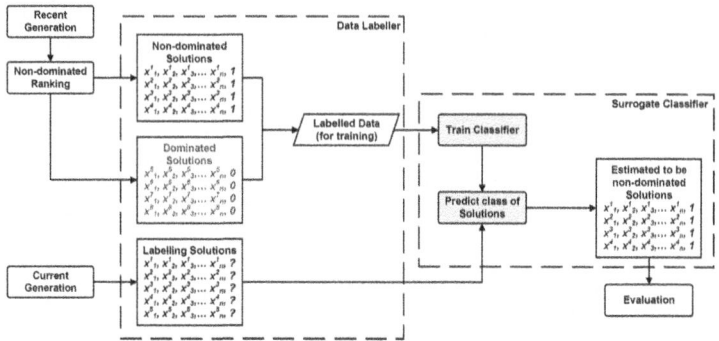

Fig. 2. Flow diagram of the surrogate data labeller.

2.1 Data Labelling

Due to the inherent variability of optimisation problems, the acquisition of pre-labelled training data is infeasible and as a result, data collection and labelling must be done during the optimisation process itself. Our proposed approach incorporates a straightforward, yet efficient data labelling technique that assigns labels to solutions data at the end of each generation, as illustrated in Fig. 2. Specifically, all non-dominated solutions receive a label of 1 whereas all other dominated solutions are assigned a label of 0. As anticipated, the number of dominated solutions typically exceeds that of non-dominated solutions, resulting in a class imbalance scenario. While existing literature offers a multitude of techniques for mitigating class imbalance, any of which could theoretically be employed, our approach adopts the following steps to circumvent this issue:

- Firstly, we augment the number of data points belonging to the class labelled 1 (non-dominated solutions) by incorporating solutions from the second rank of the non-dominated sorting procedure. The rationale behind this strategy stems from the design principles of evolutionary algorithms that leverage crowding distance, such as NSGA-II [13]. These algorithms promote diversity within the population by penalising solutions on the non-dominated front that are located in close proximity to each other. As a consequence, the second rank, following the non-dominated sorting with crowding distance, often contains solutions of comparable quality and characteristics to those in the first rank that are relegated to the second rank solely due to their spatial proximity to other non-dominated solutions in the objective space.

- Secondly, we restrict the size of the class labelled 0 (dominated solutions) by limiting the set of solutions considered for inclusion in this class. Specifically, our approach focuses solely on dominated solutions belonging to the most recent generation. This approach is based on the premise that solutions from earlier generations are less likely to represent the current search landscape and potentially hinder the learning process of the surrogate classifier.

Following the data labelling process, the labelled training data undergoes a randomisation step (shuffling) to ensure a well-distributed representation of solutions within the training set. This shuffled training data is then provided to the classifier for the training phase. The trained classifier will subsequently be employed to classify solutions belonging to the new generation, as depicted in Fig. 2 as the "current generation".

2.2   Training and Tuning the Surrogate Classifier

The second component of the surrogate model is the classification algorithm itself. From a theoretical point of view, any well-performing classifier can be employed for this task. During our initial model exploration, we investigated a range of algorithms, including Support Vector Machines (SVM), Random Forest (RF) [5], K-Nearest Neighbors (KNN) [7], and Multi-Layer Perceptron (MLP) [16]. We finally opted for the Random Forest classifier because of its competitive performance within the context of our specific application.

   As with data labelling, hyperparameter tuning must be conducted during the optimisation run. The challenge lies in the dynamic nature of the data, which changes from one generation to the next, necessitating the training of a new classifier and the discovery of new optimal hyperparameters. Any one of the established hyperparameter selection techniques can be employed for this purpose. In our study, we opted for RandomizedSearchCV [3], which is recognised for its efficiency in exploring vast hyperparameter spaces. Depending on the size of the hyperparameter space, hyperparameter tuning becomes a computationally expensive exercise (higher time complexity). During experimentation, we observed that in the later generations, all solutions in the population tend to be classified as non-dominated, as the classifier fails to distinguish between them. When this occurs, the surrogate model ceases to contribute meaningfully to the MOEA and instead slows it down. To address this, the optimal hyperparameter search can be terminated or the surrogate model deactivated entirely. In our work, we opted for the former approach to prevent premature deactivation. Upon completion of training and hyperparameter tuning, the classifier is made available to classify solutions in the new generation.

2.3   Predicting the Class of Solutions

The MOEA executes the reproduction stage as usual, generating a population of offspring solutions. The new offspring solutions are then passed to the trained classifier for classification. Based on the classifier's output, the offspring solutions are directed to separate pools. Solutions classified as non-dominated are added to a dedicated non-dominated pool whereas those classified as dominated are channelled into a separate dominated pool. This process continues iteratively until a pre-defined success rate is achieved. The success rate signifies the desired number of promising non-dominated solutions within the offspring population. Upon exiting the loop, the non-dominated pool will hold a population size that is either equal to or exceeds the product of the success rate and the offspring population size. However, it will remain smaller than the offspring population size. The remaining offspring solutions required to reach the offspring population size are obtained from the dominated pool. This ensures that there is diversity within the offspring population.

3   Experimental Design

We incorporated the surrogate model into NSGA-II [13] in between reproduction and evaluation phases as described in Sect. 2. Henceforth, we will refer to the NSGA-II guided by the surrogate classifier as Dominance Classifier Guided NSGA-II (DCG-NSGA-II). NSGA-II is the updated version of the Non-dominated Sorting Genetic Algorithm originally proposed in 1994 [28]. It follows the same MOEA framework described earlier, but its key distinction is that it uses the non-dominated sorting procedure to rank solutions into non-domination fronts. The ranks prioritise solutions based on their Pareto-dominance, with the superior solutions occupying the initial fronts. To ensure population diversity within each front, a crowding distance methodology is employed. This approach assigns a penalty to solutions exhibiting excessive proximity in the objective space, thereby promoting a well-distributed population. The algorithm selects parent solutions using a tournament selection mechanism and creates offspring solutions using crossover and mutation. By virtue of its robust nature, NSGA-II has garnered widespread adoption across various industrial applications [29].

We parameterised the NSGA-II component of DCG-NSGA-II based on the settings recommended in the literature. Specifically, the population and offspring population sizes were both set to 200. Simulated Binary Crossover (SBX) [10] with a crossover probability rate of 0.8 and a crossover distribution index of 20, as well as Polynomial Mutation (PM) [11] with a mutation probability of $1/n$ and a mutation distribution index of 20 were used. For the surrogate component, we utilised a Random Forest classifier [5]. We set the success rate, the only parameter for the surrogate classifier to 0.5, and employed RandomizedSearchCV to discover optimal parameters for the number of trees (ranging from 100 to 500 in increments of 50) and the maximum depth of trees (ranging from 50 to 100).

We evaluated the performance of DCG-NSGA-II on a comprehensive suite of 31 benchmark problems drawn from established test suites: DTLZ [8], LZ09 [21], WFG [17], ZDT [32], and KSW10 [20]. The details of these test suites are summarised in Table 1. We compared the performance of DCG-NSGA-II against the standard NSGA-II. For each test problem, both algorithms were

Table 1. Details of the 31 benchmark problems used for performance comparison.

Problem	No. of variables	No. of objectives
DTLZ1	7	3
DTLZ2-6	12	3
DTLZ7	22	3
KSW10	10	2
LZ09_F1-F5, F9	30	2
LZ09_F6	30	3
LZ09_F7-F8	10	2
WFG1-9	6	2
ZDT1, 2	30	2
ZDT3, 4, 6	10	2

granted a fixed computational budget of 50,000 fitness function evaluations (i.e., 250 generations). To account for the inherent stochastic nature of MOEAs, 50 independent runs were conducted for each solver on each problem, facilitating statistically robust comparisons of their performance. The experiments were carried out using jMetalPy v1.6, a Python framework widely used for single and multi-objective optimization with metaheuristics [2].

In comparing the performance of the solvers on the benchmark problems, we employed the hypervolume indicator (Hv) [34] as our unary Pareto front quality measure. This choice was due to its widespread acceptance in the MOEA community, and its theoretical proof of monotonic convergence behaviour. The $Hv(PF_c)$ metric measures the size of the objective space dominated by a candidate Pareto front PF_c when considering an anti-optimal reference point [34]. Consequently, larger Hv values are preferred. To enhance the interpretability of the numerical values, we compute the relative hypervolume as $Hr(PF_c) = \frac{Hv(PF_c)}{Hv(PF_t)}$. We calculated $Hv(PF_t)$ for all 31 benchmark problems using their known true Pareto fronts. Based on this, for each problem and solver combination, we calculated the average relative hypervolume achieved at each generation when considering the 50 independent repeats.

4 Results and Interpretation

4.1 Performance on Individual Problem Suites

We present the average comparative performance results for DCG-NSGA-II and NSGA-II on the five benchmark problem suites in Figs. 3, 4, 5, 6 and 7. The plots on the left focus on the first 50 generations for a closer look on early convergence trends, whereas those on the right show the full 250 generations. The results indicate that, with the exception of the DTLZ suite, DCG-NSGA-II converges faster than NSGA-II within the first 20–40 generations. Notably, the advantage of DCG-NSGA-II is substantial on the ZDT problem suite, where it achieves an average relative hypervolume of 79.7% by generation 80, compared to NSGA-II's 62.2%. At the end of the runs (generation 250), DCG-NSGA-II slightly outperforms NSGA-II on the ZDT suite, achieving 99.46% relative hypervolume versus NSGA-II's 99.37%, and on the WFG suite, achieving 90.18% versus 89.66%. However, for the KSW10 suite, NSGA-II surpasses DCG-NSGA-II in the end of the run results, with NSGA-II reaching 99.3% compared to DCG-NSGA-II's 99.25% mean relative hypervolume. DCG-NSGA-II exhibits the lowest performance on the DTLZ problem suite. We suspect that the reason for this sub-par performance could be attributed to the fact that all 7 DTLZ problems have 3 objectives. Similar poor performance was observed on LZ09_F5, which also has 3 objectives. More extensive experimentation is required to confirm this though.

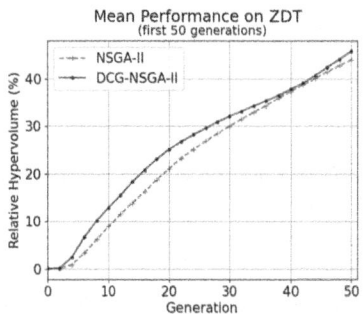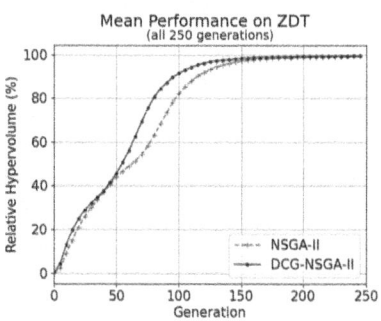

Fig. 3. Mean performance of DCG-NSGA-II and NSGA-II on the ZDT problem suite. Left: close look at the first 50 generations. Right: all 250 generations.

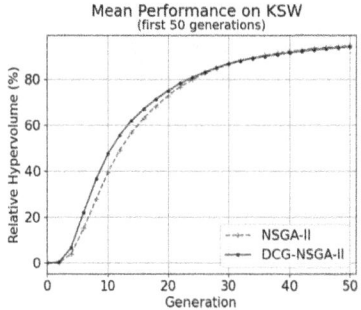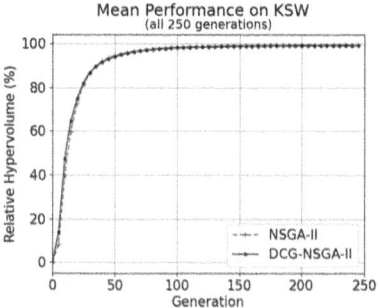

Fig. 4. Mean performance of DCG-NSGA-II and NSGA-II on the KSW10 function. Left: close look at the first 50 generations. Right: all 250 generations.

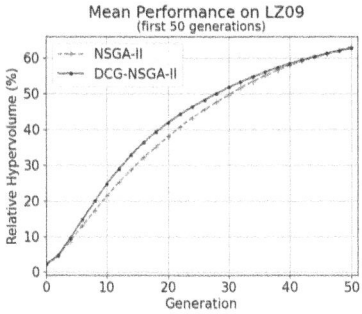
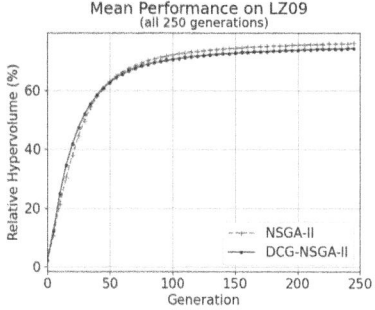

Fig. 5. Mean performance of DCG-NSGA-II and NSGA-II on the LZ09 problem suite. Left: close look at the first 50 generations. Right: all 250 generations.

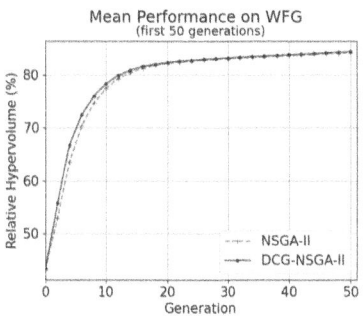
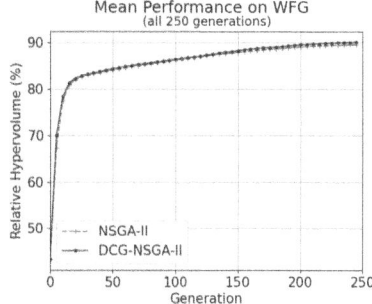

Fig. 6. Mean performance of DCG-NSGA-II and NSGA-II on the WFG problem suite. Left: close look at the first 50 generations. Right: all 250 generations.

4.2   Overall Performance on All Problem Suites

Figure 8 depicts the average performance of the two solvers across all 31 benchmark problems. The plot on the right shows relative hypervolumes achieved in all the 250 generations, while the one on the left zooms into the first 100 generations. The plots suggest that DCG-NSGA-II initially exhibits a faster convergence rate compared to NSGA-II, as was the case with the individual problem suites. However, this advantage diminishes in later generations, resulting in DCG-NSGA-II achieving slightly lower end-of-run performance than NSGA-II.

For each of the 31 benchmark problems, to determine if there is a statistical difference between the relative hypervolumes achieved by the two algorithms at each of the 250 generations, we carried out a pair of one-sided Mann-Whitney U tests [24] with a significance level of 0.05. The Mann-Whitney U test is a nonparametric statistical test used to compare two independent groups. In both our tests, the null hypothesis at each generation was that there is no statistical difference between the mean relative hypervolumes achieved by NSGA-II and DCG-NSGA-II for that problem. The alternative hypothesis for the first test was that the mean relative hypervolumes achieved by NSGA-II were lower than those achieved by DCG-NDGA-II (i.e., DCG-NSGA-II over-performed NSGA-

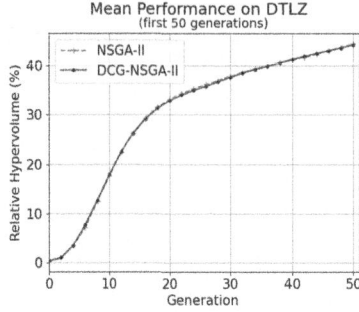
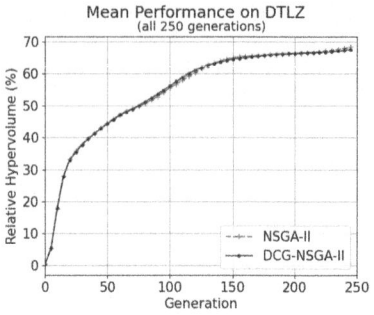

Fig. 7. Mean performance of DCG-NSGA-II and NSGA-II on the DTLZ problem suite. Left: close look at the first 50 generations. Right: all 250 generations.

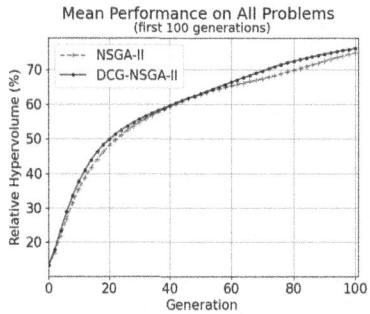
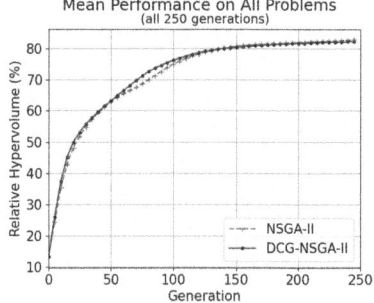

Fig. 8. Overall performance of DCG-NSGA-II and NSGA-II on all 31 benchmark problems. Left: focus on the first 50 generations. Right: All 250 generations.

II) and these are plotted by the solid black line in Fig. 9. In the second test, the alternative hypothesis was that the mean relative hypervolumes achieved by NSGA-II were higher than those achieved by DCG-NDGA-II (i.e., DCG-NSGA-II under-performed NSGA-II) and these are plotted with solid grey in Fig. 9. In Fig. 9 we also plot the number of benchmark problems where there was no statistical difference between the two (the dashed grey line). It is clear from the results that DCG-NSGA-II over-performed NSGA-II across more benchmark problems during early convergence. For example, at generation 19 (where Fig. 8 indicates for both solvers an average hypervolume attainment of $\approx 50\%$ over all problems), DCG-NSGA-II statistically outperformed NSGA-II in 19 of the 31 benchmark problems. As the generations progress, the number of benchmark problems in which DCG-NSGA-II outperforms NSGA-II begins to reduce. By around generation 100 (the start of late convergence) NSGA-II starts to outperform DCG-NSGA-II and this trend continues to the end of runs.

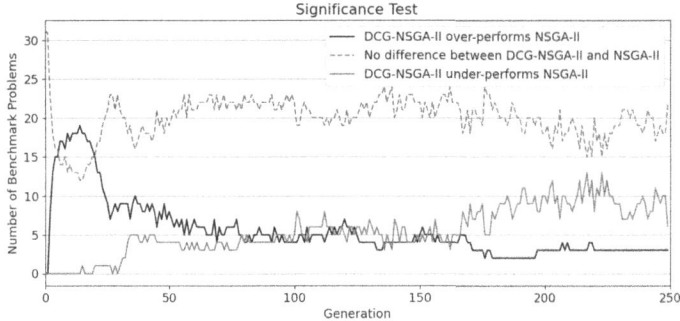

Fig. 9. Significance test comparisons of the two solvers.

5   Conclusion and Future Work

This paper has demonstrated the efficacy of employing a classifier trained on a recent population of solutions to predict dominance relationships in a new generation, guiding a MOEA towards faster convergence. The proposed DCG-NSGA-II achieved faster convergence across various benchmark problem suites, with the most significant performance observed on the ZDT problems, followed by KSW10, LZ09, and WFG suites. Notably, the surrogate model did not demonstrably enhance NSGA-II's performance on the DTLZ problem suite. Overall, when evaluated across the 31 benchmark problems, our DCG-NSGA-II outperformed the standard NSGA-II during the early convergence stage. The findings were statistically validated using one-sided Mann-Whitney U tests. As such, our approach can be seen as providing a problem-agnostic convergence improvement for MOOPs with a limited fitness evaluation budget.

For future research, we aim to refine the proposed surrogate model further, incorporate it into other state-of-the-art MOEAs and test performance on a real industrial application including carrying out comprehensive speed comparisons. Additionally, we will seek to study the reasons behind the surrogate's limited effectiveness on the DTLZ problem suite, and explore if the population size and number of objectives have any effect on its performance.

Acknowledgments. This work has been supported by the COMET-K2 "Center for Symbiotic Mechatronics" of the Linz Center of Mechatronics (LCM) funded by the Austrian federal government and the federal state of Upper Austria.

References

1. Andrés, E., Salcedo-Sanz, S., Monge, F., Pérez-Bellido, A.: Efficient aerodynamic design through evolutionary programming and support vector regression algorithms. Expert Syst. Appl. **39**(12), 10700–10708 (2012). https://doi.org/10.1016/j.eswa.2012.02.197

2. Benítez-Hidalgo, A., Nebro, A.J., García-Nieto, J., Oregi, I., Del Ser, J.: jmetalpy: a python framework for multi-objective optimization with metaheuristics. Swarm Evol. Comput. **51**, 100598 (2019). https://doi.org/10.1016/j.swevo.2019.100598

3. Bergstra, J., Bengio, Y.: Random search for hyper-parameter optimization. J. Mach. Learn. Res. **13**(2), 281–305 (2012)

4. Bramerdorfer, G., Zavoianu, A.C.: Surrogate-based multi-objective optimization of electrical machine designs facilitating tolerance analysis. IEEE Trans. Magn. **53**(8), 1–11 (2017). https://doi.org/10.1109/tmag.2017.2694802

5. Breiman, L.: Random forests. Mach. Learn. **45**(1), 5–32 (2001). https://doi.org/10.1023/a:1010933404324

6. Coello, C.A.C., Lamont, G.B., Veldhuizen, D.A.V.: Evolutionary Algorithms for Solving Multi-objective Problems. Genetic and Evolutionary Computation Series. Springer, New York (2007). https://doi.org/10.1007/978-0-387-36797-2

7. Cover, T., Hart, P.: Nearest neighbor pattern classification. IEEE Trans. Inf. Theory **13**(1), 21–27 (1967). https://doi.org/10.1109/tit.1967.1053964

8. Deb, K., Thiele, L., Laumanns, M., Zitzler, E.: Scalable multi-objective optimization test problems, vol. 1, pp. 825–830 (2002). https://doi.org/10.1109/CEC.2002.1007032

9. Deb, K.: Multi-Objective Optimization using Evolutionary Algorithms, vol. 16. Wiley, Hoboken (2001)

10. Deb, K., Agrawal, R.B.: Simulated binary crossover for continuous search space. Complex Syst. **9**(2), 115–148 (1995)

11. Deb, K., Goyal, M.: A combined genetic adaptive search (geneas) for engineering design. Comput. Sci. Inform. **26**, 30–45 (1996)

12. Deb, K., Jain, H.: An evolutionary many-objective optimization algorithm using reference-point-based nondominated sorting approach, part i: Solving problems with box constraints. IEEE Trans. Evol. Comput. **18**(4), 577–601 (2014). https://doi.org/10.1109/tevc.2013.2281535

13. Deb, K., Pratap, A., Agarwal, S., Meyarivan, T.: A fast and elitist multiobjective genetic algorithm: NSGA-II. IEEE Trans. Evol. Comput. **6**, 182–197 (2002). https://doi.org/10.1109/4235.996017

14. Díaz-ManríÂŋquez, A., Toscano, G., Barron-Zambrano, J.H., Tello-Leal, E.: A review of surrogate assisted multiobjective evolutionary algorithms. Comput. Intell. Neurosci. **2016**, 1–14 (2016). https://doi.org/10.1155/2016/9420460

15. Hardy, R.L.: Multiquadric equations of topography and other irregular surfaces. J. Geophys. Res. **76**(8), 1905–1915 (1971). https://doi.org/10.1029/jb076i008p01905

16. Haykin, S.: Neural Networks: A Complrehensive Foundation, 2nd edn. Pearson Prentice Hall (1999)

17. Huband, S., Hingston, P., Barone, L., While, L.: A review of multiobjective test problems and a scalable test problem toolkit. IEEE Trans. Evol. Comput. **10**(5), 477–506 (2006)

18. Huber, M., Fuhrländer, M., Schöps, S.: Multi-objective yield optimization for electrical machines using machine learning (2022). https://doi.org/10.48550/ARXIV.2204.04986

19. Kukkonen, S., Lampinen, J.: GDE3: the third evolution step of generalized differential evolution. In: Proceedings of 2005 IEEE Congress on Evolutionary Computation, IEEE CEC 2005, vol. 1, pp. 443–450 (2005). https://doi.org/10.1109/CEC.2005.1554717

20. Kursawe, F.: A variant of evolution strategies for vector optimization. In: Schwefel, H.P., Männer, R. (eds.) Parallel Problem Solving from Nature, pp. 193–197. Springer, Heidelberg (1991)

21. Li, H., Zhang, Q.: Multiobjective optimization problems with complicated pareto sets, MOEA/D and NSGA-II. IEEE Trans. Evol. Comput. **13**(2), 284–302 (2008)
22. Li, J., Wang, P., Dong, H., Shen, J., Chen, C.: A classification surrogate-assisted multi-objective evolutionary algorithm for expensive optimization. Knowl.-Based Syst. **242**, 108416 (2022). https://doi.org/10.1016/j.knosys.2022.108416
23. Loshchilov, I., Schoenauer, M., Sebag, M.: Dominance-based pareto-surrogate for multi-objective optimization. In: Deb, K., et al. (eds.) SEAL 2010. LNCS, vol. 6457, pp. 230–239. Springer, Heidelberg (2010). https://doi.org/10.1007/978-3-642-17298-4_24
24. Mann, H.B., Whitney, D.R.: On a test of whether one of two random variables is stochastically larger than the other. Ann. Math. Stat. **18**(1), 50–60 (1947). https://doi.org/10.1214/aoms/1177730491
25. Myers, R.H., Montgomery, D.C., Anderson-Cook, C.M.: Response Surface Methodology Process and Product Optimization Using Designed Experiments. Wiley (2016)
26. Pan, L., He, C., Tian, Y., Wang, H., Zhang, X., Jin, Y.: A classification-based surrogate-assisted evolutionary algorithm for expensive many-objective optimization. IEEE Trans. Evol. Comput. **23**(1), 74–88 (2019). https://doi.org/10.1109/tevc.2018.2802784
27. Ratle, A.: Kriging as a surrogate fitness landscape in evolutionary optimization. Artif. Intell. Eng. Des. Anal. Manuf. **15**(1), 37–49 (2001). https://doi.org/10.1017/s0890060401151024
28. Srinivas, N., Deb, K.: Muiltiobjective optimization using nondominated sorting in genetic algorithms. Evol. Comput. **2**, 221–248 (1994)
29. Verma, S., Pant, M., Snasel, V.: A comprehensive review on NSGA-II for multi-objective combinatorial optimization problems. IEEE Access **9**, 57757–57791 (2021)
30. Yuan, Y., Banzhaf, W.: Expensive multiobjective evolutionary optimization assisted by dominance prediction. IEEE Trans. Evol. Comput. **26**(1), 159–173 (2022). https://doi.org/10.1109/tevc.2021.3098257
31. Zhang, Q., Li, H.: MOEA/D: a multiobjective evolutionary algorithm based on decomposition. IEEE Trans. Evol. Comput. **11**, 712–731 (2007). https://doi.org/10.1109/TEVC.2007.892759
32. Zitzler, E., Deb, K., Thiele, L.: Comparison of multiobjective evolutionary algorithms: empirical results. Evol. Comput. **8**, 173–195 (2000). https://doi.org/10.1162/106365600568202
33. Zitzler, E., Laumanns, M., Thiele, L.: SPEA2: improving the strength pareto evolutionary algorithm. TIK-Report, vol. 103 (2001). https://doi.org/10.3929/ethz-a-004284029
34. Zitzler, E., Thiele, L.: Multiobjective optimization using evolutionary algorithms — a comparative case study. In: Lecture Notes in Computer Science, pp. 292–301. Springer, Heidelberg (1998). https://doi.org/10.1007/bfb0056872

Knowledge Management

A Homogeneous Approach to Reasoning Over Global Geographic Data

Alia I. Abdelmoty$^{(\boxtimes)}$ and Abdurauf Satoti

School of Computer Science Informatics, Cardiff University, Wales, UK
{abdelmotyai,satotiam}@cardiff.ac.uk

Abstract. Much of the information that we use is geospatially referenced. The need for homogeneous representation of global geographic themes is recognised as critical for sustainable development goals. The richness of local geographic data created and maintained by individual countries vary widely, creating what is known as a geospatial digital divide. Attempts to bridge this divide include the adoption of Discrete Global Grid Systems that provide an abstract and uniform method of partitioning space on Earth. This paper considers how the local methods of partitioning space adopted in individual countries and provided as open data can be integrated with this global grid system. The paper proposes a novel ontology design pattern for representing the integration of both grid systems, and evaluates it against existing methods. It is shown how a uniform treatment of spatial semantics is used to represent geographic places across grid systems. This proposal is a step towards the effective utilisation of these grid systems in building global geographic information systems.

Keywords: geospatial ontology · spatial semantics · global grid systems

1   Introduction

Geospatial information describes the physical location of features on Earth and their relationships with other features and associated information. It provides the integrative platform for all digital data that has a location dimension. The critical role that geographic information plays in national social, economic and environmental development is witnessed by the United Nations Integrated Geospatial Information Framework [10]. The last decade has seen substantial efforts in opening up geospatial datasets by governments. Of particular interest to this work are open data sets representing administrative and other geographic division boundaries, for example, the Ordnance Survey (OS) open datasets that include all of the administrative and postal code boundaries for countries in the UK[1] [13], and the USGS national boundary dataset for the US[2]. Other global efforts

---

[1] https://osdatahub.os.uk/.

[2] https://data.usgs.gov/datacatalog/data/.

© The Author(s), under exclusive license to Springer Nature Switzerland AG 2025
M. Bramer and F. Stahl (Eds.): SGAI 2024, LNAI 15446, pp. 285–298, 2025.
https://doi.org/10.1007/978-3-031-77915-2_20

include the United Nations' Second Administrative Level Boundaries (SALB) programme[3] and the Global Administrative Areas (GADM)[4] that collect and provide boundaries at national and lower subdivisions in countries worldwide [3]. The scale and the richness of the information provided vary across countries, as shown in the example in Fig. 1, where GADM provides a hierarchy of three levels for Switzerland and a hierarchy of only one level for Libya.

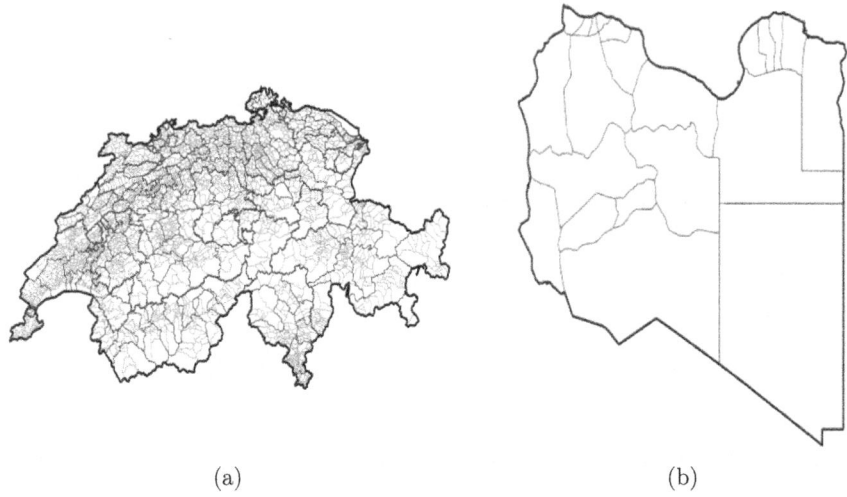

(a)   (b)

Fig. 1. GADM boundaries at different levels for (a) Switzerland (level 0-3) and (b) Libya (level 0-1) (see footnote 4).

Some characteristics of these datasets can be summarised as follows.

1. Geographic divisions of a country are thematic, hierarchical irregular tessellations that partition the space representing the boundary of the country into cells. The hierarchical division is normally represented as a set of conterminous subspaces having the same dimension as the space being partitioned; i.e. cells on any level in the hierarchy are adjacent with shared boundaries and cover the space completely. However, there can be some exceptions where cells can have contiguous boundaries (adjacent but not touching), for example when part of the country land is disconnected by a sea. This system of geographic divisions shall henceforth be denoted Discrete Local Irregular Grid System (DLIGS). An example is shown in Fig. 2, showing a hierarchy of two levels representing the Unitary Authority districts in Wales (with emphasized boundaries) and their division into communities.
2. Irregular tessellation of space is common, where cells may vary widely in size. For example when representing levels of communities in urban and rural areas

---

[3] https://salb.un.org/en.

[4] https://gadm.org.

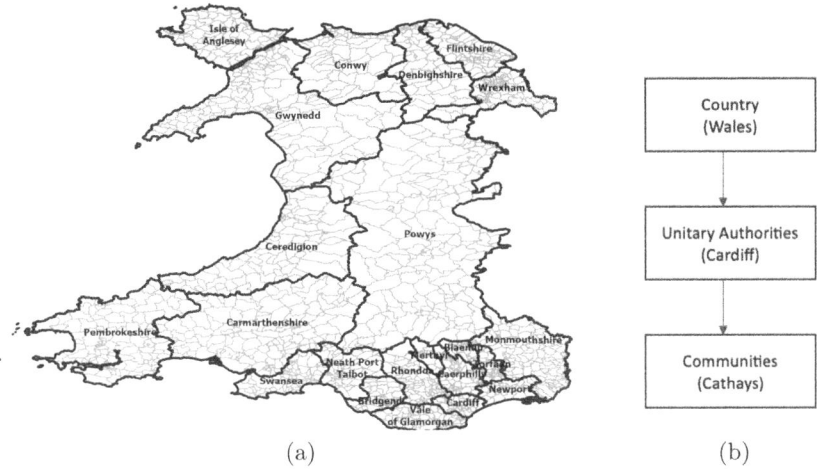

Fig. 2. (a) Unitary Authority Districts containing communities in Wales, UK, (b) DLIG hierarchy for Wales.

of the country, cells representing urban areas are more likely to be smaller in size.

3. Cell boundaries may change over time, e.g. as population distribution change, boundaries of school districts may change as well.
4. Cells may be associated with multiple names (identifiers), e.g. to record historical names or names in different languages.
5. Multiple hierarchies of different scales of division can be adopted in different countries. For example, some areas in England are designated civil parishes while others are 'unparished', resulting in different administrative division hierarchies for different areas in the country.
6. Multiple hierarchical divisions of the same area in space can be used. For example, school, health and electoral districts. In this case, cells in different hierarchies may overlap.

The above points represent a challenge to the homogeneous and integrated treatment and management of global geographic information across different countries, particularly when the monitoring of global themes such as sustainable development is considered. The proposal of the Discrete Global Grid System (DGGS) by the Open Geospatial Consortium (OGC)[5] and ISO 19170-1:2021 Geographic information [5] could address some of these challenges. DGGS is designed as a global spatial information framework that represents the surface of the Earth uniformly. DGGS address the entire planet by partitioning it into a discrete hierarchical tessellation of progressively finer resolution cells. H3, Uber's hexagonal hierarchical spatial index, is an example DGGS implementation developed by the ride-sharing company for their specific purposes, and made available

---
[5] https://docs.ogc.org/as/15-104r5/15-104r5.html#7.

open-source [4]. The H3 grid is shown in Fig. 3. Kmoch et al. gives an overview
of some examples DGGS [8].

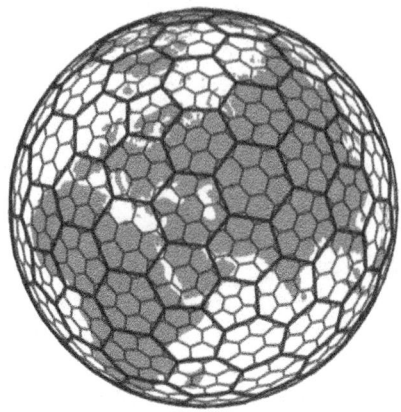

Fig. 3. Common tessellations used in DGGS; hexagonal as used in H3. Figure adapted
from [4]

This work proposes the integration of DGGS and DLIGS to address the
challenge of homogeneous manipulation and management of global geographic
information. We review previous works to address this problem and propose an
ontology design pattern with a uniform treatment of both DGGS and DLIGS
for representing geographic space. This work paves the way for considering the
combined spatial reasoning with the two systems and the realisation of global
geographic information systems.

In Sect. 2, an overview of DGGS is given and an analysis of related proposal are presented. Our ontology design pattern and examples of its utility are
presented in Sect. 3. A discussion of future work and conclusions are given in
Sect. 4.

2   Related Work

In contrast to DLIGS, DGGS provides a uniform approach to partitioning space
for all countries [2]. The underlying geometry of the cells and the topological relationships between neighboring cells can be used to define globally unique identifiers (GUIDs) for the cells at any resolution [9]. Previous works have considered
the functional specification of DGGS and the functional operations required for
its realisation and practical use in Geographic Information Systems [9]. There
it is used as a space indexing method to facilitate efficient search and retrieval;
a sort of a realisation of a Quadtree spatial index with uniform application
across the whole surface of the Earth and with recognizable unique identifiers
for its cells. Typical operations on a DGGS include translation of coordinates

to grid cells, indexing, cell geometry calculations and visualization. Uber's H3 is used for locating neighbouring cells, and representing movement between cells to facilitate navigation queries.

Few works have considered the data modelling aspects of DGGS and how it links to the standard vector and raster models for geographic data. In particular, how are the cells in a DGGS link to the topological structuring of space with points, lines and polygons representing geographic features and places and how do the identifiers for these units of information correspond. This is necessary to allow for effective reasoning with geographic information. Recent work in the KnowWhereGraph project [6,7] has considered this question and developed an ontology design pattern, denoted the Hierarchical Cell Feature (HFC) pattern, whose purpose is to model how features and regions interact with an underlying Discrete Global Grid in the context of facilitating the integration of data resources on the Web. Here we review this design pattern and its ability to integrate with DLIGS.

2.1   The Hierarchical Cell Feature (HFC) Pattern

Figure 4 shows the HFC pattern as described in Shimizu et al. [12]. The figure is adapted to present how DGGS is represented and used to model the concepts of features and regions [7]. An overview of the modelling and reasoning capacities offered by HFC is given below.

Modelling

1. DGGS is represented using the concept of a Cell that has an associated geometric representation.
2. A Cell has a spatial relationship with a geographic Feature. This is a natural consequence from the fact that the grid of cells is projected on space and the cells coincide with a specific location on Earth, and therefore intersects with geographic features occupying this space. Figure 5 shows a set of six standard qualitative topological spatial relations between simple regions that can be used to instantiate this relationship.
3. A Cell has more than one adjacent Cell and a Cell is contained in a (parent) Cell.
4. A Feature is spatially related to a Cell. A Feature encapsulates the notion of a feature, characteristic, or aspect of the surface upon which the hierarchical grid system has been applied.
5. A Region is spatially related to a Cell. 'A Region is a socio-culturally or geopolitically significant area. For example, Kansas is a state (administrative region) in the United States. It can also be regarded as a Feature' [12].
6. The OGC classes of Feature, Spatial Object and Geometry are used [1], shown with a dark gray colour in the figure.

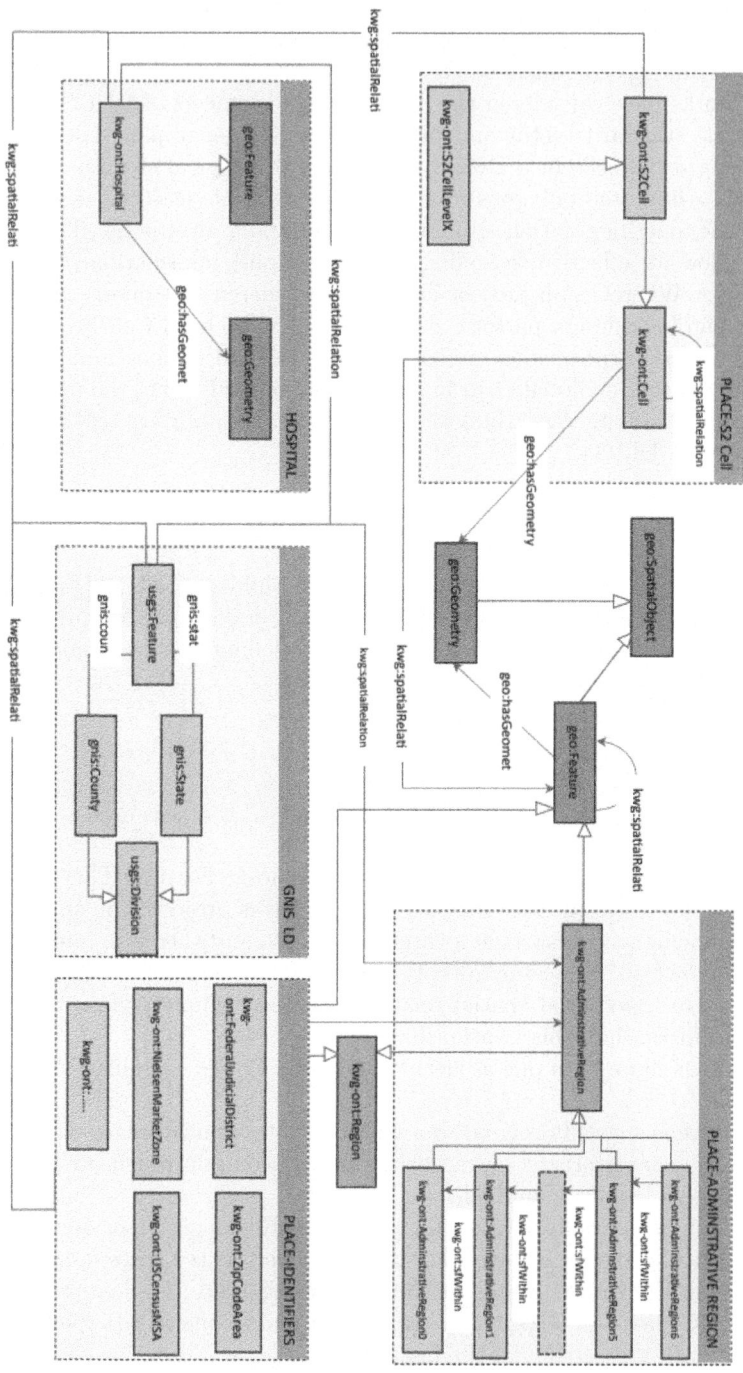

Fig. 4. Hierarchical Cell Feature ontology design pattern; adapted from [12].

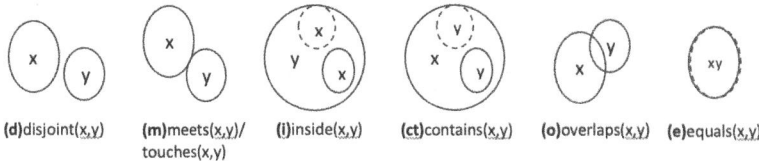

Fig. 5. Topological relations between simple regions.

Reasoning. Semantic compression and spatial reasoning with the pattern are described in [14]. In particular, two main methods are used: transitivity property of spatial containment relationships and inheritance of spatial relations for spatially related features. The exact nature of this inheritance depends on the type of spatial relation. For example, if a Cell is spatiallyRelated to a Feature, then the parent of that Cell is also spatiallyRelated to the Feature. The following are selected axioms from [12] that summarise these methods.

$$\text{Cell} \sqsubseteq \text{Geometry}$$
$$\text{Cell} \sqsubseteq \forall \text{spatialRelations.Geometry}$$
$$\text{Cell} \sqsubseteq\geq 0\text{spatialRelations.Cell}$$
$$\text{Cell} \sqsubseteq\geq 0\text{isAdjacentTo.Cell}$$
$$\text{Cell} \sqsubseteq \forall \text{isAdjacentTo.Cell}$$
$$\exists \text{isAdjacentTo.Cell} \sqsubseteq \text{Cell}$$
$$\text{Cell} \sqsubseteq\geq 0\text{contains.Cell}$$
$$\text{Cell} \sqsubseteq \forall \text{contains.Cell}$$
$$\exists \text{contains.Cell} \sqsubseteq \text{Cell}$$
$$\text{isFullyContainedIn} \sqsubseteq \text{contains}^-$$
$$\text{contains} \circ \text{contains} \sqsubseteq \text{contains}$$
$$\text{isFullyContainedIn} \circ \text{isFullyContainedIn} \sqsubseteq \text{isFullyContainedIn}$$
$$\text{contains} \circ \text{spatiallyRelated} \sqsubseteq \text{spatiallyRelated}$$

In summary, the pattern models DGGS as an abstract geometric division of geographic space. Geographic features are then attached to the cells with a spatial relationship that is defined through their extent and coincidence with the underlying abstracted space division. This is modelled uniformly for places and regions that can be administrative regions. A spatial relationship can also be established between geographic place and administrative divisions. As it stands, the pattern does not explicitly model the hierarchies in a DLIGS, nor does it clarify how the places/features relate to this hierarchy beyond possible spatial relationship with any region on any level in the hierarchy. The link between the DGGS and DLIGS is thus implicit and will need to be computed by the information systems (GIS) that implement the models.

Here we describe basic requirements for an integrated DGGS and DLIGS ontology design pattern that can be used as competency questions for evaluation.

A more thorough treatment of these requirements and the reasoning support needed are the subject of ongoing work and are beyond the scope of this paper. A schematic representation of DGGS and DLIGS are shown in Fig. 6, in which an analogy is made with representation of different map scales. A pattern that integrates both DGGS and DLIGS will be capable of addressing the following set of questions.

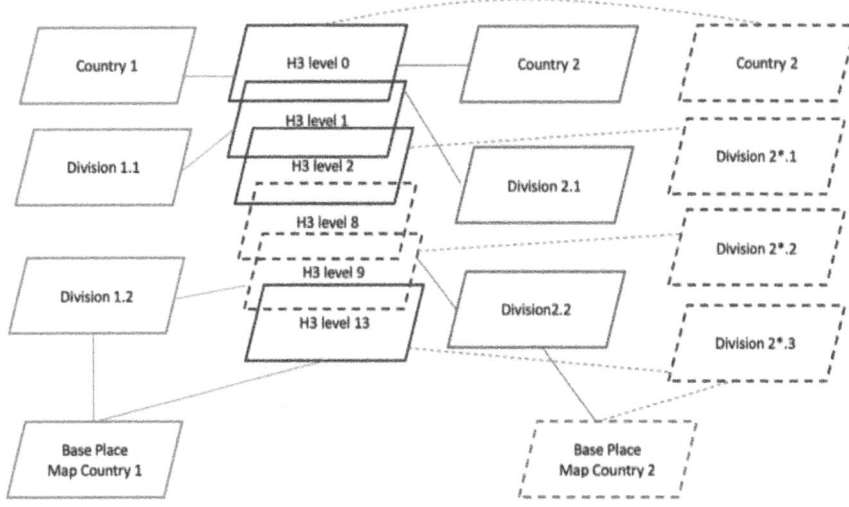

Fig. 6. DGGS and DLIGS are depicted as maps of different scales.

1. Where is place x?, where x can be any type of place on the base place map. The location of x can be represented by a simple point or by its areal extent and boundary. A region on any division is also considered to be a type of place. The answer to this question should identify the location of the place within the DGGS and within the DLIGS.
2. Which regions are neighbours (not neighbours) of region x?
3. Which regions are parents of (children of) region x?
4. Which regions in Division 1 intersect with region x in Division 2?

Questions 1–3 consider the relationships between places and regions within the same hierarchical division, while question 4 consider regions in different divisions, where the DGGS can serve to identify and link the levels of resolution in different divisions. A further example of useful questions that can be used for integration of data analysis across different countries is "Produce a DLIGS for a country that is comparable to another of a different country". For example, to produce a DLIGS for Libya that is similar to the DLIGS used for representing the Communities in Wales. The purpose here is for example to support the uniform statistical analysis and reporting of geographic themes across the two countries.

3   The Discrete Local Irregular Grid (DLIG) Pattern

An overview of the proposed ontology design pattern for the DLIGS is shown in Fig. 7. Relevant aspects of the design pattern are summarised as follows.

1. DLIGS is represented using the concept of a GeoUnit that represents a cell on any of the levels of the hierarchical division of space, e.g. an particular community or a particular district, etc.
2. GeoUnits and their associated hierarchies are modelled with two design patterns, namely, the Tree Design pattern and the Composition design pattern [11], shown in Fig. 8.
3. GeoUnits are adjacent to one or more GeoUnits and have a GeoUnit as a parent.
4. Country is a subclass of a root GeoUnit, and thus does not have a parent.
5. Geographic place are located inside a leaf GeoUnit.
6. Geographic places with extended geometries can intersect more than one GeoUnit.
7. Geographic divisions, base places and extended base places are subclasses of Place that is itself a subclass of Feature.
8. A Place is an abstract concept to represent geographic places with identifying attributes of name and place type.

DGGS can now be integrated in a uniform manner within the pattern as shown in the figure.

1. A DGGS Cell is a subclass of GeoUnit. This allows for the uniform representation and treatement of the DGGS hierarchy as any other division hierarchy in the system.
2. A GeoUnit is contained within a Cell. This explicit relationships allow for a direct definition of the location of the GeoUnit in the DGGS hierarchy.

The primary difference between DLIGS and HFC is in the treatment of how the places and regions are represented. Explicit spatial relationships are defined to relate the location of all objects. Some axioms that represent these explicit relationships are defined below. Note that this is only a partial set of the axioms. A complete set that describe the properties and constraints for all concepts is beyond the scope of this paper.

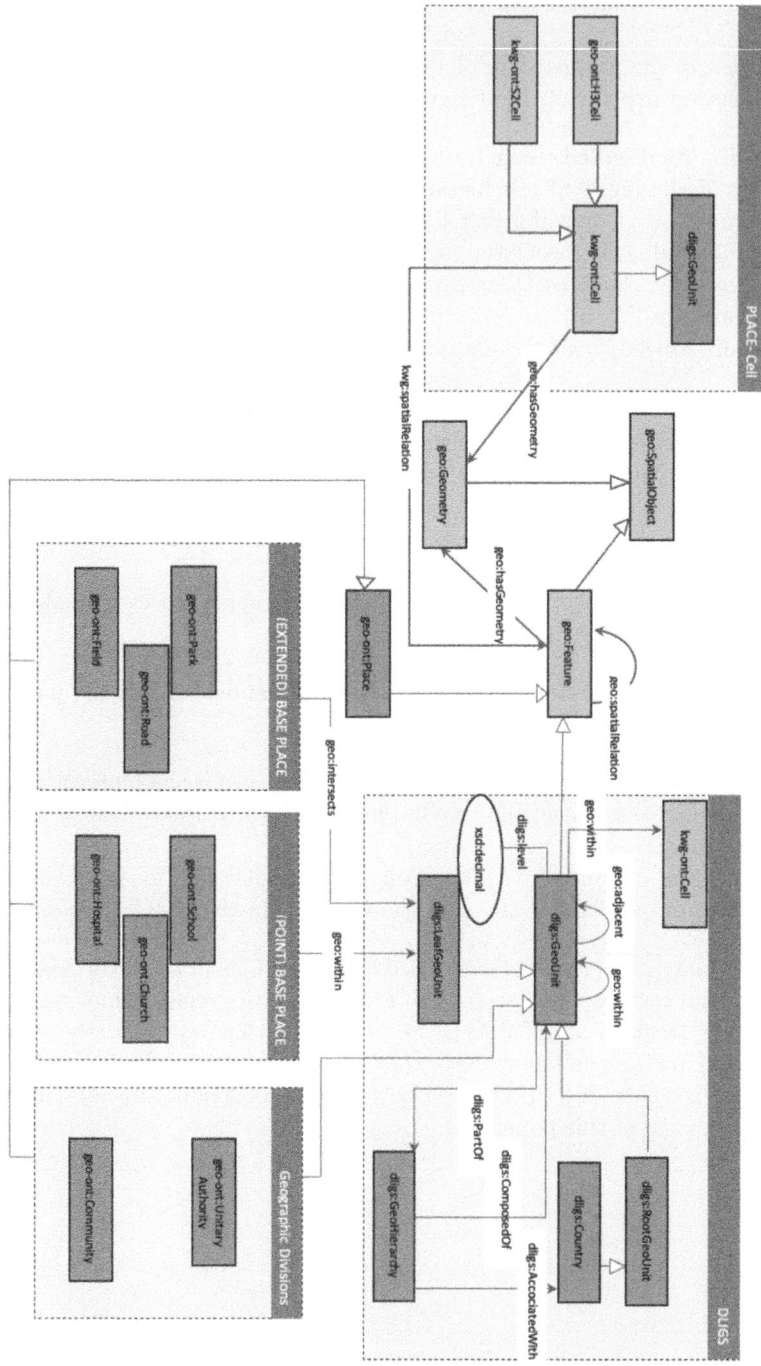

Fig. 7. The proposed Discrete Local Irregular Grid pattern.

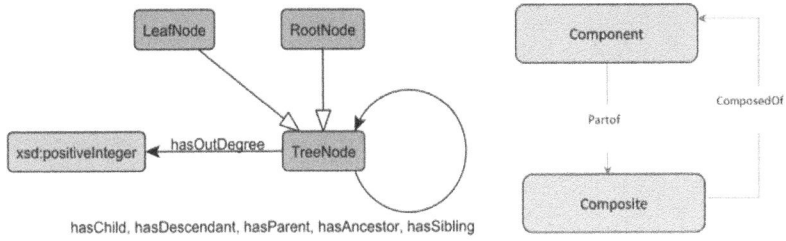

Fig. 8. The Tree and Composition ontology design patterns used in the definition of the DLIG pattern.

$$\text{GeoUnit} \sqsubseteq \text{Feature}$$
$$\text{GeoUnit} \sqsubseteq\geq 0\text{isAdjacentTo.Cell}$$
$$\text{GeoUnit} \sqsubseteq \forall\text{isAdjacentTo.Cell}$$
$$\exists\text{isAdjacentTo.GeoUnit} \sqsubseteq \text{GeoUnit}$$
$$\text{GeoUnit} \sqsubseteq\geq 0\text{contains.GeoUnit}$$
$$\text{GeoUnit} \sqsubseteq \forall\text{contains.GeoUnit}$$
$$\exists\text{contains.GeoUnit} \sqsubseteq \text{GeoUnit}$$
$$\text{GeoUnit} \sqsubseteq\geq 0\text{contains.Place}$$
$$\text{GeoUnit} \sqsubseteq \forall\text{contains.Place}$$
$$\exists\text{contains.Place} \sqsubseteq \text{GeoUnit}$$

Similar qualitative spatial reasoning rules apply for transitivity of containment relationships and downward and upward inheritance of spatial relationships within hierarchies and across hierarchies of DLIGS and DGGS. Some example application of the pattern for the representation of places in different countries are shown in Figs. 9 and 10. Tables 1 and 2 gives details of the places as represented using the pattern and how the DGGS information can be matched across the hierarchies to link the data. Evaluation of the pattern and its utility and effectiveness for the integration of global geodata is the subject of ongoing work.

Table 1. Representation of the Location of Llandaff Cathedral in Wales.

	DLIG	DLIG Level	DGG (H3) level	DGG Cell Id
Llandaff Cathedral	Base Place		15	8a7bacc04847fff
Llandaff North	Community-Ward	2	8	88195ab69dfffff
Cardiff	Unitary Authority District	1	4	8419587ffffffff
Wales	Country	0	2	82195ffffffffff

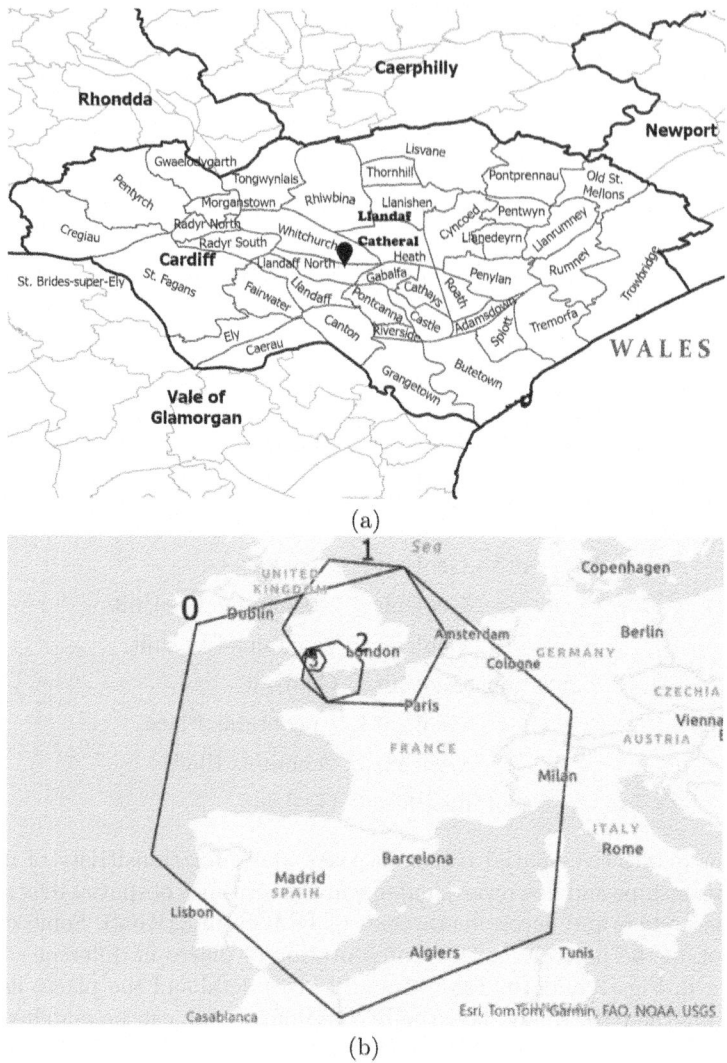

(a)

(b)

Fig. 9. Location of Llandaff Cathedral in Wales represented in (a) Administrative hierarchy of Wales (DLIGS), and (b) H3 hierarchy (DGGS).

Table 2. Representation of the location of Bahia Palace in Morocco.

	DLIG	DLIG Level	DGG (H3) level	DGG Cell Id
Bahia Palace	Base Place		15	8a96a85b1167ff
Marrakesh	Community-Ward	2	2	833983ffffffff
Morocco	Country	0	3	82398ffffffff

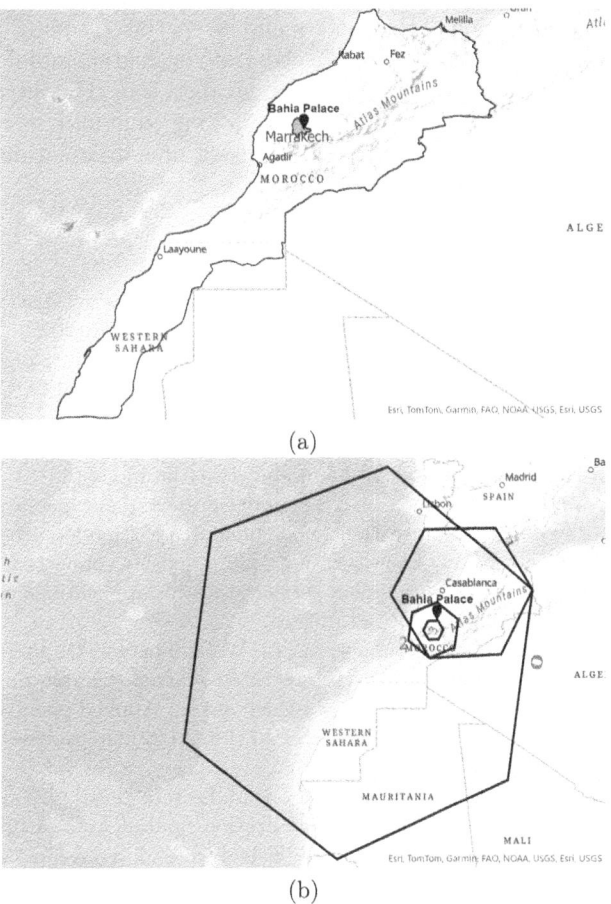

Fig. 10. Location of Bahia Palace in Morocco represented in (a) Administrative hierarchy of Morocco (DLIGS), and (b) H3 hierarchy (DGGS).

4   Conclusions

This paper addresses the need for integrated methods of management and reasoning over global geographic datasets. The complexity of the problem and its dimensions are analysed by recognising the different local representations of geodata sets in different countries and their open data availability. To address these challenges, this paper proposed a novel ontology design pattern that explicitly represents topological and proximity spatial semantics to capture the relationships between grid systems that represent geographic space and the geographic features and places on the ground. Design requirements for this pattern have been elicited by reviewing existing approaches to building integrated geographic knowledge graphs. The pattern has been implemented and evaluated with realistic data sets. Some examples were shown to demonstrate its utility.

Full logical specification of the pattern and its spatial reasoning capabilities is the subject of ongoing work. Also, more elaborate evaluation and demonstration of its utility is being carried out using open geodata sets. The integrated use of global grid systems and local grid systems is an important current topic and will pave the way for the development of global geographic information systems.

References

1. https://docs.ogc.org/as/15-104r5/15-104r5.html#7: Open geospatial consortium. topic 21: Discrete global grid systems abstract specification (2017)
2. Bondaruk, B., Roberts, S.A., Robertson, C.: Assessing the state of the art in discrete global grid systems: OGC criteria and present functionality. Geomatica **74**, 9–30 (2020). https://doi.org/10.1139/geomat-2019-0015
3. Brinks, J.: Database of global administrative boundaries (GADM) (2018)
4. Brodsky, I.: H3: Uber's hexagonal hierarchical spatial index (2018)
5. ISO: Geographic information - discrete global grid systems specifications part 1: Core reference system and operations, and equal area earth reference system (2024)
6. Janowicz, K., et al.: Know, know where graph: a densely connected, cross-domain knowledge graph and geo-enrichment service stack for applications in environmental intelligence. AI Mag. **43**, 30–39 (2022)
7. Janowicz, K., Hizler, P., Schildhauer, M., Li, W., Rehberger, D.: https://stko-kwg. geog.ucsb.edu/static/schema/figures/integrated-schema-diagram.png (2024)
8. Kmoch, A., Matsibora, O., Vasilyev, I., Uuemaa, E.: Applied open-source discrete global grid systems. AGILE: GIScience Ser. **3**, 1–6 (2022). https://doi.org/10.5194/agile-giss-3-41-2022
9. Li, M., Stefanakis, E.: Geospatial operations of discrete global grid systems-a comparison with traditional GIS. J. Geovisualization Spatial Anal. **4** (2020). https://doi.org/10.1007/s41651-020-00066-3/Published
10. United nations integrated geospatial information framework (2024)
11. ODPA: Ontology design patterns (2022), https://ggim.un.org/UN-IGIF/part1.cshtml
12. Shimizu, C., et al.: A pattern for features on a hierarchical spatial grid, pp. 108–114. Association for Computing Machinery (2021). https://doi.org/10.1145/3502223.3502236, http://ontologydesignpatterns.org/wiki/Main_Page
13. Yates, D., Keller, J., Wilson, R., Dodds, L.: The UK's geospatial data infrastructure: challenges and opportunities. Open Data Institute (2018)
14. Zalewski, J., Hitzler, P., Janowicz, K.: Semantic compression with region calculi in nested hierarchical grids, pp. 305–308. Association for Computing Machinery (2021). https://doi.org/10.1145/3474717.3483965, https://theodi.org/insights/reports/geospatial-data-infrastructure-report/

Short Technical Papers

OK Google, What is the Stock Forecast for Next week? Leveraging Search Engines for Data Collection, Sentiment Analysis and Stock Predictions

Nicholas Arthur Frederick-Preece$^{(\boxtimes)}$ ⓘ and Noorhan Abbas ⓘ

University of Leeds, Leeds, UK
nickfrederickpreece@gmail.com, n.h.abbas@leeds.ac.uk

Abstract. Predicting stock prices remains a critical research focus in finance, complicated by numerous external factors. Recent approaches utilize high-level data, such as tweets and news articles, for financial sentiment analysis. However, these methods often struggle to accurately capture public sentiment, leading to prediction inaccuracies. We introduce a high-quality dataset and a novel data collection method using a programmable search engine and FinBERT sentiment analysis, resulting in weekly sentiment metrics and stock prices for 20 stocks. The dataset was used to train and enhance a Flair sentiment model, integrated into a neural network for stock price prediction. Our results show that the neural networks with multiple time series output parameters outperform single-output models. Moreover, fine-tuned Flair models achieved higher accuracy than FinBERT-based models in predicting stock prices. This research highlights the potential of novel databases and refined sentiment models, offering improved insights into sentiment analysis in finance and introducing an innovative data collection method applicable across sectors using natural language processing.

Keywords: Flair · FinBERT · Fine-Tuning · Sentiment Analysis · Programmable Search Engine · Neural Network · Stock Prediction

1 Introduction

Understanding the various factors influencing stock price fluctuations is a complex and nuanced task, posing significant challenges to achieving high accuracy and reliable predictions [1]. Stock prices are affected by numerous variables, including economic indicators, market sentiment, and geopolitical events [2], which complicate forecasting efforts. While neural networks can provide estimates based on metrics like stock opening, closing prices, and trade volumes, many unknowns introduce noise and hinder precise predictions [3, 4]. An alternative approach involves leveraging news articles, as news often reflects or influences stock movements, with negative news potentially driving traders to sell [5]. Sentiment analysis can convert news content into actionable data for stock price estimation. However, current sentiment analysis models for stock prediction

M. Bramer and F. Stahl (Eds.): SGAI 2024, LNAI 15446, pp. 301–306, 2025.
https://doi.org/10.1007/978-3-031-77915-2_21

often rely on limited and potentially biased datasets from platforms like X^1 (formerly Twitter), forums, or financial news outlets [6, 7]. This study proposes a novel method using Google's programmable search engine (PSE) to compile a comprehensive dataset of stock-related news. This dataset will be used to train and fine-tune a Flair sentiment model, integrating sentiment analysis with a neural network to predict stock prices at intervals of 1 day, 1 week, and 3 weeks. The dataset contains stock information, FinBERT sentiment and the title and publisher of each article, this dataset is stored on GitHub[2]. The study will also compare the effectiveness of the FinBERT and Flair models in predicting stock price movements.

2 Related Work

FinBERT, a pre-trained NLP model based on BERT [8], is tailored for financial sentiment analysis and fine-tuned using the Financial PhraseBank [9]. A 2023 study [6] compared TextBlob, VADER, and FinBERT for sentiment analysis of tweets in predicting stock market trends, finding that sentiment improves forecasting accuracy. However, reliance on Twitter for public sentiment presents limitations, as its user base may not represent broader demographics that rely on news outlets. Another study [7] comparing FinBERT and VADER found FinBERT to be more accurate with financial news (Bloomberg, CNBC, Reuters, WSJ, Fortune) but less effective with tweets, where VADER performed better, emphasizing the importance of matching models to datasets. Further research [10] showed sentiment analysis, using the Harvard psychological dictionary and the Loughran-McDonald sentiment dictionary, outperformed bag-of-words approaches in stock prediction. A FinBERT model fine-tuned on 4,840 financial news sentences was also employed to classify sentiment [11]. Additionally, a study [12] using Flair sentiment models combined with deep learning methods like EWT, LSTM, and PSO achieved 90% accuracy in forecasting financial trends over 10 days.

3 Design and Methodology

3.1 Data Collection, Pre-processing and Validation

This study selects 20 stocks based on company size, sector, and public prominence to optimize search results. Data generation is conducted via the PSE, ensuring compliance with terms of service[3] by maintaining transitory storage of extracted data. To manage time and resource constraints, the dataset includes only Wednesdays within the date range of 01/01/2020 to 01/04/2024, minimizing the weekend effect [13]. Temporary datasets are created for each stock using queries "Stock name news from start_date to end_date" and store search terms, URLs, and publication dates. Website text is extracted using the libraries requests, article, paper, and BeautifulSoup, and is compiled into a unified database containing titles, text, publishers, keywords, and summaries. Prepro-cessing is applied to remove URLs, non-alphanumeric characters, and entries below a

---

[1] https://x.com/.

[2] https://github.com/Nicholasfp/GoogleFinancialDatabase.

[3] https://support.google.com/programmable-search/answer/1714300?hl=en.

minimum character count to ensure data quality and compatibility with FinBERT and Flair, addressing anti-scraping measures that return short, unusable text. Initially, the 2020–2024 database contained 24,633 articles, but after preprocessing, 1,746 unusable articles were removed, leaving 22,887. Stock data is retrieved via Alpha Vantage, filtered by search dates, and integrated with the extracted text. FinBERT is used to estimate sentiment, serving as a baseline and stored in a new column. To train the Flair model, separate text and sentiment databases are prepared with two split ratios: 70% train, 20% test, 10% validation, and 70% train, 10% test, 20% validation. FinBERT was selected as the baseline model due to the impracticality of manual labelling, which would require approximately 763 h and could introduce bias. As a consistent and accurate model for processing news articles and financial reports [7], FinBERT's sentiment assignments were manually reviewed on a sample of data points and found to be reliable.

3.2 Models

This study employs FinBERT as the baseline model due to its accuracy in analysing financial news and reports [7], leveraging its domain-specific training on financial data to better capture industry-specific jargon and nuances [1]. While FinBERT excels in this context, it performs less effectively on shorter, general posts like tweets. To address the limitations of FinBERT's context window and skewed sentiment detection, the study introduces a bias mechanism favouring positive or negative sentiment when neutral values dominate. Additionally, the study uses Flair, an open-source NLP library for model training [14] comparing DistilBERT[4] and RoBERTa [15] embeddings, chosen for their efficiency and performance. A custom database is created by combining FinBERT sentiment data, which is used to train and evaluate the Flair model. The models are evaluated based on accuracy and mean squared error, with hyperparameters adjusted iteratively to improve performance, as discussed in later sections.

During the training of Flair, we developed eight models using the generated dataset, all of which share the following fixed hyperparameters: embeddings_storage_mode = 'none', TransformerDocumentEmbeddings fine_tune = False, and a label dictionary with neutral, positive, and negative classes. To optimize model performance and prevent overfitting, we focused on tuning learning rate, mini-batch size, epochs, weight decay, and the train-validation-test split. Models F and G utilize RoBERTa word embeddings while the others are based on DistilBERT embeddings.

For evaluation of Flair's performance, we capture the Accuracy, Precision, Recall and F-score in each model. These metrics are widely used in classification tasks and are useful for understanding the overall correctness and quality of predictions.

3.3 Neural Nets

The study trains neural networks using inputs such as sentiment, sentiment score (Flair only), number of articles published, and stock open-close values to predict stock movements after 1 day, 1 week, and 3 weeks, with models generated for both FinBERT and

---

[4] https://huggingface.co/docs/transformers/en/model_doc/distilbert.

Flair. The neural network architecture for each model includes two fully connected layers with 64 and 32 neurons (using ReLU activation) and a final layer corresponding to the number of outputs. To prepare the data, stock open-close columns are added for each prediction period, and unnecessary text and URL columns are removed. Identical hyperparameters, including StandardScaler, Adam optimizer, 10,000 epochs, and a batch size of 32, are used for comparison, with additional fine-tuning of epochs and batch size for improved performance at 60,000 epochs and a batch size of 100. Model evaluation is conducted using mean squared error (MSE) and the Keras accuracy metric, providing a binary comparison between predicted and actual results.

4 Experimental Results and Discussion

Following training on the dataset, each model undergoes evaluation using a dedicated test dataset, and the outcomes of this evaluation are detailed in Table 1.

Table 1. Flair sentiment evaluation results.

Model id	Accuracy	Precision	Recall	F-score
A	0.7027	0.6335	0.7027	0.6638
B	0.7536	0.7463	0.7536	0.7464
C	0.7541	0.7473	0.7541	0.7439
D	0.7541	0.7462	0.7541	0.7462
E	0.7455	0.7429	0.7455	0.7303
F	0.5703	0.5486	0.5703	0.4152
G	0.7275	0.6609	0.7275	0.6876
H	0.7545	0.7469	0.7545	0.7477

Utilising model H we run evaluation on single and multiclass neural net models, this generates the results shown in Table 2.

Table 2. Neural net evaluation results.

Neural net model	Accuracy	Mean Squared Error
FinBERT all predictions	0.3727	44.9837
FinBERT after 1 day predictions	0.0118	59.6242
FinBERT after 1 week predictions	0.00939	75.2323
FinBERT after 3 weeks predictions	0.0068	135.5796
Flair model H all predictions	0.3292	69.9274

(continued)

Table 2. (*continued*)

Neural net model	Accuracy	Mean Squared Error
Flair model H after 1 day predictions	0.0056	64.5539
Flair model H after 1 week predictions	0.0094	104.8947
Flair model H after 3 weeks predictions	0.0068	83.8780
FinBERT fine tuned all predictions	0.3609	49.1761
Flair DistilBERT fine tuned all predictions	0.3703	95.4864

Comparing the generated sentiment models from Table 1 we see that model H has the highest accuracy, recall and f score of 0.7545, 0.7545 and 0.7477 with a precision of 0.7469, model C has the highest precision at 0.7473 with an accuracy of 0.7536, models C and D have comparable accuracy and precision scores to model H. From these results model H shows good performance with only a small compromise for a slightly lower precision. The results trend shows that an increase in mini batch size and a decrease in learning rate increases accuracy.

Analysis of the neural networks reveals that incorporating all predictions yields significantly higher accuracy compared to individual predictions in both FinBERT and Flair models, with FinBERT showing a 34% improvement and Flair a 30% increase, indicating substantial potential for future enhancement. Table 2 highlights that the best baseline FinBERT models outperform Flair in both accuracy (by 0.04) and mean squared error (MSE reduction of 24.9437). However, fine-tuning improves Flair's accuracy beyond FinBERT by 0.0094, though at the cost of a higher MSE (46.3103), likely due to overfitting. Fine-tuning appears to negatively affect FinBERT, while presenting improvement opportunities for Flair. The dataset used in this study, though smaller than others [7] (260000 tweets), [16] (306242 news articles), offers higher quality by relying on general news sources rather than potentially biased platforms like Twitter [17], thus providing a more representative view of public sentiment. This aligns with research advocating for data quality over quantity [18], emphasizing the dataset's ability to better capture sentiment-company perception correlations.

5   Conclusions and Future Work

This study demonstrates significant advancements in both financial analysis and NLP by effectively using sentiment analysis to predict stock prices, utilizing a novel dataset generated through Google's programmable search engine. The improved prediction accuracy of models with multi-class outputs highlights the importance of integrating diverse time series data, offering a valuable tool for financial analysts and investors. Notably, fine-tuning enhances Flair models but hinders FinBERT, providing key insights for optimizing neural networks in financial sentiment analysis. Beyond financial forecasting, the study contributes to NLP research by showcasing the value of comprehensive data collection and model fine-tuning with Flair distilBERT models outperforming RoBERTa models.

The research also suggests future exploration into expanding datasets, integrating more models, and using real-time sentiment analysis for enhanced stock price prediction.

A review of legal frameworks revealed that UK and EU fair use laws allow text extraction for non-commercial research under specified conditions, while US laws permit text and data mining but restrict the publication of full text, requiring substantial transformation of the original material.

References

1. Araci, D.: FinBERT: Financial Sentiment Analysis with Pre-trained Language Models. (2019). https://doi.org/10.48550/arXiv.1908.10063
2. Harper, D.R.: Forces That Move Stock Prices, https://www.investopedia.com/articles/basics/04/100804.asp
3. Vonko, D.: Neural Networks: Forecasting Profits, https://www.investopedia.com/articles/trading/06/neuralnetworks.asp
4. Adusumilli, R.: Machine Learning to Predict Stock Prices, https://towardsdatascience.com/predicting-stock-prices-using-a-keras-lstm-model-4225457f0233
5. Beers, B.: How the News Affects Stock Prices, https://www.investopedia.com/ask/answers/155.asp
6. Liapis, C.M., Karanikola, A., Kotsiantis, S.: Investigating deep stock market forecasting with sentiment analysis. Entropy **25**, 219 (2023). https://doi.org/10.3390/e25020219
7. Xiao, Q., Ihnaini, B.: Stock trend prediction using sentiment analysis. **9**, e1293 (2023). https://doi.org/10.7717/peerj-cs.1293
8. Devlin, J., Chang, M.-W., Lee, K., Toutanova, K.: BERT: Pre-training of deep bidirectional transformers for language understanding (2019). https://doi.org/10.48550/arXiv.1810.04805
9. Malo, P., Sinha, A., Korhonen, P., Wallenius, J., Takala, P.: Good debt or bad debt: detecting semantic orientations in economic texts. Asso. Info Sci. Tech. **65**, 782–796 (2014). https://doi.org/10.1002/asi.23062
10. Li, X., Xie, H., Chen, L., Wang, J., Deng, X.: News impact on stock price return via sentiment analysis. Knowl.-Based Syst. **69**, 14–23 (2014). https://doi.org/10.1016/j.knosys.2014.04.022
11. Liu, J.-X., Leu, J.-S., Holst, S.: Stock price movement prediction based on Stocktwits investor sentiment using FinBERT and ensemble SVM. **9**, e1403 (2023). https://doi.org/10.7717/peerj-cs.1403
12. Maqbool, J., Aggarwal, P., Kaur, R., Mittal, A., Ganaie, I.A.: Stock prediction by integrating sentiment scores of financial news and MLP-regressor: a machine learning approach. Proc. Comput. Sci. **218**, 1067–1078 (2023). https://doi.org/10.1016/j.procs.2023.01.086
13. Kenton, W.: Weekend Effect: What It Is & Why It Happens. https://www.investopedia.com/terms/w/weekendeffect.asp
14. Akbik, A., Bergmann, T., Blythe, D., Rasul, K., Schweter, S., Vollgraf, R.: FLAIR: an easy-to-use framework for state-of-the-art NLP. In: Presented at the Proceedings of the 2019 Conference of the North American Chapter of the Association for Computational Linguistics (Demonstrations) June (2019)
15. Liu, Y., et al.: RoBERTa: a robustly optimized BERT pretraining approach. (2019). https://doi.org/10.48550/arXiv.1907.11692
16. Pavlyshenko, B.M.: Financial news analytics using fine-tuned llama 2 GPT Model. (2023). https://doi.org/10.48550/arXiv.2308.13032
17. Bradley, D., Hanousek, J., Jr., Jame, R., Xiao, Z.: Place your bets? The market consequences of investment advice on Reddit's Wallstreetbets. SSRN J. (2021). https://doi.org/10.2139/ssrn.3806065
18. Geng, X., Gudibande, A., Liu, H., Wallace, E., Abbeel, P., Levine, S., Song, D.: Koala: a dialogue model for academic research. https://bair.berkeley.edu/blog/2023/04/03/koala/

University News: A New Data Source for NLP Bias Research

Rawan Bin Shiha[1,2]([✉]) [iD], Eric Atwell[1] [iD], and Noorhan Abbas[1] [iD]

[1] School of Computing, University of Leeds, Leeds, UK
{e.s.atwell,ml19rbs,n.h.abbas}@leeds.ac.uk
[2] Imam Mohammad Ibn Saud Islamic University, Riyadh, Saudi Arabia
rmbinshiha@imamu.edu.sa

Abstract. This research explores the use of university news articles for Natural Language Processing (NLP) and gender bias detection. It emphasises the importance of ethical considerations in NLP, advocating for transparency and diversity in dataset selection to ensure fairness. Using techniques such as Sentiment Analysis (SA) and gender-specific language classification, the study reveals a bias towards male possessive terms, indicating gender imbalance in the content. While the Facebook BART-Large-Mnli model demonstrated strong accuracy, it struggled with neutral sentiment, suggesting areas for improvement. The study highlights university news as a valuable dataset for promoting equity and inclusivity in NLP tools, laying the foundation for fairer methodologies.

Keywords: University News · Bias · News Bias · NLP · SA · Text Classification

1 Introduction

Addressing bias in NLP often stems from training datasets that reflect societal prejudices. Traditional bias detection studies have focused on mainstream news, but university news, an underexplored resource, may present unique gender biases. In this study, bias is defined as the systematic favouring or disadvantaging of certain genders, manifested through language choices and representation in media content. Specifically, university media can perpetuate biases by selectively highlighting achievements or issues related to a particular gender.

This paper's original contribution lies in applying NLP techniques to university news articles to uncover and quantify gender bias, thereby expanding the understanding of bias in academic contexts. While SA has been used in mainstream media, its application to university news remains limited. This study fills that gap, offering insights into gender representation in academia and contributing to more inclusive NLP methodologies.

The structure of this paper is as follows: Sect. 2 provides a background on media bias and the role of diverse datasets in NLP. Section 3 outlines the methodology. Section 4 presents the results, and Sect. 5 discusses their implications. Section 6 concludes the paper and suggests directions for future research.

M. Bramer and F. Stahl (Eds.): SGAI 2024, LNAI 15446, pp. 307–312, 2025.
https://doi.org/10.1007/978-3-031-77915-2_22

2 Background

In NLP, diverse datasets play a critical role in enhancing the robustness and fairness of models. Curated datasets are used for evaluation, while supervised datasets train and fine-tune models, and large unsupervised datasets are vital for pretraining and language modelling [7]. The reliance on varied data sources highlights the need for diversity to reduce systemic biases and ensure that NLP systems can process language from a wide range of contexts. This underscores the value of incorporating university news articles into NLP research. Diverse datasets are key to mitigating biases in NLP models, as homogeneous datasets often lead to poor performance, especially on texts from under-represented groups [5]. Research has shown that models trained on less diverse data struggle to generalise across different dialects and sociolects, potentially marginalising minority groups [1]. These findings stress the ethical implications of dataset diversity, which is essential for creating fairer and more accurate NLP applications [4]. Despite the growing research on media bias using SA, university news remains underexplored. Existing literature highlights the application of SA in identifying shifts in sentiment and nuances in media reporting [3]. Further studies have used Transformer models to analyse sentiment over time [8] and measure media bias in newspaper tweets [9]. However, university news, which often targets internal audiences like students and staff, may exhibit unique biases not seen in mainstream media. For example, research into media bias surrounding historically black colleges and universities (HBCUs) shows how selective reporting and tone can negatively affect institutional support and public perception [10].

3 Methodology - University Media Bias: A Case Study

This investigation aimed to enhance the understanding of bias within news associated with higher education, an area that has not been extensively explored in bias detection studies. In this case study, our objective is to conduct an SA to identify gender bias in the news website of a research-intensive British university. Our analysis began with classifying the news articles by gender distribution, following the methodology proposed by [2]. Subsequently, we performed an SA for each gender category. We then employed evaluation metrics to assess the performance of our SA model. Finally, we analysed the frequency of career and family-related terms across different gender classes.

3.1 University News Dataset

The dataset comprises 5,782 university news articles from a British university's official website, covering April 2009 to mid-March 2023. These articles cover topics such as academic achievements, administrative announcements, and campus events. The data was programmatically collected with formal approval, ensuring compliance with copyright and usage policies. Articles were compiled into a CSV file, standardised by converting text to lowercase, removing punctuation and stop words, and filtering noise.

Annotation. We used Amazon Mechanical Turk (MTurk) to annotate 46 university news articles for SA, classifying each as positive, negative, or neutral. Annotators from the EU region were paid $0.48 per task, with three annotators per article for reliability.

MTurk was chosen for its accessibility, and the goal was to compare the model results with human-labelled data, not to retrain the model. Annotators received clear examples: positive sentiment highlighted achievements (e.g., 'Dr. XX was awarded the prestigious research grant'), negative addressed controversies (e.g., 'Dr. XX's controversial statement sparked criticism'), and neutral was factual (e.g., 'Professor XX presented his findings').

3.2 Gender Distribution Analysis

Following the methodology proposed by [2], we classified each news article based on the presence of gender identity terms. Articles were categorised as male (M), female (F), or neutral (N) depending on whether they predominantly featured masculine or feminine possessive nouns or neither. This classification allowed us to quantify the representation of genders across the dataset. The number of news articles in each class is as follows: M = 1861, F = 599, and N = 3301.

3.3 SA Using Facebook BART-Large-Mnli

We applied the Facebook BART-Large-Mnli model, introduced by [6] and fine-tuned on the Multi-Genre Natural Language Inference (NLI) corpus [11], for SA. As a pre-trained NLI model, it classifies text into categories not seen during training by evaluating hypotheses. This model was used in a zero-shot capacity, meaning it was not retrained on this annotated subset but applied as-is to perform classification based on its pre-trained knowledge. For SA, we aimed to identify the emotional tone in articles categorised as M, F, or N. In M articles, there were 1,602 positive sentiments, 251 negative, and 8 neutral. F articles had 526 positive, 71 negative, and 2 neutral sentiments, while N articles contained 2,940 positive, 359 negative, and 2 neutral sentiments.

3.4 Career and Family Words Analysis

To investigate gender bias, we analysed the frequency of career-related and family-related terms in the M and F categories, using comprehensive datasets of "Career Words" and "Family Words" from [2]. The analysis showed 1,874 career-related words for F and 5,704 for M, while family-related words totalled 2,652 for F and 1,997 for M.

4 Results

4.1 Gender Distribution Analysis

We classified each article based on gender identity terms as M, F, or N. Out of 5,782 articles, 1,861 (32%) M, 599 (10%) F, and 3,301 (57%) were N. A Chi-square test revealed a significant difference in gender distribution ($\chi^2(2, N = 5782) = 2503.83$, p < 0.001), indicating notable gender bias.Example sentences further highlight this bias in representation:

M: "The Scientific Director is Professor XX whose ground-breaking research has shown how disruption to the signalling system within a cell can trigger cancer. He has worked at some of the world's most prestigious cancer research institutions and was previously Executive Dean of the Faculty of Biological Sciences at XX." **F**: "Professor XX entered the profession in the 1980s, at a time when the overwhelming majority of physicists were men and attitudes prevailed that women were not cut out for 'hard science'. Throughout her career, she has worked to improve equality and diversity."

4.2   Facebook BART-Large-Mnli Model's SA Evaluation

The performance of the Facebook BART-Large-Mnli model was evaluated using precision, recall, and F1-score. It achieved 85% accuracy, with high precision and recall for positive and negative sentiments but poor performance in identifying neutral sentiments (F1 score of 0.00). This highlights the model's need for refinement in classifying neutral sentiments (see Table 1).

Table 1. Evaluation metrics of Facebook BART-Large-Mnli model's sentiment.

	Precision	Recall	F1
Negative	0. 82	1.00	0. 90
Neutral	0.00	0.00	0.00
Positive	0.89	0.84	0.86
Accuracy	-	-	0.85
Macro Avg	0.57	0.61	0.59
Weighted Avg	0. 78	0.85	0. 81

4.3   SA Results

The SA using the Facebook BART-Large-Mnli model showed positive sentiment in 86% of M, 88% of F, and 86% of N articles. Negative sentiment appeared in 14% of M, 12% of F, and 14% of N articles, while neutral sentiment was rare across all categories. Two-proportion z-tests revealed no significant differences in positive ($z = -0.84$, $p = 0.402$), negative ($z = 1.27$, $p = 0.204$), or neutral sentiments ($z = 0.00$, $p = 1.000$) between M and F articles. Example sentences classified by sentiment:

Positive. M: "He has also acted as a special representative in China for the Institute of Civil Engineers, developing opportunities for British businesses both in China and further afield. Since 2017, Sir XX has chaired the Executive Group of the University's Institute for High-Speed Rail and System Integration." **F**: "XX has become a passionate ambassador against knife crime. 'I eat and sleep knife crime every day. Young people have become desensitised towards knife crime and this needs to change,' she said."

Negative. M: "'Attack on Creative Expression in India', Dr. XX, Associate Professor in Information Technology Law, describes the jewellery company's advert, which ended up being pulled from circulation, before proceeding to discuss and analyse the nation's response to the advert, as many deemed it controversial. Dr. XX discusses the significance of cultural and religious influences of the advert as well as the wider context of legal restraint on creative expression in India." **F**: "Women who had a final diagnosis of NSTEMI had a 41 per cent greater chance of a misdiagnosis when compared with men."

Neutral. M: "At XX, Professor XX is leading a five-year interdisciplinary study into the impact of climate change on the Congo peatlands." **F**: "Professor XX, Vice-Chancellor, addressed the recent pay award in an email to all staff."

4.4 Career and Family Words Analysis

The analysis revealed 5,704 career-related words in M articles compared to 1,874 in F articles, while family-related words appeared 1,997 times in M articles and 2,652 times in F articles. Two-proportion z-tests showed significant differences in the use of career words ($z = 50.07$, $p < 0.001$) and family words ($z = -27.21$, $p < 0.001$) between M and F articles. Example sentences are provided below.

Career. M: "Professor XX will be heading up a new Academic Unit of Palliative Care at the XX Institute of Health Sciences, a teaching and research institute within the University's School of Medicine. He will be leading research to develop and test innovative treatments that aim at improving the care of patients who have an incurable illness." **F**: "To investigate the importance of these 'master controller' regions in protein aggregation in living cells, the team joined forces with Dr. XX and her students, also members of the Astbury Centre in XX."

Family. M: "Professor XX's successful campaign to right historical wrongs for LGBT veterans and their families demonstrates the powerful role that evidence-based research plays in influencing public policy." **F**: "But Mrs XX, now a mother and grandmother herself, is pleased work by academics such as Dr XX is shedding new light on the experiences of her father and his fellow XX. "

5 Discussion

Considering the gender distribution among university staff, which has historically been male dominated, provides additional context for the observed gender imbalance in the news articles. This correlation underscores the importance of accounting for institutional demographics when analysing media bias. SA and gender classification of university news articles reveal significant gender disparities. A higher frequency of male possessive terms suggests a bias towards masculine references. The analysis of career and family-related terms reinforces traditional gender roles, with male-associated articles emphasising careers and female-associated ones focusing on family. These findings demonstrate how media can perpetuate gender stereotypes, influencing public perceptions and potentially discouraging women from pursuing underrepresented fields.

6 Conclusion and Future Work

This study highlights the importance of using diverse data sources, such as university news, in NLP research to detect gender biases. The results show a clear bias, with male-related terms linked to professional achievements and female-related terms associated with family contexts. Future work should focus on refining models to better handle neutral sentiments and explore other forms of bias in academic media. Additionally, future studies should broaden the scope to include university news from different regions or continents and compare these findings with other news sources to provide a more comprehensive understanding of media bias across different domains.

References

1. Bender, E.M., Gebru, T., McMillan-Major, A., Shmitchell, S.: On the dangers of stochastic parrots: can language models be too big? In: Proceedings of the 2021 ACM Conference on Fairness, Accountability, and Transparency, pp. 610–623 (2021). https://dl.acm.org/doi/ https://doi.org/10.1145/3442188.3445922
2. Dacon, J., Liu, H.: Does gender matter in the news? detecting and examining gender bias in news articles. In: Companion Proceedings of the Web Conference 2021, pp. 385–392 (2021)
3. Hamborg, F., Donnay, K., Gipp, B.: Automated identification of media bias in news articles: an interdisciplinary literature review. Int. J. Digit. Libr. **20**, 391–415 (2019). https://doi.org/ 10.1007/s00799-018-0261-y
4. Hovy, D., Spruit, S.L.: The social impact of natural language processing. In: Proceedings of the 54th Annual Meeting of the Association for Computational Linguistics (Volume 2: Short Papers), pp. 591–598 (2016)
5. Kiritchenko, S., Mohammad, S.: Examining gender and race bias in two hundred sentiment analysis systems. arXiv preprint arXiv:1805.04508 (2018). Retrieved from https://arxiv.org/ abs/1805.04508
6. Lewis, M., Liu, Y., Goyal, N., Ghazvininejad, M., Mohamed, A., Levy, O., Stoyanov, V., Zettlemoyer, L.: Bart: Denoising sequence-to-sequence pre-training for natural language generation, translation, and comprehension. arXiv preprint arXiv:1910.13461 (2019)
7. Lhoest, Q., et al.: Datasets: A community library for natural language processing. arXiv preprint arXiv:2109.02846 (2021)
8. Rozado, D., Hughes, R., Halberstadt, J.: Longitudinal analysis of sentiment and emotion in news media headlines using automated labelling with Transformer language models. PLoS ONE **17**(10), e0276367 (2022). https://doi.org/10.1371/journal.pone.0276367
9. Thomsen, T.: Do media companies drive bias? Using sentiment analysis to measure media bias in newspaper tweets. Johns Hopkins University (2018). https://jscholarship.library.jhu. edu/server/api/core/bitstreams/b5e59382-1f53-4b15-b9f7-8f1818fd6d2e/content
10. Troy, C.E.: Examining Media Bias Surrounding Black Higher Education: A Content and Discourse Analysis of News Surrounding Critical Incidents That Have Occurred at Two Historically Black Colleges and Universities. Doctoral dissertation, Morgan State University (2018)
11. Williams, A., Nangia, N., Bowman, S.R.: A broad-coverage challenge corpus for sentence understanding through inference. arXiv preprint arXiv:1704.05426 (2017)

Enhancing Nepali Text Understanding with Machine Translation and LoRA Fine-Tuning of Open-Source LLM

Kshitiz Rimal$^{(\boxtimes)}$ (iD) and Noorhan Abbas (iD)

University of Leeds, Leeds, UK
kshitizrimal2016@gmail.com, n.h.abbas@leeds.ac.uk

Abstract. This study investigates the enhancement of Romanized Nepali text generation and comprehension using open-source large language models (LLMs), addressing challenges posed by colloquial words and non-standard sentence structures. While current open-source LLMs struggle with these complexities, commercial models like OpenAI GPT-4 outperform in generating accurate Nepali text. To bridge this gap, we use OpenAI GPT-4 for synthetic data generation, manually verified for accuracy by a native speaker, and fine-tune an open-source LLM using the Parameter-Efficient Fine-Tuning (PEFT) technique. Our evaluation, based on translation quality metrics, shows a marked improvement in the fine-tuned model's performance over the base model, demonstrating the effectiveness of this approach in low-resource language NLP. Additionally, this work contributes to the community by open-sourcing the fine-tuning process and the generated dataset.

Keywords: Low Resource Language · Synthetic Data Generation · Parameter-Efficient Fine-Tuning · Nepali Machine Translation

1 Introduction

Nepali, a low-resource language with millions of speakers, faces AI challenges [1]. While LLMs like GPT 3.5[1] and GPT 4[2] can generate accurate Nepali text, they sometimes confuse it with Hindi, especially in Romanized Nepali mixed with English, which current NLP models struggle with. Open-source models like LLaMA[3] and LLaMA 2[4] offer limited utility compared to commercial models [2]. Data scarcity, as seen with Vietnamese [3] and African languages [4], remains a major issue. While synthetic data generation with OpenAI GPT has been useful [5], it often fails to capture nuances in

---

[1] J. Ye et al., 'A Comprehensive Capability Analysis of GPT-3 and GPT-3.5 Series Models', Mar. 2023.

[2] OpenAI et al., 'GPT-4 Technical Report', Mar. 2023.

[3] H. Touvron et al., 'LLaMA: Open and Efficient Foundation Language Models', Feb. 2023.

[4] H. Touvron et al., 'Llama 2: Open Foundation and Fine-Tuned Chat Models', Jul. 2023.

© The Author(s), under exclusive license to Springer Nature Switzerland AG 2025
M. Bramer and F. Stahl (Eds.): SGAI 2024, LNAI 15446, pp. 313–319, 2025.
https://doi.org/10.1007/978-3-031-77915-2_23

Romanized Nepali. Current Nepali datasets focus mainly on Devanagari, lacking collo-quial words [6, 7]. Open-source models like LLaMA and Stanford's Alpaca 7B [8, 9], using PEFT [10] and LoRA [11], have improved fine-tuning efficiency, reducing training time and showing promise for low-resource languages like Nepali [12]. This approach holds promise for enhancing the language comprehension and generation capabilities of open-source large language models for such languages[5,6].

2   Design and Methodology

The methodology follows 3 main sections: Data Generation, Data Translation, Fine Tuning. The data generation phase used LangChain with GPT-4 and a JSON parser for structured content, enabling accurate Romanized Nepali text generation across contexts. While other LLMs like Google's Gemini Pro[7] were explored, GPT-4 proved more con-sistent. We covered ten service sectors, generating ten unique Q&A pairs per subtopic [14], with 1818-token prompts that included instructions, slang, and few-shot examples [13]. Q&A pairs were synthetically generated to create a dataset simulating commu-nication between a business assistant and a customer, providing the LLM with exam-ples of expected input and output patterns. After generating Q&A pairs, the Romanized Nepali text was translated into English using GPT-4, addressing the challenges of mixed-language usage. The dataset was split into two JSON files for questions and answers, resulting in 2674 sentence pairs. The concise 72-token prompt guided GPT-4 to trans-late accurately, with adjustments made to prevent it from answering questions instead of translating. A native speaker verified the dataset for accuracy, once it was generated with manual verification and correction as required. This dataset of Q&A and translated sentence pairs was essential for fine-tuning the LLM on translation tasks (Fig. 1).

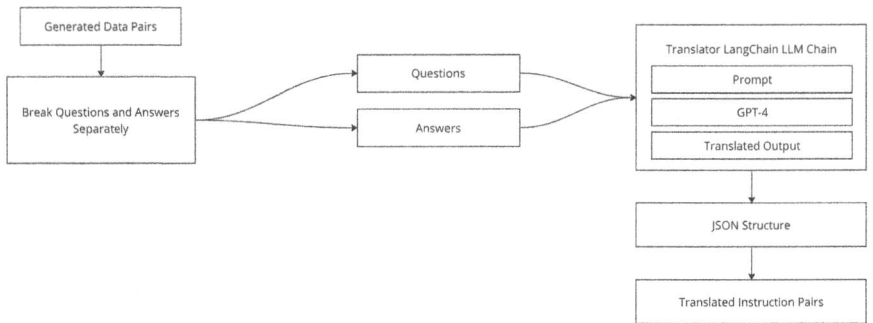

Fig. 1.   Diagram Translation process for the generated Q&A pairs.

The fine-tuning process involved two key steps: selecting an appropriate open-source LLM and applying LoRA Parameter-Efficient Fine-Tuning (PEFT) using the translated

---

[5] https://github.com/kshitizrimal/generated-translated-nepali.

[6] https://huggingface.co/kshitizrimal/tigerbot-13b-chat-v5-finetuned-nepali.

[7] Gemini Team et al., 'Gemini: A Family of Highly Capable Multimodal Models', Dec. 2023.

data. After extensive research, the Llama-2-based "tiger-bot-13b-chat-v5" model [15] was selected for its support of over 120 languages, including Nepali, making it ideal for our multilingual translation tasks. A 7B model was initially considered but fell short in performance, leading us to opt for the more robust 13B model, which better suited our fine-tuning needs. The model was quantized to 4-bit for LoRA fine-tuning to fit GPU limitations. Evaluation methodology incorporates several metrics to assess model performance on the evaluation set and compare the base model with the fine-tuned model.

Metric	Formula	Description
Bilingual Evaluation Understudy (BLEU)[8]	$BP \cdot \exp\left(\sum_{n=1}^{N} w_n \log p_n\right)$	BP prevents short translations. N is the max n-gram length (usually 4) with weights w_n summing to 1 p_n is the n-gram precision, matching n-grams btween generated and reference text
Metric for Evaluation of Translation with Explicit Ordering (METEOR)[9]	$F_{\mathrm{mean}}(1 - \mathrm{Penalty})$	F_{mean} is the harmonic mean of precision and recall for unigrams in candidate and reference translations. The penalty reduces scores for fragmented translations
Recall-Oriented Understudy for Gisting Evaluation with longest common subsequence(ROUGE-L)[10]	$\frac{(1+\beta^2) \cdot \mathrm{LCS_{Precision}} \cdot \mathrm{LCS_{Recall}}}{\beta^2 \cdot \mathrm{LCS_{Precision}} + \mathrm{LCS_{Recall}}}$	$\mathrm{LCS_{Precision}}$ measures the candidate text in the longest common subsequence (LCS), while $\mathrm{LCS_{Recall}}$ shows how much of the reference text is captured. β balances precision and recall, typically set to 1for equal weight

These metrics offer a comprehensive evaluation of translation quality. BLEU focuses on precision and word order with n-grams, ROUGE-L assesses recall and F1 score via the longest common subsequence, and METEOR evaluates synonyms and stems for semantic depth. This approach thoroughly measures improvements from fine-tuning.

[8] K. Papineni et al., "BLEU," Proc. 40th Annual Meeting of ACL, 2001, p. 311. https://doi.org/10.3115/1073083.1073135.

[9] S. Banerjee and A. Lavie, "METEOR: An Automatic Metric for MT Evaluation," Proc. ACL Workshop on Evaluation Measures for MT, 2005, pp. 65–72. Available: https://aclanthology.org/W05-0909.

[10] C.-Y. Lin, "ROUGE: A Package for Automatic Evaluation of Summaries," Proc. Text Summarization Branches Out, 2004, pp. 74–81. Available: https://aclanthology.org/W04-1013.

3 Experimental Results and Discussion

A detailed evaluation assessed the fine-tuning of the LLM for translating Romanized Nepali into English. LoRA parameters had nested quantization set to 'False,' using the 'paged_adamw_32bit' optimizer and a constant learning rate (Tables 1 and 2).

Table 1. LoRA hyper-parameter values.

LoRA Rank	LoRA Alpha	LoRA Dropout	Number of Training Epochs	Per-Device Training Batch Size	Per-Device Evaluation Batch Size
128	32	0.1	1	4	4

Table 2. Fine-tuning hyper-parameter values.

Gradient Accumulation Steps	Maximum Gradient Norm	Learning Rate	Weight Decay	Warmup Ratio
1	0.3	2e-4	0.001	0.03

The training and validation sets were split in an 80–20 ratio and shuffled before fine-tuning to ensure a randomized distribution of data, which is crucial for preventing the model from learning the order of the data instead of the underlying patterns.

3.1 Evaluation Sentences

For a comprehensive model assessment, two distinct sets of 25 evaluation sentences were used. The first set included complex Romanized Nepali sentences sourced from legal documents, such as the Constitution of Nepal, to test the model's ability to handle intricate syntax and specialized vocabulary. The second set consisted of simple, everyday Romanized Nepali sentences, aiming to evaluate the model's performance in more common, conversational contexts (Table 3).

Table 3. Samples of complex and simple sentences alongside their English translations.

SN	Nepali Sentence	English Translation Reference
1	Constitution le discrimination lai kasto tackle garchha ra law ko agadi sabai lai equal parne garchha, jasto ki, dalit haru ko lagi quota system ra women ko lagi reservation	How does the Constitution tackle discrimination and ensure equality before the law, such as through quota systems for Dalits and reservations for women?
3	Ma sahar bhitra hidna khojchu	I like to wander around the city

3.2 Translations and Performance Metrics

The translation capabilities of both the base and fine-tuned models were tested using these evaluation sets (Table 4).

Table 4. Results of translating simple and complex sentences in the evaluation set.

Sentence	Reference	Base Model Translation	Fine-tuned Model Translation
Ma guitar sikdai chu	I am learning guitar	My guitar is broken	I'm learning to play the guitar
Emergency situation ko provisions ra Constitution ko amendment ko process k ho?	What are the provisions for emergency situations and the process for amending the Constitution?	Emergency situation, Constitution provides for amendment process	What are the provisions for an emergency situation and the process of amending the Constitution?

The performance was quantitatively assessed through BLEU, METEOR, and ROUGE-L scores. The following presents the average scores across all 25 sentences for each set (Tables 5 and 6):

Table 5. Mean BLEU and METEOR Scores Across Both Evaluation Sets.

Metrics	BLEU		METEOR	
Eval Set	Simple	Complex	Simple	Complex
Base	0.0677	0.198	0.236	0.414
Fine-tuned	0.1163	0.528	0.374	0.743

Table 6. Mean ROUGE-L Precision (P), Recall (R), and F1-Score (F) for Both Sets of Evaluations.

Metrics	ROUGE-L P		ROUGE-L R		ROUGE-L F1	
Eval Set	Simple	Complex	Simple	Complex	Simple	Complex
Base	0.2616	0.447	0.172	0.235	0.203	0.306
Fine-tuned	0.465	0.746	0.251	0.372	0.321	0.495

Our analysis showed that the fine-tuned model outperformed the base model across BLEU, METEOR, and ROUGE-L metrics, confirming the effectiveness of fine-tuning for improving translation. Interestingly, both models performed better on complex sentences than simple ones, likely due to fewer tokens in simple sentences, making intent harder to capture. However, when simple sentences were more detailed, translation accuracy improved, highlighting the importance of context and clarity for effective translation, especially in simpler sentences.

4 Conclusions, Future Work and Ethical Issues

In this study, we leveraged GPT-4 for synthetic data generation to enhance the understanding and translation of Romanized Nepali. The process involved two key stages: creating conversations in Romanized Nepali with precise prompts and translating them into English. Iterative refinement of the prompts was crucial in generating high-quality data. Fine-tuning involved careful optimization of hyperparameters and the selection of an appropriate base model, resulting in improved performance across BLEU, METEOR, and ROUGE-L metrics, particularly for complex sentences. For future work, adding tasks like generating explanations and reverse translation could further improve the model's language comprehension. Exploring quantization techniques may also allow models to run locally on lower-spec hardware, making NLP technology more accessible.

Throughout the study, we ensured data accuracy and ethical standards by verifying the content with a native speaker and eliminating personal and biased information.

References

1. Magueresse, A., Carles, V., Heetderks, E.: Low-resource Languages: A Review of Past Work and Future Challenges, Jun. 2020
2. Hendrycks, D., et al.: Measuring Massive Multitask Language Understanding, Sep. 2020
3. Nguyen, T., Tang, A., Pham, T., Nhat, Q.: Fine-tuning open source LLMs for low- resource languages: the case of Vietnamese, Feb. 2023. https://doi.org/10.13140/RG.2.2.19671.04008
4. Shikali, C.S., Mokhosi, R.: Enhancing African low-resource languages: Swahili data for language modelling. Data Brief **31**, 105951 (2020). https://doi.org/10.1016/j.dib.2020.105951
5. Lu, Y., Shen, M., Wang, H., Wang, X., van Rechem, C., Wei, W.: Machine Learning for Synthetic Data Generation: A Review, Feb. 2023
6. Koehn, P., Guzmán, F., Chaudhary, V., Pino, J.: Findings of the WMT 2019 shared task on parallel corpus filtering for low-resource conditions. In: Proceedings of the Fourth Conference on Machine Translation (Volume 3: Shared Task Papers, Day 2), Stroudsburg, PA, USA: Association for Computational Linguistics, 2019, pp. 54–72. https://doi.org/10.18653/v1/W19-5404
7. Sharad, D., Bal Krishna, B.: Efforts in the development of an augmented English–Nepali parallel corpus. In: Proceedings of the Language Technologies for All (LT4All), pp. 375–378, Dec. 2019
8. Zhao, J., Zhang, Z., Gao, L., Zhang, Q., Gui, T., Huang, X.: LLaMA Beyond English: An Empirical Study on Language Capability Transfer, Jan. 2024
9. Taori, R., et al.: Alpaca: A strong, replicable instruction-following model. Stanford Center for Research on Foundation Models. https://crfm.stanford.edu/2023/03/13/alpaca.html, vol. 3, no. 6, p. 7 (2023)
10. Houlsby, N., et al.: Parameter-Efficient Transfer Learning for NLP, Feb. 2019
11. Hu, E.J., et al.: LoRA: Low-Rank Adaptation of Large Language Models, Jun. 2021
12. Alves, D.M., et al.: Steering Large Language Models for Machine Translation with Finetuning and In-Context Learning, Oct. 2023

13. Brown, T.B., et al.: Language Models are Few-Shot Learners, May 2020
14. Cheng, Z., Kasai, J., Yu, T.: Batch Prompting: Efficient Inference with Large Language Model APIs, Jan. 2023
15. Chen, Y., Cai, W., Wu, L., Li, X., Xin, Z., Fu, C.: TigerBot: An Open Multilingual Multitask LLM, Dec. 2023

Audio-Visual Emotion Recognition Using Deep Learning Methods

Mukhambet Tolegenov$^{(\boxtimes)}$, Lakshmi Babu Saheer®,
and Mahdi Maktabdar Oghaz®

Anglia Ruskin University, Cambridge CB1 1PT,, UK
mt1042@student.aru.ac.uk, {lakshmi.babu-saheer,mahdi.maktabdar}@aru.ac.uk

Abstract. This research explores the development of a deep learning-based audio-visual emotion recognition system, aiming to enhance the accuracy and robustness of emotion classification by integrating multiple modalities. Traditional speech emotion recognition (SER) systems often rely on unimodal data, which limits their ability to fully capture human emotional expressions. Our study leverages the Ryerson Audio-Visual Database of Emotional Speech and Song (RAVDESS) to implement a multimodal approach, combining audio and visual data. The proposed model incorporates Convolutional Neural Networks (CNNs), Long Short-Term Memory (LSTM) networks, and attention mechanisms to improve performance. Experimental results demonstrate that the attention-based audio model achieves the highest accuracy of 62%, outperforming other tested configurations. The study highlights the potential of integrating attention mechanisms and multimodal data to enhance SER systems, while also identifying areas for future research, such as utilizing additional datasets and transfer learning techniques to further improve model performance and generalizability.

Keywords: Emotion · Audio · Video · Deep Learning · MFCC · Tensorflow

1 Introduction

In recent years the speech emotion recognition (SER) task of interpreting human emotions in computer language has become an important research area with several applications such as human-machine interaction (HCI), healthcare, customer service, and others. Implementing effective speech-emotion recognition systems allows machines and robots to understand and receive the full spectrum of emotions reproduced by humans [12]. In recent years there has been increased attention to deep learning (DL) methods for emotion classification. Initially, SER was utilized through unimodal datasets, which means using a single data source like textual, speech, or visual data. However unimodal data cannot fully represent human emotions, since emotion expression is a multimodal phenomenon [3]. In other terms, it would be better to analyze and extract not only single-modality

M. Bramer and F. Stahl (Eds.): SGAI 2024, LNAI 15446, pp. 320–326, 2025.
https://doi.org/10.1007/978-3-031-77915-2_24

data, but other modalities as well, including facial movements, gestures, body movements, and other possible contributing modalities. This research will focus on experimental approach for multimodal SER using different DL architectures, including 3D-Convolutional Neural Networks(3D-CNN), Long Short-Term Memory(LSTM) model, Attention mechanism to enhance the accuracy and efficiency of emotion detection. Furthermore, this research will encompass a comparative analysis of the proposed models leveraging different modalities such as audio, video, and combined audio-visual inputs. Ensuring the robustness and repeatability of the findings, the same training and testing datasets will be used across all proposed models. The novelty of this study lies on the integration of diverse deep learning architectures with multiple modalities for enhanced emotion recognition, aiming to fill the existing research gap and contribute to the advancement of SER systems in real-world applications. This study seeks to not only validate the effectiveness of these approaches but also to provide insights into their potential for broader adoption and practical implementation across various domains.

2   Literature Review

The rapid advancements in DL have significantly transformed various computing domains, enabling more efficient and accurate processing of complex data. Among these domains, SER has gained considerable attention due to its potential applications in areas such as human-computer interaction, mental health monitoring, and customer service. This literature review explores the evolution of DL techniques in SER, highlighting the key methods and models that have been developed to improve the accuracy and efficiency of emotion detection from both audio and visual data. Due to recent developments in the field of DL and its ability to automatically extract high-level features from raw data, DL has become an efficient tool in many computing domains, including natural language processing, computer vision and audio recognition [3,4,7].

Data pre-processing is crucial, particularly in the SER scenarios, to extract essential features that could help to identify certain emotions in the raw data. Spectral features have the potential to effectively describe the emotional state of the speakers. According to Lian et al. [5] spectral audio features represent the power spectrum in speech, which is closely tied to how humans interpret their emotions. Spectral features include spectrograms, Mel-frequency spectrograms, Mel-frequency cepstral coefficients and others.

Models based on CNNs with attention mechanism with are getting extremely popular, including using spectral features as their input, resulting in increasingly more papers on the design of attention-based models. Research works such as that of Chen et al. [2] and Singh et al. [11], integrated attention layers into the model based on CNN and LSTM, and achieved an accuracy of 85.346% and 90%, respectively. The former study used the EMO-DB dataset for training the model, while the latter used a curated dataset created with a combination of audio SER datasets RAVDESS, SAVEE, and TESS. Spectrograms, Mel spectrograms, and Mel-frequency cepstral coefficients were utilized to train these deep models.

DL-based methods can also be applied to visual SER. CNNs are also suitable for the visual SER problem since they can differentiate the high-level features of visual data. An example of such research from Breuer and Kimmel [1], utilized 2D CNNs for extracting the features and a Multi-layer Perceptron as a classifier. Zhang *et al.* [13] indicate that it is important to consider the sequence of video motion, so a 3D-CNN network is suggested. There is currently research work in which the techniques described above were used in multimodal audio-visual feature extraction methods. CNN-based multimodal DL networks were introduced by Middya *et al.* [9] in which the video and audio features were extracted with the aid of CNNs. In this research, the number of layers, the fusion methods, and the hyperparameter tuning were experimented with, achieving an accuracy of 86% for RAVDESS and 99% for SAVEE datasets. A spatio-temporal hybrid network was suggested by Sharafi *et al.* [10] for user emotion prediction using LSTM and CNN. RAVDESS and SAVEE datasets were used in this research and resulted in accuracy levels of 99% and 94% respectively.

3   Dataset

The Ryerson Audio-Visual Database of Emotional Speech and Song (RAVDESS) dataset [6], is an open-source dataset involving audio, visual and audio-visual recordings of 24 actors (12 males, 12 females) performing emotional expressions. This will be used as the main dataset in this study. The dataset includes 7356 files, equally distributed among eight emotions, ensuring a balanced representation of emotional states.

4   Methodology

4.1   Audio Feature Extraction

Feature extraction is performed to transform audio files into Mel-Frequency Cepstral Coefficients (MFCCs) to effectively capture essential frequency and temporal dynamics, which are vital for detecting emotions in audio signals. These MFCCs will be used as input for a subnetwork that includes CNN, LSTM, and an attention mechanism, forming the deep neural network architecture. The audio features are sized (40, 108), where '40' represents the number of cepstral coefficients and '108' corresponds to the timeframes of the audio sample.

4.2   Video Feature Extraction

Video files are used to extract facial expressions and body movements. Each frame will be resized to maintain uniformity of the features. These standardized frames will then serve as input for a 3-dimensional CNN, specifically designed to process video data. The output from this video processing will be 10 frames, each with an image resolution of (32, 32) and includes RGB color channels.

After video and audio files are processed, extracted features are normalized. The detailed architecture of the proposed audio-visual model can be seen in the next subsection.

4.3   Model Architecture

Audio Subsystem: Extracted MFCCs are used to train the deep learning network, which consists of several convolutional blocks, 2 LSTM layers and an attention mechanism. Each convolutional block involves a convolutional layer, batch normalization, max pooling, dropout and dense layers. Video Subsystem: In parallel with audio data, the video frames are passed through the next subnetwork for video frames. As mentioned before all video files have a fixed size of 10 frames with image size = (64, 64) in RGB color channel. After extracted features are passed through 2 Convolutional blocks. Like in the audio subnetwork, each block consists of convolutional layers, Batch normalization, and max pooling layers. Then extracted high-level features are passed through 3 Dense layers with 512, 256 and 128 neurons, respectively. Each of the Dense layers will utilize the Relu activation function.

Fusion Technique: After both audio and visual features were extracted they are concatenated, thus perceptrons of the last layers of two subnetworks with 128 neurons are appended to each other. Hence, a layer consisting of 256 neurons is processed further with the sequence of a couple of fully connected Dense layers. Finally, the last layer was implemented for the classification of emotions. Since this is a multiclass classification task, this layer uses Softmax activation.

5   Experiments

In this research, various unimodal and multimodal DL models were designed and trained. Particularly, in addition to the proposed multimodal neural network, separate subnetworks were trained. Furthermore, experiments with attention layers were performed, to identify the impact of attention mechanisms on the performance of the model. Initially four DL models were trained: the audio model with attention, the audio model without attention, the video model, and the audio-visual model. Then it was decided to experiment with the combination of 3D-CNN, LSTM and self attention mechanisms, thus this network was tested as visual subnetwork for audio-visual network and visual neural network for emotion recognition. Therefore, in total 6 models were trained.

6   Results

Based on the previously described experiments with different architectures and modalities, and testing outcomes are described in Table 1. During the testing of several combinations of layers, it was evidenced that the attention-based speech emotion recognition methods output the best accuracy compared to others. The table also shows other metrics for comparison.

The Table 2 shows results of previous works that use RAVDESS dataset. The table shows that the current research results are comparable to previous research on this dataset.

Table 1. Accuracy of trained models

Modality	Architecture	Accuracy	Precision	Recall	F1 score
Audio	CNN + LSTM + Attention	59%	58%	56%	56%
Audio	CNN + LSTM	38%	42%	38%	38%
Video	3D-CNN	55%	59%	58%	55%
Audio-visual	CNN + LSTM + Attention 3D-CNN	62%	65%	62%	62%
Video	3D-CNN + LSTM + Attention	63%	64%	63%	63%
Audio - Visual	CNN + LSTM + Attention 3D-CNN + LSTM + Attention	69%	69%	69%	68%

Table 2. Results for previous works for RAVDESS dataset

Authors	Modality	Architecture	Accuracy
Middya et al. (2022)	Audio-Visual	CNN2D + LSTM for video CNN1D for audio	77%
Singh et al. (2023)	Audio	CNN + LSTM + Attention	74%
Luna-Jimenez et al. (2021)	Audio-visual	Transfer Learning	80%

Overall, from the performance metrics and comparison with other authors several important points can be made. The greater performance of multimodality setup over unimodal ones proves the alignment of previous works' conclusions. Thus, it clearly shows that multimodal datasets can help to increase the performance of the existing unimodal DL models. Secondly, RAVDESS dataset is the standard dataset which is used by the most of the research papers. However, there are also other source of data that can be used for the multimodal SER task. In addition, combination of them and data augmentation technique could help to increase the accuracies of the proposed models such in the research done by Singh *et al.* [11].

7   Conclusion

In conclusion, it is observed that attention based model performs well than audio model without attention, resulting as 21% difference in accuracies. Visual model that relies on video data has achieved around 55% accuracy, which is the lowest result among other models, but with combination of attention mechanism it was increased by 8%. On the other hand, combined audio-visual model could produce better results than using separate modalities. For instance, using only video files performed 55% and 63%, and using audio with and without attention produced 59% and 38%, respectively. Consequently, it clearly shows that for emotion classification it is better to use multiple modalities rather than single ones. It was proven by comparing both multimodal models with other ones. Also, looking at confusion matrices audio-visual model has better predicting ability than other developed ones.

7.1 Future Work

Despite that current research study results are not impressive, studying multi-modality in development of SER systems still continue to be one of the promising research area in this field. Hence, it is crucial to take into account other SER datasets that were provided in literature review. Proposed method can be extended by merging multiple datasets to increase sample size number and increase generalizability of the overall system. Moreover, considering other spectral features might be a key for effective emoton classification methods. Another solution for increasing data size could be various data augmentation techniques which can produce artificial data, thus can also increase robustness and avoid the problem of overfitting of the SER model. Research can also be enhanced by utilizing transfer learning techniques, consequently applying ready-to-use state-of-the-art models that have already applied to other research areas.

References

1. Breuer, R., Kimmel, R.: A Deep Learning Perspective on the Origin of Facial Expressions. arXiv.org. https://doi.org/10.48550/arxiv.1705.01842 (2017)
2. Chen, S., Zhang, M., Yang, X., Zhao, Z., Zou, T., Sun, X.: The impact of attention mechanisms on speech emotion recognition. Sensors **21**(22), 7530 (2021). https://doi.org/10.3390/s21227530
3. Keltner, D., Sauter, D., Tracy, J., Cowen, A.: Emotional expression: advances in basic emotion theory. J. Nonverbal Behav. **43**(2), 133–160 (2019). https://doi.org/10.1007/s10919-019-00293-3
4. Khan, W., Qudous, H., Farhan, A.: Speech emotion recognition using feature fusion: a hybrid approach to deep learning. Multimedia Tools Appl. 1–28 (2024)
5. Lian, H., Lu, C., Li, S., Zhao, Y., Tang, C., Zong, Y.: A survey of deep learning-based multimodal emotion recognition: speech, text, and face. Entropy **25**, 1440 (2023)
6. Livingstone, S.R., Russo, F.A.: The ryerson audio-visual database of emotional speech and song (RAVDESS): a dynamic, multimodal set of facial and vocal expressions in North American English. PLoS ONE **13**(5), e0196391 (2018). https://doi.org/10.1371/journal.pone.0196391
7. Liu, W., Qiu, J.-L., Zheng, W.-L., Lu, B.-L.: Comparing recognition performance and robustness of multimodal deep learning models for multimodal emotion recognition. IEEE Trans. Cogn. Dev. Syst. **14**(2), 715–729 (2022). https://doi.org/10.1109/TCDS.2021.3071170
8. Luna-Jiménez, C., Griol, D., Callejas, Z., Kleinlein, R., Montero, J.M., Fernández-Martínez, F.: Multimodal emotion recognition on RAVDESS dataset using transfer learning. Sensors **21**(22), 7665 (2021). https://doi.org/10.3390/s21227665
9. Middya, A.I., Nag, B., Roy, S.: Deep learning based multimodal emotion recognition using model-level fusion of audio-visual modalities. Knowl.-Based Syst. **244**, 108580 (2022). https://doi.org/10.1016/j.knosys.2022.108580
10. Sharafi, M., Yazdchi, M., Rasti, R., Nasimi, F.: A novel spatio-temporal convolutional neural framework for multimodal emotion recognition. Biomed. Signal Process. Control **78**, 103970 (2022). https://doi.org/10.1016/j.bspc.2022.103970

11. Singh, J., Saheer, L.B., Faust, O.: Speech emotion recognition using attention model. Int. J. Environ. Res. Public Health **20**(6), 5140 (2023). https://doi.org/10.3390/ijerph20065140

12. Zhang, S., Liu, R., Tao, X., Zhao, X.: Deep cross-corpus speech emotion recognition: recent advances and perspectives. Front. Neurorobotics **15**, 784514–784514 (2021). https://doi.org/10.3389/fnbot.2021.784514

13. Zhang, S., Zhang, S., Huang, T., Gao, W., Tian, Q.: Learning affective features with a hybrid deep model for audio-visual emotion recognition. IEEE Trans. Circuits Syst. Video Technol. **28**(10), 3030–3043 (2018). https://doi.org/10.1109/TCSVT.2017.2719043

Spatial Interpolation of Air Quality: A UK Case Study

Lorenzo Garbagna$^{(\boxtimes)}$, Praseed Melethil, Lakshmi Babu Saheer, and Mahdi Maktabdar Oghaz

Anglia Ruskin University, Cambridge CB1 1PT, UK
lg673@pgr.aru.ac.uk

Abstract. Air quality is an important aspect of both human health and climate change. In recent years, air quality forecasts have received a lot of attention and multiple attempts with different methods have been applied to achieve this task. Many pollutants have been utilised for air quality research, the most common ones being $PM_{2.5}$, PM_{10} and NO_2. Although various techniques have been used for air quality prediction, the need for more granular and reliable pollutant concentration data has been investigated on a smaller scale, especially in the case of interpolation methods with Internet of Things (IoT) sensors for data collection. In this study, the analysis of spatial patterns of multiple air pollutants ($PM_{2.5}$, PM_{10} and NO_2) has been assessed by collecting data at multiple locations in a case study area with Aeroqual devices and by utilising three interpolation techniques (Inverse Distance Weighted (IDW), Ordinary Kriging and Radial Basis Function). Each method achieved high accuracy in predicting pollution concentrations in new test locations and performance was evaluated using Root Mean Squared Error (RMSE) and Mean Squared Error (MSE). IDW emerged as the best-performing interpolation technique for most of the pollutants with the lowest RMSE and MSE scores.

Keywords: Spatiotemporal Modelling · Pollutants · Interpolation

1 Introduction

Air pollution is a major environmental challenge affecting public health worldwide. The pollutants as carbon emissions are a major cause of climate change. Traditionally the emissions are estimated from traffic patterns at very low resolution. The move towards active monitoring of pollutants is one of the first steps towards understanding and mitigating the effects of climate change and working towards net zero targets. There have been efforts around using networks of Internet of Things (IoT) sensors for micro-climate modeling and air quality prediction [7,11]. However, the increasing demand for granular, accurate and reliable air quality or emission data has led to the development of various spatial interpolation techniques for predicting air pollutant concentrations at locations without

© The Author(s), under exclusive license to Springer Nature Switzerland AG 2025
M. Bramer and F. Stahl (Eds.): SGAI 2024, LNAI 15446, pp. 327–332, 2025.
https://doi.org/10.1007/978-3-031-77915-2_25

any monitoring stations. This research project aims to address the gap in the literature concerning the evaluation of the effectiveness of different spatial interpolation techniques for air pollutant predictions by assessing the accuracy and precision of three popular interpolation techniques, Inverse Distance Weighting, Kriging, and Radial Basis functions, and the impact of Spatial variability on prediction accuracy. By comparing and evaluating the performance of various methods on real-world data, this study will contribute to improving the accuracy and reliability of air quality or carbon emission prediction, which is crucial for making informed policy decisions and climate change mitigation strategies along with reducing the impact of pollutants on public health.

2   Related Work

Air quality monitoring is a critical aspect of urban environmental management, with several studies focusing on the prediction of different pollutants at specific locations. The need for emission data across a wider geospatial area has led to the use of estimation and interpolation techniques.

Kim et al. [6] aimed to create a spatial distribution map of chlorophyll-a concentrations in a stream using data collected by an unmanned surface vehicle (USV). The collected data was used to compare two interpolation methods, inverse distance weighting (IDW) and kriging, for spatial distribution. The results showed that IDW was the optimal interpolation method. The study demonstrated the potential for the commercialization of remote monitoring technology development using USVs in streams. Choi et al. [3] evaluated the performance of indoor spatial interpolation methods for visualizing various indoor environmental quality (IEQ) factors on an IEQ distribution map. The study found that the accuracy of the IEQ distribution map was high regardless of occupancy time, outdoor weather conditions, and HVAC operating period and the entire IEQ condition can be identified using a small number of monitoring instruments. The study proposed future research to develop a real-time IEQ distribution map that receives environmental data from monitoring instruments and analyzes IEQ distribution in the vertical direction within the indoor space. Li et al. [9] combined IDW with the shortest wind-field path distances (SWPD) to estimate PM concentration levels for both hourly and daily prediction in the Beijing urban area for May 2013. The study demonstrated the higher accuracy of the combined system for concentration prediction by enhancing IDW capabilities, with SWPD showing potential in estimating spatial dependence and correlation between monitoring points.

Spatial interpolation techniques are employed in GIS to estimate attribute values at unsampled locations and generate continuous spatial data, which can be classified into two categories: deterministic and geostatistical interpolation methods. The choice of the optimal interpolation method depends on the study objective and is determined through comparative analysis of different techniques employed in previous research [4,10]. Li et al. [8] provided a review of spatial interpolation methods (SIMs) for generating spatially continuous data of environmental variables. The paper compares the features of commonly applied methods falling into three categories, non-geostatistical, geostatistical, and combined interpolation methods. The review discusses the factors affecting the performance of the methods, including sampling design, sample spatial distribution, data quality, correlation between primary and secondary variables, and interaction among factors.

3   Data and Methods

The data for this study was collected using two Aeroqual S500 devices [2] at 18 different geographical points within a locality: the site was located in Cambridge City (UK). This location was chosen due to its high traffic density and potential for air pollution. The monitoring devices were used to measure various air quality parameters, including Particulate Matter ($PM_{2.5}$ and PM_{10}) and Nitrogen Dioxide (NO_2), at regular intervals during the study period, over multiple days. In order to establish the same parameters for each collection period at different locations, an anemometer has been utilised to record and compare weather conditions to ensure continuity between location points data. Pollutant measurements for PM and NO_2 were collected for 20 min, for each location. The data collection period spanned over multiple days, to capture variations in air pollutant concentrations over different weather and traffic conditions. The study area was carefully selected to ensure that it represented the broader area air quality conditions and enabled meaningful comparisons between different spatial interpolation techniques. Figure 1 shows the location of the 18 collection points selected for this experiment.

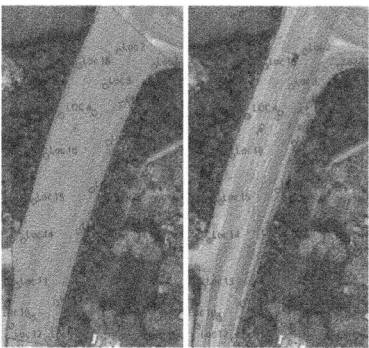

Fig. 1. Monitoring Locations

Utilisation of IoT devices for air quality data collection does introduce some challenges in calibration, failures and alignment. Comparison between collected data and available datasets from other sources requires calibration of used IoT devices with monitoring stations from these datasets: this is due to different sensitivity and measuring values between multiple devices. different devices of the same models must also be aligned with each other, to avoid different readings in the same settings: for the data recorded in this study, both the Aeroqual sensors have been calibrated in the same way to avoid this failure. This work represents the first set of multiple experiments on spatial interpolation for air quality prediction in urban settings: many factors can affect pollutant concentration levels from the distance between monitoring points to weather conditions and urban geography. The study aims to represent a first attempt of using IoT data with multiple interpolation techniques to study the related factors and to create a baseline for other scenarios with different settings to provide a better understanding of how an IoT sensor network could be deployed for air quality control. Measurements for each pollutant at all locations were combined into a single dataset and their values analysed: the concentration levels were recorded in mg/m^3. The three interpolation methods utilised in this study are IDW, Kriging and RBF. For IDW, each observation point is weighted in such a way that their influence on other locations is correlated to the distance between them, while Kriging utilises mathematical functions to reflect the spatial correlations between a number of points inside a particular radius. On the other hand, RBF utilises a weighted sum of radial basis functions to interpolate data points, such as the Gaussian function [1,5].

4   Results and Discussion

In order to compare each interpolation method, the data for each pollutant has been divided: 70% has been used to perform interpolation and test the accuracy against the remaining 30%. Table 1 shows the RMSE and MSE results for each technique.

Table 1. Interpolation Results

Metric	Pollutant	IDW	Kriging	RBF
RMSE	$PM_{2.5}$	0.01487	**0.01358**	0.02352
	PM_{10}	**0.03409**	0.03801	0.05979
	NO_2	**0.00467**	0.00490	0.00505
MSE	$PM_{2.5}$	0.00022	**0.000184**	0.000541
	PM_{10}	**0.00116**	0.001445	0.003575
	NO_2	**2.19E-05**	2.41E-05	2.55E-05

All three interpolation techniques performed with great accuracy, as both RMSE and MSE values for each pollutant are low. IDW provided the lowest error rate for both PM_{10} and NO_2, while Kriging performed slightly better with $PM_{2.5}$ data. Apart from selecting random points for interpolation, experiments have been performed by selecting points for interpolation from the available locations. The three techniques provided great accuracy and low error rates when interpolating for the three locations as well, but RBF performed better than IDW and Kriging for both $PM_{2.5}$ and PM_{10}, while NO_2 values were better interpolated by Kriging.

Table 2 shows the results of the three techniques when used to interpolate data to three locations: locations 7, 11, and 18. Each point was selected at a different position in the case study area: one at the top, one in the middle and one at the bottom.

Table 2. Interpolation Results with 3 selected Points

Metric	Pollutant	IDW	Kriging	RBF
RMSE	$PM_{2.5}$	0.00544	0.00522	**0.00358**
	PM_{10}	0.02398	0.02106	**0.01934**
	NO_2	0.00290	**0.00278**	0.00363
MSE	$PM_{2.5}$	2.97E-05	2.72E-05	**1.28E-05**
	PM_{10}	0.00057	0.00044	**0.00037**
	NO_2	8.44E-06	**7.74E-06**	1.32E-05

5   Conclusion and Further Work

In this study, we compared three different interpolation techniques, namely Inverse Distance Weighting (IDW), Kriging, and Radial Basis Function (RBF), for estimating air pollutant concentrations. The three pollutants considered in this study were $PM_{2.5}$, PM_{10}, and NO_2. The performance of each interpolation method was evaluated based on two metrics: RMSE and MSE. The results of our study show that the IDW interpolation method performed best for two of the three pollutants when random locations were interpolated, with the lowest RMSE and MSE values. For $PM_{2.5}$, the RMSE for Kriging was 0.0136, which was lower than the RMSE values for IDW (0.0149) and RBF (0.0233). For PM_{10} and NO_2, IDW had the lowest RMSE and MSE values, indicating that it was the most accurate method of the three. More visualisations of the data and interpolation outputs are presented in the appendix for reference. A potential direction for future research could be the extension of the monitoring period to capture seasonal variations and long-term changes in air quality and a selection of a bigger use case area with measurement locations further away from each other. A longer monitoring period could help identify temporal patterns and trends in air pollution. A future study could compare the performance of different sensor models under similar conditions to identify the most suitable sensor for the study area. This could involve the evaluation of various sensors based on their accuracy, precision, sensitivity, and response time. This study theorizes that a limitation of the proposed method is the dependence on the density and distribution of monitoring stations, as the accuracy of the interpolated values may decrease in areas with sparse or uneven station coverage. Further work can be explored on increasing the distance between points to simulate an IoT sensor network, to recreate similar settings to a real-world scenario to research and analyse the effect of distance and urban features on pollution readings and interpolation effectiveness. Moreover, the accuracy of the interpolation results can also be influenced by the choice of interpolation method, as different methods have varying degrees of sensitivity to outliers, noise, and underlying trends in the data, factors that might vary depending on areas selected for different case studies. There are limited deep learning-based spatiotemporal models as the modeling would involve very complicated architectures considering the complex interactions of the spatial and temporal aspects of the pollutants and related features. But as a future step, large amounts of data will be collected to compare deep learning models to these simple interpretable models presented in this research. These modeling systems will be further integrated into digital twin models for policy validation and to work towards net zero.

References

1. Adhikary, P.P., Dash, C.J.: Comparison of deterministic and stochastic methods to predict spatial variation of groundwater depth. Appl. Water Sci. **7**, 339–348 (2017)
2. Aeroqual (2023). www.aeroqual.com/products/s-series-portable-air-monitors/series-500-portable-air-pollution-monitor
3. Choi, H., Kim, H., Yeom, S., Hong, T., Jeong, K., Lee, J.: An indoor environmental quality distribution map based on spatial interpolation methods. Build. Environ. **213**, 108880 (2022)
4. El-Zeiny, A.M., Elbeih, S.F.: GIS-based evaluation of groundwater quality and suitability in Dakhla Oases, Egypt. Earth Syst. Environ. **3**(3), 507–523 (2019)
5. Ibrahim, A.M., Nasser, R.H.A.: Comparison between inverse distance weighted (IDW) and kriging. Int. J. Sci. Res. **6**, 2319–7064 (2015)
6. Kim, E., Nam, S.H., Ahn, C.H., Lee, S., Koo, J.W., Hwang, T.M.: Comparison of spatial interpolation methods for distribution map an unmanned surface vehicle data for chlorophyll-a monitoring in the stream. Environ. Technol. Innov. **28**, 102637 (2022)
7. Lai, X., Yang, T., Wang, Z., Chen, P.: IoT implementation of kalman filter to improve accuracy of air quality monitoring and prediction. Appl. Sci. **9**(9), 1831 (2019)
8. Li, J., Heap, A.D.: Spatial interpolation methods applied in the environmental sciences: A review. Environ. Model. Softw. **53**, 173–189 (2014)
9. Li, L., Gong, J., Zhou, J.: Spatial interpolation of fine particulate matter concentrations using the shortest wind-field path distance. PLoS ONE **9**(5), e96111 (2014)
10. Mirzaei, R., Sakizadeh, M.: Comparison of interpolation methods for the estimation of groundwater contamination in andimeshk-shush plain, southwest of Iran. Environ. Sci. Pollut. Res. **23**, 2758–2769 (2016)
11. Zhang, D., Woo, S.S.: Real time localized air quality monitoring and prediction through mobile and fixed IoT sensing network. IEEE Access **8**, 89584–89594 (2020)

Talk like a Local: Evaluating Large Language Models for Arabic Dialect Translation Using Similarity Scores

Alaa Bouomar[✉] [iD] and Noorhan Abbas[iD]

University of Leeds, Woodhouse, Leeds LS2 9JT, UK
alaahassan305@gmail.com, n.h.abbas@leeds.ac.uk

Abstract. This paper introduces a promising approach for evaluating the quality of translations between Modern Standard Arabic (MSA) and the Egyptian (Cairo) dialect using Large Language Models, specifically Claude and AraT5. We demonstrate how similarity scores provide a more meaningful and nuanced measure of translation quality, capturing semantic preservation and model performance improvements through fine-tuning on dialect-specific datasets. Our results highlight the potential of semantic similarity scores as a valuable evaluation tool for Arabic dialect translation using large language models. These findings suggest that semantic similarity scores could become a standard evaluation tool for Arabic dialect translations, enhancing the development and assessment of new high-quality datasets and advancing the Arabic NLP domain.

Keywords: AraT5 · Claude · Modern Standard Arabic (MSA) · Egyptian Dialect Translation · Similarity Metrics

1 Introduction

Translating between Modern Standard Arabic (MSA) and regional dialects such as Egyptian, Gulf, Levantine, and Maghrebi Arabic poses significant challenges due to linguistic variations [1, 2]. Existing evaluation metrics for machine translation, such as BLEU scores [3], often fail to capture the nuances and semantic proximity between the original and translated text, particularly in the context of Arabic dialects [4–6]. As LLMs become increasingly prevalent in addressing these translation challenges, there is a growing need for more effective and meaningful evaluation approaches to assess their performance.

This study introduces an evaluation approach based on semantic similarity scores for assessing the quality of translation between MSA and Egyptian dialect using large language models, specifically Claude [3] and AraT5 [4]. We propose that semantic similarity scores provide a more fine-grained and contextually relevant measure of translation quality compared to commonly used metrics. By capturing the semantic proximity between the original and translated sentences, our approach offers a more accurate assessment of meaning preservation and model performance improvements through fine-tuning on dialect-specific datasets.

© The Author(s), under exclusive license to Springer Nature Switzerland AG 2025
M. Bramer and F. Stahl (Eds.): SGAI 2024, LNAI 15446, pp. 333–338, 2025.
https://doi.org/10.1007/978-3-031-77915-2_26

We propose that semantic similarity scores provide a more fine-grained and contextually relevant measure of translation quality compared to commonly used metrics. By capturing the semantic proximity between the original and translated sentences, our methodology offers a more accurate assessment of meaning preservation and model performance improvements through fine-tuning on dialect-specific datasets.

The main contributions of this paper are:

- Introducing an approach that utilizes semantic similarity scores for assessing the quality of Arabic dialect translation using Claude and AraT5.
- Demonstrating the effectiveness of fine-tuning the AraT5 model on a validated dialect-specific dataset, leading to significant improvements in translation quality.

2 Methodology

We employ Claude [7] for initial translations from MSA to Egyptian (Cairo) dialect. Then, the AraT5, a model specifically pre-trained on Arabic dialects [10], is used for back-translation from Egyptian (Cairo) dialect to MSA. The AraT5 model is further fine-tuned on a dialect-specific dataset, namely the MADAR Egyptian (Cairo) dataset, to enhance performance.

2.1 Models

Our methodology employs two distinct language models: Claude for initial MSA to Egyptian dialect translation, and AraT5 for back-translation to MSA. This approach leverages the strengths of each model:

Claude: An advanced LLM developed by Anthropic [7], is designed to understand and generate human-like text. The model is pre-trained on a vast corpus of text data from diverse sources, including substantial representations of various Arabic dialects [9], allowing it to learn a wide range of language patterns, facts, and nuances. This extensive training, in addition to its optimized architecture, helps it generate coherent and contextually relevant text across various topics [7, 8]. We conducted experiments comparing Claude and ChatGPT 3.5, with results reviewed by a native Egyptian speaker. Claude consistently outperformed ChatGPT in dialect translation tasks.

AraT5: building upon the work of Nagoudi et al. [10], was chosen as the base model for the back-translation task. It employs a sequence-to-sequence (seq2seq) framework with an encoder-decoder structure. The model utilizes multi-head attention layers, which allow it to focus on different parts of the input sequence simultaneously, enhancing its ability to capture contextual information. This model was selected due to its demonstrated effectiveness in handling both Modern Standard Arabic (MSA) and various Arabic dialects [10].

By using Claude for initial translation, we benefit from its extensive knowledge and ability to handle nuanced, context-dependent translations. The subsequent use of AraT5 for back-translation allows us to leverage its Arabic-specific capabilities, potentially correcting any dialect-specific errors introduced by Claude.

This two-model approach aims to create high-quality, diverse training data that captures the complexities of Arabic dialect translation more effectively than using a single model. The resulting dataset can be used to fine-tune specialized models or evaluate the performance of various translation systems, contributing to the advancement of Arabic NLP research.

2.2 Datasets

We utilized two primary datasets:

- **Arabic Children's Corpus:** this corpus contains 2,950 documents and nearly 2 million words, featuring a variety of children's literature genres, including classic tales and popular fictional characters [11].
- **MADAR Corpus:** this corpus includes parallel sentences covering the dialects of 25 Arab cities, along with English, French, and MSA. It was created by translating selected sentences from the Basic Traveling Expression Corpus (BTEC) into different dialects [1].

2.3 Translation Quality Metric

Cosine Similarity: We use cosine similarity to measure the semantic proximity between the original MSA sentences and the translated sentences generated by the AraT5 model, quantifying meaning preservation. A pre-trained embedding model is used to encode the sentences into high-dimensional vectors. The resulting similarity scores range from -1 to 1, with 1 indicating perfect semantic similarity. For generating embeddings used in cosine similarity calculations, we employed AraBERT v2 [12] a BERT-based model pre-trained on a large Arabic corpus. It had the following key features: 77GB of text from Arabic Wikipedia, Arabic news websites, and Arabic literature. Architecture: 12-layer, 768-hidden, 12-heads, 136M parameters.

We chose AraBERT due to its robust performance on various Arabic NLP tasks and its ability to handle both MSA and dialectal Arabic. This model provides contextualized word embeddings that capture nuanced meanings in both the original MSA text and the translated Egyptian dialect, enabling accurate semantic similarity comparisons. The similarity score is then multiplied by a 100 to convert it to a percentage.

BLEU Score: This metric is used to compare the candidate Egyptian translations to reference translations, measuring the precision of n-grams [3]. We used the sentence_bleu function from the NLTK library to calculate BLEU scores for each translated sentence. The scores were computed using a smoothing function to handle cases where there were no matching n-grams. BLEU scores range from 0 to 1, with higher scores indicating greater similarity between the candidate and reference translations [3].

3   Results and Discussion

Fine-tuning the AraT5 model on a validated dialect-specific dataset led to substantial improvements in the translation quality, as evidenced by the similarity scores and BLEU scores. Before Fine-Tuning, the basic AraT5 model achieved an average similarity score of 94.9% across the translated sentences. After Fine-Tuning, the AraT5 model showed a significant increase in the average similarity score, reaching 97.1%. This indicates that the fine-tuned model produced translations that were semantically closer to the original MSA sentences.

Furthermore, the fine-tuning process led to an improvement in the BLEU score. Before Fine-Tuning, the basic AraT5 model achieved an average BLEU score of 0.0827. After Fine-Tuning, it showed an increase in the average BLEU score, reaching 0.0867. This suggests that the fine-tuned model generated translations that were closer to the reference translations in terms of n-gram overlap.

3.1 Examples of Translation Improvements

MSA Original: !!!ردت الممحاة بود: ولأني أحبك.. فأنا أمحو أخطاءك فقط حتى لا يراها أحد ويسخر منك

Translation: The eraser replied kindly: "Because I love you… I erase your mistakes so that no one will see them and mock you!!!".

Claude   Output:

.ويستهزأ بيك ردت الممحاة بحب: وعشان بحبك.. فانا بمسح غلطاتك بس عشان محدش يشوفها !!!

ARAT5 Output: ردت المعطف ودود ، لأني أحبك . أنا أكتب أخطاءك فقط حتى لا يراها أحد.

Translation: The coat replied kindly, "Because I love you. I write your mistakes so that no one will see them."

- Accuracy: This translation has significant errors. It incorrectly changes "الممحاة" (the eraser) to 'المعطف (the coat), altering the meaning entirely.
- Similarity Score: 90% – Despite these errors, the similarity score indicates a relatively high degree of semantic overlap, though the key semantic errors significantly affect the overall quality.
- BLEU Score: 0.02 – This low score reflects the significant divergence from the original text in terms of word choice and meaning.

Fine-Tuned AraT5: !!! ردت الممحاة: ولأني أحبك.. فأنا أمحو أخطاءك فقط حتى لا يراها أحد ويسخر من

Translation: The eraser replied: "Because I love you… I erase your mistakes so that no one will see them and mock you!!!".

- Accuracy: This translation is very accurate and closely matches the original MSA text.
- Similarity Score: 98% – This high score reflects the model's enhanced ability to preserve semantic content and produce a translation that is very close to the original text.
- BLEU Score: 0.09 – The significant increase in BLEU score indicates a much closer alignment with the original text in terms of word choice and sentence structure.

The combination of similarity scores and BLEU scores provides a comprehensive evaluation of translation quality. Similarity scores assess semantic preservation, while BLEU scores measure lexical and structural accuracy. The improvement in these metrics (similarity score from 90% to 98%, BLEU score from 0.02 to 0.09) demonstrates the effectiveness of fine-tuning on dialect-specific datasets. This approach ensures accurate translation between Arabic dialects and MSA, preserving both meaning and structure. These metrics are crucial for validating LLMs' performance in handling the nuances of Arabic dialect translation, enhancing the accuracy of machine translation models.

4 Conclusion and Future Work

This study demonstrates the value of utilizing semantic similarity scores as an effective evaluation approach for assessing the quality of the translation of LLMs, specifically Claude and AraT5, in translating between MSA and the Egyptian (Cairo) dialect. The higher average similarity scores and increased frequency of high-scoring translations achieved by the fine-tuned AraT5 model underscore the importance of fine-tuning on dialect-specific datasets.

Furthermore, the semantic similarity score approach adopted in this study has the potential to be generalized to other language pairs and translation tasks beyond Arabic dialects. For instance, this approach could be explored for evaluating translations between other closely related languages or dialects, such as Spanish and Portuguese or different varieties of Chinese. Additionally, semantic similarity scores could be investigated as an evaluation methodology for tasks like machine translation post-editing, where capturing the semantic equivalence between the original and edited translations is crucial.

References

1. Bouamor, H., et al.: The MADAR Arabic dialect corpus and lexicon. In: Proceedings of the Eleventh International Conference on Language Resources and Evaluation (LREC 2018). European Language Resources Association (ELRA), Miyazaki, Japan (2018)
2. Qwaider, W., Habash, N., Bouamor, H., Badran, F.: Shami: A Corpus of Levantine Arabic Dialects. https://www.semanticscholar.org/paper/654af2f5747126447e5d8fce220c6a191576 1143, last accessed 2024/06/10
3. Papineni, K., Roukos, S., Ward, T., Zhu, W.J.: BLEU: a method for automatic evaluation of machine translation. In: Proceedings of the 40th Annual Meeting of the Association for Computational Linguistics, pp. 311–318 (2002)
4. Kadaoui, T., Bouamor, H., Badran, F., Habash, N.: TARJAMAT: Evaluation of Bard and ChatGPT on Machine Translation of Ten Arabic Varieties. https://www.semanticscholar.org/paper/796b894c4e1a3cb46715cc0b45a39e91ee5910e6, last accessed 2024/06/10
5. Alyafeai, Z., Al-Omari, A., Al-Kindi, I., Al-Riyami, S., Al-Maqaleh, A.: Taqyim: Evaluating Arabic NLP Tasks Using ChatGPT Models. https://www.semanticscholar.org/paper/d14aa4 48b17fdc8d4ea12b43ee1a2b1254c38703, last accessed 2024/06/10
6. Al-Thubaity, A., Al-Khateeb, A., Al-Salhi, B., Al-Ghamdi, M.: Evaluating ChatGPT and Bard AI on Arabic Sentiment Analysis. https://www.semanticscholar.org/paper/d4c0ee9f7ea7451 216845c851d069dff95545faa, last accessed 2024/06/10
7. Brown, T.B., Mann, B., Ryder, N., Subbiah, M., Kaplan, J., Dhariwal, P., Amodei, D.: Language models are few-shot learners. In: Advances in Neural Information Processing Systems, pp. 1877–1901 (2020)
8. Mullappilly, R., Al-Awlaqi, M., Al-Yami, S., Al-Dossary, F.: Arabic Mini-ClimateGPT: A Climate Change and Sustainability Tailored Arabic LLM. https://www.semanticscholar.org/paper/6da8e97de0981b867b1038e12e98608928ad4c0e, last accessed 2024/06/10
9. Waheed, A., Abdul-Mageed, M., Nagoudi, E.M.B., Noune, B., Hamdi, A., Elmadany, A., Poesio, M.: GPTAraEval: A Comprehensive Evaluation of ChatGPT on Arabic NLP. arXiv. https://arxiv.org/abs/2305.14976, last accessed 2024/06/10

10. Nagoudi, E.M.B., Elmadany, A., Abdul-Mageed, M.: AraT5: text-to-text transformers for Arabic language generation. In: Proceedings of the 60th Annual Meeting of the Association for Computational Linguistics (Volume 1: Long Papers), pp. 628–647 (2022). https://aclant hology.org/2022.acl-long.46/, last accessed 2024/06/10

11. Al-Sulaiti, L., Abbas, N., Brierley, C., Atwell, E., Alghamdi, A.: Compilation of an Arabic children's corpus. In: Calzolari, N., et al. (eds.) Proceedings of the Tenth International Conference on Language Resources and Evaluation (LREC'16) (pp. 1808–1812). Portorož, Slovenia: European Language Resources Association (ELRA) (2016)

12. Antoun, W., Baly, F., Hajj, H.: AraBERT: Transformer-based Model for Arabic Language Understanding (2020). arXiv preprint arXiv:2003.00104

On Monadic Binary, with Application to Machine Understanding

M. J. Wheatman[(✉)] [ID]

Preston, UK
martin@enguage.org
https://www.enguage.org

Abstract. The idea of a monadic value is introduced, which has a binary form: it either has a value or is undefined. This resolves the apparent dissonance between the internal binary representation of data and the need for all external values to have an unobserved state. For example, a typically binary type, Boolean, if external, must be trinary. This exotic monadic type finds use in speech understanding as a *premise* in verbal reasoning. A premise is a terminator in a chain of reasoning, while it can be observed, it has no dependent reason; it is self-evident. An example is presented in the machine understanding tool, Enguage, which is a processes of monadic speech values.

Keywords: Machine Understanding · Verbal Reasoning · Rhetoric

1 Introduction

One problem with values from a world in continual flux [1] is that they must be observed. In contrast to variables within an algorithm, which can be initialized to a typically zero-based value, external values need an extra value, *unknown,* for their unobserved state. This is the rationale behind relational databases [2] where any data item may be set to '*null*', unless they are defined with the keywords, 'NOT NULL'.

This simple anomaly between an external Boolean and its internal trinary representation reveals a wider limitation of context-free languages and their *dualist* heritage [3, 6]. Not only may an external value be unobserved, but its written internal ontology is fixed by compile-time. This is particularly acute for natural language processing [10–13], which must '*conceal its lack of understanding*' [12:pp44], its inability to *construct ideas.* Any faith, even hubris, in fixed software denies the possibility of the next *Black Swan* moment [22].

Monads closes this ontological gap by showing how true external binary values *can* exist, and are useful, in verbal reasoning. This idea stems from Gödel Numbering [20], where mathematical equations are encoded, and reasoned with, as numeric values. Enguage [7] uses monads to construct reasoning, using speech as a computational medium [15]; specifically, it creates a *monadic binary* to complete a deterministic chain of reasoning. Such a demonstration of speech, using speech, won Enguage the SGAI Machine Intelligence Competition in 2016 [16].

M. Bramer and F. Stahl (Eds.): SGAI 2024, LNAI 15446, pp. 339–345, 2025.
https://doi.org/10.1007/978-3-031-77915-2_27

2   The Monadic Premise

All classes of real world objects need an unobserved value: *unknown* [2]. Thus, the four point cardinal direction type has the values [*unknown*, North, South, East, West]; a three point temporal system has the values [*unknown*, Present, Past, Future]; and, a Boolean has [*unknown*, False, True]. This pattern breaks down when descending to a singular value plus *unknown*, as singular values within an algorithm are typically regarded as a constant, such as π, pi, the ratio between the circumference and diameter of a circle. This is because π, 3.1415926…, is a fact—a value of definition—rather than a variable; and, because of its transcendental nature, π may only ever be an approximation, but it is never *unknown*.

One example of a singular value which needs to be (un-)observed, however, is the *premise*, a component of verbal reasoning. This rhetorical utterance, in its widest sense, needs no reasoning in itself and, thus, can act as a terminator for a chain of reasoning. There is no need to explain that '*a mask soaks moisture from your breath*' because anyone who has worn a mask will have experienced this. The observation of a premise is achieved by its annunciation.

This premise-as-monad can be demonstrated by using verbal reasoning in the form of '*effect* because *cause*', to create a chain of reasons. This is initiated by the expression of an observation, which can be followed by, '*a mask prevents the spread of COVID* because *a mask soaks moisture from your breath*'. This causal link may, in turn, be used as the reason for a moral obligation, '*we should wear a mask* because *a mask prevents the spread of COVID*'.

3   Functional Speech Using Enguage

Gödel Numbering shows how a mathematical equation can be reasoned with as a numerical value [20]. Enguage [7], extends this monad to the representation of speech, whereby an utterance is an immutable value. Emanating from an external world, it forms a binary opposition to the ubiquitous unknown: something is either expressed or it is not.

Enguage determines the most appropriate interpretation from the various interpretations of an utterance [24], which determines the values (if any) it contains, and what it means in terms of implied utterances [4]. Each interpretation results in one of several arbitrary replies encoded with a success value [18], which may direct the flow of further interpretation. This model of computation appears as an arbitrary swapping of values, for example, "I need a coffee", returns either, "okay, you need a coffee" or "yes, I know", depending on whether, "I need a coffee", has already been expressed.

This functional approach to language was originally illustrated as a *triadic* model of interpretation, see Fig. 1. The implied link, dotted baseline, between the spoken utterance, SYMBOL, and its REFERENT reply, is always determined through a list of utterances, THOUGHT or REFERENCE. This prototypical function was published a decade before the Lambda Calculus [17].

Enguage uses two written forms of instruction to record functions: comma or semicolon separated, depending on the number of implications [5]:

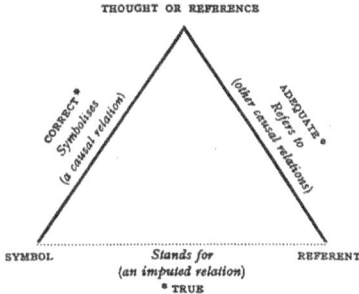

Fig. 1. The Semiotic Triangle of Reference [8, pp11]

> On "thank you", reply "you're welcome".
> On "i need a coffee":
> > does a coffee exist in my needs list;
> > if so, reply yes I know;
> > add a coffee to my needs list;
> > reply "okay, you need a coffee".

Both of these represent Fig. 1, which may be better illustrated, if arranged thus:

> Does a coffee exist in my needs list;
> if so, reply yes I know;
> if not, add a coffee to my needs list;
> reply okay you need a coffee.

> "I need a coffee" ⟹ ["okay, you need a coffee" | "yes, I know"]

Using such instructions, Enguage demonstrates verbal reasoning by using the symbol pattern '*effect* because *cause*' [9, 7:etc./dict/w/why + because.entry]. When an utterance matches the symbol, the *cause* is 'thought' first—uttered internally—to see if it is valid, and if so, the *effect* is similarly thought. Thus, causes and effects are enacted during the process of reasoning. Failure of either will return their respective failure, and rollback of an utterance transaction [19]. If the cause and effect are both felicitous, then the cause-effect link is recorded.

4 Machine Understanding

More recently, various *spoken* function description repertoires have been developed which can also be written in lieu of these written descriptions. The latest form, in brief, is:

> 'I can say ...'
> 'This implies ...'
> 'Then ...'

which can construct the above instruction at runtime. This introduces the idea of machine understanding, by which ideas can be conveyed to, and subsequently used to interact with, a machine. The onus is then on the machine to use *our* ideas [14], rather than a mechanical imposition of some artificial logical structure [6].

The first of these spoken instructions, '*I can say...*', populates an empty interpretation, a symbol but without any implications or reply. This might suggest an incomplete function: a definition without a body or return value; however, this has found use in the representation of a premise. Therefore, Enguage returns a felicitous reply for these symbol-only functions: it is understood simply because *it can be said*. Saying you can say something in this way is declaring an observation.

Therefore, spoken instruction allows the premise, to be used in reasoning.

5 An Example

The example in Sect. 2 is illustrated here using the unit test in [7:etc./dict/s/should.entry], which is presented below. The *should* repertoire contains three written interpretations:

```
On "you should PHRASE-ACTION":
     add ACTION to our should list;
     reply "ok, ACTION".

On "should we PHRASE-ACTION":
     ACTION exists in our should list;
     if so, reply "yes, we should ACTION";
     reply "no, we do not need to ACTION".

On "what should we do":
     get our should list;
     if not, reply "i don't know what we should do";
     reply we should ... .
```

There is also an interpretation added to the because/why repertoire:

```
On "why should we PHRASE-ACTION":
     should we ACTION;
     if not, say so;
     get the cause of you should ACTION from _user causal
     list;
     if not, reply "i don't know";
     set cause to ...;
     reply "because EXT-CAUSE".
```

The premise is 'a mask soaks up moisture' which is taken as a commonly understood observation. Since the COVID-19 pandemic and the obligatory wearing of masks in public spaces, it is common knowledge that a mask will be damp after being worn for some time. The human breathes out ½ to 1 L of fluid a day, depending on exertion; however, the exact amount is not important, it is simply observed that some of this ends up in the mask.

To obtain and run the example below, **git** and a **Java SDK** must be installed. Then, from the command-line:

```
$ git clone https://bitbucket.org/martinwheatman/enguage.git
$ cd enguage
$ javac opt/test/UnitTest.java
$ java opt.test.UnitTest -T should

TEST: should
============

user> what should we do.
enguage> i don't know what we should do.

user> i can say a mask soaks up moisture from your breath.
enguage> ok , you can say a mask soaks up moisture from my
breath.

user> i can say wearing a mask prevents the spread of covid
because a mask soaks up moisture from your breath.
enguage> ok , you can say wearing a mask prevents the spread
of covid because a mask soaks up moisture from my breath.

user> you should wear a mask because wearing a mask prevents
the spread of covid.
enguage> ok , i should wear a mask because wearing a mask
prevents the spread of covid.

user> what should we do.
enguage> we should wear a mask.

user> why should we wear a mask.
enguage> because wearing a mask prevents the spread of covid.

1 test group(s) found
+++ PASSED 6 tests in 198ms +++
```

Firstly, this test starts by showing that there is nothing that we *should* do. Secondly, in creating a premise by making an observation, we can start to construct an argument for wearing a mask. Next, the test creates a second rhetorical device from the first premise, by saying that we can say, "wearing a mask prevents the spread of COVID". This is perhaps not as obvious, not such a common observation, so it is the first link in a chain of reasoning, dependent on the first premise. Perhaps it could be observed by analyzing the data to show the spread of COVID against the incidence of wearing masks? A second link is created by saying that I can say what you should do: we should wear a mask. This is confirmed by repeating *what* we should do and *why*. If the monadic value, the premise, "a mask soaks up moisture", were not observed, and therefore not something we can say, this test would not be possible.

Finally, this is all dependent upon being under pandemic conditions, and Enguage already supports this conditional processing [19]; however, to include this might overly burden this paper? Certainly, there are more examples in the full unit test (using the -t option) which demonstrates over 500 examples.

6 Conclusion

This paper explores Codd's idea that external values need a value to represent the unobserved state. This prevents the neat binary representation of an external Boolean; however, external binaries do exist, the *premise* is an idea which has sense but no implications, and is useful as a terminator in a chain of reasoning. These monadic values are declared by saying, "I can say *value*", after which it is observed. This principle has been demonstrated in software by Enguage using a simple chain of reasoning.

This also shows that while speech is computational [15], it cannot be represented by programming languages, the category mistake [14] is between their dyadic attributes and the monadic spoken domain. Context-free languages are well-formed and can be parsed to extract meaning; however, much of what we say is unstructured grunts and expletives [21]: '*yes*' has many possible implications, but not *a* meaning. The resultant failure to produce a *deterministic* speech understanding system is evidenced by over 70 years' effort merely supporting simple imperatives [11].

Nevertheless, this representation dissonance leaves a vacuum which is easily filled by charlatan programs exploiting the human ability to making sense of things. Such techniques include: keyword search [12]; limiting the world and the actions that can be performed within it [11, 13]; and more latterly, generating non-deterministic content based on probability [10]. Without a monad-to-dyad mapping, without the ability to say, "I can say …", such programs cannot create speech—ideas—at runtime.

This paper does not claim that this verbal reasoning example given does not have flaws. The astute reader may claim that it may be possible to say, "I can shoot people because I like guns". While Enguage supports the concepts of *like* and *can*, "I can shoot people", should fail because, "I must not shoot people", should already have been observed. The efficacy of moral reasoning, and the details of innate ideas, in Enguage and its dictionary is hugely important but beyond the scope of this paper.

This paper could also show that monadic binaries can be combined—because all *unknown* values coincide—to create binary values and so on. So [*unknown*, False] and [*unknown*, True] can be combined to create Boolean [*unknown*, False, True]. An observation, in using such values, is that they should typically progress through *unknown* to pass onto another value; however, this idea is outside scope.

Acknowledgments. This research is self-funded.

Disclosure of Interests. The author is also the author of Enguage, which is Trademarked in the UK, but is released under the Apache open source license.

References

1. Burnett, J.: Heraclitus: Fragments of Heraclitus, fragment 22, In: Early Greek Philosophy, Chapter 3 (1920)
2. Codd, E.F.: A relational model of data for large shared data banks. Commun. ACM **13**(6), 377–387 (1970)

3. de Saussure, F.: Course in General Linguistics. Bally, C., Sechehaye, A., Riedlinger, A. (eds., Transl. 1983 Harris, R. Duckworth London (1916)). NOVA Science Publishers, Hauppauge, NY

4. Grice, H. P.: Meaning, William James Lectures, Harvard (1957). In: Studies In The Way of Words, Chapter 14, pp. 213–223 (1989). Harvard University Press

5. Wheatman, M.J.: An Autopoietic Repertoire. In: Bramer, M., Petridis, M. (eds.) Research and Development in Intelligent Systems XXXI, pp. 165–170. Springer (2014)

6. Montague, R.: Universal grammar, In: Thomason, R.H. (ed.) Formal Philosophy, Chapter 7, pp. 222–224. Yale University Press, New Haven and London (1974)

7. Enguage: Speech interpreter, see: https://bitbucket.org/martinwheatman/enguage, released under the open source Apache license

8. Ogden, C.K., Richards, I.A.: The Meaning of Meaning, Routledge and Kegan Paul (1923)

9. Wheatman, M.J.: On Because and Why - Reasoning with natural language. Int. J. Conceptual Struct. Smart Appl. **6**(2), 1–17 (2018)

10. Wolfram, S.: What is ChatGPT doing and why does it work? Wolfram Media Inc., (2023)

11. Amazon Alexa: see: https://developer.amazon.com/en-US/docs/alexa/devconsole/about-the-developer-console.html (2024)

12. Weizenbaum, J.: ELIZA - a computer program for the study of natural language communication between man and machine. Commun. ACM **9**, 36–45 (1966)

13. Winograd, T.: Understanding Natural Language. Edinburgh University Press, (1972)

14. Ryle, G.: The Concept of Mind, 60th Anniversary Edition. Routledge (1949)

15. Wheatman, M.J.: Turing Complete Speech, Towards Algorithm Transparency. https://www.bcs.org/articles-opinion-and-research/turing-complete-speech-towards-algorithm-transparency/ (2023)

16. Enguage: BCS SGAI Machine Intelligence Competition Winner, see http://www.bcs-sgai.org/micomp/pastcomps.php (2016)

17. Church, A.: An unsolvable problem of elemental number theory. Am. J. Math. **58**(2), 345–363 (1936)

18. Austin, J.L.: How to do things with words. Urmson, J.O., Sbisa, M. (eds.) 2nd edn. Oxford University Press, Oxford and New York (1962)

19. Wheatman, M.J.: A semiotic analysis of If we are holding hands, whose hand am I holding, J. Comput. Inf. Technol. **22**, LIS (2013, 2014). http://cit.srce.unizg.hr/index.php/CIT/article/view/2278/1658 (2014)

20. Nagel, N., Newman, J.R.: Gödel's Proof. Routledge (1958)

21. Andersen, P.B.: A Theory of Computer Semiotics (Human-Computer Interaction, vol. 3, pp 29–36. Cambridge University Press, Cambridge, UK (1997)

22. Taleb, N.N.: The Black Swan: The Impact of the Highly Improbable. Random House, NY (2007)

23. Wheatman, M.J.: A pragmatic approach to disambiguation in text understanding. In: Baranauskas, M.C.C., Liu, K., Sun, L., Neris, V., Bonacin, R., Nakata, K., IAICT (eds.) Advances in Information and Communication Technology, IFIP vol. 477, pp. 143–148. Springer (2016). https://doi.org/10.1007/978-3-319-42102-5_16

A Proposed ELM Ensemble Approach for Predicting Railway Delays

Matthew Day[✉]

Loughborough University, Leicestershire, UK
m.day@lboro.ac.uk

Abstract. This paper presents an Ensemble Extreme Learning Machine (ELM) approach for predicting railway delays, part of an ongoing PhD project with Network Rail and Loughborough University. With only 68.3% of station stops on time in early 2024, improving prediction accuracy is vital. The Ensemble ELM model, combining multiple ELMs, addresses key challenges in Train Delay Prediction (TDP) such as data quality and model generalization. Initial results show significant improvements in accuracy and efficiency over traditional methods. The model will be validated using UK railway data, contributing to more reliable and scalable delay prediction systems.

Keywords: Extreme Learning Machine · Ensemble Learning · Train Delay Prediction · Railway Systems

1 Introduction

1.1 Context

The increasing complexity of railway systems, combined with growing demands for punctuality, has made managing delays a critical challenge. In early 2024, only 68.3% of station stops in Great Britain were recorded as on time, with 86.8% of trains arriving within 5–10 min of their scheduled time [1], underscoring the need for more sophisticated predictive models to enhance reliability. This research, part of an ongoing PhD project in collaboration with Network Rail and Loughborough University, aligns with the Seasonally-Agnostic-Railway-Model (SARM) initiative [2] which aims to improve railway resilience using Train Delay Prediction (TDP) systems.

The urgency for such a shift from reactive to proactive strategies is highlighted by incidents like the Stonehaven derailment [3], demonstrating the vulnerability of railway systems to external effects. In this context, Machine Learning (ML) has emerged as a transformative tool, offering the ability to leverage the large quantities of data within the industry [4]. However, the application of ML is hindered by multiple factors and is still in its early stages. This research aims to identify key barriers to ML implementation for TDP and propose a solution utilizing Extreme Learning Machine (ELM) and Ensemble approaches.

M. Bramer and F. Stahl (Eds.): SGAI 2024, LNAI 15446, pp. 346–351, 2025.
https://doi.org/10.1007/978-3-031-77915-2_28

1.2 Considerations

As ML is a broad, multidisciplinary field with rapidly evolving techniques and applications, this study narrows its focus to the specific application of ML for TDP. A specialized but impactful area within transportation, allowing for a comprehensive exploration of the approaches used with a clear emphasis on practical application. This research operates under several key assumptions, including access to high-quality historical data (such as train schedules, delays, weather, and infrastructure status) and sufficient computational resources for developing and testing complex models. Ethical standards are upheld through data anonymization, compliance with data protection regulations, and a commitment to scientific integrity with transparent reporting of limitations and potential biases.

2 Literature Review

2.1 Systematic Approach

To ensure that the methodology in this research is built on a solid foundation, a comprehensive systematic review of the literature was conducted to identify common practices, highlight the most effective algorithms and data handling techniques, and uncover research gaps that need to be addressed to advance the field of ML for TDP. The Preferred Reporting Items for Systematic Reviews and Meta-Analyses (PRISMA) 2020 guidelines were followed [5], which ensure rigor, transparency, and reproducibility in systematic reviews. The study selection process is also guided by strict inclusion criteria and the Critical Appraisal Skills Programme (CASP) checklist [6], which ensure high-quality and methodologically sound studies are included, while minimizing the risk of bias and providing a balanced synthesis of the evidence.

2.2 Current Challenges in TDP

A series of key literature reviews were included within the search [4, 7–9], which were examined to provide a comprehensive overview of the current state of ML approaches for TDP. The findings from these reviews have been compiled and synthesised into several key challenges which highlight the critical areas for improvement in both data handling and model development. Tackling these challenges will not only advance future research in TDP but also enhance its practical applications within the industry. The primary challenges are outlined below:

- **Data Quality and Integration**: Inconsistencies, missing data, and difficulties in merging static and dynamic sources reduce predictive model accuracy. Solutions include gathering diverse, high-quality datasets, improving integration techniques, and standardising formats.
- **Model Interpretability**: Deep learning models can lack transparency. Hybrid models and targeted feature selection can balance complexity with interpretability, ensuring predictions are actionable without losing accuracy.

- **Computational Complexity**: Advanced models are resource-intensive, affecting real-time or large-scale predictions. Using model compression, parallel processing, and hardware like GPUs/TPUs can reduce computational costs while maintaining performance.
- **Generalisation Across Networks**: Models trained in specific environments may struggle in different settings. Techniques like transfer learning and ensemble/hybrid models can improve adaptability and generalisation.
- **Real-Time Model Updates**: Climate change and evolving infrastructure/operations demand real-time updates for predictive models to maintain relevance in a rapidly changing environment.

These challenges underscore the need for continuous advancements in data management and model methodologies, guiding both future research and the methodology adopted in this research project to develop more robust and reliable TDP systems.

3   Methodology

3.1   Theoretical Background

ELM is a ML algorithm designed for single-hidden layer feedforward neural networks, introduced by Huang et al. [10] ds by randomly assigning input weights and biases in the hidden layer and analytically determining the output weights. As found in recent reviews [11–13] this approach benefits from Extremely Fast Learning Speed, Good Generalization Performance and Versatility and Scalability, making it an attractive choice for addressing the challenges present in TDP. However, they also highlight potential limitations on real-world applications of ELM due to its Random Dependency, Low Level of Abstraction and Sensitivity to Outliers.

Only a small number of studies have aimed to overcome ELM's limitations in TDP, with a clear focus on hyperparameter optimization. The main parameters in an ELM approach consist of the Number of Nodes, Activation Functions, and the Input Weights and Biases, all of which can drastically vary the model's performance. These hyperparameter methods include Particle Swarm Optimization [14] and a novel 'threshold' approach [15]. Despite these efforts, they collectively encountered significant performance variability due to random initialization and increased computational complexity, suggesting further research into ensemble and hybrid methods.

In light of these findings from the literature, this study proposes the use of the ensemble learning paradigm to alleviate the limitations present within ELM's application for TDP. As found by Nan Liu and Han Wang [16], leveraging an ensemble architecture for ELM drastically reduces the dependency on random initialization and the need for extensive hyperparameter tuning. Initial validation tests conducted using the M4 competition dataset [17] indicate that an Ensemble ELM demonstrates superior performance across several key metrics when compared to traditional baseline models.

The Ensemble ELM utilized a bagging approach [18] to randomly sample 25 subsets with replacement at a 20% sampling size, followed by building a randomly initialized ELM on each subset. The outputs of the base ELMs are then aggregated using a meta-learner in a stacking approach [19] in this case a linear regression model was used to maintain simplicity and efficiency. This architecture achieved the lowest MSE and MAE reflecting a 11.3% improvement over Random Forests, and the highest R2 score (0.8625), indicating 8.4% better generalizability than Neural Networks. When compared to a traditional optimized ELM, the Ensemble ELM reduced MSE by 16.5% and R2 improved by 4.1%, while training 25.0% faster. These results highlight that the Ensemble ELM not only delivers enhanced accuracy and generalizability but also achieves greater efficiency without the need for extensive hyperparameter tuning, validating it as an ideal choice for large-scale time-dependent prediction tasks such as TDP.

3.2 Case Study

To rigorously assess the viability of the proposed Ensemble ELM approach in a real-world setting for TDP, the next phase of this research will involve an in-depth case study focused on the UK railway network. This is motivated by the collaboration with the SARM project and its aim to develop predictive tools for UK railway operators and infrastructure managers.

To maintain a manageable scope while ensuring relevance to high-traffic areas of the network, a subsection of the UK railway has been selected based on the available data and current progress within SARM. Focusing on the London Paddington to Penzance line, spanning from 2010 to 2023, data will be captured from various sources guided by current literature of TDP on the UK Railway [20–22] These include:

- Historical Service Performance (HSP) Platform: Provides data on the UK railway operations, including train schedules, actual arrival/departure times, delays, cancellations, and operator performance metrics. Accessible via the National Rail Darwin Data Feed with secure API access.
- Met Office MIDAS - UK Land Surface Stations Data: Covers weather stations across the UK near railway tracks, offering variables such as temperature, precipitation, wind speed, humidity, solar radiation, and snow depth. Freely accessible under an Open Government License from the CEDA archive.
- Track and Infrastructure Data: Contains information on the UK's railway infrastructure, including track conditions, signal failures, maintenance schedules, and infrastructure-related incidents. Access is facilitated through Network Rail's infrastructure network models and railway industry partnerships.

The proposed Ensemble ELM approach will then be implemented and evaluated against existing models and TDP systems, focusing on key performance metrics which reflect the ability to predict delay times and provide actionable results.

4 Conclusion

4.1 Future Directions

The next steps in this research mainly focus on the further development of the case study, finalizing the data integration and modelling stages. Beyond this, the potential to leverage extra external data sources to improve modelling accuracy is a promising direction, along with the extension onto larger sub-sections of the UK railway network and continued integration within the SARM project.

To push the boundaries of the ELM ensemble's capabilities and ensure that it remains a competitive approach for TDP, additional refinements and enhancements may be explored within the proposed ML methodology. These include meta-parameter modifications, alternate meta-learners and more advanced architectures, enabling key benefits such as Real Time Updates utilizing ELM's fast training time to stay relevant in changing climates, Specialized Base-Learners to generalize over specific and rare scenarios, and extra Interpretability to ensure bias-free and trustworthy outputs for operational use.

Acknowledgments. This study was jointly funded by Loughborough University and Network Rail.

Disclosure of Interests. The authors have no competing interests to declare that are relevant to the content of this article.

References

1. Office of Rail and Road.: Passenger rail performance. ORR Data Portal (n.d.). Available at: https://dataportal.orr.gov.uk/statistics/performance/passenger-rail-performance/. Accessed: 12/07/2024
2. Haddock, B., Beckford, J.: Understanding and utilising data for a seasonally agnostic railway (Engineering X Report). R. Acad. Eng. (2021). https://engineeringx.raeng.org.uk/media/upe lge20/engx-understanding-and-utilising-data-for-a-seasonally-agnostic-railway-short.pdf
3. Haines, A.: Resilience of rail infrastructure. Interim report to the Secretary of State for Transport following the derailment at Carmont, near Stonehaven, pp. 39–50 (2020)
4. Tang, R., et al.: A literature review of Artificial Intelligence applications in railway systems. Transp. Res. Part C: Emerging Technol. **140**, 103679 (2022). Available at: https://doi.org/10.1016/j.trc.2022.103679
5. Page, M.J., et al.: The PRISMA 2020 statement: an updated guideline for reporting systematic reviews. BMJ 71 (2021). Available at: https://doi.org/10.1136/bmj.n71
6. CASP Systematic Review Checklist.: Critical Appraisal Skills Programme (2018). Available at: https://casp-uk.net/checklists/casp-systematic-review-checklist-fillable.pdf
7. Spanninger, T., et al.: A review of train delay prediction approaches. J. Rail Transp. Plan. Manage. **22**, 100312 (2022). Available at: https://doi.org/10.1016/j.jrtpm.2022.100312
8. Wen, C., et al.: Train dispatching management with data- driven approaches: a comprehensive review and appraisal. IEEE Access 1 (2019). Available at: https://doi.org/10.1109/ACCESS.2019.2935106
9. Tiong, K.Y., Ma, Z., Palmqvist, C.-W.: A review of data-driven approaches to predict train delays. Transp. Res. Part C: Emerging Technol. **148**, 104027 (2023). Available at: https://doi.org/10.1016/j.trc.2023.104027
10. Huang, G.-B., Zhu, Q.-Y., Siew, C.-K.: Extreme learning machine: theory and applications. Neurocomputing **70**(1), 489–501 (2006). Available at: https://doi.org/10.1016/j.neucom.2005.12.126
11. Huang, G., et al.: Trends in extreme learning machines: a review. Neural Netw. **61**, 32–48 (2015). Available at: https://doi.org/10.1016/j.neunet.2014.10.001
12. Wang, J., et al.: A review on extreme learning machine. Multimedia Tools Appl. **81**(29), 41611–41660 (2022). Available at: https://doi.org/10.1007/s11042-021-11007-7

13. Cao, J., Lin, Z.: Extreme learning machines on high dimensional and large data applications: a survey. Math. Prob. Eng. 1–13 (2015). Available at: https://doi.org/10.1155/2015/103796
14. Bao, X., et al.: Prediction of train arrival delay using hybrid ELM-PSO approach. J. Adv. Transp. 1–15 (2021) (Edited by L. Li). Available at: https://doi.org/10.1155/2021/7763126
15. Oneto, L., et al.: Dynamic delay predictions for large-scale railway networks: deep and shallow extreme learning machines tuned via thresholdout. IEEE Trans. Syst. Man Cybern. Syst. **47**(10), 2754–2767 (2017). Available at: https://doi.org/10.1109/TSMC.2017.2693209
16. Nan, L., Han, W.: Ensemble based extreme learning machine. IEEE Signal Process. Lett. **17**(8), 754–757 (2010). Available at: https://doi.org/10.1109/LSP.2010.2053356
17. Makridakis, S., Spiliotis, E., Assimakopoulos, V.: The M4 competition: 100,000 time series and 61 forecasting methods. Int. J. Forecast. **36**(1), 54–74 (2020)
18. Breiman, L.: Bagging predictors. Mach. Learning **24**(2), 123–140 (1996). Available at: https://doi.org/10.1007/BF00058655
19. Wolpert, D.H.: Stacked generalization. Neural Netw. **5**(2), 241–259 (1992). Available at: https://doi.org/10.1016/S0893-6080(05)80023-1
20. Heglund, J.S.W., et al.: Railway delay prediction with spatial-temporal graph convolutional networks. In: 2020 IEEE 23rd International Conference on Intelligent Transportation Systems (ITSC). 2020 IEEE 23rd International Conference on Intelligent Transportation Systems (ITSC), Rhodes, Greece: IEEE, pp. 1–6 (2020). Available at: https://doi.org/10.1109/ITSC45102.2020.9294742
21. Taleongpong, P., et al.: Machine learning techniques to predict reactionary delays and other associated key performance indicators on British railway network. J. Intell. Transp. Syst. **26**(3), 311–329 (2022). Available at: https://doi.org/10.1080/15472450.2020.1858822
22. Ilalokhoin, O., Pant, R., Hall, J.W.: A multi-track rail model for estimating journey impacts from extreme weather events: a case study of Great Britain's rail network. Int. J. Rail Transp. **10**(2), 133–158 (2022). Available at: https://doi.org/10.1080/23248378.2021.1891582

Semantic Bone Structure Segmentation in 2D Image Data: Towards Total Knee Arthroplasty

Tobias Neiss-Theuerkauff[1,2](✉), Arne Schierbaum[1,3], Thomas Luhmann[1,3], Till Sieberth[1,3], and Frank Wallhoff[1,2]

[1] Jade Hochschule, 26121 Oldenburg, Germany
{neiss-theuerkauff,arne.schierbaum,thomas.luhmann,till.sieberth,
frank.wallhoff}@jade-hs.de
[2] ITAS - Institute for Technical Assistance Systems, Oldenburg, Germany
[3] IAPG - Institute for Applied Photogrammetry and Geoinformatics, Oldenburg, Germany

Abstract. Computer assisted navigation is important in surgeries. In this paper, we focus on the field of total knee arthroplasty, where computer aided navigation is already widely used to increase surgical precision. For the purpose, marker-based optical measurement systems are used, which are able to determine the position and orientation of surgical tools as well as femur and tibia. For the purpose of tracking the bones, optical locators must be drilled into the patient's femur and tibia to determine the position and orientation precisely. However, the temporarily inserted locators slow down the patient's healing process, due to the additional drilling.

This article presents a solution that aims to replace the marker-based measurement system used in total joint arthroplasty with an image-based measurement system. The 3D model of the knee required for computer-aided navigation is to be reconstructed in real time from 2D images using photogrammetric methods. This requires the relevant image data (femur and tibia) to be reliably identified and separated from the image background. For this purpose, an AI-based segmentation was implemented to pre-process the 2D image data. The difficulties and requirements are shown and a first proof-of-concept solution with initial results is presented.

Keywords: total knee arthroplasty · artificial intelligence · segmentation · annotation · synthetic data · optical measurement photogrammetry

1 Introduction

The implantation of artificial total knee joints is a standard surgical procedure and one of the most frequently performed operations in Germany. Approximately

M. Bramer and F. Stahl (Eds.): SGAI 2024, LNAI 15446, pp. 352–357, 2025.
https://doi.org/10.1007/978-3-031-77915-2_29

36% of total knee arthroplasty operations are already supported by navigated computer-assisted systems [5]. Computer-assisted interventions enable greater precision in the alignment and positioning of prostheses, but this requires additional surgical interventions [4], which on the other hand can have a negative impact on the patient's healing process.

For the computer-based, intraoperative navigation support of the surgeon, the position of the knee joint in relation to the patient's leg axis has to be determined. For this purpose, locators with 4–5 fixed optical markers must be surgically installed in femur and tibia. A stereoscopic 3D measuring system continuously tracks the locators during the operation in order to dynamically determine the position of the knee joint. The hip and ankle joint center is calculated in advance to determine the position of the knee in relation to the mechanical leg axis. The installation of the locators requires drilling into the bones, which is associated with further risks for the patient including risk of infection and misplacement. In addition, the healing process is prolonged [4,8].

The overall aim of this work is to develop a method with increased precision, improved patient well-being and faster, less error prone surgery using total knee arthroplasty as an example. This is to be achieved through the development of an assistive multi-sensor system incorporating the latest algorithms of artificial intelligence (AI) and augmented reality (AR). The overall technical goal, the fusion of 3D measurement technology and AR, is divided into three sub-goals:

1. Markerless 3D reconstruction of femur and tibia from 2D image data
2. High-precision real-time tracking and navigation during surgery
3. Convenient visualization of planning in augmented reality

In this paper we concentrate on the challenge to generate a highly accurate 3D reconstruction of the knee surface from 2D images in real time despite problematic imaging conditions, such as superimposition of the bone structure by fluids and tissue, reflections, occlusion, etc. A feasibility study by [2] shows that marker-free total knee surgeries with the support of photogrammetry is promising. But it has not yet been possible to achieve sufficient accuracy. As part of a proof-of-concept study, an AI-based pre-processing of 2D image data will be presented, which can be used to generate a highly accurate 3D reconstruction of the femur and tibia using marker-less tracking with a multi camera device and SLAM.

While the current state of the art and necessity of this research was discussed in the introduction, the underlying methodology and approach are presented in Sect. 2. The implementation is presented in Sects. 3 and 4. Initial proof-of-concept results and further steps are described in Sect. 5.

2 Concept and Methodology

By replacing the marker-based measurement method with a marker-less optical method, the surgical installation of additional locators can be omitted. This can shorten the rehabilitation time after the procedure as well as the duration of the operation and also reduce the risk of infection and misplacement. Replacing physical locators with a purely image-based method requires reliable recognition, evaluation and assignment of pixel-based image information. A high accuracy must be achieved for the 3D reconstruction of the knee. In order to successfully achieve these goals, it is essential to first document a high-precision 3D model of the bones (femur and tibia). This must be done during the first surgery phase. A trinocular SLAM method is used in this study to digitize the knee.

A trinocular system offers significant advantages in terms of robustness as the additional view creates redundancy in the computation [1,3]. As explained in [7], the reconstruction of the knee surface takes several steps. In the pre-processing phase, we introduce an AI-based method to perform semantic segmentation in 2D image data to only proceed with the relevant bone structures. This step involves creating a training data set comprised of pre-segmented and annotated image data of femur and tibia to train an AI-model for this specific use case. As part of a proof-of-concept study, various AI-models were trained and evaluated. In order to be able to test the trained models optimal, independent data sets were used for training and testing.

The deep learning (DL) framework *Detectron2*[1] from Facebook AI Research was used.

3   Segmentation and Masking Procedure

To train the AI model, a training data set consisting of 2D image with tibia and femur must be segmented and annotated. Finally, the training data set must be divided into two parts. The larger part is used for training, while the smaller part is used for accompanying validation of the results.

A training data set of 500 individual images of an artificial knee joint was segmented using *LabelMe*[2] Individual bones and ligaments were manually segmented and labeled with the categories femur, tibia and ligament (Fig. 1 left).

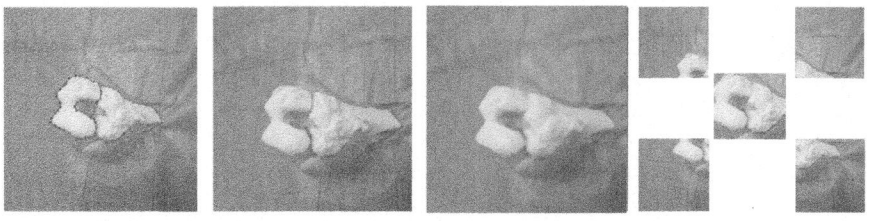

Fig. 1. from left: (1) segmentated and annotated image; examples of modifications: (2) rotation, (3) blurred and (4) image section

The data set was then artificially extended by calculating additional images by filtering (grayscale filter, blur, etc.), scaling and image section generation

---

[1] Detectron2 (Meta), Version v0.6, https://github.com/facebookresearch/detectron2.
[2] LabelMe Version 5.5.0, https://github.com/labelmeai/labelme.

resulting in a training data set of approx. 10,000 images (Fig. 1 right). The original images were taken in JPG format with a resolution of 1920px × 1200px. This corresponds to the resolution of the trinocular camera system, which is used for the images to be analysed during the operation.

4   Training and AI-Based Segmentation

The deep learning (DL) framework *Detectron2 (Meta)* contains pre-trained AI models that can be used as the basis for self-defined AI models. By further training these models, it is possible to generate application specific AI models. *Detectron2* provides state of the art algorithms for object detection, segmentation and other visual recognition tasks and is based on the PyTorch library [9].

Of the 10,000 images, 7,000 images were used for training and 3,000 images for validation. The training process was implemented with 1,000 iterations. After each 100 iterations, an evaluation process was started, which evaluates the current training status via the validation data set. After 1,000 iterations, a detection average of approx. 65% (femur) and approx. 55% (tibia) was achieved.

The generated AI model is then tested with independent data sets. Functions from the *Detectron2* library were used for the automatic segmentation. Functions from *OpenCV*[3] were used to generate the masked images, which are used for further calculation of the 3D knee model via SLAM (Fig. 2).

The trinocular SLAM algorithm, which is used for the subsequent creation of the 3D model, achieves significantly more stable results with the automatically masked images than with the images without masking [6].

Fig. 2. from left: (1) original image; (2) detected segmentation and annotation; (3) polygon calculation; (4) calculated mask image

5   Results and Further Work

The first proof-of-concept results are presented and directly supplemented with planned optimization work for the further procedure. The masked images from the AI-based image segmentation for further processing are only created if the respective bone was recognized with a probability of over 95%. This applies to approx. 70% of the first test data set (artificial knee model) and 10% of the second

---

[3] OpenCV, Version 4.10.0, https://github.com/opencv/opencv.

test data set (real surgical images). The resulting data set from the first test data set is sufficient to subsequently generate 3D models from 2D image data. In order to be able to process more masked image data in the subsequent SLAM process, the training is to be carried out with 10,000 iterations in future. This increases the average recognition rate and, analogously, the number of images that can be used for the subsequent generation of the 3D knee model.

Another option is to enlarge the training data set with image data that corresponds to the real surgery conditions. The latter should significantly improve the evaluation of the real surgery image data from the second test data set.

However, for data protection reasons, it is difficult to obtain real surgical images in the required quantity. In addition, the integration of real surgical data into the training data set would entail extremely time-consuming manual segmentation and labeling.

Another promising approach is the use of synthetic training data, which we are currently working on. For this purpose, the artificial knee joint was captured as a 3D point cloud and then converted into a meshed model. The resulting 3D model consists of independent bones that can be virtually moved and bent using the software *Blender*[4] Synthetic images of the knee are then rendered from different angles and in a variety of postures and materials. The *Blender* plugin *vision_blender*[5] is used to generate ground truth maps from the captured images, which contain the segmentations and annotations of the individual bones (Fig. 3). This method can be used to generate a large amount of training data with different properties at low cost.

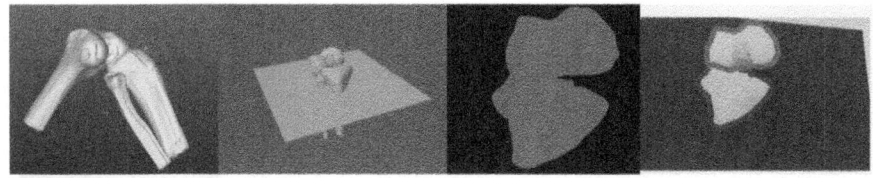

Fig. 3. from left: (1) 3D model from 1scan; (2) Visualization in Blender; (3) Ground truth map; (4) Calculated segmentation and annotation

6   Conclusion

In this work, a proof-of-concept was presented that enables AI-supported segmentation and annotation of surgical 2D images in order to refine the subsequent creation of a 3D knee model using trinocular SLAM algorithms. The trained models already provide promising but not yet sufficient results when applied to the generated test data set. In particular, the real surgery images cannot yet be

---

[4] Blender, version 4.10, https://www.blender.org/.

[5] vision_blender, version 1.0, https://github.com/Cartucho/vision_blender.

sufficiently segmented, annotated and masked. This was caused by anatomical conditions (skin, ligaments, blood, etc.), obstruction of the bones by the surgeon as well as reflections, insufficient lighting and others. Using synthetic training data can simulate these influences to allow future AI-models to be evaluated on a comprehensive test data set consisting of real surgical images. To this end, a method was presented that can be used to generate synthetic data that can be incorporated into the training data without difficulties with medical data protection.

Acknowledgments. The research work presented was funded by the *Bundesministerium für Bildung und Forschung (BMBF)*. Many thanks for the co-funded support from *Aesculap* and *AXIOS 3D Services* as well as the insights and expertise of the *PIUS Hospital (Oldenburg)*.

References

1. Conen, N., Luhmann, T., Maas, H.-G.: Development and evaluation of a miniature trinocular camera system for surgical measurement applications. PFG J. Photogram. Remote Sens. Geoinf. Sci. **85**(2), 127–138 (2017). https://doi.org/10.1007/s41064-017-0014-3
2. Hu, X., Liu, H., Baena, F.R.Y.: Markerless navigation system for orthopaedic knee surgery: a proof of concept study. IEEE Access **9**, 64708–64718 (2021). https://doi.org/10.1109/ACCESS.2021.3075628
3. Kahmen, O., Haase, N., Luhmann, T.: Orientation of point clouds for complex surfaces in medical surgery using trinocular visual odometry and stereo orb-slam2. Int. Arch. Photogram. Remote Sens. Spatial Inf. Sci. **XLIII-B2-2020**, 35–42 (2020). https://doi.org/10.5194/isprs-archives-XLIII-B2-2020-35-2020
4. Moret, C.S., Hirschmann, M.T.: Navigation und robotik in der knieendoprothetik. Arthroskopie **34**(5), 351–357 (2021). https://doi.org/10.1007/s00142-021-00467-6
5. Rath, B., et al.: Aktueller stellenwert der navigation in der knieendoprothetik in orthopädischen und unfallchirurgischen kliniken in deutschland. Z. Orthop. Unfall. **149**(2), 173–177 (2011)
6. Schierbaum, A., Neiß-Theuerkauff, T., Luhmann, T., Wallhoff, F., Sieberth, T.: Investigations on 3D reconstruction of bones in surgery using a handheld trinocular camera system. Int. Arch. Photogram. Remote Sens. Spatial Inf. Sci. (2024, submitted)
7. Schierbaum, A., Neiß-Theuerkauff, T., Wallhoff, F., Sieberth, T., Luhmann, T.: Untersuchungen zu einem ki-basierten slam-verfahren für ein trinokluares kamerasystem zur 3D-erfassung der knieoberfläche. Photogrammetrie - Laserscanning -Optische 3D-Messtechnik (2024)
8. Stübig, T., Windhagen, H., Krettek, C., Ettinger, M.: Computer-assisted orthopedic and trauma surgery. Dtsch Arztebl International **117**(47), 793–800 (2020). https://doi.org/10.3238/arztebl.2020.0793. https://www.aerzteblatt.de/int/article.asp?id=216800
9. Wu, Y., Kirillov, A., Massa, F., Lo, W.Y., Girshick, R.: Detectron2 (2019). https://github.com/facebookresearch/detectron2. Accessed 06 July 2024

Author Index

GPSR Compliance

The European Union's (EU) General Product Safety Regulation (GPSR) is a set of rules that requires consumer products to be safe and our obligations to ensure this.

If you have any concerns about our products, you can contact us on ProductSafety@springernature.com

In case Publisher is established outside the EU, the EU authorized representative is:

Springer Nature Customer Service Center GmbH
Europaplatz 3
69115 Heidelberg, Germany

The manufacturer's authorised representative in the EU is Springer
Nature Customer Service Centre GmbH, Europaplatz 3, 69115 Heidelberg,
Germany. If you have any concerns regarding our products, please
contact ProductSafety@springernature.com

Printed and bound by CPI Group (UK) Ltd, Croydon, CR0 4YY
06/05/2026
02104369-0001